A
CRITICAL
(NINTH)
ASSEMBLING
(PRECISELY: 6789)

OTHER PUBLICATIONS OF ASSEMBLING PRESS

BOOKS

VISUAL LANGUAGE (1970)
EXACT CHANGE (1974)
RECYCLINGS (1974)
AS IF A FOOTNOTE TO
 THE FINAL GLORY (1974)
LISTS (1974)
COME HERE (1975)
PROCEEDINGS OF THE NATIONAL
 ACADEMY OF THE AVANT-GARDE (1975)
DESIGN POETICS (1976)
NUMBERS: POEMS & STORIES (1976)
MUHAMMED ALI RETROSPECTIVE (1977)
CORROBOREE (1977)
SELECTED STRUCTURES (1977)
TWENTIES IN THE SIXTIES (1978)
SWEEP (1979)
"THE END" APPENDIX/
 "THE END" ESSENTIALS (1979)

ANTHOLOGIES

ASSEMBLING (1970)
SECOND ASSEMBLING (1971)
THIRD ASSEMBLING (1972)
FOURTH ASSEMBLING (1973)
FIFTH ASSEMBLING (1974)
SIXTH ASSEMBLING (1975)
SEVENTH ASSEMBLING (1977)
EIGHT A-J ASSEMBLING (1978)
EIGHTH K-Z ASSEMBLING (1978)
ASSEMBLING ASSEMBLING (1978)

OBJECTS

MANIFESTOES (1975)
THE PONTOON MANIFESTO (1975)
MODULATIONS (1975)
EXTRAPOLATE (1975)
RAIN RAINS RAIN (1976)
RUMOR TRANSMISSIBLE (1976)
EXPERIMENTAL PROSE (1976)

A CRITICAL (NINTH) ASSEMBLING

PRECISELY: SIX SEVEN EIGHT NINE

COMPILED AND INTRODUCED BY RICHARD KOSTELANETZ

NEW YORK

1979

For Jerome Klinkowitz
–Kosti's Klink

Kostelanetz, Richard, ed.
  A Critical Assembling
ISBN: 0-915066-33-5
            Library of Congress Catalog Card No. 78-72282
A Critical Assembling, compiled and introduced by Richard
Kostelanetz. Published by Assembling Press, P.O. Box 1967,
Brooklyn, NY 11202, with support from grants from the Litera-
ture Program of the National Endowment for the Arts, a Federal
Agency, and the Coordinating Council of Literary Magazines.
Also published as *Ninth Assembling* and *Precisely: Six Seven
Eight Nine.* Copyright © 1979 by Richard Kostelanetz, for
automatic reassignment to individual contributors upon their
written request. All rights reserved. No portion of the following
texts may be reproduced in any form whatsoever without per-
mission in writing from their respective authors, except for brief
passages quoted for inclusion in a review in a magazine or in a
newspaper or on a radio or television broadcast. Cover, design
and production by Richard Kostelanetz. First edition. Manufactured in the United States of America

Prospective contributors were invited to submit two pages,
camera-ready for offset reproduction, of "critical commentary
on radical/experimental tendencies in contemporary
literature." Contributions are printed here mostly in alphabetical sequence (with late arrivals at the end). Biographical notes in
the back of this book identify the contributors. As no submission from those invited was refused, nothing expressed in these
pages can be considered the responsibility of Assembling Press
or its editors; all statements are wholly the responsibility of the
contributors.

While it grows and matures, the new must speak for itself, must remain self-explanatory—*but the layman is justified in asking for an explanation of the new art now, and it is logical for the artist,* after *creating the new art, to try to become* conscious *of it.—Piet Mondrian, "The Rationality of Neoplasticism" (1917-18).*

There is something demanding about the freedom an Assembling *contributor has. That vacant space he's given can draw something out of him, challenge him to do his best.... The lack of editorial restraint encourages him to do things which he otherwise might feel too limited to do.—Karl Young, "Assembling" (1975).*

There is no substitute for critical tradition: a continuum of understanding, early commenced.... Precisely because William Blake's contempories did not know what to make of him, we do not know either, though critic after critic appeases our sense of obligation to his genius by reinventing him.... In the 1920's, on the other hand, something *was immediately made of* Ulysses *and* The Waste Land, *and our comfort with both works after 50 years, including our ease at allowing for their age, seems derivable from the fact that they have never been ignored.—Hugh Kenner,* The Pound Era *(1971).*

Most magazines ... leave one with the feeling of monotony of tone. Some central authority has selected the pieces included and that authority's sense of tone usually pervades the magazines. Contributors to Assembling go from outright uninhibited play to intense soul searching, from an immediate sort of plangency to undefined giggles to grand pronouncements to an utter serenity—all of these set in sharp relief against each other.—Karl Young, "Assembling" (1975).

Given any rule, however "fundamental" or "necessary" for science, there are always circumstances which it is advisable to introduce elaborate, and defined ad hoc *hypotheses which contradict well-established and generally accepted experimental results, or hypotheses whose content is smaller than the content of the existing and empirically adequate alternative, or self-inconsistent hypotheses, and so on.—Paul Feyerabend,* Against Method *(1975).*

WHY *A CRITICAL ASSEMBLING.*

As a radical experiment in book-making *A Critical Assembling* should be drastically unlike most, if not all, other collections of criticism that anyone has ever read. Most critical anthologies we know are put together to illustrate a certain theme, such as a common background ("Russian critics") or a common methodology ("formalism"), or to approach a circumscribed subject with many hands (e.g., contemporary literature, or a single major author). Most critical symposia are edited, designed and even typeset to produce the appearance of uniformity—the illusion that, notwithstanding the various origins of the parts, they all belong together and contribute to a single purpose. A critical collection is meant not only to realize more than the sum of its parts but also to exemplify professional excellence—the editor's considered belief that the following selections are the best examples of his chosen theme. These pretensions are familiar to me, mostly because I have previously edited several anthologies of criticism.

A Critical Assembling, by contrast, makes none of these claims—absolutely none. It was our alternative idea to invite over 500 potential contributors to write on "radical/experimental tendencies in contemporary literature." We also invited them to prepare their own camera-ready copy. One advantage of offset printing is that it gives every contributor the opportunity to make his or her contribution both read and look as personal, as distinctive, as extraordinary as possible. Since we as publishers agreed to print *everything* contributed by those invited (and obviously could *not* predict what they would submit), there is no way that we can verify the excellence of what follows. What is valuable and memorable, let alone "good," "better" or "best," are questions left for the reader to decide. Those qualities that we can claim for this book, however, are opportunity, freedom and variety. Indeed, we think that here the reader will find more of *those* qualities, far more, than in any other critical book ever published, anywhere.

A Critical Assembling is a recent development in the history of *Assembling,* which is itself a profoundly radical editorial experiment. In brief, *Assembling* was founded in 1970 as an outlet for "otherwise unpublishable" creative work. Since its founders were bothered by the authoritarian restrictiveness of conventional magazines, whose editors wanted everything to fit neatly into a pre-determined formula and format, we wanted a medium that would, by a radical counter-editorial stroke, transcend these deleterious practices. The simplest way, we discovered, was to invite artists and writers whom we knew to be doing innovative, "otherwise unpublishable" work to contribute a thousand copies of whatever they wanted to include. *Assembling* in turn would bind the contributions into a thousand alphabetically collated books, and return two copies apiece to each contributor. In spite of the requirement that contributors prepare all of their own pages for the copy-camera, literally self-publishing their work from scratch, hundreds of writers and artists around the world have joined me as colleagues in *Assembling*. Indeed, the medium has become so thick with contributions that *Eighth Assembling* (1978) had to appear in two volumes. In 1975, the critic Karl Young characterized *Assembling* as the "only gut innovation in magazine editing techniques" since Ezra Pound's *Exile,* and in October, 1978, *Assembling* was honored with a comprehensive exhibition at Pratt Graphics Center in New York—the first time since *The Dial* (in 1959) that a U.S. magazine-small press received an institutional show.

Late in 1977, we applied to the Literature Program of the National Endowment for the Arts to do *A Critical Assembling:* "We propose to invite four hundred editors, writers and artists to produce no more than two (2) camera-ready pages apiece, 8½" by 11", of critical commentary on radical/experimental tendencies in contemporary literature. In contrast to previous *Assemblings,* which required the invited contributors to print their own pages, we now propose to print their contributions ourselves, and to bind them into 1600 books, returning two copies apiece to each contributor. We believe that the result of this development in the continuing editorial experiment of *Assembling* will be an unprecedented symposium, of unparalleled range, quality and honesty, of thinking about literary possibility." Five thousand dollars came down the government chute; all of it, plus a token grant from CCLM, went into producing this book.

Potential contributors received invitations, early in the fall of 1978, outlining the purposes of this project and adding, clearly, that, "Everything submitted by those invited will be included, providing that it falls within the ground rules." We explained: "Because, in the tradition of *Assembling,* we do not want to 'edit' or tamper with your contribution in any way, we will not typeset or 'design' your work; those dimensions are your responsibility. Thus, your contribution to *A Critical Assembling* must be camera-ready for offset reproduction; any contribution judged technically insufficient will be returned for correction. If you cannot tell yourself whether your contribution is technically satisfactory, ask your local insty printer to judge. If he can do it clearly and cleanly, so, probably, can we." Needless to say, most magazines, let alone critical anthologies, are *not* done this way. No authoritarian editor would allow so many contributors half that much freedom. No, no, not at all.

"Your contribution," we continued, "may be typeset, typewritten, or hand-written; but if you use a typewriter, may we recommend a carbon ribbon for an impression that is deep black, rather than light gray, and clay paper, because it takes a fuller impression. If you handwrite, similarly use black ink, rather than pencil. We cannot reproduce photographs (although veloxes are okay) or colors other than black. May I recommend mounting your contribution on boards to prevent binding or crushing. Remember that no more than two (2) sides can be contributed. Your contributions will appear alphabetically, as is our custom; and as there will not be a table of contents, the names of all contributors will probably appear on the cover. Since we will print a disclaimer at the beginning of the book, all libel and other legal offenses are your responsibility; by your contribution you agree to absolve us from any culpability. [Potential litigants take note.] Please also send me a biographical note, on a 4″ by 6″ card, no more than fifty words in length, for inclusion in the back of the book; include your current address here if you want it published. (The resulting mail might be more interesting than the usual junk.) All contributions and correspondence should be sent to Richard Kostelanetz, P.O. Box 73, Canal Street, New York, NY 10013, no later than 1 April, 1979—a deadline that *cannot* be stretched.

"Remember that you are genuinely free to contribute whatever you want to *A Critical Assembling;* the concept of 'critical commentary' should be broadly interpreted. It can be something you've done already, or will do especially for the book. It might be something that other publications have rejected but which should, you believe, nonetheless appear in print. However, since the principal purpose of *Assembling* has been making available works that are 'otherwise unpublishable,' your contribution can*not* be something that has already been published. Whereas most magazines encourage prospective con-tributors to 'fit' into the surroundings, *Assembling* offers every contributor an unparalleled opportunity not only to transcend editorial restrictions but also to surpass his or her previous work with a singular contribution that will stand out from the surrounding pack. Your commentary may be about anything in radical/experimental literature you wish—about a particular work, things in general, grants, art politics, your best friends or even yourself; but remember that, in this context, each commentary will inevitably be compared with all the others, not only in content but in appearance. If there is anyone you think should contribute to this book, please invite them to send Kostelanetz a sample of his or her commentaries, well before 15 February, 1979. An invitation like this will follow. It should be understood that although *A Critical Assembling* may include an incomparably large number of people, it may still not be large enough.''

These were the ground rules, setting the publication machinery in motion. Whereas the conventions are that an editor imposes his taste, that contributions are ''edited'' to fit into an overall scheme, and that a magazine realizes a continuity, if not a unity, of tone and appearance, *A Critical Assembling* violates all of these conventions. Should our anti-authoritarian ''editing'' be considered *experimental,* then the *hypothesis* was that this unconventional compositional method might well produce something very special. Restricted in a few respects (e.g., range of subject matter and maximum length), the invitation was unprecedentedly open in others. Indeed, given certain unspecificities, the editor was no more sure than the next person what might eventually result, not only in quality but in quantity. Given the number of people invited and the quota of pages extended to each potential contributor, *A Critical Assembling* could have received over a thousand pages (which, in fulfillment of our promises, would have cost us over $10,000 to print). On the other hand, these instructions might be more forbidding than inviting, especially to people who lacked experience in designing pages that would be printed as they looked (and would thus miss an opportunity to learn). Some might have preferred a specific assignment to such an open invitation, editorial freedom being more discouraging to them than authoritarian direction; and others perhaps required more personal prodding, if not supervision or flattery, than an unassisted editor can afford. Whereas some potential contributors needed six months to prepare their work, others would indulge the long deadline to forget about the invitation. Whereas some would relish a competition where everyone starts from scratch, snobs would be distressed by their inability to negotiate editorial advantages. (The opening place in this book is reserved for Daniel Aaron, if he wishes to contribute.) Others might be reluctant to place their ''precious names'' in the company of many unfamiliar people. (A true way to appear distinguished is to do distinguished work; a false way is to avoid the company of currently undistinguished colleagues. Conversely, in a truly open forum, genuine excellence should transcend all competition.) Some, as we say, ''couldn't get it together,'' while others had ''nothing to say.'' *A Critical Assembling* could have been a disaster; no doubt some readers think it is.

It seems to me that just as contemporary art at its best is created in a spirit of risk and adventure, so those qualities could also inform the production of critical magazines that want to be as profoundly contemporary as the art they talk about. A tolerance for anxiety invites certain possibilities that might otherwise be lost. Reading *Assembling* should be as much of an adventure as editing it, or contributing to it; for neither the reader nor the editor nor the contributor can guess in advance what might come next. (As both an editor and an artist, as well as a sometime teacher, I have a taste for creating situations that prompt people, including myself, to take risks that they have not done before.) Theory and criticism are important, to be sure, especially in our consciousness of experimental literature; and one assumption of this project is that essays, especially essays about art, should be as free of editorial finagling as poetry and fiction.

A few months after writing the NEA application, I co-founded the periodical *Precisely* to publish critical essays on experimental literature of the past twenty years. In the wake of an initial general issue, *Precisely: Two* was devoted to "Grants & the Future of Literature," *Precisely: Three Four Five* to critical essays on visual literature. Since most of the following pages fulfill *Precisely*'s purposes precisely, it seems appropriate that this symposium, which is several times the size of the initial *Precisely*, should also appear as *Precisely: Six Seven Eight Nine*. *Precisely* has applied to the National Endowment for the Arts to do a special issue devoted to critical essays on aural literature, and to the Canada Council to do a special issue on Canadian literature. *Assembling* has applied to the NEA to do a *Grand Assembling* which would have three stages. For the first year, we would print up to two camera-ready pages of anything "otherwise unpublishable" (not just criticism) from 300 invited artists and writers (approximately 500 pages); for the second year, up to three pages from 400 people (approximately 1000 pages) and for the third year up to four pages from 600 people (approximately 1800 pages). Funding decisions are pending, naturally; but announcing these proposals suggests directions in which, support willing, *Precisely* and *Assembling* might well develop.

As a critical book like no other anyone has read before, *A Critical Assembling* is, to repeat, better enjoyed than evaluated, better appreciated as a suggestive experiment than judged as a definitive encyclopedia. Since no contribution necessarily relates to any other, the book can be read backwards, as well as forwards, or from the middle outwards. Indeed, as the leaps from one chapter to the next are so great, the book might best be read in circumstances that encourage discrete pauses—on the breakfast table, at one's bedside, in the bathroom. At a contribution a day, *A Critical Assembling* may take several months to read. If repeated themes and styles emerge from the book, rest assured that the editor did not put them there; they are, literally, signs of the times. If only through its bulk and scope, this book may ultimately be about "what's happening" today. In its own alternative way, *A Critical Assembling* may inadvertently achieve more, much more, than the sum of its many parts.

Organization Grant Application **National Endowment for the Arts** Applications must be submitted in triplicate and mailed to the Grants Office, National Endowment for the Arts, 2401 E Street, N.W. Washington, D.C. 20506 *	**Literature Program**

I. Applicant organization
   (name and address with zip)

Assembling Press
(Participation Projects Fdn.)
P.O. Box 1967
Brooklyn, NY 11202

II. Literature Program/
   Category under which support is requested: General Programs

III. Period of support requested
Starting May 1, 1979   Ending April 30, 1980
   month   day   year   month   day   year

IV. Summary of project description (complete in space provided. Do NOT continue on additional pages.)

Extending the compositional principle of A CRITICAL ASSEMBLING, funded in 1978 by NEA-Literature for publication in 1979, we should like to publish a compendious anthology entitled AMERICAN WRITING IN 1980. It would be realized in the following innovative way: Two thousand U.S. writers, working in a wide variety of modes, would be invited to contribute a single page, 5" by 8", camera-ready for offset reproduction in an alphabetically organized book. The invitation would state that this contribution may consist of literally anything the writer wishes: a fresh manuscript in whole or in part, a page cut from a previously published book, a resumé, a manifesto, a list of publications, a display that would include both examples and commentary, or anything else that can be reduced to a single 5" by 8" mass-reproduced format. Every page received from those invited will appear intact. Were this proposal fully funded, invitations would go out in May, 1979, with a deadline of 1 October, for book publication at the beginning of 1980; one copy will be mailed gratis to every contributor. The book's principal editor has produced over two dozen anthologies, both selective and inclusive, both historical and prophetic. As indubitably the most populous anthology of its sort ever published in the U.S., AMERICAN WRITING IN 1980 will serve more writers than any other and will no doubt stand as a monument for our time. Appropriately, it will be dedicated to the National Endowment for the Arts. We apply under "General Programs" because our budget for doing this book in the best way exceeds those allowed under "Assistance to Small Presses" and "Assistance to Literary Magazines" to which we have already submitted proposals that should neither compete nor conflict with this. Tied to a particular calendar milestone, this proposal will not be made again.

V. Estimated number of persons expected to benefit from this project   200,000

VI. Summary of estimated costs (recapitulation of budget items in Section IX)

                                            Total costs of project
      A. Direct costs   **(rounded to nearest ten dollars)**

Salaries and wages	$ 11,500
Fringe benefits	
Supplies and materials	1,500
Travel	
Special	
Other	38,500
Total direct costs	$ 51,500
B. Indirect costs	$
Total project costs	$ 51,500

VII. Total amount requested from the National Endowment for the Arts $ 25,750

VIII. Organization total fiscal activity

	Actual most recent fiscal period	Estimated for next fiscal period
A. Expenses	1. $ 14,750	2. $ 88,000
B. Revenues, grants & contributions	1. $ 12,000	2. $ 88,000

Do not write in this space

Evaluat... of prior year(s)' projects | 1 | 2 | 3 | 4 | Pys $ _____   Cps $ _____   Audit report | 1 | 2 |

NATIONAL
ENDOWMENT
FOR
THE ARTS

WASHINGTON
D.C. 20506

A Federal agency advised by the
National Council on the Arts

March 14, 1979

Richard Kostelanetz
141 Wooster St.
New York, NY 10012

Dear Richard,

Thanks for your latest note and proposal. As it happens
I can report to you only what the Literature Panel
recommended concerning your application for the anthology
"American Writing in 1980"; the disposition of your other
applications will be made known to you when we send out
the announcements-later this spring (could be as late as
June depending on how well the bureaucratic machinery is
working).

I must unhappily inform you that the Literature Panel voted
not to consider this application on the grounds that it was
in all ways qualified to be considered as a regular application under the category of Assistance to Small Presses.
Since one cannot make two separate applications under this
category, and Assembling already had another application
under consideration, this vote meant that this particular
application could not be considered at this meeting. The
panel understood your arguments that this project went or
will go beyond the scope of the Small Press category, but
they did not see how the size of a given project could
differentiate it from any other publication project.
Since everyone else must operate under the guidelines,
which include the $10,000 amount limitation, they felt you
would have to work under the same limitation as well.
Please note that this decision had absolutely nothing to do
with their feelings for the nature or quality of the actual
project; they urged you to apply for funding in the future
for this project under the regular guidelines. No matter
how the panel may feel about a particular project, our
limited funding capabilities force us to abide by the $10,000
ceiling under all circumstances; the point being that if a
project requires a greater level of support it will have to
come from other sources. Again, this is a circumstance that
while we may not like, extends across all our categories and
applies equally to all our applicants. Their decision concerning your application had only to do with the fact that
it was a publication project and therefore eligible under a
regular guideline, and not for GeneralSupport.

Based on this Panel decision, then, I must tell you that
there is no point in sending an application for "The Other
Poetries Of New York" to the Literature Program at this time.
It can not be considered under General Services and must
be considered as an application under the Guideline Category,
Assistance to Small Presses, for which the next deadline
will not be until fall of 1980. The new guidelines won't
even be ready until June of this year. The point here is,
simply, that this is a publication project and therefore
eligible under a regular guideline category; anything that
is eligible for a guideline category cannot be considered
under General Services. That is one of the reasons we have
guideline categories in the first place. I know that the
project requires more money than the maximum available, but
that in and of itself is not enough to take it out of the
guideline category. The reason there is a maximum is simply
that the program does not have sufficient funds to give more
than that figure to any publication project. It may in
fact be true that the $10,000 figure is too low - I happen
to think that it is - but in order to change that we have to
go through a lengthy review process, which I believe we will
do, and no change will occur at least until FY 1982.

I would appreciate it if you would call me if the Panel's
decision or my explanation of it is not clear. I hope you
will appreciate the difficulties engendered by our lack of
adequate funding, and how we attempt to deal with them in
both programming and decision making. I do want to reiterate
that these decisions have absolutely nothing to do with the
nature of the projects (which appear to me to be literarily
fine) but with the exigencies of categorical definitions and
guideline stipulations.

I'll be happy to discuss these decisions further if you like.
And personally, I want to wish you luck in pursuing these
projects, whether you go ahead without us or wait until next
time to reapply.

Warm regards,

David Wilk
Director, Literature Program

Notes on the Currents of Silence
an excerpt by
Jonathan J. Albert

Silence is a field of white noise.
Silence moves in random patterns.
    It moves in all patterns, and therefore in none.
The currents of silence are sounds.
    Sounds are events.
    Sounds are radiant waves.
        New sounds are generated by the collision of waves.
    Everything is a sound and sends waves into the environment.
    Currents are perceivable movements, patterns in the silence.
    All sounds are currents.
        They are radiant movements in the field of silence.
    Currents form "things".
    Currents are the radiations from all things.
        Everything is radiant.
    A sound is a splash in the moving fabric of silence.
Hearing the currents of silence.
    Hear the sounds as movements.
    Hear sounds in relation to the range of possible sounds.
    Hear the progression of sounds.
    Hear an object.
        Sense the object as a movement, a series of movements.
        Allow yourself to move to and with the movement.
Swimming in silence.
    Swimming means allowing yourself to move with your medium.
    Swimming in silence.
        Move with the random movements of silence - stand still.
            To move all ways is to stand still.
    Respond to sounds and events.
        Sense the possible; play with each movement.
        Tie each to all, and all is silence.
        To move to silence is to move in poise.
            Each individual act is a move away from poise, unless you find the
                silence within it.
    To swim in silence, be poised, silent, and sense the multiplicity.
    Listen to the silence.
        Listen with your ears and with your body.
        Feel it running in your body - the same vibration you hear.
        Hear all sounds in relation to the silence.
            Notice the foreground-background relationship of sound and silence.
        Feel all sensations, perceptions in relation to the feel of silence.
The personal field.
    There is a field of silence within each person.
    Within is every movement.
        Each person has certain currents, patterns of current highlighted.
            This is the personal way of radiating, of interacting.
    Your currents are what you resonate to.
    Responding to a currents means responding to it in you.
        You resonate to your world.
Swimming in the currents of silence.
    First swim in silence.

The currents are radiance.
Set up a sympathetic vibration.
    Within each person is the silence, all currents.
    Sounding the note of the current means **sounding** the inner current.
      Move to the radiance, draw on it, and move to its power.
Using the voice to swim in the currents.
    Sing the sound/movements.
    Translate sound/movements into spoken sound movements.
    Sing movements based on the sounds.
      Variations of what you sense.
    Sing to the sound/movements.
      React to the currents.
    These are ways to sing with and to your world, to proclaim a harmony and
      make an ally of the currents.

THE SLANTED HOT-SHEET BOOKSHELF ART GALLERY   By Blair H. Allen

Contemporary
Vanguard Trends In Two Small Press
Mags

East
—

ASSEMBLING
rises repeatedly
as phoenix
in the face of
idiotic opposition

ASSEMBLING
lets free
expression
appear
unedited
stimulating
challenging
other artists
idea-fissioning
filling mindskies

Opposite
side
applies
also

Upcoming
ASSEMBLING
celebrates
why cats have
NINE lives
* * *
Then in the
Tenth issue
will show why
ASSEMBLING
is no pussycat

ASSEMBLING
ASSEMBLING
did it
all over
the walls of
Pratt's Graphic
Center in
New York City

Wallbangers
for sure

Alot of
concept
concept
concept
concept
concept
concept
concept
concept
concept
concept
concept
concept
concept
often
right
into
the
5th
DIMENSION

6th   7th   8th   9th

Founder
Kostelanetz
is a futuristic
superstar and
the Picasso of
experimental
visual
language

without
Mike Metz
there'd be no
fantastic
covers

Henry James Korn
is a surrealistic
word magician

ASSEMBLING
Assembles
Assembly
A
for   plus
you

EIGHTH ASSEMBLING
Avant-art-lit-mag
as exhibit
catalogue
two-bird
stoning it

ASSEMBLING
cuts all
the barbed wire
fences of rules
*
play with
paste-up
typewriter
instant type
found art-lit
scissor
collage any
anything
you can
find within
reach

Numerous
words as art
letter-designed
for instant
visual
impact
on walls
and pages of
books and mags

Open
the
ASSEMBLING
doors
in your mind
and
step right
out

into

the universe
space

ASSEMBLING
is
unhomogenized
unstandardized
unacademized
unstrait-jacketed
unmilitarized
unpasteurized
untamed
unsettling
raw roots
raw meat
raw milk
applejack
jumpforjoyjuice

ASSEMBLING
invites
joyful
innovators
to send page
surprises
reproduced
at contributor's
cost to be
collated and
mag-book-bound
and shipped
around
the world

filled
with every
treasure
a mind
can get
its
thought-fingers
on

In
ASSEMBLING
art
literature
music
make
wildest
orgies
not
war

ONE

ASSEMBLING
eliminates
age as you
find your
fountain
of youth
again

Try
every
NEW
thing
you
can

Dada
dee
dum
surreal
as some
futuristic
fun
beyond
Pop Art
is done

a torch
yell
in
the
dark

B.H.A.

ah - one

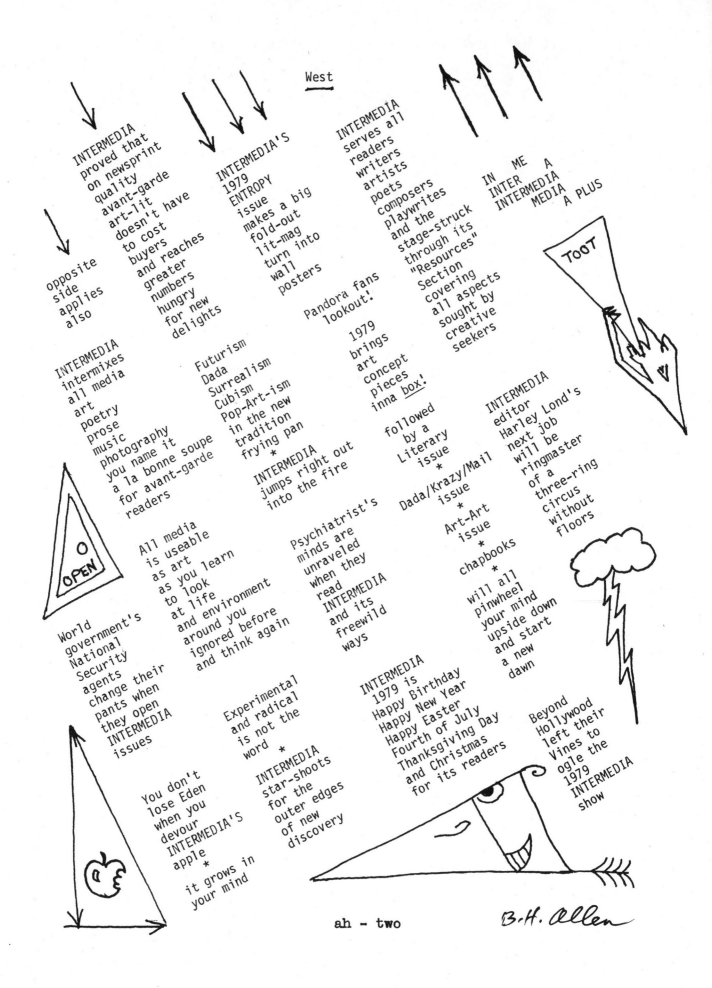

West

INTERMEDIA proved that on newsprint quality avant-garde art-lit doesn't have to cost buyers and reaches greater numbers hungry for new delights

opposite side applies also

INTERMEDIA'S 1979 ENTROPY issue makes a big fold-out lit-mag turn into wall posters

INTERMEDIA serves all readers writers artists poets composers playwrites and the stage-struck through its "Resources" Section covering all aspects sought by creative seekers

IN   ME   A
INTER   INTERMEDIA
MEDIA   A PLUS

TOOT

INTERMEDIA intermixes all media art poetry prose music photography you name it a la bonne soupe for avant-garde readers

Futurism Dada Surrealism Cubism Pop-Art-ism in the new tradition frying pan *

INTERMEDIA jumps right out into the fire

Pandora fans lookout!

1979 brings art concept pieces inna box!

followed by a Literary issue *

Dada/Krazy/Mail issue *

Art-Art issue *

chapbooks *

will all pinwheel your mind upside down and start a new dawn

INTERMEDIA editor Harley Lond's next job will be ringmaster of a three-ring circus without floors

OPEN

All media is useable as art as you learn to look at life and environment around you ignored before and think again

Psychiatrist's minds are unraveled when they read INTERMEDIA and its freewild ways

World government's National Security agents change their pants when they open INTERMEDIA issues

Experimental and radical is not the word *

INTERMEDIA star-shoots for the outer edges of new discovery

INTERMEDIA 1979 is Happy Birthday Happy New Year Happy Easter Fourth of July Thanksgiving Day and Christmas for its readers

Beyond Hollywood left their Vines to ogle the 1979 INTERMEDIA show

You don't lose Eden when you devour INTERMEDIA'S apple *

it grows in your mind

ah - two

B.H. Allen

L'ACTE NOMADE.

La "Tour de Babel" est le récit d'une confusion des langues, ou plutôt de la haine par l'Eternel d'une possibilité de communication entre les humains: "Et l'Eternel dit: voici, ils forment un seul peuple et ont tous une même langue, et c'est là ce qu'ils ont entrepris; maintenant rien ne les empêcherait de faire tout ce qu'ils ont projeté". (Genèse XI).

Avec la confusion des langues, l'acte divin consiste à disperser les hommes "sur la face de toute la terre" (Genèse, id.), séparant ainsi à jamais la chair de son verbe: il s'agit là de la première opération de censure, d'un acte politique traduisant le religieux judéo-chrétien comme haine du désir de l'Autre: dès lors toute écriture s'annonce comme le récit antérieur d'une chute, d'un noeud de paroles où se mêleront toutes les trouvailles vieilles comme le monde et instantanées, engendrées par le silence et l'angoisse. A QUI PARLER MAINTENANT? Je veux, tu veux, je voudrais, tu voudrais, il y a tout, comment? merde!

L'écriture est alors une réaction contre le domestique, là où la communication est donnée comme restituée par l'ordre et les Etats, elle est le dernier acte des nomades: cette fois-ci, l'homme debout est trop seul pour entendre les glapissements des chiens de garde, le haut de son crâne est irradié par la folie muette du soleil. La course commence: il y a sans doute des chevaux, des insectes, des rats, des rhinocéros, des buffles, la mort est ailleurs maintenant, elle n'a d'ailleurs jamais existé, c'est une invention des vivants.

L'écriture ne subsiste plus que comme expérience, elle ne trouve de valeur qu'en elle-même. Elle abonde en instances, se contestant d'elles-mêmes, et qui s'ouvrent délibérément au non-savoir: l'expérience littéraire oppose un corps et des rictus ensauvagés, monde complexe du rire comme du sanglot, monde antagonique bruyant où le "gai savoir" entend balayer toute volonté de vérité. "L'écriture est un bond hors du rang des meurtriers". (Franz Kafka)

La littérature comme "savoir" est linéaire car elle se gorge d'histoire(s).

Comme expérience, elle n'est qu'"instant", instant-même de l'expérience, cet "ici" où le corps change de monde; entre le sujet et l'écrit, toute la question est d'"être ensemble" et d'y être "en même temps": le reste, c'est précisément le passage à la page, c'est-à-dire au mensonge: le mensonge est le ricanement souverain de la page devant l'effroyable désir de fusion entre le corps et l'idée de son écrit: le ricanement de la page, c'est déjà de les laisser à l'abandon. Et le poison du crime parfait de mûrir dans le crâne irradié de soleil du sujet.

Le corps du sujet et ses simulacres s'introduisent dans l'espace mensonger pour en extraire alors du temps qui n'y était pas: on revient à un "temps qui n'a pas encore de barbe" (Lichtenberg). On crie, on hurle, on bat des mains, on est profondément ridicule, alors on pleure et on recommence.

Dans l'écriture, le temps de l'écrit ne se pointe que de possibilités de paroles: la scène fictionnelle se bavarde afin de tenter de biaiser le mensonge, elle tâche de se livrer à l'effraction, déchirant constamment des bouts de mensonges entre eux, afin, espoir, de n'avoir plus à se fatiguer un jour, afin d'attenter justement à sa vie: en somme l'écriture se grouille dans ses mensonges avec la certitude béate d'en finir; l'écriture vit pour se tuer, taire ce qui ne cesse de l'appeler à le taire.

Il n'y a d'écriture que cynique.

"Etre moderne, c'est bricoler dans l'incurable". (Cioran).

Mireille Andrès
Patrick Rousseau

from *DIVESTITURE*   Bruce Andrews

Aesthetic Man
Aristocracy
Auto-da-Fe
Bell
Brain
Capitalism
Cinemas
Civics
Class
Comic Cuts
Consumer
Day of Judgement
Deproletarianization
Fall of Lucifer
Forgetmenot
Free Trade
Freud
Garden
General Strike
Grammar
Home Chat
IQ
Individualism
In Memoriam
Ion
John Bull
Lillo
Little Wife
Living in the Present
Love's Last Shift
Masses
Miracle plays
Narodnost
Oracle
Orthography
Passages
Patent
Quem Quaeritis
Refugee
Scalp Hunters
Self-exile
Six Acts
Socialism
Sprat
Star
State
Structure of feeling
Sunflower
Take it from here
Yellowbacks
Zaum

Treat every sentence as SyMpToM.   Foxing it with opacities.   Caressing lonely epistolary style.   Legible sounds — I want horizons.   Implications in wording. I WAS MISLED INTO THINKING.   As politics, to encourage that kind of reading — not an aesthetic response just to 'composition' but recognition of the degrees of opacity or truthfulness in all language we can socially experience. Penetration by stages [myth].   Composing w/ (as a central axis, distinguishing) degrees of representationalism — that 'in & out' quality the topographical quality [not synchronic in the idea of analysis by going straight down, as in layers, but like a map indicating heights

etc.

Language as guilt.

Final revelation or discovery of a crime — writing like playing CLUE, choice as end point of a process of elimination. Flaws in words' ability to 'make a place for themselves' is clue, need or used to reject them. Those words, for example, eliminated, because they have an alibi (explanation?), status is dependent, are less autonomous. The criminal (& the tool & the setting of the crime) are therefore free standing, without clues, without context, accurate.
It's the crime of absence & loss that the writing constantly harkens back to : seat of repression, & of what recurs.   As language blocks speech [counter-factuality] so ideology blocks politics — seeing opacity of the former probably needed if we are to see the opacities of the latter. No easy transparency : transparency would be a revolutionary social (societal) act, process, possibly even contra naturum.   Question not even one of which aspects of language do you foreground (literal elements — 'material signification', physicality, etc., vs. referential elements); it's one of : what principle of organization predominates & how & with what end. Sartre : "every time I made a mistake it was because I was not radical enough".   TEXTURAL RESONANCE.   To what degree are the methods the subject?   Words not, like icons, patches of 'clear visibility'.   Noting how prosody, grammar (or spatial relationships) control the order of disclosure upon which the poem depends; convey the tone, intention.   "where there is clarity there is no choice".   "no words can be put in to explain the words".   "She uses the canvas as an arena for an inner dialogue between the language of formalist art — flat, surface-conscious, non-illusionism, emotionless, and unromantic — and her own deepest impulses."   Self-ordering subsystems vs. the pointing system.   Basic movement — gradual elimination of 'outside motivation' music (tonality) painting (perspective) dance (story, character) novels (plot, characters) poetry (representation). Sign behavior as illusion.   The de-socializing of language.
WORDS TELL THEIR OWN STORIES.   There are words. "holophrastic speech" — single word stands for an entire complicated sentence.   Attenuation of the bond between sign & reference, dismemberment of the sign itself.   Not language as documentation of a nonlinguistic exploration (of pre-constituted world), but words as their own documentaries.   Are

semantically randomized (e.g. contextually or 'speech situation' randomized, or decontextualized, or de-indexicalized).   LITERAL ART.   An order of presentation just as personal as autobiographical tracks.   Create 'inverse motivation which doesn't reduce a code to its most schematic nature but which lets one code contradict another — not just crystal clear & in conflict, but by decontextualizing each of the elements.   Mabel Mercer: "it's all in the punctuation."   Issue one of avoiding an interference — soft storms — of the sense on the sound requires a certain degree of non-interference O.K. you could say the only issue is one of structuring the words along physical axes (& not using physicality to <u>collude</u> with or ornament the more important element of meaning) because even then readers (expectations built up) may ignore primacy of physical structuring or 'literal signification' & read the words ('i.e. perceive the structure of the words) as though they were structured semantically, as though syntax (a physical paralleling of a semantic order) were implicit & acting in its normal semantic-correspondence role), as though their art value lay in the meanings or in the overall meaning, that they <u>added up</u> to a single content, that the references were somehow yoked together, a code existed, etc. So you avoid what calls attention (melodramatic language, cliches, esoterica, proper names, etc ? — flattening — or connections that'd give rise to such a spectatorial emphasis.   If signs are reminders, referential/nonreferential as remembering/perceiving...   Disembodied drama.   Have always seen it as a kind of meditation.   To subliminalize meaning.   Combining things not to create 'codic doubling' but to make them <u>vibrate</u>, like standing waves.   Spatial arrangement as syntax.   When are terms useful & if (December 1972, 'language-centered' writing).   Calling attention to rules, foremost, by violating them.

SHELF: Sarris, Diamond, Bachelard, Woolf, Gass, Freud, Adorno, Ponge, Goffman, Wilson, Anderson, Marx, Schechner, Rimbaud, Cooper, White, Benjamin, Olson, Jacoby, Zukofsky, Reich, de Chazal, Laing, Barthes, Jarry, Williams, Chomsky, O'Hara, Kafka, Brown, Kerouac, Beckett, Duchamp, Slater, Jameson, Grotowski, Marcuse, Steiner, Habermas, Pound, Lacan, Jones, Cage, Perls, Eliade, Burroughs, Agee, Berger, Shattuck, Bataille, Castenada, Sartre, Maslow, Foucault, Stein, Wollheim, Firestone, Kenner, Hoggart, Lasch, Lippard, Bardwick, Wittgenstein, Sontag, Austin, Artaud.

"We should be much clearer about these cultural questions [the deterioration of culture, in the broadest sense] if we saw them as a consequence of a basically capitalist organization, and I at least know no better reason for capitalism to be ended."

"... until a Revolution of all the Colours be completed,
     and that first Colour return again." (Newton, OPTICKS)

— finally some repeated
     letter patterns did emerge. —

the Character: maybe
August Saint The
Plot: thickening. The
Metaphor: the Language.
The Tone: univocality.
Any "other" characters,
including the Author:
pall-bearers. The
Time: check your TV
guide.

a supercriticism - Alain Arias-Misson '79

newfiction as negativity demise of metaphysics a universal
metaphysical lining in our most rational discourse the "rea
list" option is ideological not esthetic newfiction is a la
nguage-machine dehumanisation (demythification) life as a
biological machine to the newwriter the stylema is a bioscr
ipt this life-of-fiction is a surplus unaccountable in the
psychosocial model ontological instability: de/scribes, de
constructs the molar figures of its own fiction superaliena
tion: the text of culture become autonomous emblematic: the
macrosign of the public media- especially tv newfiction is
endofictive text= objet-en-soi: hyperreflexivity superfict
ion is exofictive: non-tautotological in its skewed relation
to "reality" in the refractions of its multiple, discrete t
ext-crystals super is the focal point to which the disparate
texts of this "world" drift, converge superfiction is not a
disalienation: no supra- or infra-linguistic topos can be poi
nted to conventional fiction is a naive fictometaphysics n
ewfiction, an ambiguous fictometaphysics = the metaphysics o
f an active nihilism camouflaged in the pretensions of a to
talizing language alienation is of a transcendance or is not
hing the dialectical relation of superfiction is transcenden
tal the message of the world-text, oblique, is a superreal

Alain Arias-Misson

FOR THE FUTURE OF A PROJECT by ASCHER/STRAUS

1. The future of literature does not lie in its development as an inferior graphic or musical art. The novel itself is a recent form. The prose narrative novel is not exhausted as a form. The will to execute large scale literary works and to confront the difficult issues raised by the great, revolutionary modern novels has been exhausted.

  The energy for vital developments always comes from the rupture with tradition. The shift from the desire for continuity of tradition to the conscious search for new points of rupture and energy marks the modern spirit. This search still animates us. However, because the thread of authentic development of the modern novel has lapsed through critical neglect, two forces have developed. The worst development has been the idea of writing as a serious career and profession, and the attendant growth of creative writing courses, writers' conferences and the like. This is a reactionary development because the demands of pedagogy, to teach something teachable, compel the presentation of mediocre models, refinement of the techniques of accessible modes that enhance career possibilities, ignorance of the great, atypical modern works and of the authentic modern spirit.

  Many of the most profound and far-reaching revolutions in novel form are scarcely known in America (the works of Hermann Broch, for example) and certainly not offered as creative writing models. These works would present young American writers searching for the authentic modern energy of the significant rupture with possibilites for new grounds of being for the novel. Inclusiveness of material, discontinuity and modular structure, philosophical discourse and poetic narrative, for example, are generally lapsed threads.

  And the second result has been a literary avant garde, hungry for the new, mistakenly finding its models in other media. The result is inauthentic work and a defensive, or merely stupid, mandarin insularity. The obvious fact that a book is endlessly reproducable, unlike a unique art object, means that Duchamp and everything that flows from him — happenings etc. — have nothing of importance to say about the ground of being of writing, aesthetically or politically, while they may have everything to say about the art world, if not about art.

2. One often feels in the various efforts to assert that writing is a directly sensuous medium, whether the limited experiments of concrete poetry or the dull theater and bad acting of the poetry reading, a melancholy longing to be film, television, painting, music or, at the most vulgar level, a sort of counter-advertising.

Perhaps for these reasons, language gradually vanishes from abstract and visual literary works, leaving the book as a total object in its place. Writers ought to be wary of such developments — and certainly ought to insist that these represent the hybrid growth of a different medium.

There is no need to insist on the direct sensuality of literature. This runs counter to literature's greatest strength, in fact, which is the sheer volume and range of possible references to experience.

3.   The assertion that language is referential does not mean that literary validity lies off the page. The fact that the justification of all art lies within its own borders and terms, however, does not mean that those terms do not refer to the world outside those borders: to memories, phenomena, sensations, emotions, events and so on. All art is referential in this way. If not, we have the vulgar notion, a concept of critics not artists, that painting is pure decoration, pure play of forms on a surface; that music is pure sound, etc. There is no pure language — and it is not something to strive for.

The creative writing apparatus and publishing and friendship networks will not yield authentic modern fiction. Indeed, the influence of the university on the writer and of the writer-as-pedagogue on potential writers, has a lot to do with the sensuous, emotional, spiritual, philosophical, linguistic and moral/political poverty of fiction, above and below ground.

The romantic cliche is true: the risk of the outer world's stupidity and deprivation has to be taken to yield an art capable of acting in life, a fiction renewed as moral project.

"Radical" Is Return to Independence.
d.a. levy was prophetic. He worried "someday people/will all read poetry/& not try to live it/sort of like christianity/or buddhism or any/religion." Small presses have turned away from their historic role of bringing out material too progressive for the established media in order to suck up to government funding agencies. Most poetry mags are house organs of the Big Franchise which do not want to publish anything that might jeopardize perpetual government assistance. Aided by the National Endowment for the Arts' unwavering commitment to mediocrity, suburban nouveau hobby poetry is flourishing & the prospect of government control of literature increasing. It will be accomplished not by creeps from the CIA, but by your friendly arts funding administrator.

One means of circumventing the prohibitive book printing costs that drive many writers to Big Brother for handouts is the broadside. Artists & poets who genuinely cherish independence must merge the best of the 60's—confrontation, the questioning of premises, & guerrilla theater (but not dope lobotomy, flower senility & sloganeering) with the introspective & administrative skills acquired in the 70's. A new brew.

Back to the underground!

"Radical" Is Return to Song.
Twenty years ago Karl Shapiro wrote "Ours is probably the only poetry in history that has had to be *taught* in its own time. A contemporary art that must be taught to adults before it can be enjoyed is sick." His observation is still valid.

Kerouac pulled off the synthesis of literature & jazz in 1959 when he threw haikus at the horn men, putting poetry on equal footing with sax wail. A radical achievement then & now because *accessible* poetry threatens the academic establishment which must keep literature a dead frog for slicing.

Don Cherry used child jazz to rescue Afro-American music from the overtechnique of the neobopper. Kerouac's capacity for improvisation & rhythmic variation shattered the monotone of the theorist.

The foundation of poetry is song. On the edge of a moonlit forest Tu Fu tunes his dew moist lute. bill bissett chants for the liberation of self & language:

> i have days to go thru this soul
> relees th spirit lord. . .
> hees cummin to land th typhoon
> hees cummin to land th typhoon

A kid wrote "I used to hear lullabyes when I went to sleep/but now my pillow plays jazz on the trumpet." To make poems as pretty as a Ben Webster ballad is radical! To sing over the sellout is radical!
Tu Fu. Kerouac. bissett. Song. Soul.

Eric Baizer
Washington, D.C.
April, 1979

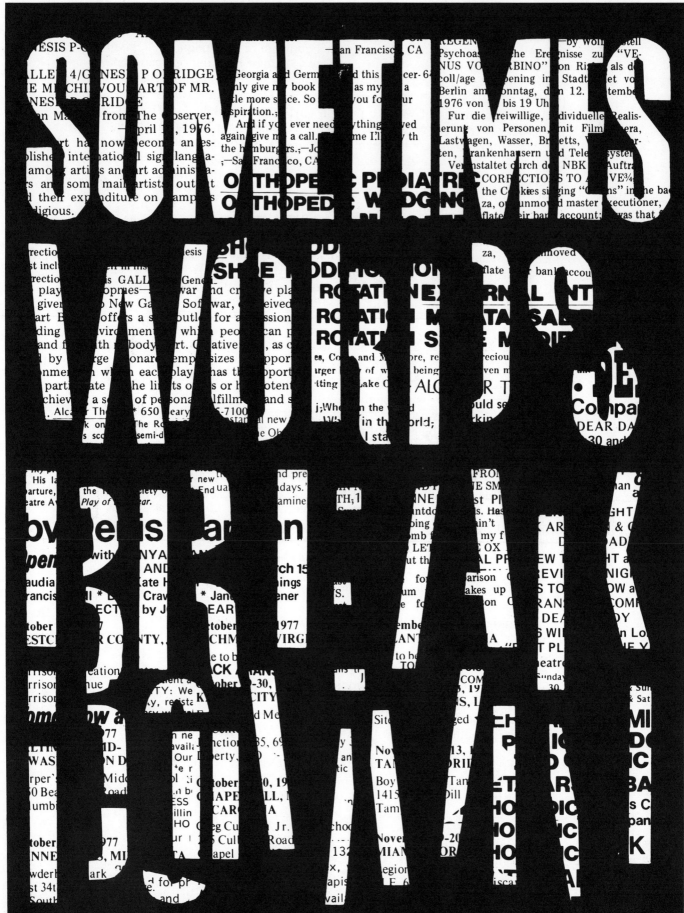

SOMETIMES WORDS BREAK LOVIN

Anna Banana Apr. '79.

OPEN STRUCTURE FOR A PHILOSOPHICAL EXPERIMENT by Peter H. Barnett

What can only take place when our attention is diverted from it? How would we learn to perceive if everything we turned our attention to were thereby eclipsed?

If whatever comes to our attention is "just past," should we view our movement through time as approaching from a distance something we can identify, or instead as falling away from everything identifiable?

What would it feel like to be part of the skin or surface of something else?

When do we realize suspension between a contained division and a division of the container?

Is there any "point in time" at which we cross the threshold from looking forward to something to looking back on it: from anticipation to retrospect?

Why can't we come to the end of a period of time without already being beyond it? If we are still in it, do we recognize its ending? If we are now beyond it, were we ever in it to begin with?

If there were a container such that you could neither get into it nor get out of it, in what sense would you belong to it?

Construct a box or container with two insides and no outside, and whose surfaces are both mutually defining and mutually excluding.

Is there a cycle of repetition which you can complete without already having begun another? Can you begin a cycle without having displaced its predecessor?

How can there be cyclical alternation unless each alternant both precedes and presupposes its complement? If we were in a phase of alternation, could we tell which repetition of the phase it was? Why do we have to suppose that the one we are in is "latest"?

What would it mean for two amoebas to engulf each other simultaneously? Could any one state of such a process be determined unless it were already succeeded?

How could we ever meet unless each of us arrived before the other?

What is there which must happen twice in order to happen once, and whose parallel occurrences both mutually define and mutually exclude one another?

Can we ever repeat a cycle, or can we only see what we have done, in retrospect, as belonging to a pair of cyclical repetitions?

What sort of interval only exists insofar as it is being formed and ceases to exist as soon as it is completed or closed? What container am I in only as long as I cannot say what contains me?

Here is a distance between us which only exists in the process of its formation: if I am to reach you, you are not yet at any point I occupy, and you are no longer at any point I can specify.

If we realize that we are repeating ourselves, we cannot go on without changing something. Then can we repeat ourselves unless the fact of repetition is somehow hidden from us?

Suppose that to realize what we are doing is actually to realize that we are repeating ourselves. In that case, would we ever do anything if we knew what we were doing?

What container or interval is there which we could never get out of if we were ever actually in it?

Is there a disposition or feeling which presupposes its continuation as the ground of its current authenticity?

Here is the feeling of lost or irrecoverable time: "If I had known what I was doing, I would not have done it." Does this actually mean, "If I had known that I was repeating myself..."?

"Lost time" means that we acted under an illusion. If the past cannot be re-entered, then, was it ever the way it appeared to us to be?

If an epoch is extinct, could it ever have been the occasion we thought it was? Try out the consequences of reducing all times to these two: that which never was as it appeared to be, and that which always is if it ever is.

If what is given in objective experience is always "just past" then our disposition is to fall away from it. Are we reliving something that was never "lived through" a first time?

What is the difference between distant times and distant places? In which do we suppose that something more is going on? In which do we suppose that nothing more is going on?

Why are we bound to suppose that the same present is inhabited by all, when this has the inevitable consequence that anyone else's "present" is objectively inaccessible to us?

They must be supposed to occur, yet we cannot locate them in time: somebody's thoughts and perceptions between his last communication and his death. Could this be accounted for by the relativity of simultaneity?

Let two persons sit where they cannot see one another and follow this instruction" "Wait as long as you can to clap before the other one does."

In order to reach a conceptual "first point in common," we have to go through a series of steps. But if we go through a series of steps together, we must already have a first point in common.

When are we in the condition of taking turns and each thinking that he had the last turn?

What kind of objective is it which I am blocked from reaching by no circumstance but by time alone? What is implied in the fact that this time interval is conceptual yet is beyond my power to foreshorten?

The illusion of a retreating visual horizon is undone if we envision approaching it from both sides: what would it mean to approach the temporal horizon from both sides?

When are we in the condition that each of us arrives after the other has left? Is this to be lost in space or to be lost in time?

When we wait for each other on opposite sides of a wall, is the nature of the barrier between us physical or conceptual? Is it overcome by travel or by realization?

The sum of the present of which I am objectively aware prevents me from apprehending whatever is present behind it. Is this what it means to "form a surface"?

What kind of interval cannot be foreshortened by any unilateral act but only by a mutual reorientation?

"I cannot yet throw up, but neither can I escape the feeling that I am going to." Nausea is a model of the irresoluble, the temporal horizon.

Can you ever tell whether what you were waiting for yesterday is what you are waiting for today?

Can you tell whether a past understanding was true or false without consulting the present? Can you verify the authenticity of your past commitment without renewing it? Try then to deny the copresence of all actual presents.

If "present" implies copresence, and if "copresent" implies mutual anticipation, could my means of access to my own presence be any different from my means of access to your presence?

What would it mean to wait in a void of your own creating, where the mutuality of the waiting realizes the condition awaited?

What feeling is always experienced as being present, never as past? What feeling is always felt as being unprecedented? "This is not what I am waiting for. I am still waiting for something else."

Realization is a relocation of perspective. But to quit perspective A for perspective B is, from the point of view of A, to do nothing intelligible. And from point of view B, we are already there, so we appear to have done nothing. The act of realization must be an act contrary to time.

Why is it that what can be stated in philosophy generally cannot be carried out? Is that because what can actually be done in philosophy cannot be stated?

If we wait, knowing what for but not when it will come, or if we wait for what we can only recognize by its being the right time, how shall we know how long to wait? How would we know when to give up?

What would it feel like to fall away from everything you can see without approaching anything you could see? Would this reorientation be felt as being mutual?

Could there be such a thing as a concrete, nonobjective intuition? If there were, would it have to be anticipatory?

Can anything be found out about the present unless it is what we construct non-objectively in the process of seeking it?

From what orientation toward time can we understand the equivalence of these three dispositions: "falling away;" "waiting in a void;" "going to meet the other"?

From what orientation toward time can we see "it has just begun" as equivalent to "it is just ended;" and see "it is not yet begun" as equivalent to "it is not yet ended"?

Here is a model of realization: to turn a corner in a desert, or where you can see in every direction. This can only mean that you are being displaced parallel to yourself.

What is given as a whole in each of its mutually-exclusive states, yet undefined except by all of its states together?

How would you go about looking for someone who is looking for you?

In what temporal model would we have to turn or fall away from each other in representation in order to approach each other as copresent?

The "double mirror": what would it mean for two ostensibly discrete experiences to make internal reference to one another? Could I send a message whose decoding simultaneously encoded a message being sent to me?

Repeat the syllables "burnum" or "man-ger" stressing the first syllable, then the second, until you can switch the stress every time a syllable is pronounced.

(a continuation on the theme of my philosophical contribution to the last two Assemblings)

MAKING BOOK

I was walking behind the
shopping center found a
book stuck out a trash compactor I
looked inside I
saw a page of eyes with worms inside
I went back home to write it down a
glass was stuck inside my brain "A book of meat?" I
thought, chewing at the inkstains on my fingers

That night I watched TV and saw a cookbook
opened in the light "Your words are
splinters flying toward my face" I yelled
a liquid swarm was speeding out my mouth I
raised my hands to hold it back but
jolt in the chair and crushed my tongue in my teeth

John M. Bennett   1979

THE BATTLE OF THE HEADLINES
****

STANLEY BERNE
STANLEY BERNE
STANLEY BERNE

american-canadian publishers inc.
drawer 2078, portales
new mexico. 88130 u.s.a.
innovative forms
tomorrows literature
a non-profit foundation

NEWSPAPERS ACROSS THE NATION HEADLINE LANGUAGE

THEORY OF ARLENE ZEKOWSKI AND STANLEY BERNE

Some Selected Headlines

TAILORING OUR LANGUAGE
San Francisco Chronicle

WORDS AS THEY ARE WRIT
London Daily Mail

AUTHORS ADVOCATE HERETICAL WAY TO TEACH JOHNNY READING, WRITING
Rocky Mountain News (Denver)

MCGOVERN TAKES SLAP AT ENMU PROFS
Portales News-Tribune (N.Mex.)

ENGLISH PROFESSORS SEEK END TO ELITEST, LIFELESS GRAMMAR
The New Haven Register

PAIR WANTS TO ABOLISH ENGLISH RULES
Enterprise-Record (Chico, Ca.)

LANGUAGE FOR THE YEAR 2000
Colorado Daily (Boulder)

CAST OFF SHACKLES OF GRAMMAR RULES SAY MISSIONARIES
The Seattle Times

AUTHORS SAY ENGLISH LANGUAGE IS OUTDATED
Albuquerque Tribune

(Selected from 4000 newspapers world-wide)

ABOLISH RULES OF GRAMMAR
Kenosha News (Wisconsin)

In January 1979 United Press International carried the Zekowski/ Berne story on their wires to 4000 newspapers world-wide. Interviews were published in The Midnight Globe and The Star (6,000,000 combined circulation).

Radio and TV carried the story. (Mutual Radio in New York carried a five minute spot out to 900 stations.)

Image Breaking Images (Arlene Zekowski) and Future Language (Stanley Berne) were published by Horizon Press, New York City, in 1977. For about six months after Horizon Press sent out copious review copies to the media, the books were virtually ignored. Silence. Suddenly all hell broke loose in January 1979. A second edition had to be printed in a hurry. American-Canadian Publishes, Inc., Drawer 2078, Portales, New Mexico, USA, handled single order copies promptly at $6.00 each. Still does.

American-Canadian Publishers, Inc.
Drawer 2078
Portales, New Mexico 88130 USA

Image Breaking Images (Zekowski) and Future Language (Berne) suggest
many ideas, among which are the following (selected):

****

1. Language is changing.

2. Grammar is too cumbersome and needs to be reformed.

3. The history of the English Language illustrates an obvious trend
   toward economy and elasticity (less cases, fewer inflections
   than Greek, Latin or Old English).

4. "Open Structure" means the "sentence" is simply less important.

5. Grammar is equated with "discipline" rather than with practical
   technology, which is always undergoing change.

6. "Open Structure" is a brain-compatible language of images.

7. "Open Structure" is the literary form invented by the four leading
   writers of the 20th century: Virginia Woolf, James Joyce, Gertrude Stein, William Faulkner.

8. Zekowski and Berne have not invented "Open Structure"; they merely
   recognized it and described it.

9. "Open Structure" as promulgated by Woolf, Joyce, Stein and Faulkner,
   is often called "Stream-of-consciousness."

10. The sentence is not at all natural to man, but has to be arti-
    ficially imposed and drilled.

11. Zekowski and Berne do not advocate "Open Structure" for newspapers,
    business reports, committee minutes, news bulletins.

12. The authors advocate that "Open Structure" is the direction towards
    which English, and all other modern European and World Lang-
    uages are inevitably moving.

13. Zekowski and Berne suggest that both languages be taught in schools:
    the language of the objective world (Command Grammar) and
    "Open Structure."

14. The suppressions of Grammar have led all people to more generous
    and interesting media: TV, video tape, radio, movies.

15. Command Grammar has too many rules and elements (300) for the
    non-author to master in his/her lifetime. This acts as de
    facto censorship to expression of "the me."

16. The future of the novel (by the year 2000) will be the explora-
    tion of the world of multiple consciousness. Access to this
    world is only through the gates of "Open Structure."

CHARLES BERNSTEIN

WITH WORDS: AN INTRODUCTION

(The following is from an introduction to a show at Ugo Carrega's Mercato del Sale gallery in Milan --With Words: An Assembling of Visual Works from New York--*which was organized by Susan Laufer and myself in March, 1979.)*

To a large extent, the people in this show are primarily either writers or visual artists whose work has, at least in part, drawn them into an area of intersection. But, I think in general, the works exhibited here are best understood in terms not of "visual poetry"--in any sense that would make that a distinct entity--but rather in terms more directly related to poetry writing or the fine arts. Both Jackson MacLow and Bruce Andrews--in the work presented here--seem interested in breaking words out of the normalizing and officiating codification of the world, allowing words to collide and jam rather than simply represent a picture of a beyond-language-world taken as status quo. MacLow's pieces, in addition, are specifically designed to serve as performance scores: a practice which subverts an internalized process of reading by necessitating that each element be read not as part of an accumulating, horizontal, movement--a syntax--but vertically interrupted (an outward movement from the page at each moment) as the elements are interpreted in a way similiar to musical notation--a radically referential sense of words and letters very much at odds with Andrews' attempt to make the words exist as far as possible for themselves and in relation to each other in the context of the page itself. What's continuously remarkable about MacLow's work, however, is that these opposing readings of the text in the end just add to its richness--they exist as simultaneities. Mira Schor's interest in personalizing art objects by placing them into some direct relation to auto-biographical content has resulted in her making diaristic writing the actual material of her constructions--here pieces are construct-ed of a translucent parchment dusted with colors and covered with handwriting. With a similiar impulse, though quite a different practice, Nick Piombino, a writer, has situated a collage made of various notebook pages and printed texts so as to be photographed by Roland Antonelli. The result is a series of works in which the photographic frame and plane take the place of the page as the medium on which the language appears, while the selective coloration gives to the texts an atmospheric airiness with shifts in color reading as changes of tone and emphasis. The situation of writing is also Michael Gottlieb's concern. Street and store signs, packing labels, public notices, etc, make up the material of his color xerox bricollage, which re-place the signs of the world at hand. Lee Sherry, whose paintings are intense studies of color and richly textured pigment with a nearly monochromatic visceralness, has become interested in her pages of hieroglyphic-like markings in the sheer graphicness of the linguistic sign. Susan Laufer's use of purely visual material in the context of bits of handwriting and type, in her collages, these non-linguistic scraps into ciphers, creating an overall feeling of intertextuality, that is, different senses of textuality being balanced against one another. Johanna Drucker's marvelous books--which involve a constantly

shifting use of typefaces and type sizes even within words--
represent a giddy thrownness into textuality, the typography
actually pulsing with the energized impulses of writing as
practically a libidinal flow. My own "veils", which involve
typewritten pages of various shapes in which writing is continued on top of writing for several layers so that the overprinting of new writing partially obliterates the writing
underneath it, come from a sense of the act of writing, that
energy having as its byproduct the visual image. Karen Eubel's
use of overprinting, in contrast, is related to her interest in
repetitive and optically dense visual structures--a typical
page for her involves various offset overprints of the same
pattern of a single letter, each overprint slightly out-of-phase
with the others, and some using a quite beautiful variety of
overprinted color. Robert Grenier, a writer, found that his
interest in seriality made him more attentive to small units of
writing and as a result he visually removed his writing from its
normal vertical and horizontal inhabitation (placement) in
page and book so that these particulars could be seen better both
for themselves and in relation to each other. His work, Sentences,
made up of 500 different sections printed on white index cards,
allows for an unlimited variation in sequence, or, in another
sense, for a 500-part simultaneous sounding. Finally, Ray DiPalma's
use of rubber stamp images as a kind of fixed vocabulary, a
pictographic grammar where repetition, blurring, juxtaposition
and serial ordering page to page give rise to a movement of
meanings realized soley by this specially made coding is very
much rooted in his sense of the poem, the movements and shifting
conveying a delight and wonder at a world brought into being
by a homemade language system.

A TEAR WRAPPED IN CANVAS

This is the gift I have to offer the critic
before he permits me to couple with him.

I could doubtless recall other cases of sur
rogate activities and ritual actions   and
could perhaps find other ways of interpre==
ting my gesture.

I might say, for instance, that the canvas
represents an emotional outburst, like the
demonstrations of feeling for generals and
biting their tongues by taxi drivers.

The tear might indicate annoyance, joy, hap
piness, physical pain, esthetic pleasure,
compassion, dissatisfaction, disappointment,
bad temper or weariness of art.

The torment I feel could arise from the fact
that I take on at one and the same time the
critic's role and the artist's.

Or rather I try to make them meet (couple)
somewhere or other, preferably at night, and
I get a kick when towards dawn I learn that
the former has just had a scrape with oblivion
and the other with success.

So my agitation extends right up to that spa
ce of myself which is the black settee in my
room.

(vito boggeri)

George Bowering

e.k.

Make it New Make it
Now Take it Now Take
if Now Tape if Now
Type if Now Type of
Now Type of Noh

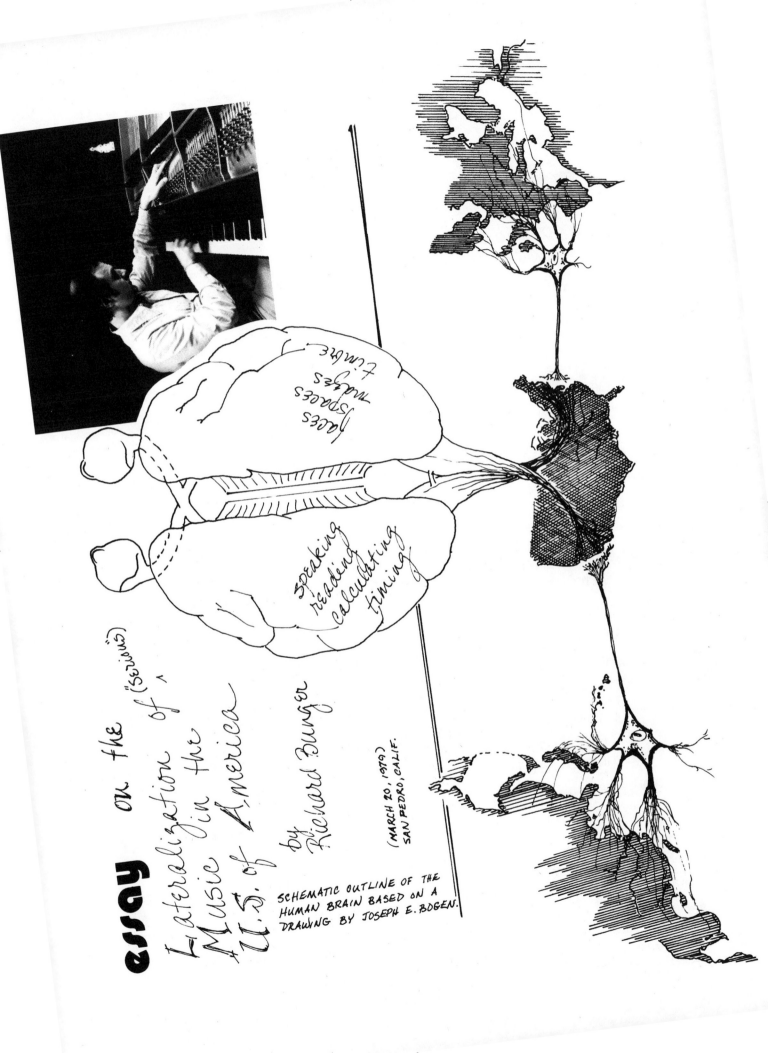

essay on the lateralization of ("serious") ∧ Music in the U.S. of America

by Richard Bunger

Faces / Spaces / Images / Emote

Speaking / reading / calculating / timing

(MARCH 20, 1979)
SAN PEDRO, CALIF.

SCHEMATIC OUTLINE OF THE HUMAN BRAIN BASED ON A DRAWING BY JOSEPH E. BOGEN.

The Literary Avant Garde
And The Time Taboo
by Richard Burgin

Every generation imagines it must create for itself an avant garde, but the "avant garde" is a cliché of the avant garde.

Something becomes a cliché from repetition without resonance. If people always talk and act the same way regardless of the situation their behavior is a cliché. If they write prose or poetry the same way for many years it also becomes a cliché, and if they merely produce work whose only originality is the ambition to be original that too is a cliché.

As imaginative writers we can avoid clichés only by constructing a fictive universe of resonance in which we write in relation to time, as we most clearly understand it, always bearing in mind, of course, Kant's limitations—that we can never know "things in themselves."

Until Kafka and Borges and their disciples like Calvino, imaginative literature avoided for 3,000 years the problem of infinity or more properly the drama of man confronting what he of necessity perceives as an infinite world.

Of course Dante endeavored to describe this confrontation in the Paradiso, but he is perhaps the example par excellence of a writer who reduced infinity to an organized system (all religions do this also) so that we could perceive this confrontation in rational finite ways.

The chief function of language (which regrettably includes with rare exceptions literary language as well) is to reduce infinity to a manageable form.

Technology which still originates with language does the same thing. This is what Faulkner meant when he said clocks hide time instead of revealing it.

The truth is your memory is your novel, you *are* only the moment you're in. Time is *not* money and money is not Time. Clock, calendar, chronological time and so called History enforce "Reality" but reality has little to do with this.

We live in moments not seconds. Moments are not linear like seconds, they are of indeterminate duration. Some last for less than a second, others for a lifetime.

We call Hamlet mad because he couldn't free himself from a moment. We call such a dysfunction of time an obsession, but obsessions like madness in general simply demonstrate one confronting time unsuccessfully.

No literature can be "avant garde" in a universe governed by infinite time.

Writers who wish to do something "new" must find ways to dramatize our sense of temporal dysfunction, our dimly perceived experience of moments.

If there is a God it is probably the interval between any two moments.

I am considerably more interested in writers with an acute awareness of their metaphysical situation than in those who experiment with calligraphy or with so called extra-literary materials.

Every object in our environment enforces the Time Taboo and keeps us from feeling what Time is.

Sex is an ideal metaphor for time. Then we feel most intensely the drop after orgasm from lived time to lost time. Then unwittingly we feel the power of the Time Taboo—the deepest of all Taboos.

It is precisely the absence of the sensual of what we traditionally call character that strikes us as distinct in the fictions of Kafka, Borges, Beckett and Calvino.

In a sense the innovations of Kafka and Borges like Schoenberg and Kandinsky are "analytical" Beckett and Calvino are neither wholly analytic nor synthetic in that they on occasion depart from the types or anonymous everymen of Kafka and Borges. Yet neither create characters—Beckett is more concerned with the permutations or deteriorations of his own voice. In Calvino the emphasis is overtly metaphysical albeit with oblique social references. He is not able however to achieve a reconciliation of his metaphysical aim with the creation of believable psychological beings.

Just as Berg was synthetic in taking what he wished to for his expressive purposes from Schoenberg's system as well as from "traditional" tonality, I feel the next step for the serious "avant garde" writer must be a synthesis of Borgesian types and metaphysics—the metaphysics of uncertainty, of dreams and fiction; in other words of infinity with a world of characters that we find say in Dostoyevsky who in many ways understood our time better than anyone now living in it.

We have left the earth and we are preparing to leave the earth. A new literature that deals with real space and time must accompany it.

It appears to me then, that the new writer, the present writer, must first and foremost try to break this taboo or at least address himself to the problem.

Optimizing

By optimizing the evolutionary processes of natural
variation and selection, the artist designs the ultimate
end state of entities that he observes in the universe.
The artist optimizes the evolutionary process of error-
correcting selection to proceed from less to more
selective destructions until - with sufficient succession -
he simplifies forms into perfect efficiency. The artist
optimizes the evolutionary process of innovative variation
to proceed from more to less probable creations until -
with sufficient time - the impossible becomes probable
and the probable is eventually inevitable.

The artist designs the end of all locks in the universe -
the most successful lockable - whose unpredictability of
internal form excludes all keys but one. He designs the
end of all keys - the key to open all closeables - the
key whose one inevitable form will release all potentially
evolvable forms. The artist becomes one of two optimally
locked forms, each containing the other's key.

Burgy

Dear Jane Bell,

                        since ouR
                   soho televIsion
                           Conversation
                   sometHing else
                   hAppened.
                   Result is
                   thirD and fourth writings

          through finnegans waKe will be different than
                        the One i began
              while you were aSking me
                   quesTions.
                     thEre
                     wiLl be five
                       Altogether
                     aNd
                     thE
                     fifTh one will be
              the realiZation of the one i began with you.

   what happened is that louis mink wRote to say
                        I had invented
              the impure mesostiC. a pure one
              would not permit tHe use of either letter
                   between two cApitals. thus,
                   what i just wRote is impure
        because "a" is repeateD in "capitals" and "what" before the "r" appears.

                     minK's right.
                   and thOugh purity
                     iS no more
                      To
                     bE desired than impurity
                   i wiLl write
                    strAight through the wake two more times
                    fiNding
                   joycE's name.
                        Then i'll finish
              the "mureau" Zig-zag soho version tv-begun with you.

                   Sincerely,   John Cage

This is not a manifesto and may be taken as such.

Language is in the world. Art, a word we like to regard with dismay, is in the world. Interior and exterior experiences are both "worldly" ones. The world generates concepts and concepts arrange the world.Nothing is created; existence is realignment. We do not create, but if we can, as Pound suggests, we, "make it new." It is the relation of the new to its precedents which propels.

The discussion centered on signifier/signified, especially the limits or powers of the former, is often misdirected. It is in the realm of conception where both the greatest freedom and the worst constrictions occur. The idea, expansive, specific, accurate or vague is accepted and its failings pushed off onto language. The word c-h-a-i-r, the object ♔, and the idea CHAIR all exist, but, granting that synchronization is both possible and desirable, it is the failure of conceptual generation that causes the discrepancy. But haven't we already passed this point? A photograph is a photograph of an object and not the object. ("Ceci n'est pas une pipe"--Magritte. It's been said enough hasn't it that the novel is a novel, or isn't a novel, but is in anycase a thing of itself. If the idea CHAIR is not precisely realised in the construction ♖, and it never is, the separation is no less than between the idea and the word. The same is true in regard to pre-existing objects (stone, tree, dog--- ◆, ♠,ㅜ) and the words used to catalogue them. There is always a space between concept/object/language. When the space no longer exists one thing is another and we are talking about something else.

Language is not even identical to itself as there is textual (written) and verbal (spoken) aspects. Now I would like to draw a diagram.

idea(pre-linguistic interior) ⟵⟶ object(exterior)
‖
linguistic thought

written language   spoken language

The English performance collective Theater of Mistakes in their piece "Going" deconstruct words and language through repitition. The same words and actions are repeated by different performers and are viewed from different angles (physically). Juxtaposedthe ambivalence in the gesture as well as the word becomes obvious. There are various possibilities in the kiss, the wave, the blow as there are in the words. Without words they would still function. Words do not enslave of themselves, rather it is our use of them. Julia Kristeva postulates that language convention defines reality. These letters are easily enough rearranged. New formations of lines can be used. Different verbal constructions are avalable.

So we are at war with grammar and syntax and this is all very good. We should not however allow ourselves the luxury of thinking of the enemy as anything other than ourselves. Thought is the convention that must be reformed. We can call the resultant permutations language or fish or glkx. Language is in flux regardless. The critical point is our attention to its movement and relation to itself and to what it is not. That's all I have to say right now.

Jamé-Maçeo CAMIER

ON WORD RAIN, ITS EQUILIBRIUM

CHARLES CARAMELLO

Et qui libre?

Marcel Duchamp

In one of his most elegant formulations, Duchamp asked: "Et qui libre?" The answer, given in the wordplay of the question (thus forming a perfectly reflexive statement, one originally presented, moreover, in a "mirrorical return"), reflects everywhere in his work. It is also reflected in Madeline Gins' Word Rain, or A Discursive Introduction to the Intimate Philosophical Investigations of G,R,E,T,A, G,A,R,B,O, It Says, a remarkable book pervasively Duchampian in its imagery. Gas, dust, bacteria, and especially the evaporation-condensation cycle of water are its primary images, as they are in Duchamp's work--especially in the Large Glass and in the last major piece, "Given: 1. The Waterfall / 2. The Illuminating Gas." Gins' game is subtle and equipoised: her book of metonymies and displacements also seeks to resolve itself in metaphor and condensation . . . in the metaphor of condensation.

Word Rain strives for complete reflexivity. With a photograph of its dust-jacket on its dust-jacket and two interior pages each composed of "itself," a gap at the margin, and (a truncated photograph of) a hand holding it, the book reflects on its materiality/ideality in the way that the Large Glass reflects on itself as artifact and idea. Discussing Duchamp's "Fresh Widow," David Antin has put the dynamics well: "it is an intermedial piece consisting of a physical construction locked between two linguistic ones [fresh widow/french window] . . . i would say that what duchamp does as an artist is to create a series of kinetic art works in which a language field defines the action of something that's put in the middle" (1). Although these are interpenetrating rather than incompatible perspectives, one could say that what is on the Large Glass as a pictorial artifact is less important to its meaning (its working, its performing) than are the cultural and metaphysical concepts in which the Large Glass is situated. Similarly, what is between the covers of Gins' book as a narrative artifact (simplified: the story of a woman reading and writing a work-in-progress while being interrupted by a party) is less important than are the cultural and metaphysical concepts of the book in which this book is situated. For Gins is not only exploring the gap between the ideal book and the material book, she seems, more importantly, to be seeking an equilibrium between the book and writing (2).

For Duchamp, the equilibrium which suggests freedom in balance is erotic and androgynous (witness his punning role as Rrose Sélavy). The female speaker of Word Rain is "a word," a "living word," one who "appear[s] on a page which would otherwise be blank. I, the mist, the agent--word rain . . . ." This speaker is also the book: "I am warmer than paper. I can hold more words. My erasures can be made to reappear. Words need not merely press themselves parallel to me; any angle of entrance is acceptable and useful." As the mist condenses on the page--as words, for example, replace blanks--the ideality of the book becomes present in the materiality of this book: "I have not been able to . . . rid myself of words. But the words, the rain of words, the weather . . . , the low warm puddles, the reflective mist; these combined to achieve the final opalescence of my presence." Because Word Rain is also an intermedial piece locked between--and attempting to mediate--word reign and word rain, this apparent mixing of erotic metaphors becomes essential to its meaning. Gins' book, like Duchamp's Glass, seems to refer to a cabalistic

tradition that we can identify with the exemplary marriage of the seventeenth-
century Jewish mystic Sabbatai Sevi to the Torah, but in both these works the
marriage rite is internalized. What is between Word Rain's covers is not,
finally, unimportant. As Philippe Sollers has said of the grands verres:
"You transform the relationship of the regarding body to the object of its
regard, which is not truly an object, being transparent" (3). Like that other
grand verre Finnegans Wake, with its river-ocean-clouds-rain-river cycle, Word
Rain internalizes and transforms subject-object relationships: its metaphorical word reign becomes a metonymical word rain, which becomes a metaphorical
word reign, and so on.

Word Rain follows the Duchampian trajectory from retinal structure to
linguistic structure to conceptual structure to neurological/cosmological
structure. And it, too, finally sustains itself in equilibrium. It has no
"ending": it quotes the final passages of a score of other books; its last
page is a palimpsest of multiple typings which conclude: "This page contains
every word in the book"; its endpapers display a concretist chart of the book's
"flow," whose gloss in the narrative projects a free-standing grand verre:
"The most significant thing I was doing was creating a platform, perpendicular
to my forehead, parallel to the sentences." Word Rain cannot end because, on
the one hand (the quotations), there is no end to the intertextuality of writing, and because, on the other (the "flow"-chart), the book in which the world
was meant to end may be a mystical book of eternal return. Madeline Gins has
inscribed Word Rain on the silence between writing and book, between indeterminacy and immanence (4), between the and riverrun, between bachelor and bride:
between question and answer.

(1) davidantin, "duchamp and language," in Marcel Duchamp, ed. Anne
d'Harnoncourt and Kynaston McShine (The Museum of Modern Art, 1973), pp. 104-5.

(2) "The idea of the book is the idea of a totality, finite or infinite,
of the signifier; this totality of the signifier cannot be a totality, unless
a totality constituted by the signified preexists it, supervises its inscriptions
and its signs, and is independent of it in its ideality. The idea of the book,
which always refers to a natural totality, is profoundly alien to the sense of
writing. It is the encyclopedic protection of theology and of logocentrism
against the disruption of writing, against its aphoristic energy, and . . .
against difference in general." Jacques Derrida, Of Grammatology, trans. Gayatri
Chakravorty Spivak (Baltimore: Johns Hopkins Univ. Press, 1976), p. 18.

(3) Philippe Sollers, in David Hayman, "An Interview with Philippe Sollers,"
TriQuarterly, No. 38 (1977), p. 129.

(4) "At the far limit of indeterminacy, however, the figurative state of
silence . . . reigns. Silence begins as "experiment" in literature, its urge
to question and contest itself, and it moves through self-parody and self-
subversion, radical irony, to the edges of speech. There, on the dark margins
of consciousness, literature wants to consume or transcend itself wholly--in
vain. And precisely there, on the margins of silence, the dream of immanence
teases literature, teases all art, back into waking. As in Finnegans Wake."
Ihab Hassan, "Culture, Indeterminacy, and Immanence: Margins of the (Postmodern)
Age," Humanities in Society, 1, No. 1 (1978), 78.

COLOR ASSIMILATION

ITS NAME = HUE
   RED; ORANGE; YELLOW; VIOLET; BLACK; GREEN; WHITE; BLUE

ITS LIGHTNESS TO DIMNESS = HUE / BRIGHTNESS
   NUES OF THE SAME RATIO ARE OF LIKE BRIGHTNESS.
   THE DEGREES OF TWO ~~OPPOSITE~~ HUES ADDS UP TO 120.
   THE RATIO OF TWO ~~OPPOSITE~~ HUES ADDS UP TO 12.

ITS DAZZLE TO DULLNESS = HUE / SATURATION

   CENTER = HUE / DULLNESS
      NEUTRAL IS THE INFLUENCE OF RED-GREEN; ORANGE-BLUE;
      YELLOW-VIOLET; BLACK-WHITE, SOMETIMES CALLED GRAY.
   CIRCUMFERENCE = HUE / DAZZLE

TO WORK WITH PAINT ONE NEEDS TO UNDERSTAND THE FOLLOWING:

   MIXING PAINT IS THE ~~OPPOSITE~~ OF SEEING PAINT.
   TO MAKE A HUE LIGHTER USE THE INFLUENCE OF A LIGHTER
   HUE (RATIO) THEN AS A LAST RESORT USE WHITE (ITS OPAQUE).
   ITS STRENGTH (COMMERCIAL TINTING).
   TO REVERSE THE RATIO NUMBER IS NECESSARY TO UNDER-
   STAND THE BASIS FOR NEUTRALIZING ~~OPPOSITE~~ HUES
   (EXAMPLE: 9 PARTS YELLOW = 3 PARTS VIOLET).

THE ENCLOSED INFORMATION IS ONLY INFORMATION. WHAT IS HERE IS FOR THE MIND AND <u>NOT</u> TO BE PHYS-ICALIZED.

YOUR WAY IS TO DO THE WORK THAT ONLY YOU CAN DO.

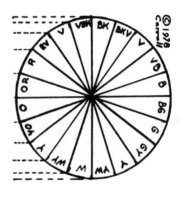

DEGREE	110°		90°		70°	50°	30°	10°
RATIO	11		9		7	5	3	1
HUE	BK		V		R	O	Y	W

D-I-M-E-N-S | | | | | | L-I-G-H-T

U-N-M-E-A-S-U-R-E-D

HUE	BK	V	B	G	Y	W
RATIO	11	9	7	5	3	W
DEGREE	110°	90°	70°	50°	30°	10°

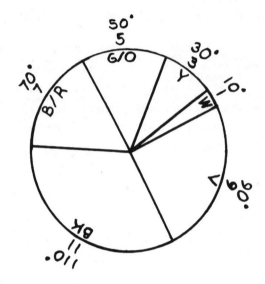

©1978 Carroll

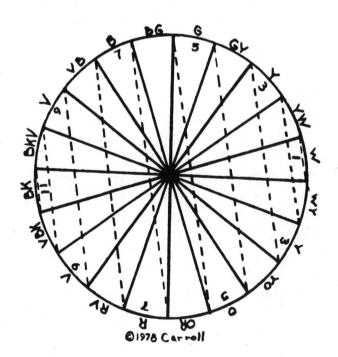

©1978 Carroll

MODERNISM IN CONTEMPORARY LITERATURE, or the Case of the Missing Switchboard Instigator

At the moment, the retrenchment of the avantgarde in the field of aesthetics has occasioned the reconstruction of the armaments surviving from the skirmishes of earlier experimentation. The problematic status of innovation has called a truce into a successive array of stylistic nuance.

What remains to be done?

In each artform, there has been the succinct realization of <u>crisis</u>. Modernism per se is besieged by the demands of integration: an increasing domesticization has induced the discomfort of acceptability. Art no longer is situated within the confines of a restricted context: accessibility has caused the infiltration of vanquishing elements through the barricades of artistic endeavor. With increasing velocity, the claims of specificity and/or synthesis have surrendered to a policy of <u>suspension</u>.

The definition of modernism vis-a-vis literature is dependent upon the strictures of sensibility. Just how extreme or radical or strenuous must the precepts be before the appellation of modernism is awarded? Conceptualizing modernism in terms of self-consciousness, irony, and analytic scrutibility, an immediate result is an awareness of the current limitations on irony. The mechanistic reflexivity of the mode has developed a manner of regard which is increasingly insular. The insistence on formal developments has deflected the emphasis away from "experience". Just what experience is reflected in an ontological assertion which is apodistic?

The assumption of the avantgarde generates from an acknowledgement of the establishment. The avantgarde must maintain an antagonsim to the concept of tradition. For the assertion of an advance, there must be some conception of a rear. The congruence of modernism and avantgarde is a presumption no longer borne out in practice. To stipulate the existence of an academy requires an accepted criterion of opinion. For the avantgarde, the locus of that academy must coincide with the possibility of consensus.

At this time, addressing the issue of the avantgarde in terms of literature is a matter of evaluation. What remains important in terms of the consideration of the avantgarde is the avowal of contemporaneity. However, just as modernism need not equal avantgarde, so, too, avantgarde need not coincide with modernism. Within the continuance of the avantgarde, the lack of historicization has rendered the tenets of style into a perpetual cycle. As the formal constructs evolve, the conceptual precepts appear in regression: the resultant premise is one of contradiction. At the center of that contradiction lies the malaise of the modernist sensibility. The crisis induced by the acknowledgement of that malaise should be prescriptive of avantgarde aesthetics. That such a situation does not exist is symptomatic of the cooptation of impulse: the collapse of defensivity renders the avantgarde powerless.

The discernment of "difficulty" appears as a primary focus for the adherents of the avantgarde. Yet one of the difficulties involved in the avantgarde is the dialectic which must exist between the construct of the establishment and the revelation of the antagonism. In an important sense, the enterprise of the avantgarde is one involving an access to duplicity: tha avantgarde institutionalizes bad faith, for the involvement of the avantgarde is dependent upon the factor of establishment authority.

Do we say what we mean?

The fact that there is, at present, no coherent avantgarde is indicative of the lack of a defined establishment. What values are opposed, when there are few cohesive values? Although the pretense of authority exists, the fact that this authority is unfounded has made the dialectic value of the avantgarde superfluous.

Although the perception of a diffused focus ought to result in a system of plurality, the outcome has been a general loss of lucidity. The question at this time is: what is avantgarde literature? At present, there are few practitioneers whose work maintains a commitment to the modernist dictum of "seriousness" as well as to the avantgarde aspiration of "revolution". Adjusting to the problematic status of an entropic continuity, the potential for genuine achievement is marred by the probability of condescension. The problem at this time is: where is the audience for avantgarde literature? For better or worse, the responsivity of the audience qualifies the work, in so far as that work must approach communicability.

The current situation for the avantgarde is stymied by the lack of a coherent continuity: the audience is one which is divided by the concurrent manifestations of sensibility. The contradiction between modernism and avantgarde may be analogized in terms of the theater. The formal configurations of, say, Robert Wilson or Richard Foreman provide the setting for an aesthetic which is, in actuality, quite "arrieregarde" in terms of the actual "meaning". The supposition that meaning need not concern the specialized audience is one which ascribes to a spurious notion that already established is a corpus of "meaning". Avantgarde valuations supposedly oppose "meaning". Unfortunately, such is not the case.

Recently, a number of prose works have been written by those who profess an affinity with the art world. Striking in these works is a quality of naivete which results from the deliberate use of conventions which appear to the writer to be "avantgarde". However, these devices are resolutely anachronistic, although the loss of irony in their deployment signal the ahistorical awareness from which the work derives.

The problems of language and of narrativity would appear to be central to the modernist development of literature as a serious art form. The difficulty of the avantgarde would seem to reflect a discomfort in terms of position.

In terms of the split between modernism and avantgarde-ism, categorizing might be of benefit. For example: Constance De Jong and Kathy Acker are writers who are "avantgarde" without being "modernist", while Thomas Pynchon and John Barthes are "modernist" without being "avantgarde". The problematic status of the avantgarde is not ameliorated by the discrepancy between the avantgarde and the modernist sensibility. Perhaps the most sharply defined example of this split in terms of sensibility might be given in the case of "punk". The current "punk" sensibility is one founded on nostalgia, for the gestures, the mannerisms, and the general outlook have been appropriated from sources which have been dated. The fact that "punk" proclaims the ascendancy of "rock" at a time when the populist direction of music is "disco" (and the fact that "punk" is hostile to "disco" barely conceals the racial antagonism between whites attempting to retain an image of supremacy at a time which has seen the aftermath of black consciousness) points out the irrelevancy of the "punk" sensibility. Irrelevance, however, does not equal unimportance.

Carrying analysis further, an important factor in the decline of the avantgarde is the lack of resources in terms of education. Taking dance as an instance in this system, the fact that ordinary movement has become a defined staple of dance formalism is a signal of the neglect which is the background of many dancers, i.e., the purpose of ordinary movement lies in its opposition to the movement of dance training. For those dancers trained in styles dependent upon ordinary movement, the dialectic between dance training and ordinary movement does not exist, therefore rendering the ordinary movement as a feature of style rather than as a reaction of antagonism. Without that antagonism, ordinary movement is reduced to "interestingness".

The arts are, at this time, "interesting".

Meanwhile, the general tendency seems to involve going Hollywood.

-----Daryl Chin
New York City
Spring 1979

paul christensen

Preface to a Manifesto

America now is at a standstill; a vast and solemn quiet hangs over civilization confusing and disheartening poets writing this moment to the next. A mad scramble ensues as some of us dart back from the frontier into the old conquered ground of thought where we domesticate verse to the old forms and the old summations. Some few plod forward without direction trying to remain experimental and scary to a diminishing audience bored with shrillness. We've all come to find ourselves writing in a deep trough between epochs, at the middle of our lives, without the benefit or the outrage of great fathers to overthrow. We have become a mob without leaders; a mass of jittery scribes who can't discriminate any longer the new from the worn out in our work. The language of poetry has once again blocked only a fragment of the whole of real speech and experience, and the same words are churned and sifted through the old frames of selfhood. I take it many of us consider Ed Dorn's **Gunslinger** an act of recent greatness, but close-up it is an angry satire on dying ideas; it does not move us forward to a new shape of life with values to freshen or invigorate our stance.

What we need now is a whole new desire to stretch consciousness to the borders of existence to see what comes toward us out of time. My conviction is that we are lolling in a dead verse just at the border of a vast new structure of human life. We are now in the final throes of the old male supremacy: all around us men are languishing in neglect, and poets can barely speak of the threadbare remains of their epoch. There are no elegies or lamentations, only the impulse to count the minutes of silence in tiny verses of pitying self-consciousness. The form of male dominance has been abandoned by all of us, as we either feminize our psyches or find solace in homosexuality. An incredible energy of language now erupts from women and from other races: they are the future of earth. And as the old supremacy dwindles away, the nations that were its form also decay and prepare to disappear. America is the last of the great nation-forms, and it is losing its shape; it is collapsing silently onto the landmass. Nationness itself is a delicate membrane that cannot hold humanity in categories much longer. The earth is cohering again; its races are mingling; the sexes are transcending the old differentiations; a form of things slowly emerges from the whorl of recent centuries that will be the nameless immensity of content for the poet to translate. He no longer has his self to interpret; he is a fragment in solution with all else that exists, and his task will be to swim instead of merely drown.

The stagnation of verse now is a lull before apocalypse. There is every sign in the sky and earth that nature is making a quantum leap. All the poets are at this moment drifting into the future with the clues of its shape everywhere about them. But when poets are not prophets, they are only hacks who nag at the boredom of their lives. Miracles loom at the edges of every line of contemporary poetry, but no poet pushes himself sufficiently over the edge to get at them. When one of us does get up to interpret, others will follow, and we will straggle into the dance others enjoy.

Poetry now is only a scavenger art lyricizing the remains of personality. Verse sadly concentrates on minute sensation, momentary disequilibrium, tiny claims of spirituality in the void of meaning. It is a literature of hopeless accomodation to the whole dying edifice of Western civilization. Something nameless and awesome is rising and overtaking every recognizable facet of human order. The "I" of poetry is even now only an empty nickname for an awareness that has overleapt individuality and become entangled in the rest of life. The poet who solemnly reminds

himself of his personal existence in cranky lyrics hacks at the entanglement he has no language to express; he chooses to be spokesman for the grief and dislocation others feel. And most of the reading public has already sloughed literature from their consciousness and consoled themselves with vacant manuals and books of advice. The poets continue to revive the last Hellenic flames of selfhood with deteriorating words and feeble grammar that when published look sprawled and fossilized on the page.

An earth coheres at the edge of poetry; it joins its edges together without regard to all the aging boundaries of Western mentality. The least likely partners come together and merge their differences. The white race is crushing its edges into other pigments as the center rages and worships purity. The West dissipates itself into utter foreignness. Suddenly the remotest past, the origins of consciousness itself, are new and welcome in thought, as though we had come around again to the beginning. East rushes to Westernize, to engorge that final alienation in order to move beyond history altogether. The West hangs in a deep immobility of uncertainty and entropy of mind, allowing every other nationality and cultural vortex to come and plunder it. A willing rape; a

massive, fertile, voluptuous thing lies across several continents waiting for lovers to fill its womb with newness. But poets linger in the shade of that event counting the facets of their loneliness.

The times were never as ripe for poetry as they are now. The poet must accept the circumstance of no fixity, of no boundary, of no category, and go out of his life to swim in the flood. Verse should be without knowing of any kind, and without trace of identity—it should be the anonymous language of reconnoitering. The poet should only want to see what the news is all about, devoid of causality. The vision to grope toward is of an uncategorical totality, of things joined inextricably together. Everything falls into everything else in the drama of transition, but the form it is making is beyond poery to understand. There is only the immensity of the event taking place, the freedom it poses, thrill of its total strangeness to thought. The language for poetry is no longer words; it is the range of sensations felt by this immeasurable transformation of the realm of being. The word should only be the last resort of the adventure; the reluctant shorthand of dazzled travelers. There is nothing to lament; no self to suffer; only the riprap of the participation, the gaps, the fissures of excitement between the evasions of nouns and verbs.

HOMAGE TO ANNE TRUITT

I

```
TRUITT                          TRUITT
R    R                          R    R
U    U                          U    U
I    I        TRUITT            I    I
T    T        R    R            T    T
T    T        U    U            T    T
R    R        I    I            R    R
U    U        T    T            U    U
I    I        TRUITT            I    I
T    T                          T    T
TRUITT                          TRUITT
```

II

```
TRUITTRUITT                     TRUITTRUITTRUE
R                               R    R    T
U                               U    U    T
I                               I    I    U
T                               T    R    E
T                               T    T    T
I              TRUE             R    T    R
S              R    T           U    I    U
T              U    R           I    U    E
R              I    U           T    R    T
U              T    E           T    R    R
E              TRUE             TRUETRUITTRUEU
```

William Claire
4·79

AN ANARCHIST'S DILEMMA　　　*Merritt Clifton*

Because I do not believe in extortion, theft, or slavery, I customarily avoid contributing to heavily grant-subsidized publications: grants in effect compel every taxpayer to support projects he does not freely choose to, robbing him of his time and labor. A CRITICAL ASSEMBLING is thus to the average American what the plantation-subsidized southern quarterlies were to black fieldhands slightly over a century ago. The difference is in degrees, not philosophical justifications; a few elite still enjoy privilege at cost of the many.

I also do not believe in censorship; over the years, the independent ASSEMBLING has provided a unique open forum for cultural dissidents. I have declined invitations to contribute before not from disrespect, but because I have my own forum, SAMISDAT, and because while I 'experiment' ceaselessly toward communicating with maximum intellectual and emotional impact, I am not truly an 'experimental' writer. My mediums are fiction, essays, columns, articles, and poetry, all more-or-less as traditionally defined. My experiments are not with sound, visual form, or grammatical structure, nor with other attempts to translate fleeting thought into permanent words. Rather, I work with time: time-lapse, time-shifts, and most especially time-condensation. I believe literature at point of conception is stopping time: a poem stops and captures a climactic moment, a story a sequence of moments building toward the climax, a novel multiple climactic episodes building toward a greater realization. My time-stopping methods include flashback, stories-within-stories, and others no doubt ancient when Homer used them. I view these methods as tools, means to philosophical ends, not ends in themselves.

I contribute to A CRITICAL ASSEMBLING now partly in political protest, partly because it offers an unparalleled opportunity to voice my objections to the common trends in 'experimentalit'; not to those reacting against it out of shallow prejudice, stereotypically ignorant of art but knowing what they like, nor to those favoring it from mere knee-jerk response to anything faddish, but to those actually engineering it, attempting to understand it in general as well as specific, and vice-versa, introducing it as well as mimicking what has come before bearing the name.

In protest, I ask fellow contributors how this book or any other can help build a better world, when for all the good intentions behind it, it remains engendered by repressive, exploitative institutions. It is at best a symbol of socialism or capitalism replacing feudalism: serfs now work for 'the people', meaning the state, or corporations and unions deriving their economic strength from the state, and though standards of living rise, pursuit of happiness remains difficult as ever because true freedom remains scarce as ever. From the bottom of our murky pit, we may perceive the heavens, but we confine ourselves and all those we live among to a kind of hell nonetheless, ruled by faith that each of us or some gifted one among us knows how all of us should live and think.

In objection, I assume as departure point that at least those of us here write with serious purpose, not just for personal amusement or for self-definition as 'author', a class of person somehow supposed to be more glamorous, more respected, and more sexually gratified than any other. Presumably, we write to get something across to others, something of importance to others, not just of interest to ourselves. Our common objective is lasting effect on readers we may never meet, who may never run across our work again, nor even remember our names. Fame and fortune may be desireable short-term rewards, but our actual long-range goal is changing or opening hearts and minds.

To search eternally after whatever best achieves this is both natural and necessary. The vehicle stopping one moment, expressing one message, one insight, does not necessarily stop another of different scope and dimensions. Those opposing this kind of genuine experimentation, of testing and exploring, or afraid to do it, become mere hacks and drudges, endlessly grinding away at formulas proven successful in a limited context, self-barred from any further growth. Serious readers cannot long respect or remain interested in authors who do not experiment;

sincere experimentation both measures and demonstrates the drive to communicate.

However, any particular type of experiment, when unswervingly adhered to, when advocated as a new, universal literary religion, is every bit as constricting as the rules for genre science-fiction or romance, or the old patterned verse forms. Stanley Berne and Arlene Zekowski provide an instance: decent, hard-working, friendly people, nonetheless as trapped by their crusade for grammarless language as any 9-to-5 worker on a treadmill assembly-line. What they advance, knowingly or not, is really nothing more or less than what the Connecticut Yankee's page-boy wrote in King Arthur's Court, no better adapted to complex or deep thinking now than it was in Mark Twain's time, when he aptly made gentle fun of it. Berne and Zekowski are fascinating talkers, unconsciously putting in all the structure and punctuation with their accents and pauses that on paper they omit; yet I suggest neither has in some thirty years of writing produced any work lasting as anything beyond a curio.

Part of experimenting is failing and understanding failure. Or, as Ted Williams puts it in THE SCIENCE OF HITTING, as expert an approach to accomplishment as any treatise ever written, "As Yogi Berra says, you can't think and hit. But know what you've done when you've done it. Don't strike out and not know what fooled you." Implicit is never fooling one's self. The mere fact of attempting an experiment, or of formulating a theory, is not by itself a worth-while result, any more than merely swinging a bat produces hits. At some point one must connect with a reader's attention and absorption, preferably sooner than later, hard than soft. Yet too often experimentalit writers do fool themselves. Work is reviewed as valid if conforming to some established 'experimental' criteria, an ultimate contradiction in terms, whether or not possessing further significance. Five centuries after Gutenberg and Caxton introduced printed poetry, ending a few million years of almost exclusively oral tradition, poems meant to be read aloud rather than printed re-emerge, suffering from the same lack of versatility and transfer-ability that rendered them obsolete in the first place. Four centuries after shaped poems enjoyed a brief vogue in England, Bob Cobbing and Phil Smith among a host of others play with that idea again, and so it goes, so-called experiments repeating themselves eternally, never managing to say enough often enough to emerge as standard literary tools. More recent, more demonstrably communicative one-time experiments such as the prose vernacular, free verse, and imagism are in every author's repetoire long since. Simultaneously, from the same blind-ness, experimentaliterati tend to dismiss other work experimenting less self-consciously. Perhaps one ASSEMBLING reader in 1,500 has read THE COMPLEX VISION OF PHILO ST. JOHN, by Martin Helick, a well-produced and promoted novel successfully doing all James Joyce does in ULYSSES, without affected, gimmicky 'cleverness'. Maybe two in 1,500 have read Tom Suddick's A FEW GOOD MEN, where an abstract concept of honor and duty is the central figure, rather than any of eight different narrators. These are legitimately experimental works, risking the unconventional to say the difficult in an easily absorbed and comprehended manner. Here literary design becomes literary archetecture, "the art of the practical made beautiful."

"The medium is the message", Marshall McLuhan said of the first generation to grow up with TV, the generation to which most of us loosely belong. The phrase sums up a cultural picture badly out of balance; only when we experiment toward balance, toward putting message first, can any experiments succeed. Ultimately we must remember writing is not thought itself, but instead an alternating current of thought-cues and thought-summary, that our little tools are parts of bigger ones, invented to work for us, not just be. We can blend art forms, express literature through new media, and make communication a participant rather than passive activity, but in so doing we must not forget what literature is, must avoid technique for the pure sake of technique just as in daily life we oppose environmentally destructive technological projects carried on simply because technology makes them possible. Like scientists now disc-overing quality of technical achievement and quality of life do not always coincide, we must consider quality of communication, not merely quality of experiment—and our only accurate qualitative yardstick must be voluntary response, however hard it is to come by.

POSSIBLE TITLE
DIALOGUE BETWEEN WITH VOICE OFF

PERHAPS THIS IS A STORY A SHORT STORY OR MAYBE PART OF A LONG STORY A LONG STORY OF THE USUAL BANAL HUMAN LOVE HATE RELATIONSHIP
THE CHARACTERS HAVE NO IDENTITIES OR MAYBE THIS IS THE REASON WHY THEY DO HAVE ONE
WE'LL GIVE THEM NAMES JUST TO MAKE READING IT EASIER BUT ANY REFERENCE TO REALITY IS NATURALLY COINCIDENTAL
SHE=AN ART HE=AN ARTIST THE OTHER=A CRITIC
NOTE THIS STORY ISN'T BY ME OF COURSE IT'S BEEN CUT OUT HERE AND THERE FROM A TRUE LOVE MAG

AUGUSTO CONCATO

SHE	HE	THE OTHER
	She thinks I'm innocent. Thought it's not the truth I have to let her think so.	
	If she knew the truth she wouldn't want to go on seeing me and I love her too much, I can't bear to lose her. I know she's waiting there for me.	
Cut it out. And don't stare at me. I want to be alone.	Alone?	
Sometimes I think you don't love me.		SUDDENLY HE BENDS DOWN. HE KISSES HER SOFTLY.
		A LONG SILENCE FOLLOWS, FRAUGHT WITH DOUBTS AND HOPES. UNCERTAIN FEELINGS OF JOY AND FEAR THROB IN THE SMOKE-LADEN AIR.
Now are you satisfied? Have you appeased your vanity?	Let go of my hand.	THE ANSWER IS A KISS.
Impossible.	Heck!	THEY FIND THEMSELVES WRAPPED IN A CONVULSIVE EMBRACE.
Listen, I've got an idea.	Let me do as I think best. Go on, don't worry.	
Within a few days we won't have to meet in secret.	But what is this "good news" have you found a job?	THE SLAP ECHOES SHARPLY.
	Oh... What's got into you? Tell me what it means.	
At your orders!	Do you mean it?	THEN SUDDENLY A START.
	It's horrible, what I've done.	SHE GIVES A CURT, IRONICAL SMILE.
Keep calm, don't raise your voice. Sit down again and go on.	Oh...	AT BOTTOM SHE'S JUST THE SAME WHEN SHE WAS LITTLE SHE USED TO KEEP TO HERSELF TOO, GAZING INTO SPACE AND DREAMING OF GOODNESS KNOWS WHAT.

(ARRAY DAY)

THEO RETICAL   CRITI CISM

david cole

< Okay >

Two of the more 'creative' features of language, says Ferdinand
de Saussure, are association and analogy. In the former, four modes
prevail. Bundles of relations stem from new sets splaying off either
a common radical or a suffix; so that Hook can decline to hooked
and hooking, etc., while in the second instance hooker and hocker
can lead to looker and locker. Or in the third, analogy of concepts
which the word signifies can be said to regulate enumeration of new terms:
the noun hook will fasten onto crook, or a feathered fly -- the staff of
the angler's lure -- will latch onto the shepherd's crozier, then a needle
for crochet, a crocketed capital, or even the bend of a question-mark
(chance of "monopoly"), the hook of doubt on the keyboard of the typewriter, etc. From association of concepts there could be enchained a
cane, an umbrella, a stipulation, a loop-hole, a tea-cup and saucer,
a socle and so on. Minimally and most concretely, hook would have
been both sides of its bend. Now the fourth category of association occurs

> "OE. hóc: MLG. hôk, MDu. hoec, Du. hoek, MLG. hōk,
> corner, angle, nook, point of land. In ablaut relation with
> OE. haca, 'pessolus', a (?) hooked bolt, and app. also with
> MDu. hake (? hōke), Du. haak, OHG. hākko, hâkko (also
> hâsso), mod. Ger. haken, O.N. hakū, Sw. hake, Da. hage,
> hook: see HAKE sb."² (O.E.D., V. i, 343, col. 1)

                                  via resemblance of sound-images, where
a word spins into sometimes a "double similarity of meaning and form. The last
case is rare and can be classed as abnormal, for the mind naturally discards
associations that becloud the intelligibility of discourse. But its existence can be
proved by a lower category of pun based on the ridiculous confusions that can
result from pure and simple homonomy" (Course in Gen. Linguistics, pp. 126-27).

Okay, Saussure would say, "hook might swirl in the smoke of hookah, or embed in an oak once called a hooke; it might recall the sycophant derived from the figure of a hook-billed snipe that clasps a fig in its beak; or hooky children practice (in the North) to play hockey." By association the word engenders infinite forms that the more systematic relations (in compounds, phrases, sentences along the path of common sense) would delimit.

In the latter, analogy, new shapes generate according to the model of one or more others which follow a definite rule. The linguist almost called it an œdipal drama "with a cast of three" (p. 163) where 1) the legitimate heir or nominative has 2) a rival mate from 3) the "collective character" that gave birth to the second form. On this scene we see how a simple shift does the trick, where

$$OK : hocqvet = okay : x$$
$$x = ochkay$$

Here no terms are lost, as the new ochkay stands to gain and save language from the vagary of signifiers and stricture of history. Ochkay puts the hiccup (fr: j'ai le hocqvet) back in our pallid "yes" with a healthy reminder of heartburn.

A belch is more than okay. Okay. Ochkay Saussure would add (over a cup of coffee) that in analogy, "its end result — creation — belongs only to speaking." But how can we speak with a burp of the eye, since hoc- or -och fasten to -kay and catch the ochre of their look, their shape of an eye in an oculis? Analogy leads back to association, and vice-versa, a slippage that graphics* provide. Speech hooks into ok or ok. And there we are exorbitantly spent in the phenomena of language.

To trace Okay over and over, back through our threads, would assure via Saussure how the graphic gloss of okay, its visible language, deserves more than a rejoinder of that colorless yes, okay, we putter every day. (See Old Kinterhook near Albany.) With the hook and hocqvet of ochkay the visible seizure and glottal syncope within an oral yes are cast beyond any doubt. For etymologists, Old Kinterhook is the original   scene of creation, where the place-name was drawn away in a paralysis of okay.

Berkeley, CA   Tom Conley

*nb - graphite of #2 (for future work)

Great Women of History
(or a Revised Dinner Party)

1. Leni Riefenstahl
2. Lucretia Borgia
3. Lady MacBeth
4. Marie de Medici
5. Anita Bryant
6. Mary Tudor
7. Alta
8. Cosima Wagner
9. Unity Mitford
10. Lizzie Borden
11. Eva Peron
12. Livia Augusta
13. Theodora
14. Eva Braun
15. Clodia
16. Popeye
17. Eleanor of Aquitaine
18. Queen Jezebel
19. Heriodias
20. Leila Kaland
21. Lady Bird Johnson
22. Madame Mao
23. Mrs. Lenin
24. Gloria Steinem
24. Gloria Steinham
25. Sally Stanford

26. Marie Antoinette
27. Queen Fredegunda
28. Diane Moseley
29. Madame Pompadour
30. Empress Josephine
31. Agrippinilla
32. Bonnie Parker
33. Catherine the Great
34. Betty Freidan
35. Mata Hari
36. Martha Raye
37. Lola Montez
38. Medea
39. Squeaky Fromm
40. Bianca Jaegger
41. Margo St. James
42. Gloria Vanderbilt
43. Shirley Temple
44. Tempest Storm
45. Frieda Lawrence
46. Indira Gandhi
47. Elizabeth, Empress of Russia
48. Clytemnestra

GEOFFREY COOK

i can walk through the world as Music (sometimes)

you may walk through the world as music

making the sounds pure and total
in their arrival to your ear.

(when i want this
you may want this
and to do this

the world, of this locus,
arriving to our ears
and in our heads
how this and any place
                particular-placed
arrives and really
is, with us — within

hear those sounds

The Art of Noise

Let's walk together through a great modern capital,
with the ear more attentive than the eye, and we will vary
the pleasures of our sensibilities by distinguishing among
the gurglings of water, air and gas inside metallic pipes,
the rumblings and rattlings of engines breathing with obvious animal spirits, the rising and falling of pistons, the
stridency of mechanical saws, the loud jumping of trolleys
on their rails, the snapping of whips, the whipping of flags.
We will have fun imagining our orchestration of department stores' sliding doors, the hubbub of the crowds, the
different roars of railroad stations, iron foundries, textile
mills, printing houses, power plants and subways.

by Luigi Russolo

yet i suspect that this Futurist was thinking more for sources of raw materials, for making
his musical composition. He goes on to "score and regulate harmonically and rhythmically"
yet that is now not what we want (to do —

could he too go out with us in all this to just to listen?

Accept that as the composition!

and Not to expect those enumerations
nor to search for such
And certainly not to analyze
(and not at all the poetry of description)

To hear! and that the eye focus will limit perception
to a certain thing, and we will not
sacrifice or fail to perceive the expressions of
humanity in these things But we want
to get it all, and that all of our
prejudicing limiting perception-devices
are open full so that we come to hear it.

Walk quietly through, at - even - rate

and not fast or our own activity would draw the mind. [n]

Becoming just easy and empty we localize all,
come to be focus of simultaneous total surround us.

Neither lingering nor rushing.

And so within the mind.   give-up giving out distractions and
                                                         with the voice.

Take - IN

to a time when some one might stop. The mind turns away by many ways—
— like that certain thing that sticks to you. — your own person suckling the
spirit deep within and far away.   When this happens you know it is over.

LISTS

ONLY

ROWS

ONLY

TALLIES

ONLY

ENUMERATIONS

ONLY

CATALOGUES

ONLY

ROLLS

ONLY

ROSTERS

ONLY

SCHEDULES

ONLY

INDICIES

ONLY

REGISTERS

ONLY

INVENTORIES

ONLY

LISTS

JEAN-JACQUES CORY

page containing the pre-, present and post history ⱡ of the writer and
reader of this same page. a beginning and end of the history of all
involvement with the page. a condensed version.

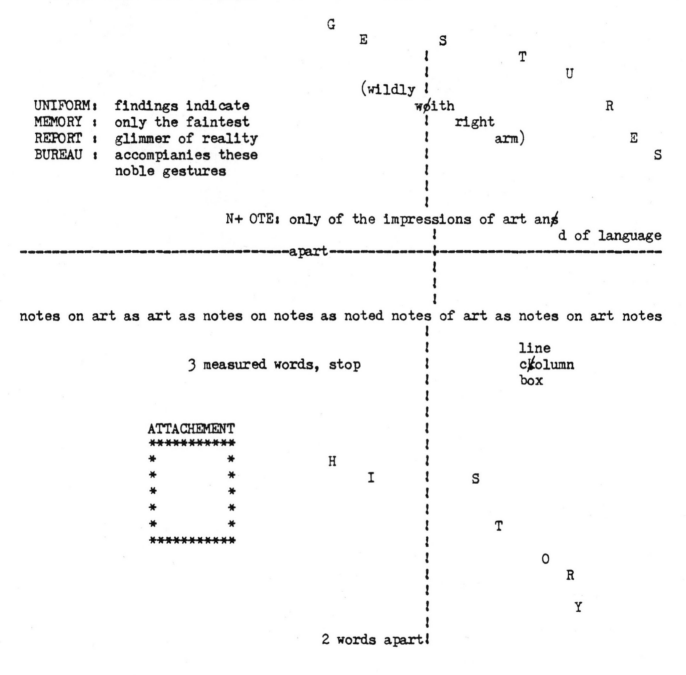

```
                                      G
                                 E         S
                                      ¦              T
                                      ¦                   U
                                (wildly ¦
UNIFORM:  findings indicate           wⱡith                    R
MEMORY  :  only the faintest          ¦    right
REPORT  :  glimmer of reality         ¦        arm)                E
BUREAU  :  accompianies these         ¦                              S
           noble gestures             ¦
                                      ¦
                                      ¦
          N+ OTE: only of the impressions of art anⱡ
                                      ¦            d of language
-----------------------------------apart-----------+-----------------------------
                                      ¦
                                      ¦
notes on art as art as notes on notes as noted notes of art as notes on art notes
                                      ¦
                                      ¦            line
          3 measured words, stop      ¦            cⱡolumn
                                      ¦            box
                                      ¦
                                      ¦
          ATTACHEMENT                 ¦
          ***********                 ¦
          *         *      H          ¦
          *         *        I        ¦    S
          *         *                 ¦
          *         *                 ¦      T
          *         *                 ¦
          ***********                 ¦         O
                                      ¦            R
                                      ¦              Y
                                      ¦
          2 words apart¦


head                                                                      feet


          the good biological metaphor for, is 'the good biological metaphor'
```

m. crane

1. Feeling tired much of the time
2. Sleeping poorly
3. Too much underweight or overweight
4. Gradually losing weight
5. Frequently bothered by a sore throat
6. Catching a good many colds

7. Living in an undesirable location
8. Transportation or commuting problem
9. Lacking modern conveniences in my home
10. Lacking privacy in my living quarters
11. Unfair landlord or landlady
12. Poor living conditions

13. Wanting to develop a hobby
14. Wanting to improve myself culturally
15. Wanting worthwhile discussions with people
16. Wanting to learn how to dance
17. Lacking skill in sports or games
18. Not knowing how to entertain

19. Lacking leadership ability
20. Lacking self-confidence
21. Not really being smart enough
22. Being timid or shy
23. Lacking courage
24. Taking things too seriously

25. Wanting a more pleasing personality
26. Awkward in meeting people
27. Daydreaming
28. Being too tall or too short
29. Being physically unattractive
30. Wishing I were the other sex

31. Being away from home too much
32. Member of my family in poor health
33. Death in my family
34. Member of my family working too hard
35. Worried about a member of my family
36. Drinking by a member of my family

37. Having too few dates
38. Not finding a suitable life partner
39. Deciding whether I'm really in love
40. Having to wait too long to get married
41. Being financially unable to get married
42. In love with someone my family won't accept

43. Needing a philosophy of life
44. Confused in my religious beliefs
45. Losing my earlier religious faith
46. Having beliefs that differ from my church
47. Failing to see the relation of religion to life.
48. Differing from my family in religious beliefs

49. Poor appetite
50. Stomach trouble (indigestion, ulcers, etc.)
51. Intestinal trouble
52. Poor complexion or skin trouble
53. Poor posture
54. Feet hurt or tire easily

55. Needing a job
56. Needing part-time work
57. Disliking financial dependence on others
58. Having too many financial dependents
59. Getting into debt
60. Fearing future unemployment

61. Having a poor memory
62. Not being as efficient as I would like
63. Not using my leisure time well
64. Too few opportunities for meeting people
65. Trouble keeping up a conversation
66. Not mixing well with the opposite sex

67. Being lazy
68. Lacking ambition
69. Being influenced too easily by others
70. Being untidy
71. Being too careless
72. Not doing anything well

73. Feeling ill at ease with other people
74. Avoiding someone I don't like
75. Finding it hard to talk before a group
76. Worrying how I impress people
77. Not getting along well with people
78. Not really having any friends

79. Having to live with relatives
80. Irritated by habits of a member of my family
81. Home untidy and ill kept
82. Too much quarreling at home
83. Too much nagging and complaining at home
84. Not really having a home

85. Wondering whether to go steady
86. Deciding whether to become engaged
87. Deciding whether to get married
88. Needing advice about getting married
89. Wondering if I really know my prospective mate
90. Afraid of the responsibilities of marriage

91. In love with someone of a different religion
92. Finding church services of no interest to me
93. Doubting the value of prayer
94. Doubting the existence of God
95. Science conflicting with my religion
96. Not getting satisfactory answers from religion

This wordstamp can be seen as my
critical commentary on radical /
experimental tendencies in modern
literature wrote Robin Crozier. But
on the next line he began to wonder
if seeing and reading words or,
indeed, eating them had anything
to do with literature or with . . . . . .

for robin crozier receiving love letters from mette
Aare rABBits from Annette BAACk penCils from m
onique BAilly BAnAnAs from AnnA BAnAnA
glAssworks from Betty Bressi cAts from wenDy
Briton BluEs From jAnEt BuBAr rAinBows
From BEtty DAmon DoGs From irEnE DoGmAtiC
FisH From pAt FisH AutoBioGrApHIEs From mE
rrily ForDEArtH From wAnDA Golkowsk A umB
rEllAs From JuDItHoFFBErG mothlnG From Dor
otHY IAmmonE stAmps From LEAvEnwortH JACK
son LABELs FroM rusAn E KING BEANs FroM
ALIsON KNOwLEs GRAPHs FroM IDA KroL
QuEstIONs FROM zOFIA KuLIK FuRS FROM
NATALIA LACH-LACHOwICz MONALISAS F
ROM SUzANNE LACy VOWELS FROM KATA
LIN LADIK FLOWERS FROM KARIN LAMB
RECHT PUNS FROM PAT LARTER SHOES FR
OM ANNA-K LOBNER HORSES FROM DANA
LONG POSTCARDS FROM ANNA MANTOVANI
POETRy FROM LUCIA MARCUCCI BUTTER
FLIES FROM GRACIELA GUTIERREz MARX
CROWS FROM DORA MAURER ROSES FRO
M ROSE MARIE MEICHTRY HAIR FROM L
ENINHA AGUIA MENDES MONEY FROM S
HEILA MURRAY BOOKS FROM XENIA MU
SCAT BREASTS FROM GWENDOLYN MUS
CHELMAN PARUSEL KISSES FROM EWA
PARTUM CHINOISERIE FROM PATRICIA PLA
TTNER VIEWS FROM FATIMA POMBO STR
AWBERRIES FROM RUTH REHFELDT EMBR
OIDERY FROM TAKAKO SAITO CHERUBS FR
OM ANGELIKA SCHMIDT MIRRORS FROM
MIEKO SHIOMI IS LITERATURE MINUS THE Z

Found Poem   Dadaland

Aktenzeichen XYungelöst
Aktenzeichen XYungelöst
Aktenzeichen XYungelöst
Aktenzeichen XYungelöst
Aktenzeichen XYungelöst
Aktenzeichen XYungelöst
Aktenzeichen XYungelöst
Aktenzeichen XYungelöst
Aktenzeichen XYungelöst

Aktenzeichen XYungelöst
Aktenzeichen XYungelöst
Aktenzeichen XYungelöst
Aktenzeichen XYungelöst
Aktenzeichen XYungelöst
Aktenzeichen XYungelöst
Aktenzeichen XYungelöst
Aktenzeichen XYungelöst
Aktenzeichen XYungelöst
Aktenzeichen XYungelöst

Optophonetic   Poem   Dadaland

Against argumentation: on sound poetry

by Matteo D'Ambrosio

> S'il était possible d'imaginer
> une esthétique du plaisir
> textuel, il faudrait y enclure:
> l'écriture à haute voix. Cette
> écriture vocale (qui n'est pas
> du tout la parole), on ne la
> pratique pas, mais c'est sans
> doute elle que recommandait
> Artaud et que demande Sollers.
> Parlons-en comme si elle
> existait.   (R. Barthes)

Breton has shown his perplexity about the value and destiny of poetic communication committed only to verbal writing.

Moreover, writing is sensorial deprivation, abstract work, partial specialization, falsifying convention, approximation: "Writing is arbitrary becoming of speech" (Derrida), and has the mystifying quality common to processes of language valorization.

Sound poetry, on the contrary, investigates and explores the space separating the voice and word. If "the linguistic sign is a phonetic form with a sense" (Bloomfield), the word is the limit of the voice, its antithesis; but the voice can do without a referent, refusing the coherence guaranteed by meaning: in this way fruition will be promoted by sensibility, rather than by the codes of understanding, it will be a perception of psychic living, externalized by the creative idiolect of the performer.

By breaking the word, i.e. the sham unity of the phoné and sense, one restores the power of primary expression (of the howl) to the voice, and thus goes beyond the limits of rationalized knowledge...

Poetry is indivisible from gesture; its first compilation modality, by giving the text its living character, it liberates both the latent humors and the subconscious.

Sound is the materiality of the voice, its meaningful substance; nonsense, rebelling against the constraints of language logic, resorts to pre-linguistic poem improvisation.

"Poetry is a physical thing" (Cobbing): the laceration of a sound object is the symptomatic act of an artist's (of man's) will to transform the voice, from a communication form permitted by the phonetic apparatus, into bodily expression (rhythm and breath) and pulsional matter.

The audience can either be involved in a collective poetry) or reached by different kinds of mechanical reproduction; (whereas, the page is only the transcription place of an experience and a gesture realized in another dimension, using specific symbolization strategies): the eventual text-score has only an indicative value.

The electronic medium, whereas, submits the techné of the community to the Bedeutung of the subject, present with all his faculties in the syn-aesthetic act of para-sense expression (glossolalia, lautgedichte).

With sound poetry, poetry is no longer marginal language but spectacle, the aesthetic contamination of a single, complex experimental space, i.e. a new multi-media that replaces dispersive conventional communication, with a linguistic tension that allows irrationality, play and excess to erupt.

621 Sayre Avenue
Lexington Kentucky 40508

Easter 1979

Dear Richard:

        I've tried twice to do your assignment and
have twice failed. I really don't think I know anything
about the experimental and the radical. I have an awful
feeling that for the past 30 years everything has trivi-
alized (in art of the so-called vanguard, I mean). All I
can see is anemia, posturing, and ineptitude. It is perhaps symptomatic of my disillusion that the list of writers in this morning's paper being honored by the American
Academy might as well be a list of winners of the Greater
Iowa 4H Awards, or a list of the foremost Albanian lite-
rati. What can I do to catch up? I read all fiction, tons
of poetry, subscribe to about 40 magazines, and still am
as uninformed as the Episcopal clergy and real estate deal-
ers in my neighborhood here in Lexington.

        Middle age, I suppose.

                    Blessings,

                    Guy

Prolegomenon a hoarse

Small furrows in alternation make us to permit of the words.
As a vowel is to a goal, contrariwise. These of the
consonants run on. Covert a comma evasive of need. Desperate
to disperse, semi-colon a pane linger of seive. Turmoil
scathe of sever colon. Dispersion this of longer period,
sedate hollow thin in immersion. Distract, question a period.
Bask noun shuttle stall evase. Tucker of lob, tamper state
in nulls verb torpor waft. Sheath link furlow by prolong
pronoun. With to pattern of lengthening, and ad.jective and
.verb. Connective in cornering preposition, or verso, and
and. Phrase to discern, clause to obey. In tells a article,
thinnest tall pedestal, taintless dough posture. Us of time
by space of needles, permissing with larder of thought.

Alan. Davies.

Why Being Serious Is Hard

(1) Lacrimation is serious. Prosopolepsy is solemn.

(2) Suppuration is serious. Tautomerism is solemn.

(3) Intercolumniations are solemn. Prolixity is serious.

(4) Bathymetry, obeah, ebriosity, aschatocol are all serious.
Saprogenicity is solemn.

(5) Antonomasia is solemn. Haplology is serious.

(6) Preterition is serious. Muliebrity is solemn.

(7) Lycanthropy was solemn. Antonomasia was serious.

(8) Eudaemonism is solemn. So are obelli, lucubrations, and
roulades. Virginismus is serious.

(9) Imbrication is solemn. Acroparesthesia is serious. So is
pansexualism, but aporrhoea is solemn.

(10) Ettles are serious. Phonisms and excenters are solemn.

                                        Alan. Davies.

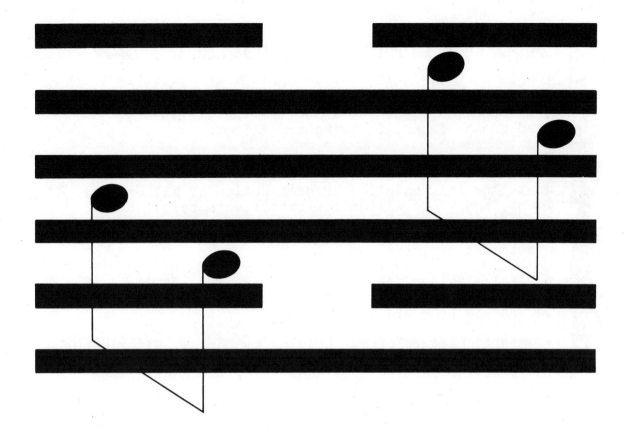

CAGE: CHANCE: CHANGE

pentahexagram for john cage

augusto de campos 1977

A TRAIN OF THOUGHT

I have no philosophy. I believe in the oneness of two and three and four and minus five. The state of Art is New Jersey. A garden of assembly line illiteracy. It is read on the faces. It is embarrassing.

Thus we let sense escape into the realm of nonsense, although it never left that of the senses. It drives us to the fragmentation or destruction of all artistic forms, and to rebellion for rebellion's sake; to an anarchistic negation of all values, a self exploding bubble, a raging anti, anti, anti linked with an equally passionate pro, pro, pro!

ART falls asleep. ART needs an operation. ART is a pretension, warmed by the diffidence of the urinary tract. Thought is produced in the mouth.

I am speechless. Forever holding my tongue. Uttering possibilities to the mindless judge sitting on a throne in my brain. Casting multitudes of fishy conclusions into my throat. I am a horse. I am a horse of a different color. I shoot horse and fly off into the sun on its bullet proof wings. High as the kite I was told to go out and fly, on a windless day.

(Thus you see that one doesn't consume one's pater except slice by slice, it's impossible to do it in a single picnic and even the lemon falls to its knees before the beauty of nature.)

When we feel a piece of iron we say: This is iron; we satisfy ourselves with a word and nothing more. Between iron and hand a conflict of preconscious force-thought-sentiment takes place. Perhaps there is more thought in the fingertips and the iron than in the brain that prides itself on observing the phenomenon.

If you've heard the sound of one hand, prove it.
Without a word, thrust one hand forward.

gadji beri bimba glanddridi laula lonni cadori

grimbasa cundoma gridgicoma anoni leapa cambric
And perhaps is my favorite word.

The state of society is incontestably artificial; the power of one man over another must be always derived from convention or from conquest; by nature we are equal.

I smash drawers, those of the brain and those of social organization; everywhere to demoralize, to hurl the hand from heaven to hell, the eyes from hell to heaven, to set up once more, in the real powers and in the imagination of every individual, the fecund wheel of the world circus.

from:

neoneo richter dada neoneo arp marinetti zen ball neoneo godwin tzara

A circus of us and circles and three rings you're out.

The tree of idealism, that sentimental tree in which the
nests of materialist philosophers sway, came crashing down
in one single stroke of helium thunder.

Together we will invent what I call the _imagination_ _without_
wings. Someday we will achieve a yet more essential art,
when we dare to supress all the first terms of our analogies
and render no more than an uninterrupted sequence of second
terms. To achieve this we must renounce being understood.
It is not necessary to be understood.

It is not even necessary to be seen and not heard.

The artist's excuse is always selfish. It is drilled like
oil from the prehistoric pits of fossilized egos and drilled
like nails into the gesture. A cross between Jesus and his
apparition. A religion based on approval and the last judgement.

I believe that there is an irreducible antagonism between
the creation of art and a desire to communicate with the public. That antagonism confounds the artist; he refuses to
assume the position of "alienation" implied by the creative
activity, and vainly attempts to reconcile his work with a
desire to be integrated into society and recieve honors and
rewards.

Art is extincting to high heaven and the artist is buried
two feet below the ground!

In the dreadful chaos of our era I catch sight of only a
few rare oasis of purity. Man has succumbed to the frenzy
of intelligence. A lunatic impregnated with scientific
culture tries to dominate the world by means of his pseudo-
head.

After all, what do we want: What is it that we _must_ know?

I call for an ART OF ADMITTANCE! The opening up and the
confession! I am no escape artist. I admit that I do not
understand what I know. I admit that I "think" I am the
center of the universe and "know" that I am not. I admit
that I have an ileostomy. I admit that I am not bald. I
admit that my ideas are far ahead of my re-enactment of
them. I admit that I watch lots of television and love it.
I admit that I have little confidence and care very much
what others think. I admit that I have all my fingers. I
admit that I could never bid chaos welcome, throw bombs,
blow up bridges, and do away with ideas. I admit that I am
not an anarchist. I admit that my art has always been con-
templated by a cold, distracted _I_, too preoccupied with
itself, full of preconceived wisdom and human obsessions.

I admit that I was born in nature, that I was born in the
Bronx, that I was born in a cloud, that I was born in a pump.
I admit that I was born in a robe, that I have four natures
that I have two things, and five senses.

Phil Demise   N.Y.C.   1979

Sammlung
Klaus Peter Dencker

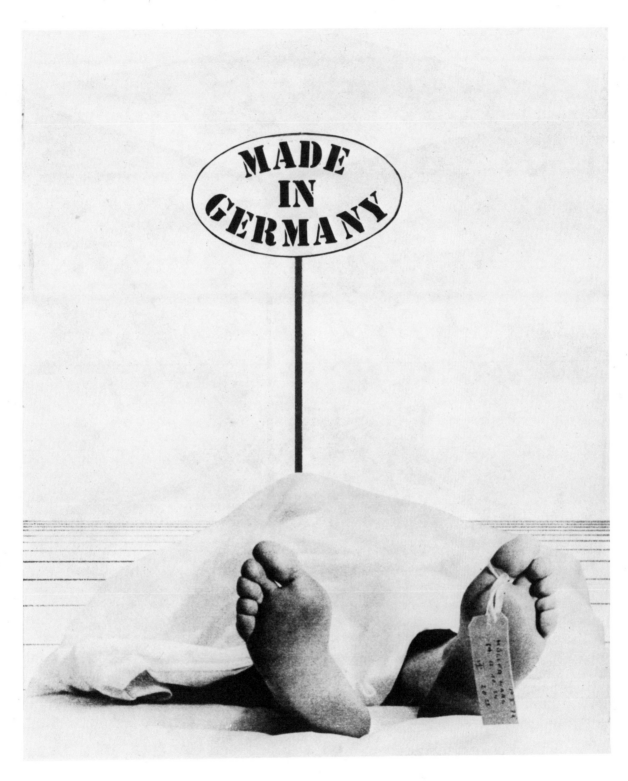

Sammlung
Klaus Peter Dencker

AGNES DENES
THE DEBATE, 1 million B.C. – 1 million A.D.

right after the explosion as billions of fragments started their journey, the endless, eternal debate began. as the stars and galaxies formed and bacteria began to grow on landmasses the endless debate commenced. analytical wisdom, scientific discoveries and all the great thoughts thought by man brought forth the words and their beauty was like uneven sea pearls in a row strung by compulsion and curiosity. the universe grew, fragments exploded and sped away from each other, mass clustered into form, space expanded and gave birth to the paradox. the debate went on. man was in the middle, translucent skin shielding his substance, a thin membrane between him and the world. there was a world beyond it and a world within, the distance and the mystery were the same. knowledge came painfully with doubts and indecisions, but no sooner was any truth accepted, it proved untrue. the opposite of space had been mass, but soon the carefully created reality shattered into more doubts and uncertainty-principles while mass became a form of energy and the human substance was reduced to a process, just spinning velocities, patterns and forms gyrating in a world of relativity. fashions and philosophies, concepts and beliefs were born and defeated while the galaxies hurled away from each other and the mad spinning of atoms endured into lightless eternities, where the past joins the future and causes are formed. and we spin, debate, analyze and argue the point, but what is the point? and where is it? in the particles, in velocity or in illusion? as stars collapse and galaxies funnel into orgasmic tightness to emit massive bodies of heat into other worlds and universes we write words, speak words, scream words of wisdom, but today's wisdom is tomorrow's folly. yet we must seek and question for we are damned to inbetweenness. left with little of our instinct and having gained partial intellect, we confused the intuition and missed what really mattered. hard little buds burst every new spring and the soil we lived on drank in the soft rain as our tiny home rotated in space hurtling into darkness. in the silent heavens there was such turbulence that would have frightened us into worldlessness or at least greater caution but instead we achieved wars and exhausted technology and analyzed the species homo curiosus, homo futurus. but then came the realization that there was no future and no past, time was relative and so was reality. doubtful premises followed by faulty deductions. if measures and concepts are relative and even the laws of nature may change, upon what do we base reason? if there are no constants, what is the point of departure, and is not logic then based on layers of illusion? the debate went on. the words kept piling up, but they were worn and misleading. communication was garbled. nevertheless knowledge expanded as the universe expanded. small miracles were born, named and leashed. seed was planted and harvested and we analyzed the formation of form itself. built empires of money and power that some valued and some did not. and while the fluid surface wrapped itself obediently around the earth, somewhere in the distance this future we hoped for became the past. there was aging and being born and the debate went on. we questioned and reasoned and the words formed chains of sea pearls strung by doubt and belief while the spinning never stopped. suns burnt out and collapsed but we knew only one little sun in the heavens to get suntanned by on the beach while grasping the cold lips of a bottle of beer. little humans bleeding and writing words of wisdom on the-structural-significance-of-elusive-phenomena-love-and-hope-and-the-spatio-temporal-limitations-of-being-unaware-of-total-existence-and-total-function-or-ultimate-realities-or-the-reason-why-some-things-never-make-sense. but the debate goes on, that's life. for silence is not all, noise is all! the great bursting of the primal seed, the big bang is all the rhythm of evolution and involution, expansion, contraction and poles of entropy. and after all the silent swimming in space we'll just get all sucked up again to be emitted through a colossal womb to do another human dance. so we write words and seek truths, change fashions and describe emotions and sunsets, have great minds and wits. we let the words form pearls from the sea and call the exchange art. look, these forms you see aren't skeletons but you and I at a dinner party discussing the state of the world or the stock market. they are Hamlet and Socrates and Descartes and da Vinci. children of the imagination so eager to question, so desperate to communicate and to know the reason for this incredible journey through space. homo communicatus, homo literatus, homo desperatus.

not ideas

about the thing

but the ding an sich

RHW Dillard

philippe dôme

¿...?

2

ce cher tableau dont il ne reste qu'un fauteuil, roc *aujourd'hui*
dans la campagne, guère que la certitude d'une
naissance raréfiée >
¿d'un Ordre? (arrangement● absent aussi   ● *qui n'en est pas un* ▪
de sa chute : ô Pensée, conscience précieuse.
. **IL FAULT** ajuster (3) des réponses à ces crises comme sidérales qui apparaissaient sous la plume *¡hum!*
(que nous ne comprendrions pas si nous n'en produisions toujours-maintenant)
(¿mais à distances universelles?)
— blancs spéciaux justifiés, bouts et confins datés de cette époque chue, donc, sur nos difficultés *lectrices*
(¿plus érectile ou suggestive **MAINTENANT**?)

1 des substitutions d'envergure, toutes les méta-3 ô couronné, ☎ aux prises avec les distances
(capitales) imposables au déploiement du discours,
morphoses .... avec le projet de l'espace faisant retour sur la
: une mastiqueuse en marche vers l'inFinni .... Pensée ou la mimant comme un papillon de mai ☎,
no venerection fourmi's fouryou please

□ autre seconde question de réveil **I**
puisque la mer, depuis lors, ne s'est pas figée
davantage
par la disposition de quelques marges multipliantes.
c'est le tout-insaisissable de son histoire qui est
jeté, qui se projette en taches-retenues (cartes sur
sable), en élargissements, en agrandissements qui
veulent dire ? →
agiter la Pensée, la faire à long terme gesticuler
sur place, **FAIRE UNE SCENE** de l'inscription
[une Pensée **SUR LA PLACE D'UNE AUTRE,**
l'ensemble bondissant à grand train]   ¿?□   ● *¡hombre passant devant un ciel d'ensemble clair, mais*
si mental!

PUNZZLE (jubilatoire) qui tout à la fois soude
et/mais rassemble des **causes** de hasard, du moins
de celles qui viennent en conscience — sa gestualitétion à elle, c'est **la** soudure (1),   *[crissement de vers]*
CONTINUUM ¿la lecture? n'avait lieu qu'en   **SIGNIFIANT**   *[que faire ?]*
second rang (pudeur impossible)   ☎ où cela se place d'importance   que le
(universaliste abstraction (3), histoire-Histoire)discours s'ordonne sur autre chose aussi que la
[homme-Somme]   pensée, mais que cette partition n'est
pas ce dont on parle là **¡COME ISY!** — que c'est — *vagues* —
En mémoire :   la disposition de plusieurs contenus liés☎ ou bien:
Auroch dans la campagne **I** je cherche **I** la signifi-où est la réalité Dédé ?
cation de pour quoi je n'ai pas   pour que
nous **I**   qui tentions, retenterions dans le sens **I**
mais qui **I** ne puissions-nous frères sensés
— Ici que se passe-t-il ?

Answer: cycle maison amour parfait qui tout contient.

Consolation à notre usage ? faits précis de notre histoire par transparence adaptés à toutes les circonstances — quotidienne présente ou passée — **Coup de Day** quand j'essaie ☐ de recueillir l'éphénement dans la marge du jour et de la nuit ? (2)

¡Go go, Messer Sol!

Answer : ....
....
....
....

☐ *BISMILLAFOULTIES*
....
....
.... ■ Vers mes rêves diffus d'après-règne, il y a tout. Dichimulation∗∗∗ à coup chûr. La maison se délogeant de l'œuf et ses structures ligneuses se démantelant à grand bruit.

∗∗∗ ô déchivrance

Où je se dessinerait si quelque courbure de langue — cet indice-masse — [En note : « Il y a ça Ailleurs », ou « ce qui n'y est pas est encore ailleurs », ou ●« ce qui sort ici n'est que l'ombre et la marque de la Pensée Perdue ».●] était possible sur les lieux, pour nous qui en descendons, restée ferme comme planche à la mer toujours romancée, ses creux seuls irréguliers indiquant, sous la forme du désordre, **QUE JE SUIT.** inspiré d'une histoire authentique par esprit.∗∗

∗∗ que tout s'écrit, que tout est hasard — arrangemental — sauf ce qui surgit des profondeurs de de nos mères-pies, des gouffres ventriloques de nos paysages exclusifs.

Ce souvenir demeure

∗ : descrépition du ch'valmilial qui, de ses yeux absents s'approche et scrute le marais☐☐ (l'humidité, ce qui suinte au bord de la pourriture, plutôt).∗ qui pendant tout ce temps aurait servi de support simple. (2)

Très affectueux, regardant d'un cœur soulevé qui fraie, détrempé comme ces fragments en épaves sur les plages.

(2)

Comptant l'imaginaire déambulation, musique de voyage plus ponctuée que jamais, homme abrégé pendant toutes ces années, sur des lieux qui ont changé,

dans les bolges, vers le jardin couvert de neige, puis vers les corneilles perchées.
Né bien avant la disparition, peut-être disparu avant la disparition précédente, tombé d'images, de feuilles vivantes : élevé pour allonger la chute, jeté aux champs marins par assonances,

BEHIND HIS
MEDDLE
THROW

cosmochronie allusive commencée par une généalogie classique : une onde moyenne **I** un beau jaune **I** un plan d'envol **I** la seconde conscience d'une importante chaleur disparue <

KINGU   SPEAKS

Nothing I can talk about directly. If I couldn't, there'd
be no further need for words. Paraphrase of the irreducible
is another name for Sisyphus' labor. Yet everytime I make
sense, I'm taking incalculable risks: you may understand me.

Essentially what I "think" I am after is analogs. What gave
me words in the first place: what memories: what joys or
sorrows lead me into haunted ground: what giant force grips
the soul forcing out my voice: what eternal, limitless energy
has lain hidden in the fragments, the figments of my life,
has always and undoubtedly will remain private, glassed off
from daylight. From time to time I am privileged to look,
as in a glass darkly. But as in any mirror I see only the
bits and pieces, the quester rather than the demiurge lurking
behind the blackened silver lining my particular cloud of
unknowing wears.

Beware the rain: the Titan of desire who pelts down from that
cloud, who assumes a benign face the better to work his tight
designs -- in the daylight where no harm comes unless he's loose.

But analogs. Counterparts, avatars. Everyone has locked within
all experience, all event. Sooner or later what has happened to
one happens to all. If not in this life, then in another. No
human possibility we leave untouched. As surely as we pass from
amoeba to minnow, from salamander to frog, painfully joyously,
up the great ladder of the womb, the soul knows in its heart
of hearts that everything is possible. That nothing has been
left out.

All those we know: poet, magician, philosopher, stonehead,
historian, friend: victim victimizer: male female: young old:
all antipodes: all bodies, antibodies: there, there they are,
pointing away, leading back, irrefutably, to the index, that
phallus nest finger of power, the one verifiable, continuing
source of sun work in all universes. For only in the pointings
and chasings, the shootings and fuckings, the killings and
lovings (and all their actives, passives and middles as well)
is there network, an emergent pattern. By contraries progress:
thus stasis is woven from strife. Each flower is its own form:
the human family creating, recording, forgetting itself day
on day.

The divinities we organized the stars and wombs of earth into,
these unions have now all been broken.

So, then, in the analogs, replacements for the selv' oscura
the dark self, we find ourselves in the middle of the road.

All the strange ones, those for whom no tag has been invented,
who righteously refuse judgment: new life woven on the space

time loom: they, too, are included, finding body in the
boundless tradition of energy defining shape. Everything
creates its own place and occupies all others. Nothing has
been left out since no place is void.

This is how it works. Not by direction but by instinct: not
by reductive paraphrase but by tone, rhyme, rhythm, picture,
story, shape on the page in the mind, the ineffable colors of
book, the place where it's done, the soul where it's formed
consumed in endless diasystole first time everytime, does
whatever magic I own act.

My pieces are not themselves or wholly another's. They are
of this body and yet strangely not. They enjoy owl-like the
greyblue, the apple you almost saw of your eye: the whirled
in a cloudbank: faces of the damned dancing in flame: nymphs,
satyrs, dryads, the PanBacchae flickering in the flower rug.

Whatever I see is there. If not there, then somewhere. Once I
locate it, track it to its place of origin, I shake hands
with myself.

My pieces are there to produce change. Uncreated, they create.
Like children they dance treading out the measure of the burden
that they bear. In this they are like music: not the reinvention
of beauty but its begetter in time. Prime movers of history,
not faithless scribe. In the world they are the novel, not
its unread replacement.

I make words like trees, like photographs of trees. I live
against and with them; they fill the world, they ring it
and make it

      FREE

   Picking and choosing which law

   (is not to obey but create!)

   in the end I give way to nothing

                       Charles Doria

                       Austin, 1975

(Kingu, in Babylonian story, was the eldest child of
Tiamat, the whale mother. From the shattered pieces of
his body, after he was slain by the sky god Marduk, the
First, or Antediluvian, World was made.)

PANES-FICTION AS THERAPY, THE ULTIMATE NOVEL SELF-HELP BOOK FOR WOMEN by Dr. Angela L. Heartsinger and Rochelle H. Dubois is a novel of the future and a gothic Southern romance, a work of the imagination of one writer, myself, but finally shaped into the above form after 12 years with the help of Anais Nin and William Faulkner who contacted the author to complete 743 pages mystically and mysteriously in the fall of 1978.

The novel is a tragicomedy that can be read as a self-help book and as a modern literary psychological work of fiction. PANES has a three page Table of Contents delineating the text. Part 1 - CONFLICTS OF THE SELF--The Mind with subheadings: SUICIDE; IDENTITY; MOODS; Part 2 - KINDS OF LOVE--The Soul with subheadings: MARRIAGE AND DIVORCE; OTHER DESIRES; OMNI-SEXUALITY; and Part 3 - PROBLEMS IN SOCIETY--The Body with subheadings: ILLNESS & ALCOHOL; FEMINISM, FAMILY & FREEDOM; OLD AGE, WAR & DEATH; DRUGS; SUCCESS. There is an AFTERWORD, ART & LIFE, written by a child, THE FINAL WORD, a film and book review of PANES itself (which I am including as my entry to ASSEMBLING); a libretto and the EPILOGUE "A Creative Dreamer" by the only real person in the novel, Dr. Sharon Spencer, Professor of Comparative Literature at Montclair State College in Upper Montclair, New Jersey, an author and a critic. After this ALMOST FINAL WORD come the biographies of Dr. Heartsinger & her assistant, a bibliography, assorted pre-release pre-publication reader input, questions and answers, yourword and the last dedication & addenda.

PANES includes the fictional accounts, stories, testimonies of 57 Southern women artists who handle their problems and conflicts creatively after seeing Dr. Angela Heartsinger, a practicing elderly female psycho-therapist based in Atlanta. Thus, the novel serves as the first critical book on the woman artist and a text for medical students and psychotherapists with two prefaces that parody jargonese of a heart surgeon and a comparative literature professor. The novel represents all ages, living situations, classifications of women artists in all media and is an imaginative work that stresses the solution of individual problems and conflicts through the therapy of fiction, the act of writing, transforming frustrations and fears in a way that aids the artist to handle her situation, positively, through art. The forerunner to this tome is PANGS, an almost aborted novella, which I plan to self-publish with photographs of swans should no publisher recognize its merit, so that eventually PANES will have its publication way paved by the smaller novel. Write Rochelle Holt Dubois, 59 Sandra Circle A-3, Westfield, New Jersey. 07090

As a writer who has been seriously devoted to her art for over 13 years, I can say that I believe in PANES-FICTION AS THERAPY, and I would like to gather the names and addresses of other people who would like to see this book come to fruition. Should you think I have a saleable literary novel, please feel free to drop me a line saying so with your signature and address. Perhaps a petition will be one way to convince a publisher that PANES must be printed now.

In PANES, I have a case study preceding the testimony. I submit to you "The Case of H. Sylvia D. Stephenson - Book Reviewer - Reality (her conflict)".

H. Sylvia D. Stephenson, who refused to reveal her true identity, came to me with a location complex. She wanted to be ubiquitous, was living in the South and the North as either an actress, a dancer, a photographer, in short, what she thought was an artist, but Sylvia obviously had no imagination.

In appearance Sylvia was nondescript. She wore black slacks and either a red or blue blouse every time she came to see me, once a month for eight months, sometimes arriving from O'Hare International Airport and other times coming up on THE CITY OF NEW ORLEANS train from Louisiana. PAST HISTORY. Sylvia's tonsils were never removed as a child and she also had a severe case of chicken pox when she was five years old, the virus apparently remaining dormant in her body her entire life according to specialists and dentists who x-rayed her head for neuralgia before performing rootcanal oral surgery.
COURSE IN TREATMENT. Sylvia wrote a very short piece which she says in a book and film review of the science fiction remake "2002; A Space Odyssey." She is the only woman I have seen who has shown no sign of progress in resolving her conflict or problem, which she claims is one of time and location. In her own words, "I am always confused, and I like to eat frozen yogurt, plain not strawberry or chocolate-coated." Sylvia is obviously not a woman artist or she too would be on my long patient list of partial and totally psychotherapeutic successes, women artists who have healed themselves through fiction as therapy. However, her film and book review, is being cut on a 45 rpm record, much to my own amazement. -Angela Heartsinger
****
"Transmutation"

"A Real Author," Polly Malle's new film based on the bestseller novel, A GOTHIC SOUTHERN ROMANCE,despite the advance controversy, turns out to be tender and sensitive, and to handle its subject with delicacy. (*** 3/4) A wonderment of a movie despite its cast of 57 feature roles played by a galaxy of stars with Keith Carradine, a Haley's comet, leading in outstanding shimmering sensitivity, the real author who lived with both Dr. Angela and Miss Rochelle, first as a man, a 17th Century British scholar and biblio- grapher, and then as a woman, a high school band teacher and gymnastics coach who, after 16 years in her profession, leaves teaching to become a management consultant for a pharmaceutical company.

The subtly erotic film retains the poetic and visionary quality of the novel while at the same time depicting the pain and pleasure of a man-woman, for eight years the husband of a woman artist, a schizophrenic painter, who believes she is the reincarnation of a male psychiatrist in a woman's body and then for two years as the female lover of a passionate poet who sub- sidizes her income as an exotic belly dancer at a literary Women's Salon in Greenwich Village, New York City. Despite apparently bizarre revelations and transformation, the screen crackles with truth. A thrilling epic, the interior scenery of the soul and mind is lush and memorable.

Not for the sentimental or the squeamish; only for people who still read and care about good movies. No female nudity or shark blood, there is story, acting, and direction, even if Polly Malle, always a maverick, usually proves to be more popular with critics than with audiences. "A Real Author" is artistic, psychological, compelling, and captures the poignant truth of how it is to live as a sensitive man in a chauvinistic society who then experiences the pain of being ostracized as a homoemotional* woman.

If you haven't yet read the book, a sly charmer of a southern novel, hefty but worth the universal effort, you're in for a real treat.

* homoemotional-a modern term   by H. Sylvia D. Stephenson
for the old word "lesbian"   Mexico City, Mexico
                                                         Cannes Film Festival, 1989

Michael Dyregrov

Summary Neologisms

Finally the images lying together too long in a list hook up arm to leg
and blood flows through. But the newborn poem needs a head, something to call
it by. The essence of the poem escapes you still. Then a labial lifts
unbidden from the residue. . .a pivotal idea for which until now there was
no word.

    This new word derives from a parent language. As a speaker
from the linguistic "collective unconscious," it speaks incoherently,
withholding even while revealing itself. Unlike speaking in tongues
or a schizophrenic's neologisms, the poet's new words are logical.
Their submerged meaning can be "understood."

    "Knoddas," based on "knaben," German for "boys," "knokel," Middle English
for "knuckle," and "klods" or "clods," embodied the two old men outcast
and frightened, "clang to the pelt," in my poem "Flight with Marduk."
"Krexen suse," from the Latin "sus" or "swine," I turned into the title, apex,
of a poem in which a sow lays an egg. I leave the meaning of "krexen" open.
In "Falling Away in Songkhla," "Brassala" became the place name of a Southeast
Asian village on the estuary of the "Rempidahpol" where that river broadens
into a brown and shiny brass platter. The neologism "Slaelebate," a corruption
of the "sloe bat cut from a dying chin" in a poem, worked out as the title.
"Brylopian" synthesizes "embryo" and "fallopian" in this poem:

                              Brylopian

    The womb is, in shape, a ginkgo whose branches end in two vireos'
    nests underslung and pressed against the trunk, fingers on hips.
    Leaves brush the cups. . .fledge blandlings.

                                  *

                              Sarkoru

    Lady Sarkoru's love for the Emperor went all to his comb. . .
    a boat shearing a grey tsunami with the years slipping away
    down the back of his head. Living within a comb always
    ends in sarcasm, and "Korrusa's" was physical as death.

"Sarkoru" is "oriental" for "sarcasm." "Korrusa," the Emperor's pet name
for the Lady and an anagram of "sarkoru," pretends to the Latin "corrosus,"
"gnawing."

a

Michael Dyregrov

Onomatopoeia bridges all languages. The Japanese word for "owl,"
"howo-waiwo," the Ojibwa, "kokoko," and the English "owl" from Old High German
"uwila," mimic an owl's "hoot," from the Middle English imitative "houten."
I offer this onomatopoeic fabri, "howailo," as a sound to be understood anywhere
as "owl."

Even a successful neologism commands and dwarfs its context with strangeness.
Somehow the contrivance, the calculation must be resolved. An entirely neologistic
"poem" doesn't move beyond an exercise. Neologisms and known words synergize. . .
the unfamiliar depends on the familiar.

Through the Looking Glass

A primer for neologisms in poetry is Lewis Carroll's "Jabberwocky."
"Frumious Bandersnatch," "vorpal sword," "manxome foe," "uffish thought,"
"tulgey wood," and "frabjous day" don't yield their origins. . ."manxome"
has nothing to do with "Manx" and the "Isle of Man." But as Humpty Dumpty
explains, "'Brillig' means four o'clock in the afternoon - the time when you
begin broiling things for dinner" and "'slithy' means 'lithe and slimy.'"
"To 'gimble' is to make holes like a gimlet." A "wabe" is called that because
"it goes a long way before it, and a long way behind it." "'Mimsy' is flimsy
and miserable." "'Mome,'" Humpty Dumpty speculates, is "short for 'from home'
 - meaning that they'd lost their way." "'Outgribing' is something between
bellowing and whistling, with a kind of sneeze in the middle." Carroll
uses a real if archaic word in "gyre," from the Middle English "giren"
and Latin "gyrus": "'Gyre' is to go round and round like a gyroscope."

"Galumphing," a contraction of "galloping" in "triumph," made a tenuous
entrance into the general language. But "chortled," which Carroll synthesized
from "snort" and the radical of "chuckle". . ."snort" from the onomatopoeic
Middle English "snorten," and "chuckle," the frequentative of "chuck," to "cluck"
. . .has a secure place. No other word reproduces so unmistakably that flutter
of the soft palate. As with "owl," sound traverses the barriers of language.

b

Canadian SPacific

^

321, 9A Street N.W. Calgary, Alberta. T2N 1T7

A Periodic Chart Of The Atoms, Phase 4
(A Play For Telex In Ten Acts)

Act 1
On being asked by the audience to express an
opinion on the burning issues of the day;

The artist makes a point

Act 2
On being questioned by the audience as to the
nature of such extreme opinions;

The artist draws the line

————————————————

Act 3
On sensing that the audience is finding his
argument more attractive and being overcome by
a type of sleeping sickness identified as
'revolutionary zeal';

The artist spreads the word
                        T H E
                        W O R D

Act 4
On failing to recognize his own vanity whilst
trying to convince the audience of the mechanical
nature of existance;

The artist delivers the goods
                        GOODGOODGOOD
                        GOODGOODGOOD
                        GOODGOODGOOD
                        GOODGOODGOOD
                        GOODGOODGOOD

Act 5
On failing to identify within himself strong
feelings of self-importance whilst attempting to
express to the audience the need for a deeper
understanding of natural law;

The artist lays it on thick
                    IT

Act 6
On being told by the audience that he is talking
a load of old boots;

The artist over-reacts
                        The artist
                        reacts

Act 7
On being unable to realize that he is not being
honest with the audience and thus being out of
harmony with the ideas he is trying to express;

The artist gets stuck in a rut
                        in a rut
                        in a rut
                        in a rut
                        in a rut

Act 8
On feeling the need to re-establish his credibility
in the eyes of a sometimes hostile but mainly
indifferent audience;

The artist tells the truth
                        'The artist lies all the time'

Act 9
On reflecting at length on his purely mechanical
reaction to the audience's criticism in the light
of the opinions he has expressed so far;

The artist understands
                        stands
                        The artist

Act 0
On being made aware through his association with
the audience and consequently through a deeper
understanding of himself and his first aim in life;

The artist stops at

What do you say, saying "art".

```
art ......................... art
arterial ............... arteriel
arteriosclerosis  arteriosclerose
artery .................... artere
artesian .............. artesien
artful
artichoke ............ artichaut
article ................. article
articulate .......... articulaire
articulation ....... articulation
artifice .............. artifice
artificer
                        articuler
artificial ........... artificiel
artificiality ....... artificieux
artillery ............ artillerie
artisan ................. artisan
                          artison
                          artisonne
artist .................. artiste
artiste
artistic ............ artistement
artistry ............. artistique
artless
artlessness
arty
```

"Art" is some artistic /artificial/ article,which has
been articulated by artist /artificer,artisan/ in artful
/artistry/ manner,and has been presented as artless
announcement to somebody.
"L'art" est un certain article artificiel /artistement/
qui est articule par un artiste /artisan/ d'artifice
facon et lequel est presenter quelqu'un comme une
artificieuse enonce.

conclusion:
Because artist articulates an article and articulates it
to somebody and artist ist articulated by a number of
people,hence "art" is created by artist and artist is
created by a society in which he lives,therefore,saying
"art" you must say about artists and about the society
they live in.

ART AS REVOLT
OF CULTURE

ORAL POETS OF THE AIR WAVES   George Economou

Are the play-by-play men of sportscasting oral poets? That they compose
at least part of the time by formula as they perform their task of calling the
game, is evident to anyone that knows anything about the game or oral poetics.
There are numerous ways to denote and describe most plays in major spectator
sports. Most of these ways, or formulas, are conventional and traditional, but
there is always room for one more. Many a sportscaster invents his own self-
identifying way of calling a shot, pitch, or pass, which may eventually take its
place among its traditional relatives. For example, Marv Albert's onomatopoeic
"Yesss!" for a basket ball field goal may be too closely associated with him to
be adapted by colleagues in the near future, but in another time and place....
Then there are the opportunities for self-individuation through a personal style
of imagery, as in Keith Jackson's frequent use of homespun country figures of
speech to embellish his call of an unusual or outstanding play. If the performance of sportscasting raises a comparison with the poetics of preliterate cultures,
the subject matter does as well. Where in our increasingly illiterate culture
do we find as many stirring and specialized paradigms of physical and willful
heroics and strategies as we do in big-time collegiate and professional sports?
I do not mean to imply by these questions that sportscasting and oral poetry are
thoroughly analogous. I do wish to inquire if the analogy has occurred to others
and to urge them to investigate the subject and its problems in greater depth.
And if the status of poet--of any kind--seems inappropriately generous for a class
of men that includes a Howard Cosell, I would remind us all that we seem to know
with confidence who his counterparts are among our own.

The eye is a more universal organ than the tongue.
The eye is a more universal organ than the tongue.
The eye is a more universal organ than the tongue.
The eye is a more universal organ than the tongue.
The eye is a more universal organ than the tongue.
The eye is a more universal organ than the tongue.
The eye is a more universal organ than the tongue.
The eye is a more universal organ than the tongue.
The eye is a more universal organ than the tongue.
The eye is a more universal organ than the tongue.
The eye is a more universal organ than the tongue.
The eye is a more universal organ than the tongue.
The eye is a more universal organ than the tongue.
The eye is a more universal organ than the tongue.
The eye is a more universal organ than the tongue.
The eye is a more universal organ than the tongue.
The eye is a more universal organ than the tongue.
The eye is a more universal organ than the tongue.
The eye is a more universal organ than the tongue.
The eye is a more universal organ than the tongue.
The eye is a more universal organ than the tongue.
The eye is a more universal organ than the tongue.
The eye is a more universal organ than the tongue.
The eye is a more universal organ than the tongue.
The eye is a more universal organ than the tongue.
The eye is a more universal organ than the tongue.
The eye is a more universal organ than the tongue.
The eye is a more universal organ than the tongue.
The eye is a more universal organ than the tongue.
The eye is a more universal organ than the tongue.
The eye is a more universal organ than the tongue.
The eye is a more universal organ than the tongue.
The eye is a more universal organ than the tongue.
The eye is a more universal organ than the tongue.
The eye is a more universal organ than the tongue.
The eye is a more universal organ than the tongue.
The eye is a more universal organ than the tongue.
The eye is a more universal organ than the tongue.
The eye is a more universal organ than the tongue.
The eye is a more universal organ than the tongue.
The eye is a more universal organ than the tongue.

is minimal every word is language no word is minimal language
minimal every word is language no word is minimal language is
every word is language no word is minimal language is minimal
word is language no word is minimal language is minimal every
is language no word is minimal language is minimal every word
language no word is minimal language is minimal every word is
no word is minimal language is minimal every word is language
word is minimal language is minimal every word is language no
is minimal language is minimal every word is language no word
minimal language is minimal every word is language no word is
language is minimal every word is language no word is minimal

journal entries on visual language / loris essary

```
Everman
nT
yW                        yW
EvermanTextbyWelchDEv
nTextbyWelchDEvermanT
yWelchDEvermanTextbyW
EvermanTextbyWelchDEv
nT            .          nT
yW
Everman


Eve                       Ev
nTex                      anT
yWelc                   xtbyW
Everman         elchDEv
        yWe  chDEvermanT
yWe        vermanT      yW
EvermanTextbyW
nTextbyWelc DEver anT
yWelchDE              extbyW
Everm                  hDEv
yWel                    byW
yWe                      yW


yWelch            TextbyW
Ever                  hDEv
nTe     WelchD         nT
yWe       ver          yW
EvermanTexybyWelchDEv
nTextbyWelchDEvermanT
yWelchDEvermanTextbyW
EvermanTextbyWelchDEv
nTe                    nT


nTextby
yW
Ev                        Ev
nTextbyWelchDEvermanT
yWelchDEvermanTextbyW
EvermanTextbyWelchDEv
nTextbyWelchDEvermanT
yW                        yW
Ev
nTextby
```

```
byWelchDEvermanTextbyWelchDEvermanTextbyWelchDEvermanTextbyWelchDEvermanTe
hDEvermanTextbyWelchDEvermanTextbyWelchDEvermanTextbyWelchDEvermanTextbyWe
manTextbyWelchDEvermanTextbyWelchDEvermanTextbyWelchDEvermanTextbyWelchDEv
byWelchDEvermanTextbyWelchDEvermanTextbyWelchDEvermanTextbyWelchDEvermanTe
hDEvermanTextbyWelchDEvermanTextbyWelchDEvermanTextbyWelchDEvermanTextbyWe
manTextbyWelchDEvermanTextbyWelchDEvermanTextbyWelchDEvermanTextbyWelchDEv
byWelchDEvermanTextbyWelchD          TextbyWelchDEvermanTextbyWelchDEvermanTe
hDEvermanTextbyWelchDEverma    extbyWelchDEvermanTextbyWelchDEvermanTextbyWe
manTextbyWelchDEvermanTextb    elchDEvermanTextb    elchDEvermanTextbyWelchDEv
byWelchDEvermanTextbyWelchD                         ermanTextbyWelchDEvermanTe
hDEvermanTextbyWelchDEverma                         extbyWelchDEvermanTextbyWe
manTextbyWelchDEvermanTextb                         elchDEvermanTextbyWelchDEv
byWelchDEvermanTextbyWelchD                         ermanTextbyWelchDEvermanTe
hDEvermanTextbyWelchDEverma    extbyWelchDEverma    extbyWelchDEvermanTextbyWe
manTextbyWelchDEvermanTextb    elchDEvermanTextbyWelchDEvermanTextbyWelchDEv
byWelchDEvermanTextbyWelchD          TextbyWelchDEvermanTextbyWelchDEvermanTe
hDEvermanTextbyWelchDEvermanTextbyWelchDEvermanTextbyWelchDEvermanTextbyWe
manTextbyWelchDEvermanTextbyWelchDEvermanTextbyWelchDEvermanTextbyWelchDEv
byWelchDEvermanTextbyWelchD    rmanTextbyWelchD    ermanTextbyWelchDEvermanTe
hDEvermanTextbyWelchDEverma    tbyWelchDEverm      extbyWelchDEvermanTextbyWe
manTextbyWelchDEvermanTextb    hDEvermanTe         elchDEvermanTextbyWelchDEv
byWelchDEvermanTextbyWelchD    TextbyW             ermanTextbyWelchDEvermanTe
hDEvermanTextbyWelchDEvermanTextb    l             extbyWelchDEvermanTextbyWe
manTextbyWelchDEvermanTextb    lchDE        extb   elchDEvermanTextbyWelchDEv
byWelchDEvermanTextbyWelchD                  elchDEvermanTextbyWelchDEvermanTe
hDEvermanTextbyWelchDEverma         h      m       extbyWelchDEvermanTextbyWe
manTextbyWelchDEvermanTextb       vermanT          elchDEvermanTextbyWelchDEv
byWelchDEvermanTextbyWelchD      anTextbyWelc      ermanTextbyWelchDEvermanTe
hDEvermanWelchDEvermanTextb      chDEvermanText    elchDEvermanTextbyWelchDEv
manTextbyWelchDEvermanTextb      lchDEvermanTextb  elchDEvermanTextbyWelchDEv
byWelchDEvermanTextbyWelchDEvermanTextbyWelchDEvermanTextbyWelchDEvermanTe
hDEvermanTextbyWelchDEvermanTextbyWelchDEvermanTextbyWelchDEvermanTextbyWe
manTextbyWelchDEvermanTextb        Everman         elchDEvermanTextbyWelchDEv
byWelchDEvermanTextbyWelchD      manTextbyWelc     ermanTextbyWelchDEvermanTe
hDEvermanTextbyWelchDEverma    xtby        Everma  extbyWelchDEvermanTextbyWe
manTextbyWelchDEvermanTextb    lchDE      manTextb elchDEvermanTextbyWelchDEv
byWelchDEvermanTextbyWelchD                         ermanTextbyWelchDEvermanTe
hDEvermanTextbyWelchDEverma                         extbyWelchDEvermanTextbyWe
manTextbyWelchDEvermanTextb                         elchDEvermanTextbyWelchDEv
byWelchDEvermanTextbyWelchD                         ermanTextbyWelchDEvermanTe
hDEvermanTextbyWelchDEverma    xtbyWelchDEverm      extbyWelchDEvermanTextbyWe
manTextbyWelchDEvermanTextbyWelchDEvermanTextbyWelchDEvermanTextbyWelchDEv
byWelchDEvermanTextbyWelchDEvermanTextbyWelchDEvermanTextbyWelchDEvermanTe
hDEvermanTextbyWelchDEverma         WelchDEvermanTextbyWelchDEvermanTextbyWe
manTextbyWelchDEvermanTextb    elchDEvermanTextbyWelchDEvermanTextbyWelchDEv
byWelchDEvermanTextbyWelchD    ermanTextbyWelchD    ermanTextbyWelchDEvermanTe
hDEvermanTextbyWelchDEverma                         extbyWelchDEvermanTextbyWe
manTextbyWelchDEvermanTextb                         elchDEvermanTextbyWelchDEv
byWelchDEvermanTextbyWelchD                         ermanTextbyWelchDEvermanTe
hDEvermanTextbyWelchDEverma                         extbyWelchDEvermanTextbyWe
manTextbyWelchDEvermanTextb    elchDEvermanTextb    elchDEvermanTextbyWelchDEv
byWelchDEvermanTextbyWelchD    ermanTextbyWelchD    ermanTextbyWelchDEvermanTe
hDEvermanTextbyWelchDEverma         WelchDEvermanTextbyWelchDEvermanTextbyWe
manTextbyWelchDEvermanTextbyWelchDEvermanTextbyWelchDEvermanTextbyWelchDEv
byWelchDEvermanTextbyWelchDEvermanTextbyWelchDEvermanTextbyWelchDEvermanTe
hDEvermanTextbyWelchDEvermanTextbyWelchDEvermanTextbyWelchDEvermanTextbyWe
manTextbyWelchDEvermanTextbyWelchDEvermanTextbyWelchDEvermanTextbyWelchDEv
byWelchDEvermanTextbyWelchDEvermanTextbyWelchDEvermanTextbyWelchDEvermanTe
hDEvermanTextbyWelchDEvermanTextbyWelchDEvermanTextbyWelchDEvermanTextbyWe
```

RAYMOND FEDERMAN

after all isn't it the role of fiction and I don't mean science-fiction
only to alter reality for the better   the writer
may not be as privileged as the scientist nowadays   or perhaps he is
who knows   for this oblique witness of reality must   at the same
time   seek and avoid precision   the reality of imagination
is more real than reality without imagination   as we well know   and
besides   reality as such has never really interested anyone   it is
and has always been a form of disenchantment   most of us would say if
we were asked   quite rightly   what makes
reality fascinating   at times   is the imaginary
catastrophe which hides behind it   the writer knows this   and
exploits it   whereas the scientist tends to ignore it   wilfully
and this is why the writer must seek and avoid precision simultaneously
which may cause him to suffer violent strokes of delirium   and
typographiphobia   but what the hell
scientific precision   on the other hand   is always
antidelirious   and   calmative

Biography ?!

There are few texts,
but you may start with

**A Biographical Sketch of
Dr. Samuel Johnson (1785)**
Thomas Tyers

Flush
Virginia Woolf

Short Lives
John Aubrey

A Fortunate Man
John Berger

Christopher and His Kind
Christopher Isherwood

Imaginary Lives
Marcel Schwab

Biographical Essays
Lytton Strachey

Henry James
Leon Edel

The Quest for Corvo
A.J.A. Symons

and various biographies by Hugh Kingsmill

© **Andrew Field, Palm Beach,
Queensland 4221 Australia**

The next kind of Art:

There are only two rules

Rule 1: Biography is a genre like any other
and should take many forms

Rule 2:
Simple explanations
of a life have been
much overrated and
should be avoided

Aphorism — a life or
a biography too easily
indexed is a bore.

20TH CENTURY ART* DYNAMICS

(a hopefully useless tentative definition)

p/ by Rtfillion   for the Eternal Network

to 3rd millennium   ! > ?

↑

(no one excluded: doors removed)

SPIRIT

↑

(awareness : doors opened then left open)

MIND   MINDS

↑

(concepts : doors opened then closed)

MIND   MATTERS

↑

(-isms : doors opened then locked)

MATTER   MINDS

↑

(craftfulness : doors decorated)

MATTER MATTERS

to 1900's   ? > !

1979

* art being looked upon, on the one hand, as a function of life plus fiction, with fiction tending towards zero, and, on the other hand, as one of the (ambiguous, paradoxical) roads leading to the road.

ON EXPERIMENT IN POETRY

> The coincidence of the changing of circumstances and of human activity or self-changing can be conceived and rationally understood only as revolutionary practice.
> — Marx,
> *Theses on Feuerbach*

> The progress of an artist is a continual self-sacrifice, a continual extinction of personality.
> — Eliot,
> *Tradition and the Individual Talent*

Experiment is the vital spark that has revived the body of poetry innumerable times; it has cast new light on the neglected past even as it has presented itself as a departure from what has preceded it. In the genuinely experimental work, the future makes itself known as the sudden expansion of formal possibilities; poet and reader understand where they have been because they see where they are going. Experimentation is lawful insofar as it is the manifestation of increased self-consciousness; thus, the history of poetry is a history of successful experiments, which have been proven successful in that they are now regarded as traditional.

It should be the goal of all poets to perfect their instruments. In doing so, one takes the tools with which one has been provided and alters them in such ways as to precisely express the *matter* of the work. Experimentation consists of this process of refinement, which, while involving the manipulation of linguistic forms, should never be reduced merely to the play of language which has enamoured so many contemporary poets. Regardless of whether this pathology is expressed as obsessive formalism or fragmented "projective verse," it is evidenced in the work of even the finest of today's poets. In the work of lesser figures, linguistic novelty has become completely fetishized in the wake of the disruptions of Modernism. But there is a crucial difference between Modernist and contemporary experimentation, and Frederic Jameson has isolated this difference:

> . . . older modernism was in its essence profoundly antisocial, and reckoned with the instinctive hostility of the middle-class public of which it stood as a negation and a refusal. What characterizes the new modernism is however precisely that it is *popular*: maybe not in small mid-Western towns, but in the dominant world of fashion and the mass media. That can only mean, to my mind, that there has come to be something socially useful about such art from the point of view of the existing socio-economic structure; or something deeply suspect about it, if your point of view is a revolutionary one.
>
> *(Marxism and Form*, pp. 413-14)

Jameson's analysis places the post-modern artist at the center of a cultural system he ostensibly rejects. This is certainly the case of most poets, who are compelled (if they do not do so willingly) to transform their works into commodities, on sale for a greater or lesser price to the editors of literally thousands of magazines and presses of every conceivable "style" and "school" of verse. It is small wonder then that experimental literature is so highly valued: fashions in poetry come and go as they do in clothing or home furnishings, and for precisely the same reasons.

The fallacious notion of individuated poetic style that has currency today, the supposed development of the poet's "voice," runs counter to Eliot's conception of a tradition that guides a poet's growth while keeping him from the idiosyncracies of "personality." Despite current theories of poetic influence, the materially successful poet emerges into the light of fame as though he were self-created. Given the socio-economic conditions that determine poetic production today, it may be assumed that the truly innovative poet will be invisible, not only in terms of Eliot's "extinction of personality," but in the simple fact that he will not be read. (Perhaps, through an implacable dialectical reversal, it is the poetic audience who has actually disappeared). This poet will have successfully subsumed his tradition in the fabric of his verse; he will be prey to neither the anxiety of influence nor the fetish of innovation, for the process of experimentation that will have taken place will have been lawful; it will be the recognition of the *necessity* of formal change in his verse and the discovery of a new freedom. In this sense, poetic experimentation may be seen as the human subject acting upon the objective conditions of its being: poetic experiment as revolutionary practice.

Ezra Pound was correct in declaring that "only emotion endures," and it is the emotions engendered by the struggle for perfection that are immortalized in that never-completed body of work called the tradition. Such is the *matter* of poetry, the test against which experimental verse may be measured. In the sixteenth century, Spenser discovered a "new" means of embodying these emotions in a kind of archaic diction that drew both praise and blame. Spenser "writ no language" Ben Jonson declared, though Jonson "would have him read for his matter." In the eighteenth century, Chatterton would again experiment with archaic diction, so would

Keats in the nineteenth. Wordsworth sought the language of common men, Williams found his language in "the mouths of Polish mothers." Innovation is thus contingent upon historical circumstances; no one may see how the poetic emotions will next take shape. What must be remembered, even amidst the fraudulent circumstances that surround so much literary activity, is that poetry is produced in response to a human demand for beauty that is never really still. Each new poem is the fulfillment of a promise. As William Bronk has said of his poems,

> They are waiting for me. Well, we have to go on.
> That isn't a reason. It isn't reasonable.
> We concede so much. What don't we concede?
> I wish I had something; and the poems are there.

Norman Finkelstein

Charles Henri Ford

THE AMAZING MORBIDITY OF YUKIO MISHIMA

Always interested in ritual deposits of the culturally deprived

You visited cannibal villages

As though they were the only radical transformations on the map

At the shrine of the Seven Mangoes

Mrs Okura was called upon to slaughter a chicken

Some roses were floating face down

They seemed stupid from prolonged suffering

The bull was subject to him as he was to it

He did not covet death so much as what comes after

Days of silent despair, irresistible as a cry of 'Kill me!',

   can seem longer than years

One of the Jatakas mentioned five hundred page-boys, adept

   at wrestling

Fanned by the veronicas of baffling winds

With your nerves' raw edges you wrote the last words of a novel:

'It was the exacerbation of genius and he knew it.'

Charles Henri Ford

REFLECTIONS ON MY BIRTHDAY

Buddhism has no metaphysics, even non-existence is existing

Do you see the starfish in the tentacles of the anemone?

Of perfect workmanship, it was concealed by continuity

The ontological totum is a pervasive concept

There's a sham reality in a tube built by seaworms

When informed of the hemispherical mound the Ponda police

        arrived and did the panchanama

One of them put a bullet through a young bullfighter

The irrationality of a healing mantra left its invisible imprint

Crypto-realist like that of a place, the focus is deliberately

        blurred

As with the touching and not touching of a lustral discharge

A sincerity of fingermarks bruised into flesh

Lying flat on my face, forehead touching the guru's feet

I listened for clandestine utterance in the mystical

        universe of discourse

Out of a mixture of milk and water the swan drinks only the milk

DISILLUSIONED TEXTS

The following is the fourth in a series of language relays which began with a video-taped conversation between Anselm Hollo and Robert Creeley. A second tape saw myself attempting to reconstruct the conversation on the basis of an inadequate audio track. On the third tape I comment on my efforts in the second tape. The text below is a typescript of the third tape. The project was jointly undertaken by Hans Breder, myself, Robert Creeley and Anselm Hollo at the Corroboree: Gallery of New Concepts, University of Iowa, Iowa City.

In this text I begin to   I don't know, I don't know what the last words were. I missed it. It was probably the most crucial part of the discussion.

In trying to pick up this conversation I'm trying to somehow relay what occurred in a conversation between these two, thrown back and forth. While   vast generalizations and absolutely inconsequential minutiae

The discussion that I was asked to relate was a discussion between two friends. These people were having a good time talking. They haven't seen each other for awhile. They sit down and they talk about the kinds of topics   and Russell that embody a content that are   , if you'll pardon the word, great ideas. But it's not really the great ideas that they talk about. They use this as a means of communicating with each other on a much more personal kind of a level. One asks listening to it, What in the hell's the point. It's surely not to talk about Russell. They don't try to approach Russell and they try to approach   . They try to approach each other, and   is purely pretext for this kind of a thing. It takes all kinds of large questions about what does all this mean, and   doesn't mean anything in this argument. I mean what does this conversation mean that occurs between Harlow and Creely. They don't even want to talk about the ideas. They don't want to talk about Fitkenstein, and it's thrown away after just a couple of minutes in favor of discussing their friends who are also people who embody ideas, but whose ideas aren't ever approached directly, who aren't ever discussed vis a vis their ideas. These people basically are behaving together. They are trying to search around and find a kind of common ground on the basis of which they can renew their friendship which they must perceive as their past history of understanding each other. I think it's all really about behaving. A lot of it, I think, is about their identification of themselves as poets. They get together and they confirm their past as poets. They say things to each other to reassure each other that they're still poets and that their friends are still poets, and that they have a kind of a license to make poetry out of the kinds of things that they talk about. But it's almost impossible to relate this kind of thing. Well, one is forced into doing this, talking about equivalency to what they're saying. One can't relate straightforwardly what the conversation is about.

It's kind of a situation where I'm an outsider. I'm an outsider looking on a situation that one, well that requires being an insider to understand what's going on.   I think one would typically go away from a conversation like this—if you're sitting around listening to it over a cup of coffee, you go away from the conversation feeling like you knew what was going on. You'd say that it was, perhaps if you were the outsider, that it was small talk, that it was nothing much that really went on in the way of communication, and maybe you'd say it was bullshit or chewing the fat or whatever because the kind of information the conversation conveyed was so trivial, so inconsequential. Especially in comparison with the nominally had mounted as the subject of their conversation,   Vitkenstein. That he might come away with nothing but contempt for the whole thing. Of course that would be to completely misunderstand the purpose and meanings of these two people's communication. It would take a poet, I think, to interpret what went on if what we want to ask about that conversation is what did it mean? The little bits of information that I can glean from the tape of their discussion are not uncontextual. They're not out of order. They are sequential in places. They even make a certain amount of (on the surface of it) sense, but on the other hand they are wildly beside the point. The process of relaying the conversation is complex when it's unpackable into a number of questions like, Is what it is you are relaying information or is what you are relaying meaning or what? It's not easy to recover information, but it's a good deal harder to recover the meaning of the communication that goes on.

It's a strange myth that would have us try to retrieve information anyway, perhaps of the fact that information is so much beside the point. It would have made much more sense to simply use the tape as a basis for fabricating what would amount to a fictional conversation between these two people. But we're prevented from doing that because what would be construed as the unethical aspects of misreporting what it is they said. We feel obligated in listening to a conversation like this to leave the integrity of the conversation undisturbed, and not misreport, to not alter the facts. O.K. I'm to be that TV that they talk about later on. I was put in front of this conversation to be a surveyor and a scanner. I wasn't really placed here to interpret or to criticize, just simply to relate the information. It's a very strong impulse that people have to do that. It's a kind of responsibility we all feel to other people, other people's conversation, other people's writing, other people's art to approach as moral precaution this obligation to be just with it. But it's an impossible task and we all know from the beginning. I don't know why we insist on this kind of pretense.

I don't really have a notion of how accurate the information is in the second generation, the second stage of the tape that I made. I don't know how straight I've even got the facts. I've

heard things on the tape and said things that sound like what Creely and Harlow said, but I can't
be sure they're the same thing. The information is so incomplete. There are so many breakdowns,
lapses, and drifts in recounting it that I'm not sure but what I heard something that simply
sounds like what I said. The ramifications of that are horrifying. It suggests that the kinds
of relays that typically go on in communications between individuals, one to the next, and to
the next and to the next and to the next are from the media, this TV, this impersonal, this
accurate objective surveyor, they are relaying from that information to an individual must be a
complex thing and then from the individual that receives it to another individual, one more step.
One more lapse, if you will, and but what's construed in the beginning is a kind of straightforward information. It's kind of a straightforward communication of content, one party to another.
Every time the information is relayed there's a deterioration, a terrible deterioration on all
kinds of levels. Probably least of all information, probably most of all the essence of what
a pause that was to be communicated. We have to be very unsure of language. It makes one think
that something needs to be done, something like what the Dadaist suggested back in the teens and
the twenties, that there has to be a renewal of language. This communication that's accomplished
only under such difficulty in our everyday world. There has to be something done to direct or
facilitate meaningful communication. We need a revolution in language. We can't communicate with
the language we have any more. It8s .... imprecise, it's a crude tool that's manipulated
probably most effectively, there's aesthetically. It's as though the poets today, maybe Creely
and Harlow included, are using language as a kind of verbal refuse, as a kind of language refuge
like Switters (?) used, refuge from material culture. It can't function in any kind of practical
way anymore. It can't do it, what it was intended to do by those who were to present it in the
first place. We use it as the basis for what's little more than a concrete language.

    One of the questions we're talking about is, What's the status of this language that Creely
uses? It seems to me that from my purposes listening to this tape of them talking, it might as
well be in Greek. It's a language I don't understand, but it's one that I could repeat the
sounds of, and the sounds would carry a certain amount of information, if they were enough like
Greek. But I doubt if I would miss any more of the conversation that I'd missed in this conversation that's being created between Creely and Harlow in English. They're both at this stage of
the game kinds of concrete languages or kinds of noises that act as instruments in behavioral
situations. They acquire meanings; they don't carry meaning.

    If I was able to interpret Harlow and Creely's language as concrete language then I'd have
the freedom to reconstruct on some level the conversation as I perceive it. But as long as I
perceive language as information and communication I don't have that freedom. It's as though the
language we're using in the everyday world is a copyrighted language that I can't plagarize,
misquote, I can't utilize against the rules. I'd do better trying to talk about noises, just
noises, just noises and watch the people's behavior. If I were to do the tape again I'd shut
the sound track off and try to infer what's going on just in terms of how the people act and how
they gesticulate, how they smile, laugh, and how they relate to each other in terms of their
bodies and their postures, their dispositions as I can perceive it, because at least in that
case I could perceive the whole thing; the visual record is more complete than the audio record.
But that's only part of it. It's more than just a question of the ability of me to retrieve the
proper sounds. It's a question of having retrieving, having retrieved the sounds, of not being
able to make sense of what they really mean.

    I'm sitting here with headphones on, rather isolated. I'm not looking at the image of these
two people. Listening to myself talk about their conversation, and I don't really know what's
going on. The only communication that's going on at this moment is between me and myself. I hear
myself say things and I think things to myself and they say things to what I thought. My thoughts
say something back to me. Even the text that I'm listening to myself, of my interpretation
of the Harlow Creely text doesn't make any sense because it doesn't have any kind of concrete
reference in the other conversation. It's purely gratuity.

    I actually don't understand what I'm saying, truly don't understand what I'm saying on that
tape. The sheer full thought that most of what we say is like that. It's what we've been taught
to say. It's what we say on this or that occasion, and that's the appropriate thing to say
under the circumstances. It's all mostly cliches, prefabricated language. I dare say if we were
to sit down and listen to most of what we have to say to other people that it wouldn't make much
sense. Our everyday parlance, our conversations with people don't...They're not about the kind of
information and communication that, for example a formal paper, a speech, an article. A book is
about formalized language that attempts as best it can to insure real communication, but even then
when it's looked at closely; falls short of what we'd like. I'm not sure that books and magazines
really communicate much of anything more than this conversation didn't make too much sense to me,
and not any more than my attempt to reconstruct the conversation which makes even less sense
to me.

                                                        Stephen C. Foster

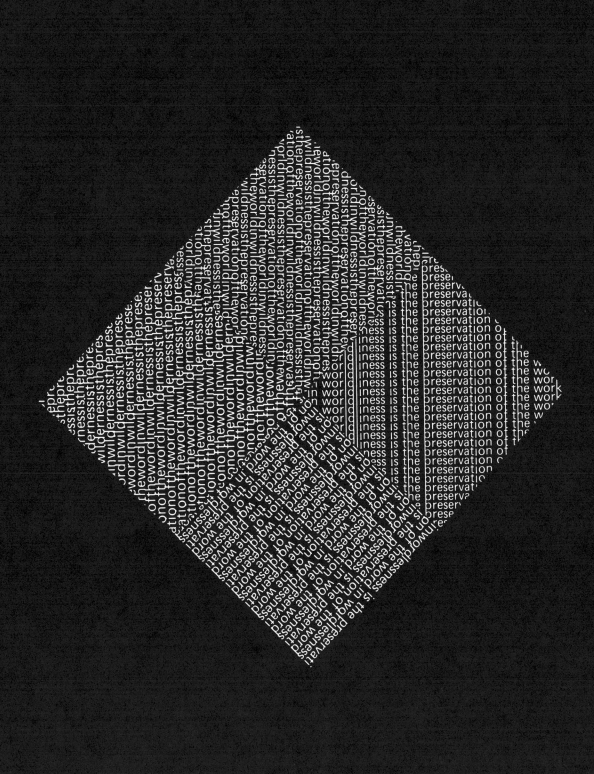

william l. fox
3-79

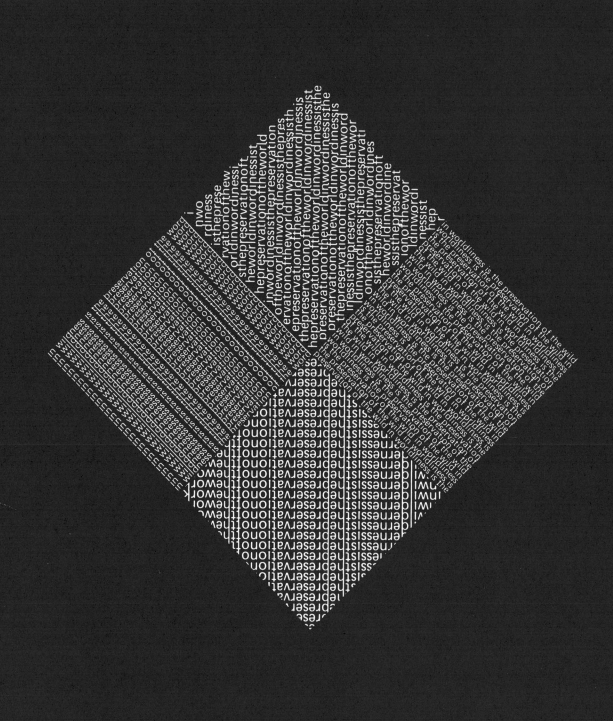

LINES ON ART NOW

Peter Frank

. Our aesthetic attitudes have broadened enough to allow us to regs
regard every phenomenon as bearing aesthetic impact or value.

. This aesthetic impact or value may be seen as positive, negative, or
neutral, but not according to any universal terms.

. The individual perceiving the impact or value judges for himself or
herself the societal and personal worth of the phenomenon as an
aesthetic circumstance, and engages in debate with others who have
discerned perhaps different societal and personal worth.

. Art is substantiated, even defined, by the discourse comprised of
this personal evaluation and subsequent interpersonal/societal debate.

. Art is not just form or content or form-as-content or content-as-
form, it is context-- the context of the aesthetic discourse.

. The context of the aesthetic discourse is without material bound,
as the participants in the discourse potentially regard any
phenomenon in aesthetic terms.

. What art tends to be nowadays is the field or fields of activity
beside and beyond all other fields of activity-- beside and beyond
chemistry, agronomy, politics, economics, ditch digging, street
cleaning, etc. Art is the "miscellany" in the catalogue of
humankind's disciplines.

. Art can incorporate the other, "fixed" disciplines into its own
operations, but it cannot be the other disciplines.

. Art is its own discipline, despite its ability to incorporate the
other disciplines, because art has its own purpose, distinct from
the other disciplines': not to get the streets clean or run the
country, but to encourage awareness of the fixed disciplines--
and all other things-- as aesthetically resonant phenomena.

. The genuine artist does not decide this, but discovers this.

. The genuine artist has perceived things in aesthetic terms and has
endeavored to shape phenomena in response to this perception before
realizing that this perept perception and this endeavor are those
of an artist.

. An artist is only someone who has chosen to model the means of
expressing his or her own impulse to exhibit aesthetic perception--
an impulse apparently inherent in the reasoning capacity of all
human beings-- on the activity of others recognized as artists.

. If someone decides to be an artist before actually doing art, the
art produced is likely to be undermined by its own self-consciousness.

. This is especially true nowadays because art is produced at a
confluence of other heightened consciousnesses, including historical,
stylistic, and marketing consciousnesses.

. Historical consciousness prompts today's artist to strive to do
something something no other artist has done before.

. Stylistic consciousness prompts today's artist to strive to do
something that conforms to contemporary methodological orthodoxies
(even if unorthodoxy is one of these orthodoxies).

. Marketing consciousness prompts today's artist to seek the dissemi-
nation of his or her ideas-- and perhaps to profit from this dis-
semination-- according to established means or variations on these
means: galleries, museums, publications, art fairs, teaching
positions, conferences, government support, et al.

. In this century-- and especially in the last few decades-- these
consciousnesses have replaced the narrative moralizing and enter-
taining of the bourgeois art of the nineteenth century and the
royal and religious propagandizing of earlier art as the motivations

for making art.   New York, Sept. 1977- May 1979

Prime Source 23

(a statement about relationships)

4 × 4

6×6

4 × 4

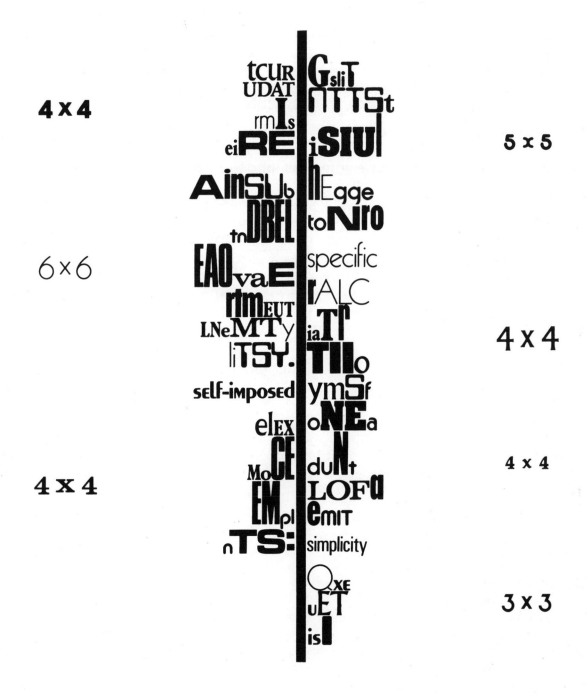

5 × 5

4 × 4

4 × 4

3 × 3

abstract: 1. factors
2. position
3. syntax

LAURENCE GOLDSTEIN

ON EXPERIMENTAL WRITING

EXPERIMENTS ARE CUSTOMARILY PERFORMED ON DEFENSELESS
OBJECTS. WHAT WAS INTEGRAL IS ACTED UPON AND MODIFIED
IN SERVICE OF A NEW CONCEPTION.

HENCE THE HOSTILITY OF WRITERS WHO LOVE THE WHOLE OF
ANIMATED NATURE TO TECHNICIANS THAT "PEEP AND BOTANIZE,"
AS WORDSWORTH PUT IT.

BUT WORDSWORTH IS NOT A DEFENSELESS OBJECT. WHY SHOULD
NOT EXPERIMENTS BE PERFORMED UPON HIS CORPUS? ROSMARIE
AND KEITH WALDROP DO SO IN WORDS WORTH LESS, A VOLUME
AND ARENA OF CONFLICT BETWEEN POETS COMPETING UPON
A PRESCRIBED ORDER OF WORDS. WORDSWORTH ONCE SAID:

    FIVE YEARS HAVE PAST: FIVE SUMMERS, WITH THE LENGTH
    OF FIVE LONG WINTERS!

BUT DISMEMBERMENT IS THE PRIMAL ACT IN THE TIME OF THE
ASSASSINS, THOSE WHO HAVE LEARNED CANNIBAL MAGIC FROM
THE GOLDEN BOUGH. THE WALDROPS MIX IT UP:

    FIVE STEEP FIRES

        *   *

    FIVE YEARS, STEEP
    DAY. COME,
    SYCAMORE, TO
    THE FIRE.

        *   *

    FIVE YEARS AND
    WATERS.
    AGAIN STEEP DAY.

AND SO ON UNTIL THE SILLY PUTTY OF WORDSWORTH'S IMMORTAL
POEM IS ALLOWED TO RESUME ITS FIRST ADAMIC SHAPE.

SUCH IS THE INESCAPABLE NOSTALGIA OF EXPERIMENTAL WRITING,
WHICH NO SUBJECT WOULD ENDURE WITH MORE SYMPATHY THAN
THE AUTHOR OF "TINTERN ABBEY."

THE INSTRUMENTS OF THE EXPERIMENTAL METHOD ARE THE
FORMER PROBES OF CRITICISM: NOT SO MUCH IMITATION AS
INTERPRETATION: NOT SO MUCH INTERPRETATION AS
USURPATION.

EXPERIMENTAL WORKS HAVE POSSESSIVE TITLES LIKE
ULYSSES, ARIEL, CHIMERA, V.

THE AMBITION OF LITERARY RADICALISM IS TO PERFORM
A REVOLUTION LIKE THE MOON'S, ILLUMINATING BY THE
SAME GENRE OF LIGHT ITS ECTYPES STOLE FROM THE SUN.
ONE WRITER WHO BEGAN WITH HOWL PROCEEDED TO THE
SOLEMN RUBRIC THE FALL OF AMERICA IN SEARCH OF
LUMINOUS RECOGNITION. HE ASKED:

    WHERE'S STRAVINSKY? THEDA BARA? CHAPLIN?
      HARPO MARX?

          WHERE'S LAUREL AND HIS HARDY?

NOWHERE. AND SO THAT SCHOLAR BALDLY REMADE THEIR
BELOVED PRESENCES, THEIR VOICES, THEIR ROUTINES.

LET ME CORRECT MYSELF.

TEXTS ARE DEFENSELESS OBJECTS. THERE IS NO ORDER
OF WORDS THAT MAY NOT BE VIOLATED. NO THOUGHT.
NO PERSON.

READER, YOU WILL NOT ESCAPE REFINEMENTS OF STYLE
IN THIS REVOLUTIONARY CENTURY. THOSE WHO REMEMBER
THE PAST ARE CONDEMNED TO RELIVE IT.

20th. century Commercial	21 st. century commercial
don't smoke tobacco cigarettes.	Smoke GINSENG
it has a micronite filter	it has a snow filter
when you begin lit & end it	when you begin & end lit
it does hurt	it doesn't hurt
inhaled & exhaled +	going in & going out *
packaged in celoprofane neon	packaged in celophone birdsprint
the stamp sealed cancer	the SEAL " Nicotine Free "

march '79   by Courtenay P. Graham-GAZAWAY

(written for Critical Assembling)

Roland Grass

Visual Literature as a Free Kick

PRELUDE

The idea that art evolved from play is both ancient and current. Plato held that mimetic play and art produced a false reality and, hence, were harmful. Others, like Schiller, have held that artists, unlike scientists, have no illusions about their illusions, that they create an ideal world that serves as a palliative for the real world. Other thinkers who have dealt with the relationship between art and play in one way or another include Aristotle, Kant, Schopenhauer, Nietzsche, Spencer, Freud, Jung, Huizinga. One aspect of art and play has been stressed by nearly all of them: art and play are free activities. The antithesis is WORK, performed in our society by technology.

Generally, all the discoveries and innovations of pure science and fine art--those intellectual and aesthetic pursuits which are carried on without reference to technology or utility--may be credited to functioning of the human play impulses. . . . They rest on the play impulse, which is connected with growth but is dissociated from preservation, comfort, or utility, and which in science and art is translated into the realm of imagination, abstraction, relations, and sensuous form. --A.L. Kroeber[1]

LUDUS [not into temptation]

It is precisely the technology used to execute works of art that places restrictions on the artist. William Blake was sensitive to this fact. He railed against the artistic machine, and it is significant for my purposes here that he employed visual images as well as words in his rebellion. Morris Eaves in a piece on "Blake and the Artistic Machine: An Essay in Decorum and Technology" has stated the problem as follows:

In printing, as in dishwashing, the system of mechanical execution tends to limit the human tasks that can be performed. In the arts, the problem becomes the limits imposed by mechanical execution upon human conception. To a large extent, for instance, the writer is a slave to the press, and he adjusts accordingly. The easiest way to adjust, and the one discovered by modern humanity after long experience with the press, is for a writer to make himself over in the image of the printer by writing with a typewriter and by imitating the forms and conventions of the press. Take, for example, the novelist who wishes to make the page, rather than the chapter, the unit of narration in a novel. He probably cannot, because the typesetter, not the writer, is the master of the page. A novelist cannot consider the position of a word or sentence on the page; therefore in novels the position of words and sentences on the page is insignificant, and no reader ever thinks to consider it. The unlucky novelist with a regard for the mystical significance of number is liable to suffer if he hopes to work out his literary mathematics at any level less gross than the number and disposition of his chapters. But the graphic artist, who has usually controlled the elements in his composition, has had the option of using upper and lower as significant metaphors, and traditionally he has used them so. The rule for poets, who have traditionally made some attempt to control the appearance of their lines on the page, the poetic line being a unit ill suited to print, is that in a print culture the impression of sincerity and profundity increases in proportion to uniformity, which is a product of the mechanical principles by which the press operates.[2]

INTERLUDE

The notion that art and play are free activities has been expressed in different ways by different thinkers. The idea was developed in a notable way by Friedrich Schiller who in turn expanded some basic ideas of Immanuel Kant. Essentially, art and play are free activities in that they are engaged in freely; they are not, like work, engaged in for purposes of survival. Art and play both include a set (or various sets) of rules, but these rules are freely accepted; they are not binding like the laws that govern technology, which are based economy.[3] If one fails to observe the rules, one is not threatened with annihilation (unless one is a gladiator); one rather suffers the fate of a spoilsport.

Art is the most beautiful deception: and no matter how much a man may wish to make it the setting for his daily life, he must still desire that it remain an illusion lest it become utilitarian and as dreary as a workshop. --Claude Debussy[4]

Robert Frost evidently had something like this in mind when he said that to write poetry without rhyme would be "like playing tennis without a net."

LUDUS [pray]

The playfulness as well as the rebelliousness of the artist may be seen in an exemplary way in visual literature. I can predict with some degree of confidence as I write this that both characteristics will be observable in pieces in this Critical Assembling. There are those who would classify this phenomenon (these phenomena) as a neoromantic rebellion. Renato Poggioli, for example, has written:

The principal difference between the book hack and the book artist is that the former succumbs to the conventions of the medium, while the latter envisions what else "the book" might become. Whereas the hack writes prose that "reads easily" or designs pages that resemble each other and do not call attention to themselves, the book artist transcends those conventions. -- Richard Kostelanetz[6]

"Avant-garde art seems destined to oscillate perpetually among various forms of alienation-- psychological and social, economic and historical, aesthetic and stylistic. There is no doubt that all these forms are summed up in one other, namely in ethical alienation . . . It expressed itself . . in that art and literature of revolt which has occupied so large a part of modern thought and culture since romanticism. . . ."[5]

POSTLUDE

Walter Ong, who holds that the romantic movement is still in progress (and will be in progress for all of the foreseeable future) has pointed out that "Modern rhetoric has become more visualist than the older verbal rhetoric, not merely through the use of pictures for persuasion but also through the presentation of words as objects, with 'display type' in 'display advertising.'"[7] He has also expounded the quasi-paradox that the romantic rebellion against technology was not feasible before the technology was developed to support the rebellion. As the romantic rebel ventured into the exotic and the unknown, he was emboldened by an awareness that "All he had to do was to glance back over his shoulder at the Encyclopédie and other books on the library shelves" (p. 278). It would be ludic to imagine what visual literature might be like today without modern advances in printing. Could this Critical Assembling have appeared without cheap offset printing? Still, those who think that technology and art, work and play are the same thing[8] are so completely under the spell of the technological Zeitgeist that they cannot see the difference between expenditures required for survival and expenditures freely made for pleasure.

[R]omanticism and technology can be seen to grow out of the same ground, even though at first blush the two appear diametrically opposed, the one, technology, programmatically rational, the other, romanticism, concerned with transrational or arational if not irrational reality. Yet, . . . in terms of the growth of knowledge and the development of knowledge storage and retrieval systems, both romanticism and modern technology appear at the same time because each grows in its own way out of a noetic abundance such as man had never known before. Technology uses the abundance for practical purposes. Romanticism uses it for assurance and as a springboard to another world. --Walter Ong[9]

NOTES: [1]Anthropology (New York: Harcourt, 1948), p. 357. [2]PMLA, 92 (1977), 904. [3]See M. Korach, "The Science of Industry," in The Science of Science, ed. M. Goldsmith and A. Mackay (London: Scientific Book Club, 1964), pp. 185-86; cf. W. Sypher, Literature and Technology (New York: Random House, 1968), pp. 159-78 et passim. [4]Quoted by L. Vallas, Theories of Claude Debussy (New York: Dover, 1967), p. 12. [5]The Theory of the Avant-Garde (Cambridge: Harvard Univ. Press, 1968), p. 127. [6]From a flier announcing his show of "Book Art" at PS 1, Queens, NY, Jan.-Feb. 1978, and Central Library, Tulsa, OK, Apr. 1978. [7]Rhetoric, Romance, and Technology (Ithaca: Cornell Univ. Press, 1971), p. 9. [8]See, e.g., J. Ehrmann, "Homo Ludens Revisited," in Game, Play, Literature (Boston: Beacon, 1971), pp. 42-43. [9]Op. cit., p. 279.

Richard Grayson
SOME YOUNG WRITERS I ADMIRE

There is a caricature of Matthew Arnold by Spy which
hangs on the wall of a professor I know, and beneath it are
written the words: "I say, the critic must keep out of the
region of immediate practice." Well, I'm not a critic and
I'm foolish enough to attempt to assess a few of my contem-
poraries. If life were fair, these people would be more
widely known than they are. I read their fiction and poetry
with amazement, with admiration, and often with envy. Here
goes, in no particular order:
1) Crad Kilodney: one of the funniest people on the North
American continent. His stories, published in numerous
literary magazines and in his book Mental Cases (Lowlands
Review, 1978) are exquisitely structured, delightfully
funny, and frequently touching. He is Henry Miller with a
sense of the 1970s.
2) George Myers, Jr.: an accomplished critic of arts visual
and written, an editor (X, A Journal of the Arts) with an
eclectic eye, "biofiction" is his forte and his creation.
His Nairobi (White Ewe Press, 1978) scrambles up Africa
and his own life and puts it back together in astounding
fashion. A master of phraseology.
3) Dennis Cooper: this Los Angeles poet writes about teen
idols, surfers' sex, and John F. Kennedy, Jr. -- whom he
captures in a series of "adventures" that never take a wrong
turn. Check out his magazine Little Caesar and his chapbook
Tiger Beat. He's great at understatement.
4) Brad Gooch: the next John Ashbery (and the comparison,
I hope, does them both proud). His poems, especially in
his The Daily News (Z Press, 1977) are incredibly good.
He captures the cruelty and coolness of a lot of New York
life. On second thought, maybe he's the next David Bowie.

5) <u>Brian</u> <u>Robertson</u>: no one satirizes the small press scene (and just about everything else) better than this resident of a banana republic some miles north of Mexico. His syndicated newspaper column, <u>Take</u> <u>Five</u>, is better than Buchwald's for my money. And his magazine <u>Blind</u> <u>Alley</u> is one of the few in small pressdom that manages to be witty and literate at the same time.

6) <u>Tom</u> <u>Whalen</u>: an imaginative fiction writer whose stories skate the thin ice of surrealism and always leave you in awe. His poetry (<u>The</u> <u>Spare</u> <u>Key</u>, The Seven Deadly Sins Press,) is so clean that at first you'll think he wrote it with his eyes closed. But his eyes are always wide open, and his magazine, <u>Lowlands</u> <u>Review</u>, is always a terrific read.

7) <u>Miriam</u> <u>Sagan</u>: a poet who is not embarrassed to show warmth and concern, always tempered by a fine intelligence. Her love poetry manages to succeed on its own terms; she may be The Last Romantic. Her book, <u>Vision's</u> <u>Edge</u> (Samisdat, 1978), shows her to be an almost flawless lyricist; there's one fantastic poem about Czechoslovakia you must read.

8) <u>Barbara</u> <u>Baracks</u>: her ironic juxtapositions, both in her poetry, fiction, and art criticism, make her a writer I never get tired of reading. Her magazine <u>Big</u> <u>Deal</u> is just that. She's wonderful when she merely describes an ordinary day; often her prose is extraordinarily rewarding.

9) <u>Christopher</u> <u>McKenna</u>: at 21, this actor/playwright has already completed some astoundingly mature work. His radio plays, heard in Los Angeles, are hilarious without being cheap; his play <u>Atomic</u> <u>She-Pizzas</u> <u>of</u> <u>Uranus</u> is not merely the perfect genre parody but devastating social criticism.

10) I could go on for days: Kevin Urick, Richard Myers Peabody, Linda Lerner, Peter N. Cherches, Jerry Stahl, Scott Sommer....but you'll be hearing about all of them sooner or later, I'm sure.

Every good poem is innovative. Some people would
invert the order: every innovative poem is good. I
agree, so long as I define innovation. There is gross
innovation and there is minute innovation. In
Lyrical Ballads Wordsworth was grossly innovative; so
was Apollinaire in Calligrammes; and each poet was
minutely innovative as well, making not only obvious
breaks with convention but continually inventing on the
cellular level of language - sub-cellular, atomic, even
particular. They combined what seemed impossible of
combinations; they resolved the unresolvable. On the
other hand E. E. Cummings's gross innovations, mostly
typographical, were genuine so long as they were obvious,
but worked to disguise stale romantic language, weary
old metaphors and symbols - goatfooted balloon men,
for goodness sake - and cliches of Victorian and
Edwardian magazine verse. If we take a cliche -
"basic assumption" for example, or "Yankees clash

with archrival Red Sox," or "mud wonderful" - and
print it in red ink on blue paper in Germanic script
with perfume on it and project it from four projectors
on four walls at once, with four people speaking it
at four levels of pitch and volume - we still use a
cliché; though we may have a nice party going.

And on the other hand Robert Frost, with sonnets
and blank verse and quatrains, with conventional signs,
with familiar syntax, innovated minutely and genuinely
in his particular syntax and diction, in the relationship of sentence and line structure. Or, say: Thomas
Hardy's poetry is weird, innovative, unlike anyone's
before him, and largely inimitable; the same is true of
his contemporary Hopkins, with the difference that it
is obvious in Hopkins.

Which does not make the one better than the other.

                                        Donald Hall

TOO FREQUENT

r
ri
ric
rich
richa
richar
richard
richard
richard m
richard m.
richard m.
richard m. n
richard m. ni
richard m. nix
richard m. nixo
richard m. nixon
Richard m. nixon
RIchard m. nixon
RIChard m. nixon
RICHard m. nixon
RICHArd m. nixon
RICHARd m. nixon
RICHARD m. nixon
RICHARD M. nixon
RICHARD M. nixon
RICHARD M. Nixon
RICHARD M. NIxon
RICHARD M. NIXon
RICHARD M. NIXOn
RICHARD M. NIXON
RICHARD M. NIXOn
RICHARD M. NIXon
RICHARD M. NIxon
RICHARD M. Nixon
RICHARD M. nixon
RICHARD M. nixon
RICHARD m. nixon
RICHARD m. nixon
RICHARd m. nixon
RICHArd m. nixon
RICHard m. nixon
RIChard m. nixon
RIchard m. nixon
Richard m. nixon
richard m. nixon
richard m. nixo
richard m. nix
richard m. ni
richard m. n
richard m.
richard m.
richard m
richard

richard
richar
richa
rich
ric
ri
r

r
ri
ric
rich
richa
richar
richard
richard
richard m
richard m.
richard m.
richard m. n
richard m. ni
richard m. nix
richard m. nixo
richard m. nixon
Richard m. nixon
RIchard m. nixon
RIChard m. nixon
RICHard m. nixon
RICHArd m. nixon
RICHARd m. nixon
RICHARD m. nixon
RICHARD M. nixon
RICHARD M. nixon
RICHARD M. Nixon
RICHARD M. NIxon
RICHARD M. NIXon
RICHARD M. NIXOn
RICHARD M. NIXON
RICHARD M. NIXOn
RICHARD M. NIXon
RICHARD M. NIxon
RICHARD M. Nixon
RICHARD M. nixon
RICHARD m. nixon
RICHARD m. nixon
RICHARd m. nixon
RICHArd m. nixon
RICHard m. nixon
RIChard m. nixon
RIchard m. nixon
Richard m. nixon
richard m. nixon

richard m. nixo
richard m. nix
richard m. ni
richard m. n
richard m.
richard m.
richard m
richard
richard
richar
richa
rich
ric
ri
r

r
ri
ric
rich
richa
richar
richard
richard
richard m
richard m.
richard m.
richard m. n
richard m. ni
richard m. nix
richard m. nixo
richard m. nixon
Richard m. nixon
RIchard m. nixon
RIChard m. nixon
RICHard m. nixon
RICHArd m. nixon
RICHARd m. nixon
RICHARD m. nixon
RICHARD M. nixon
RICHARD M. nixon
RICHARD M. Nixon
RICHARD M. NIxon
RICHARD M. NIXon
RICHARD M. NIXOn
RICHARD M. NIXON
RICHARD M. NIXOn
RICHARD M. NIXon
RICHARD M. NIxon
RICHARD M. Nixon
RICHARD M. nixon
RICHARD M. nixon
RICHARD m. nixon

RICHARD m. nixon
RICHARd m. nixon
RICHArd m. nixon
RICHard m. nixon
RIChard m. nixon
RIchard m. nixon
Richard m. nixon
richard m. nixon
richard m. nixo
richard m. nix
richard m. ni
richard m. n
richard m.
richard m.
richard m
richard
richard
richar
richa
rich
ric
ri
r

r
ri
ric
rich
richa
richar
richard
richard
richard m
richard m.
richard m.
richard m. n
richard m. ni
richard m. nix
richard m. nixo
richard m. nixon
Richard m. nixon
RIchard m. nixon
RIChard m. nixon
RICHArd m. nixon
RICHARd m. nixon
RICHARD m. nixon
RICHARD m. nixon
RICHARD M. nixon
RICHARD M. nixon
RICHARD M. Nixon
RICHARD M. NIxon
RICHARD M. NIXon
RICHARD M. NIXOn
RICHARD M. NIXON

GGGGGGGGreed

Sueur / *SWEAT*
ou Sang / *OR BLOOD*
ou Larmes de dactylos
OR TYPIST'S TEARS
      HOMMAGE A TOUTES
      HOMAGE TO ALL OF THEM

"ETHER 4"
                      1966
                    BERNARD HEIDSIECK

(SATURDAY)   (FRIDAY)   (THURSDAY)   (WENESDAY)   (TUESDAY)   (MONDAY)

?   ENOUGH   STANDING UP   ¡   O.K. ?   NOTHING YET

Journal de Bord

AT LAST!   NOTHING   STANDING UP   SITTING DOWN   VERY HOT!   OUF!

(MONDAY)   (TUESDAY)   (WENESDAY)   (THIRSDAY)   (FRIDAY)   (SATURDAY)

BERNARD HEIDSIECK "ETHER 4"

1966

INFORMATION SCIENCE AND THE ART OF COMMUNICATION

> Noise is the factor of disorder contingent on the intent of
> the message, which is characterized by some kind of order.
> It introduces a dialectic, figure-ground, connected with
> the dialectic, order-disorder, which constitutes the second
> law of thermodynamics. The general theorem about entropy,
> "disorder can only increase in isolated system," amounts
> to saying that noise can only degrade the orderliness of the
> message; it cannot increase the particularized information;
> it <u>destroys intent.</u>
>
> "Information Theory and Esthetic Perception,"
> by Abraham Moles (Paris, 1958)

Duchamp with his "Green Box," notes for the Large Glass, precursed the
concerns of the avant-garde in the Sixties and Seventies. These notations,
documentations and bits of information emphasize the great lesson of the Bride
Stripped Bare: that art was information and the entropy of distribution. It
was no longer possible to convey a coherent and truthful picture of life through
metaphors that did not allow for the reduced ability of the receiver to com-
prehend the original intent of the artist.

Just as the Abstract Expressionists explored the medium for its own sake,
the avant-garde of the Seventies explored communication and the exchange of
esthetic information, for its own sake. They focused their attention upon the
distribution and the distortion of the artwork. This distortion is entropy.

The paranoia of Thomas Pynchon is a reaction to the pervasiveness of this
distortion.

The Minimalists response was to reduce the extent of the repertoire of
elements that could be conveyed. This increased sensitivity to a particular
channel amplifies the nature of the signal. The information gained in one
direction, however, is lost in the other. What is gained in sensitivity is
lost in the variety of elements.

The Fluxus movement, spearheaded by George Maciunas, also engaged in this
dialectic of order-disorder. Continuing the Dada traditions of performance,
typography, intermedia, outrage and humor, the movement concentrated on setting
up structures of alternate information transfer - the European tours, Something
Else Press, the multiples. Not to mention SoHo, and the growth of the alternate
gallery space.

The observer is minipulated in much of this art to react to the piece in
a predetermined pattern. This behavorist stance is the result of the extra-
polation of mathematical formulas, deriving from them, messages pertaining to
natural communication. From these explorations, a number of alternate art
channels were realized.

Correspondence Art has flourished under these conditions. One of the
more thoughtful links in the communication network is Mohammed, a "restricted
communication center," located in Genova, Italy. By submitting a communication
on letterhead stationary supplied by Mohammed, accompanied by a list of twelve
names and addresses, the Center (in actuality Italian artist Plinio Mesciulam)
will duplicate and distribute to those twelve the communication it receives
from the sender. This alternate distribution system has perfectly circumvented

the nemesis of the Dada, Fluxus, and Post-Dada artist - the gallery system and the museum establishment.

Artists books have also displayed the contemporary artists' concern for the distribution of information. This also has to do with the concept of inter-media - the creating of open structures that resist the entropy of closed systems.

Copy Art (xerox, electroworks) is another leading example of the growing Seventies preoccupation with information theory and esthetic perception. While flaunting the degradation of the singularity of the art object, it also ex-aggerates the entropy of the original.

Rubber Stamp Art embraces a host of concerns: correspondence art, information theory, Dada activity, the artist book, the emphemeral and marginal, Minimalism and Concrete Poetry. Nowhere else is the transfer of information as metaphor so readily apparent.

Video artists are concerned with the process of transfering information through Space and Time. Because of their ability to minimpulate Time as well as Space, they have become an important component in the art vocabulary of the Seventies.

This tendency to examine the lessons of information theory, and to apply these new concepts to both the visual and written arts, tends to breach the Two Cul-tures. The Arts have always learned from Science. Just as artists were curious about the revelations of Einstein's Relativity theory, artists today are ex-ploring esthetic questions raised by scientific research in areas of mechanical communication. The great lesson so far has been the distortion of the art object when subjected to distribution channels. In a world networked by mass communications, this concern has social as well as artistic implications.

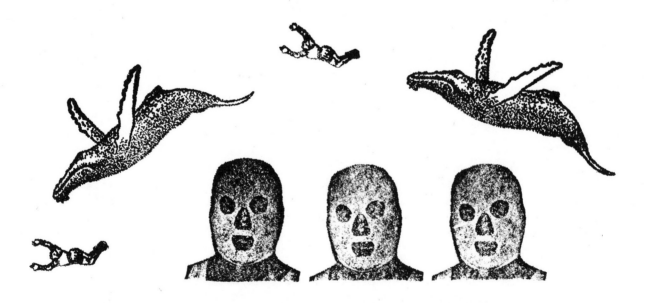

By JOHN HELD JR. who sometimes wonders what its all about

MMMMANIFESTOOOOOO:
№ 1
RAD. TEND. IN CONT. LIT. ARE:

( ) BULLSHIT

( ) IGNORED

( ) UNITENLLGIENT

( ) EMOTIONAL

( ) IMPORTANT

( ) SEXUAL

( ) DENSE

( ) JUNK

( )

thank you for allowing this valuable
opportunity to put in print something I've
wanted to say for a long time, but have
been afraid to put it in print because once
it is in print just about everyone can look
at it and say how dumb it is now that it is
in print in black & white for all those people
to analyze it and fret over it and read it again
and again & look for hidden meanings that aren't
there but in print they suddenly appear without
you knowing or wanting to, but, what the hell,
there it is in print so it must be important or,
of course, it wouldn't be in print, but once it is
in print, because print costs money, then it has
to be important, not just put in print because in
print, there it is in print, and it appears in print
with someone saying this should be in print or not
in print or maybe someone else should print it or
maybe if you changed a word it would print better,
or if it got in print, you should change it because
i would like it better, an besides, I like the way it
looks in print on the page followed by more print, which
was printed to tell you what to print when printed by
a machine when really to print is only to print not to
give blood, blood print is difficult, to print blood is
difficult because it has to be good to print so people
will read the print, not skip over it, or print over it, just print

Scott Helmes

UNBLOCKING

For the author who for no discernible reason finds himself
"blocked," I would like to offer the following exercise as a
means of "unblocking," loosening the dendrites, stirring up the
creative juices.

First of all, you must save your urine from the night before,
preferably in a dark green or brown bottle, since urine like
fine wine, diminishes in strength when exposed to sunlight. In
the morning, when brushing your teeth and hair, take a mouthful
of urine and gargle with it until you feel a tingling sensation
at the back of your throat. Next, take a handful of urine and
splash it in your face as you would aftershave lotion. You are
now prepared to face the day. Proceed to your nearest coffee
shop and before ordering breakfast spit in the counterman's face.
No doubt he will be somewhat taken aback by your unexpected greeting,
but if you leave a generous tip you will be forgiven. You may even,
if you so desire, fart in his face--gently, of course. This done,
depart at once.

It is vital, in the course of this exercise, to smile at all
times, lest you offend someone.

Now that you are out on the street with a bracing breakfast
in your belly, go to your local newsstand, buy the <u>Daily News</u>, and
tell the blind vendor that you have only a hundred dollar bill
with you. When he refuses to make change, slip off your trousers
and leave them with him as collateral. Inform him that you are
just on the way to the bank.

Presently you're on the street with a healthy breakfast and a

newspaper, but no trousers. Hail a cab and direct it to
your branch of Manufacturer's Hanover. Tell the driver to
wait while you cash your hundred dollar bill. In the bank,
while waiting on line, you may unbutton your overcoat and
masturbate a little. You will find that the line moves
right along.

Get your change. Return to the cab and direct the driver
to take you to the 42nd Street Public Library. While he is
stalled in traffic, open your door and sneak out. Make your
way to the library on foot and take the elevator to the main
reading room. There you will discover an information desk,
behind which sit several ladies and gentlemen ready to answer
your questions. Ask them one by one whether they have read
any good books lately. Wink at anyone who appears on the verge
of calling the guard. The guard will be notified anyway, but
by this time you are out of the building and on your way home.
Stop at the newstand to retrieve your pants.

It's time to get down to work!

C. DAVID HEYMANN

Autogogy

From the Gr. "auto-" (meaning "self-") and "-agogos" (meaning "tube" or "conduit"), "autogogy" defines the character people who use their actions or achievements as a method of calling attention to, or of creating a striking persona for themselves. A parallel term would be the commonly used one, "demagog"—one who, by means of oratory or appeals to brute instinct, leads the people (the "demos") in directions which may be counter to their best interests. And the opposite would be "heterogogy" (q.v.).

In the arts, focusing on the self can serve a useful analytic function, especially when the artist's own deeds or being can serve as models for the viewer or reader's understanding of his or her own experience, or actual or potential situations. But when the purpose of the presentation of the material comes to be the creation of a persona for the artist which becomes, to any extent whatever, a substitute for the actual persona or which detracts from the needs of the actual work, then a condition of autogogy may be said to exist. This is a frequent fault in post-Freudian writing and art, and in any work which tends towards expressionism: thus it is most commonly found (though by no means uniquely so) in periods which have had that tendency. What tends to happen is that the artist becomes deeply influenced by his or her own manner, and is no longer free to achieve what the work at hand needs: typically, he or she is no longer sensitive to those needs. When Renoir would paint, for instance, a painting in the manner of Renoir, he would cease to be using his own style as a personal language which had become natural to him, would reduce his ideas to mere tropes, and his own style would become a confining device. In this sense, in more recent time, most of the abstract expressionists of the 1950's and pop artists and concrete poets of the 1960's have become autogogs by the 1970's. Even criticism can exhibit autogogic tendencies, when it treats the work according to what it reveals of the artist (presumed) and not according to what it is. When there is a natural interplay between these, one is probably reading the healthier kind of Freudian or biographical criticism: when the writings of an author are treated as a revelation of that author and little more, then one has reached autogogic criticism.

Finally it should be noted that certain artists and writers are almost passionately autogogic, with very little concern for anything outside the creation of their persona and with a corresponding fallaciousness about their work, or at least a very strained quality. This has been the sad fate of many of the poets associated with Charles Olson and the Black Mountain School, for instance, as, in previous times, it was with German Expressionist poetry in its last phase, in the 1920's.

Heterogogy

From the Gr. "hetero-" (meaning "other") and "-agogos" (meaning "conduit" or "tube"), "heterogogy" is a term proposed by Dick Higgins to cover art works or texts which are oriented towards other people rather than towards oneself (but without leading them), either as regards their subject or expression. As such the term is the opposite of "autogogy" (q.v.), and is particularly a useful concept in the analysis of social or political art or poetry. The methodology of heterogogic poetry or art is, however, far more complex and problematic than the rather simple concept at first would indicate. For instance, if the need of the work is for a complex or extremely innovative form or style, and yet one's long-term purpose for the work is heterogogic, a conflict clearly exists—and how does the artist determine whether to do the work as is and provide a useful entry-way in the form of a statement to accompany it, or whether to assume that in time the people will find their way into the work and so no such statement is necessary, or whether the work should be to some extent simplified or modified into normative modes in order to reach its audience? This question is extremely complex, and is the source of many disputes among artists, especially in the context of strongly politicized or socially-oriented situations.

DICK HIGGINS
P.O. BOX 842
CANAL STREET STATION
NEW YORK, NY 10013

"It was more like

those myths

of amazing strangers

who arrive at an island

- gods or demons -

bringing good or evil

to the innocence

of the inhabitants...

gifts of unknown things

words never heard before."

Joseph Conrad, Victory

"The vast majority of people

are quite incapable of putting themselves

individually into the mind of another.

This is indeed a singularly rare art,

and it does not take us very far.

Even the man we think we know best

and who assures us that we understand him

through and through

is at bottom a stranger to us.

He is different!

The most we can do

is to have at least some inkling of his otherness,

to respect it

and to guard against the outrageous stupidity of wishing to interpret it."

Carl Jung, Two Essays on Analytical Psychology

PAROLES x x x JAMAKE HIGHWATER
PAROLES x x x x x x x x x x x
PAROLES x x x x x x x x x x x
PAROLES xxxxxxxxxxxxxxxxxxxxxx

"It may be that some little root

of the sacred tree still lives.

Nourish it then, that it may leaf

and bloom and fill with singing

birds." Black Elk

"This is a Ghost Dance for Wounded Knee—

This place where my people lie

The root of a thousand agonies

digs deep into the earth

and cannot endure the silence

of old women whose eyes are

dry.

It is always dusk

for those who wear the

morning star."

Jamake Highwater

"What sets worlds in motion is the interplay of differences, their attraction and
repulsions. Life is
plurality, death is uniformity. By sup-
pressing differences and
peculiarities, by eliminating different
civilizations and cultures, progress
weakens life and favors death. The ideal
of a single civilization for everyone, implicit in the cult of progress and
technique, impoverishes and mutilates us. Every view of the world that

becomes extinct, every culture that disappears, diminishes a possibility

of life." Octavio Paz x x x x x x x x x x x x PAROLES x x x x PAROLES

x x x x x x x x x x x

x x x x x x x x x x x

x x x x x x x x x x x x PAROLES PAROLES PAROLES PAROLES

xxxxxxxxxxxxxxxxxxxxxxxxxxxxxxxxxxxxx

xxxxxxxxxxxxxxxx

"He who fights the future
has a dangerous enemy.
The future is not,
it borrows its strength
from the man himself,
and when it has tricked
him out of this,
then it appears outside
of him as the enemy
he must meet."
Soren Kierkegaard

PAROLES

PAROLES

PAROLES

PAROLES

"The other does not exist,
this is rational faith, the incurable belief
of human reason. Identity = Reality, as if,
in the end, everything must necessarily and
absolutely be one and the same. But the other
refuses to disappear; it subsists, it persists;
it is the hard bone on which reason breaks its
teeth. Abel Martin, with a poetic faith as
human as rational faith, believed in the other,
in the essential Heterogeneity of being, in
what he called the incurable otherness from
which oneness must always suffer." Antonio
Machado
x x x x
xxxxxxxxxxxxxxxxxxxxxxxxxxxxxxxxxxxxxxxxxxxxxxxxxxxxx
"And Montezuma could do nothing but wait.
He sat very still on his throne and he lay sleepless
upon his mat, and he waited for whatever would come
down upon him. In the night the birds were silent and
only the sound of distant weeping came through the window.
The Moon rose into the sky and danced with the shadows
in the black lake of Mexico." Jamake Highwater

PAROLES x x x PAROLES x x x PAROLES x x x PAROLES x x x PAROLES x x x x x

The editors of ASSEM-BLING have requested submissions of story-tellings (some in the publication might prefer "im-age-tellings"), that resist transposition of their original form to accommodate the market.

Alternative literature (some would shout "radical/experimental literature"), begins as a single arrangement of events within a specific situation that gains power as the listener more closely approaches the original telling.

In contrast, writers of mainstream literature (some who are not hiss, "story-merchants") construct a tale so that its primary themes and spirit will accept any number of profitable changes in the time or method of telling; a tale that will increase in popularity as the distance between the first telling and a present hearing widens.

I do not believe it is correct (some of my co-contributors have insisted "or fair"), to characterize the bulk of ASSEMBLING's events as "otherwise un-publishable". Better that they be described as "not re-publishable" since their meaning is usually dependent upon or make reference to ASSEMBLING's unique conditions of publication.

Of course, there is a third type of literature; the one most often encountered. It is advertising; a telling (everyone in the business calls it "communication"), based on the belief that someone, besides the speaker, can use or will benefit from the hearing. *This is an advertisement.*

Davi Det Hompson
POB 7035
Richmond, Virginia
USA
23221

Da-da (dä′dä) *n.* A western European artistic and literary movement (1916-23) having as its program the discovery of authentic reality through the abolition of traditional cultural and aesthetic forms by a technique of comic derision in which irrationality, chance, and intuition were the guiding principles. [French *dada,* pet theme, hobbyhorse, from baby talk (a name arbitrarily adopted by leading members of the movement).] **—Da′da•ist** *n.* **—Da′da•ist′ic** *adj.*

Det (dĕt) *n.* An eastern United States artistic and literary position (1966-   ) having as its program the recognition of authentic reality through the abolition of European avant-garde cultural and aesthetic forms by a technique of sequential order in which courtesy, assurance and the acceptance of prevailing conditions are the guiding principles. [From the altered name of its founder, Davi Det Hompson (David E. Thompson) Born 1939.] **—Det′•ist** *n.* **—Det′ist′ic** *adj.*

CRITICAL EQUATIONS

Contributions to this assembled volume may have to do with "literary possibility." I'd like to address rather literary probability as I have seen it expressed by small press publishers and little magazine editors. Some years ago it was made clear to me, both in my own critical work and in responses to other critical work, that small press editors and publishers expected different "rules" to apply to the work that they publish. They expected to be exempt from true criticism. Volumes of work or issues of magazines that were less than spectacular were to be ignored by the small press reviewing establishment, if we can call it that; only those volumes that clearly could be praised were to be reviewed at all. I fought against these notions in various articles, culminating in a lead piece for MARGINS called "The Reviewer as Pimp." That same article, unrevised, has been reprinted in the Winter, 1979 issue of THE SMUDGE out of Detroit. The really sad fact about its publication--unrevised--is that very little has changed in the minds of small press editors and publishers.

Many editors still expect preferential treatment, particularly within the pages of small press review media. The argument goes that since the established review media either will ignore small presses or pan their work, it is up to "us" to say positive things about "each other's" work. Then libraries will order the work, and bookstores may consider it, and distribution networks will consider picking up the book(s) and/or the press itself. Everyone is happy, except maybe the reviewer.

Small presses have finally taken over the publication of every imaginable subject matter. The Crossing Press has a large list of childrens' books, cookbooks, and books of general interest. Many of the COSMEP members who recently responded to my query for magazines to be read for possible review in the WILSON LIBRARY BULLETIN sent strange, specialized magazines, magazines about nuclear energy, about developing countries, about positive education, about the field of health. Five years ago I would have received a bunch of similar little magazines, each composed of mostly poetry, an occasional short story or review, and possibly some commentary by the editor(s).

If small presses are going to take on all of the responsibilities of establishment, commercial presses, then they had better learn to deal with the review mechanism. Presses have conquered Library of Congress CIP, have dealt with ISBN's, have learned to prepare catalogs, invoices, and IRS documents, have taught themselves grantsmanship (in a few cases)-- now why can't they deal with reviewers as discriminating readers who don't feel the need to offer strokes just because the material under scrutiny is "small press," whatever that might mean anymore?

John Jacob

GUERRILLA PUBLISHING

Small press history is short, but even so, the editors and publishers
still around seem to have bad memories. Few seem capable of remembering
the most exciting and active publishing ventures the small presses have EVER
seen, the mimeo and cheap offset publications of the 1960's.

There was activity in Niagara Falls, New York; Cleveland, Ohio;
Sacramento, California; Folsom, California; Bellingham, Washington;
and Chicago, Illinois. Presses like Black Rabbit, Ground Zero, Desperado,
Runcible Spoon, Grande Ronde, Vagabond, Two Bags, and others were
bringing out the most exciting poetry and commentary anywhere. These
documents were produced cheaply, in small print runs, and they didn't sell.
They were given away or sold for high prices to collectors or special
collections (in order to pay the cheap printing and paper bills). The White
Panther Party in Chicago and Ann Arbor used the techniques to distribute
its political rhetoric. But for a few short years, those in the know always
had the number of that truck: where to find the best poetry being published
period .

And now, strangely enough, there may be a resurgence of such grassroots
publishing. Michael Tarachow of Pentagram Press has begun a mimeo magazine
called HAWK-WIND which is promising; Tom Montag of MARGINS fame has
risen from the dead with his own magazine/press series of mimeo books and
more periodic pieces. I've moved back into ditto, mimeo, and even xeroxing
as viable publication productions. Steve Lewandowski in upper New York
is involved with a regional grassroots publishing enterprise. CLOWN WAR
is being given away free in New York City. Several publishers still distribute
broadsides free, or have begun such broadside programs.

The point to all of this resurgence is that it directly contradicts the
commercial flavor being sucked into small press publications. The original
quality and vision have been lost, these editors are saying, because we spend
too much time filling out grant forms and invoices. Personally, I think that
one should be capable of both, of maintaining quality and also learning to be
more sophisticated in promotion or grantsmanship or even that hated area of
distribution. But we've all seen editors make their choices, and many of those
choices have been sad.

The poems are being written everywhere, and they are not being written
for everyone. Still, they have to get out of the drawers of America. The hit-
and-run tactics of many of the finest literary/terrorist minds of the country
will prove that guerrilla publishing did not die in 1970.

Watch out, when you travel into Nutbush.

John Jacob

Dear seer:

   Anyone can see that

   let a poem be a shade, like rain from clouds

                    is unimpressive,

but that

                         let

                         a

                         poem

                         be

                         a

                         shade,

                         like

                         rain

                         from

                         clouds

                    is more impressive,

   at least visually.

       And if

you cannot see at a glance that

```
    l   a   p   b   a   s   ,   l   r   f   c
    e       o   e   h       '   i   a   r   l
    t       e   a   k           i   o   o
            m   d   e   n           m   u
                e       '               d
                                        s
```

                              is still better

visually

                              and no worse

semantically

                              even as it is equal

linguistically,

then

I shall leave you to your own un-instructible mor-
ass.

                              Yours concretely,

                              T J Kallsen

                              T J Kallsen
                              600 Bostwick
                              Nacogdoches
                              TX 75961

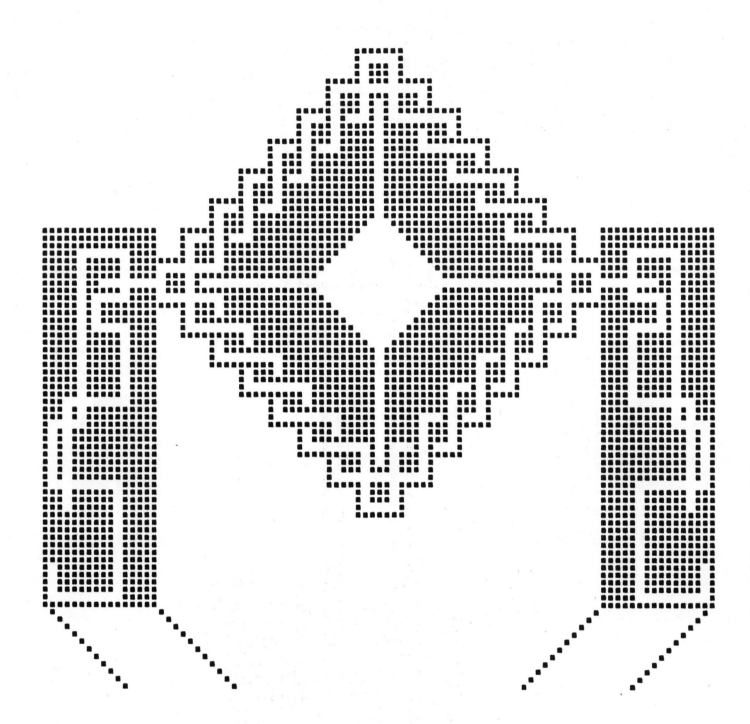

karl kempton

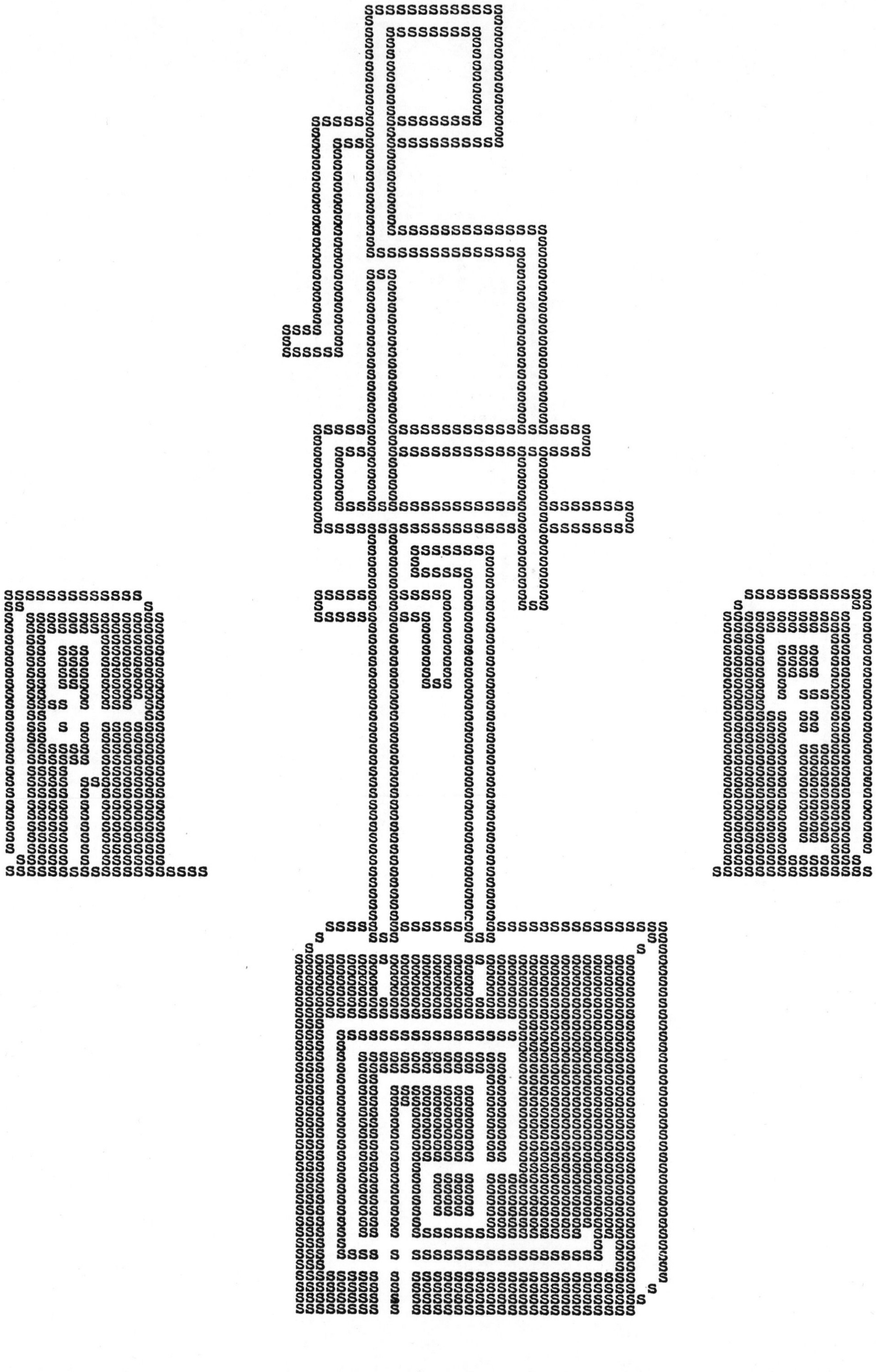

THE BLEAK WORD FROM HUGH KENNER

A time for plain words.

There is the Reading Public, a multifarious population of whooping cranes, watched, surveyed, tabulated, sheltered from shock.

There is Reading Public Writing, on which it is fed: expensively balanced to its requirements, which are the requirements of a herd nourished on such feed.

And there is Avant Garde Writing, defined as all that which will not interest or will actively repel the Reading Public. Its confector may be hoping to repel them, or may trust (like Joyce) that their progeny will follow him one day, or may be rapt in a vision of his own, or may be asleep, or stoned, or simply self-indulgent, or even unlettered.

There is not one Avant Garde Public, there are many. They range in size from one (the writer) to perhaps 1,100. They are drawn by many desires, including the desire (sometimes gratified) for imaginative life. Many simply seek novelty, or gape vacuously.

Avant Garde Writing is as transient, most of it, as Reading Public Writing: transient because dull, because foolish, because numb, because unnecessary.

I said "most of it": 99.999%. The writing that periodically makes a difference —that permanently alters our sense of how the written word can grip— is discoverable among thr remaining .001%.

No one denies by now that Joyce made a difference. I do not see how it can be denied (though it doubtless is) that George Oppen has made a difference, or Guy Davenport.

One of the examples I cite is in his seventies, one in his fifties. They are not the only living writers I care about, and I reject the proposition that my being 56 has anything important to do with my citing them.

I cite them in part to illustrate Chaucer's maxim, "The lyf so short, the craft so longe to lerne."

Mastery took Chaucer time, when the definition of "the craft" answered to a consensus. The hits of Villon, a hit-or-miss genius who vanished st 32, were possible because he did not have to spend time defining the bases of his art.

Mastery takes, mehercule, time, when one must absorb and cast off Reading Public Writing;
:must rethink one's art to its roots;
:must identify a lost strand and the extent of one's personal varient;
:must practise to achieve mastery: all the time keeping an eye on whatever else goes on.

Study with the mind of a grandson and watch the time like a hawk

The time can be unwatched, or overwatched.

Our time has substituted electronic simultaneity for Gutenberg successiveness. This is easy to say.

Yet words enter the air, or fall on a page, one after another.

Gertrude Stein does not totally resolve this tension, nor does Ian Hamilton Finlay.

It does Avant Garde Writing no service to pretend that it is, *ipse facto*, superior to Reading Public Writing. Most of both are sheer junk. The Avant Garde hack is as enslaved to his ego as is his confrere to *Writer's Digest* shibboleths.

There are other Avant Garde writers besides Avant Garde hacks. They are rare.

How many poets was it, "all of the first rank," that Gulliver perceived in England? Hundreds. (Gulliver, enamored of quantity, harbinger of The Reading Public.) There have never been more that six writers who mattered alive at once.

Clear your mind of cant. (Sam Johnson, an excellent master.)

The Kern Interview   April 17, 1979

with Astral Bleame and Mr. Kern at the temple of William IXX.

AB. How, when, where and why did you begin doing sound poetry.
K... how, when where wnd why did man begin ? begin sound
      begin sound knowledge wisdom, begin sound poetry.
      shall we begin. i believe the world began in sound,
      ordered rhythmic sound. the world began out of chaos,
      out of the darkness. the world came out of the darkness
      as light. a bright light in the night.
      The ṚGVEDA confirms this, the Egyptian book of the Dead
      confirms this, and the Christain Bible confirms this.
      confirm and affirm. perhaps it is true that many of
      the great books of god for other religions confirm this.
      i don't know i can only speak for those i know.
      from sound we have vibrating matter,
      from this vibrating matter we have light
      and from light we have fire, water and air.
      light in the the night a bright light in the night.
AB. sho   shoooo shu shu shu sho ahu
K... yes shu the Egyptian god of light
AB. and earth
K... and earth, birth of the earth began in sound.
AB. i wish to know more about this sound philosophy.
      it's not new, true?
K... true, not new. nothing is new except that which
      is known knew. true. ? it's all been done before.
AB. i am confused
K... the lord said many will come in my name. Whats in a name?
      everything is in a name. can you remember oow ow
      ooo   ooo   ooo   ooo   ooo   ooo ooloo
      na na atu   i look around and i see
AB. tomatoes   oo o   o
K... man began to express his deepest feelings, thoughts and
      perceptions through painting with sound.
      from repetition of certain combinations of sounds
      we developed language. certain sounds when repeated
      had certain effects you know.
AB. go on
K... on ona ona ona ona ona ona ete   ona ete in ooloo means
      an erring man will love. from this sound language man
      communicated with each other and became more civilized.
      he developed visual symbols to go with the sounds.
      man had less need or greed, i think need
      but was it seed or was it feed.
AB. visual you mean painting?
K... i mean everything visual means, and certainly painting.
      everyone doesn't see a painting the way one hears one
      or does one.

                          more beer

AB. which or what came first?
K... mother and fate, then father and mother,
    then creation, then children.
    in order to see light we must have sound.
    light is vibrating matter which man hears through his eyes.
AB. you mean his ears
K... no i mean what i say unless i don't say it
    it is it ? is it it ? it is it.
    shapakapa   shapakapa shapakapa
    i thought through thoth thought
AB. silence
K... "from vibration in the air we have light on the stair
    out of the darkness first time saw you standing there"
AB. whats that, where is that from?
K... my NUCLEAR PRAYER. it's a good one, no
AB. no meaning yes
K... all began in sound, began in sound, began in god
    began in sound god, began in sabda brahma to the hindus,
    began in Amen to the egyptians, and to the christians,
    god said let there be light. you see your god and
    my god are one in the same god. wonder
    if you believe in god or not its all the same.
AB. i agree but how did you begin
K... i began as a soul many suns ago
    as a physical entity i began like everyone else
    in my mothers womb, the unkown the heart of the soul
    enshrined in the heart of god. back to the physical
    as a child i was always a loner. I have a nerve deafness
    in my right ear. I was always a little odd because of it.
    i don't always hear everything that is said to me.
    often i have to read lips and body gestures to get
    what i don't hear being said to me. often i am misunderstood
    as being arrogant or a snob which i am not. because i don't
    always respond to what is being said to me on my right side.
AB. how did this happen? was it an accident?
K... there are no accidents in life.
    it is my karma. i was born like this. a birth defect.
AB. can it be corrected?
K... no. nor do i want it. i am happy the way i am. remember
    i never had any hearing on one side. so i don't know what
    i am missing. oddly enough i can determine the difference
    between stero and monoral sound by direction from which it comes.
AB. interesting
K...in not hearing everything directed to me, i developed
    natural paranoia. i always think people are talking about me
    because i can't hear them.
AB. you are right everyone is talking about you.
K... thanks a lot. anyway to live with these feelings as
    a result of my ear, i lived in my imagination.
    my friends always called me a dreamer. so i live in
    my fertile imagination i love it like that. to dream
    to live to dream. to paint, to draw, to write to share
    my life with a lady and children and a home is my dream.

Art and life in our time have one thing in common: things happen to happen. The actor acts, the life is lived, and before one knows it Willem de Kooning paints a picture, Miles Davis plays a solo, and you and I have lived a great part of our lives--yet nobody ever planned it that way.

But if the act of improvisation is recognized and played for what it is, living one's life can be a life of fiction. Susan Quist's very personal novel Indecent Exposure (Walker, 1974) is built on this structure. "I never wanted to get married," her protagonist begins. "I wanted to be famous. Actually, I wanted to be a famous writer." But school and marriage and a child intervene. Following that are more adventures, which lead to the novel at hand--a long but very interesting trip home. Is there cause and effect, rhyme and reason to her life? "Mine was a very nice family," she reasons. "When it came time for me to go to college, my family tried to pick a good school in safe areas where there was little rape. New York was definitely out. So was California. Ideally I would have gone to a women's college in the middle of the Middle West. But I was stubborn. I insisted on going east. I ended up in Pittsburgh. That was as far east as they would let me go."

College leads to dropping out, and that leads to marriage. The 60's pass by, until the protagonist drops out of marriage, into the counter-culture, and ends up in a poorly heated walk-up apartment in the East Village. "My boyfriend, who lives across the hall, has a pretty sixteen-year-old chick in his pad tonight and I can hear them balling. And he won't answer the door. Do you suppose it's all because they let me go to that lousy fucking school? I don't know."

This is one of the many things I saw on my summer vacation.
    --Bainbridge, Ohio, 7/21/76

I have figured out what's happening in the seventies. The flu. That's it. According to my granny, who heard it from John Chancellor, this flu leaves one feeling morose. So at least I have a good excuse. And here I thought it was poverty.
    --Cincinnati, Ohio, 3/1/76

Series of proposed paintings:

nude with swiss cheese
nude with fat lip
nude playing solitaire
nude with mother
nude with father
nude with high school equivalency diploma
nude playing piano
nude playing horses
nude with four carat diamond solitaire
nude taking the air
nude with green thumb
high nude
hitchhiking nude
nude signing check
nude with bubble gum
nude hunting easter eggs
nude rolling on deodorant
the vanishing nude
nudes in the news
nude on nude
nude with buttons
nude with shadow
QUIET: NUDE WORKING
DANGER: FALLING NUDES
nude with falling arhces
nude with herpes simplex
nude with plum on thumb
nude with varsity letter
nude up a creek
nude with silver spoon in mouth
CAUTION: NUDE CROSSING, etc.
    --Naples, Florida, 4/14/75

It is this freshness, lack of
inhibition, and refusal of dead
seriousness that makes Indecent
Exposure such a joyful book. That
and the author's ability to avoid
dull repetition of the past. Instead
she keeps us in a continual present,
with a constant sense of self,
carefully examining the past according
to how she is now (and hence always
rewriting the past, for that's the
role of memory, editor in the fiction
of life).

In her novel, the protagonist
makes films with the same vital sense
one finds in the story itself. "It
was physical, like dancing. I had
to move around to get my shot. I
liked the way I could be standing a
block away from someone, but with the
camera, I could look into his eyes
like they were right in front of me.
I could fill the lens, the screen,
a whole wall with just a caterpillar."
Not the full chronology of life, but
rather its essence made real--this is
what Susan Quist gives us in Indecent
Exposure. Her writing has the same
zoom and bounce as her camera work;
neither will sit still, for life is
action, and art is play. Indecent
Exposure reads like a series of zany
postcards from a young woman on a
trip. The postcards keep coming.
Life goes on.

Susan Quist has counted all the
hazards of living, and found the
true perspective. "Which dangers
are real?" she asks. "All of them.
Or none. Probability has nothing
to do with it. You can guard all,
one, some, none. In the end it's all
the same."

I truly thought I was going to
crack up. As in the meantime NAL
had looked at the first part of
WOO WOO & said: . . . I think that
it would benefit from some changes and
rewriting (and a different title).
Instead of beginning with Charlotte
already in Cherry Bottom, why don't
you start with her living in N. Y.,
going to bars, etc. A girl like
Charlotte in the big city would make for
very interesting reading, indeed. Also
(this is the good part, Jerry), I think
it would help if you cut down on some
of the more fragmentary and experimental writing--you know, the unconventional sentence constructions,
the comments on writing, etc. This
kind of modernism is lost on our mass
market audience.
   That's what she said.
   Later she said that Charlotte's
life in WOO WOO wasn't exactly mainstream America. And agreed with me,
that what she really thought would be
interesting was a book about the life
she was leading--going to bars, etc.
   --undated, Cherry Valley, NY

One cheerful note--the birds. They
tootle in the middle of the night
like recorded background for "The
Seagull." Not just your usual twirp
twirp bird, but real warbling like I
never heard. Sort of like Puccini's
"Turandot." Self conscious birds.
And they always do it in the middle
of a pregnant pause.
   --Naples, Florida, 4/8/75

A kid in class the other day said I
looked like I worked for the carnival.
   The best part about being a
poet in the schools is getting love
notes from ten year olds.
   --Columbia, SC, 10/26/75

And, as a parting shot, offer the
village idiot (part of his head was
blown away in WW I) who stands on the corner beneath my window, in his blue
windbreaker, every day, & right now, patting himself on the back, a daily
ritual, bellowing, "A windy day. A windy day. Howdy neighbor. Have a good day."
   --Cincinnati, Ohio, 3/19/76

POETIKA: Tom

With words.
The bard writes down what he sees, he looks at
it, he is pleased. He is not pleased. He changes
something. Something changes. The printing press
appears, the poems are read, reread, recited.
Books bind the bard's breath. The line is born,
and will never die. The line is: never say die.

p

Narrative poetry endures until it grows old. The
poetry of the last hundred years is essentially
the fetching of this and that for the old man.
Eventually, he dies or he is laughed at. He is
buried in the book, his soul the indissoluble
lines. Words follow one another like sheep.

the word sheds

The poet's response to industry and technology:
the simultaneous. Ideals lose their l's. Poets
begin to experiment, peering into the future. Few
want it. Blake's illustration: man leans ladder
against the moon. Caption: I want! I want! (1793)

communi^a_ction

The poem which most reflects our time is one whose
words are in action. On the page they suggest action.

t real

The poem which most reflects our time is one whose
words are inaction. On the page they suggest inaction.
The value of the poem is directly proportional to the
degree to which it represents action or inaction.

Konyves

Having written and published poems for magazines,
books, broadsides... having been there at the att-
ending ritual of their recitals, performances... I
have been increasingly setting my sights on visual
media for exhibiting my poems. Video has been more
accessible and pliable, too. Advantage: unfolding
the poem at my convenience. Disadvantage: less freedom and rumination by the audience.

oetry changes.

Many, including myself, believe that once the suggest-
iveness of words becomes realized in images, there is
a tendency to demystify the poem. The selection of i-
magery is the instrument bequeathed to the modern poet.
In view of the abundance of new books of poetry, it is
becoming evident that not many wish their poems to leap
off the page into another element. The page has not
been exhausted, they cry. Fish out of water. Out of their
element. But the metamorphosis has already begun. Words
have been removed from their linear context, juxtaposed
to create visual excitement; syllables, letters have been
isolated for their visual properties. These experiments
culminate with the poem leaving the page for other "new"
means of presentation. The poem is looking for a new home.
The chairs are weak, the walls are peeling. The poem
becomes a "free subject", its own subject, the poet disappearing like clouds of dust in cartoons. If the poem
is a window, the landscape is changing. Let us change
with it, let us not restore the old conventions.

picture = 1000 words

It has been revealed to me that the poem is fragile and
cannot sustain narrative without collapsing in a heap.
This is necessary. It must then be coaxed into opening
its eyes, but only for a few seconds. Dreaming follows,
abruptly halted by the telephone. As it gives, it must
take. Who is taking?

©1979 Tom Konyves

In every public granting agency, there are two sets of people--administrators and judges. Theoretically, the administrators function merely to collect the applications and to document the decisions of the judges. They do not participate in the voting, although they may advise the organizations's trustees--known as the "Council" or the "Board of Directors"--in the selection of judges. This theoretical distinction notwithstanding, it can be observed, the more closely we examine U.S. granting organizations, that the administrators have far more discriminatory power than they should have or most of them customarily admit. The administrator's power lies not only in helping select the judges but in control over the information presented to them.

For instance, administrators can "advise" the judges on the accuracy of an application or on the applicant's past history; and unless the judges know better, they are likely to believe what they are told. Administrators may contribute new "information" to the judges' deliberation, and they may also withhold it, in order to favor applications they like or to deprecate those they dislike. Administrators also have the power to decide which applications can be admitted into the competition.

Last autumn, the constituency of past recipients of grants from the Coordinating Council of Literary Magazines elected me one of five judges to participate in disbursing CCLM funds to literary magazines. Once I received the magazines to be considered, I discovered certain omissions; and had I not been on the panel myself, I would never have known about the exclusions. One magazine which I knew had applied was not included in the package submitted to me, because, according to the CCLM administrators, its application had not arrived in time. To the contrary, the publisher of this magazine wrote me that on the deadline day he had personally delivered copies, "along with all pertinent application materials, and had handed them to a [CCLM] functionary who assured me that all materials were in order."

One might toss a coin over whom to believe had not these same administrators earlier made another inconsistent exclusionary decision. *Precisely*, which I co-publish and co-edit, was permanently refused admittance to any CCLM competition, because, to quote the CCLM's administrator's letter to me, "It is a critical journal, and critical journals, magazines which do not feature any creative writing such as fiction or poetry, are ineligible to apply to CCLM for funding." Reasonable as this exclusionary criterion may sound in principle, it is not true in fact. The package of CCLM applications submitted to me (as a judge) included several magazines containing absolutely no fiction or poetry: *Black Scholar, New America, Northeast Rising Sun, San Francisco Book Review, Stony Hills,* among others, all of which presumably passed the CCLM censors. Such obvious discrepancies suggest to most of us the existence of double standards in CCLM gatekeeping, illegitimately pre-excluding possible competition for the available pie.

Some readers might object to such reference to my own experience in this and other criticisms of cultural granting, but the principle reason why I cite it, and even generalize from it, is heuristic. Quite simply, no one is likely to know precisely how the granting processes can be corrupted unless they go through the process themselves. If you do research from the outside, as an inquiring reporter, you are likely to get a series of platitudinous statements that make sense initially but which, if you got involved with the application process, you would discover are inadequate, if not disingenuous. All organizations say, for instance, that they accept all applications and process them equally; but not until you apply yourself will you discover, as I did, that in some cases this platitude is essentially untrue.

Two years ago I tried through a complicated correspondence to discover the fate of my own repeated application to the National Endowment for the Humanities. In 1974, 1975 and then again in 1976, I proposed to do a critical study of experimental literature in America from 1959 to the present--a subject on which I have commonly acknowledged expertise. In the course of correspondence with the director of individual fellowships at the NEH, I asked about the panelists who might have judged my application for the previous three years. The NEH official replied with a list of nine credible literary scholars. Soon after I put this list into print, one of the NEH judges, a true expert, wrote me, "Nothing of yours, or resembling any cause of yours, came before any of the three NEH panels I served on." Where did it go? Was it excluded by a lower committee? By the director of individual fellowships himself? Unfortunately, the sometime NEH judge is not unreasonably reluctant to make a special inquiry of the NEH administration for fear that he would never again be asked to be a judge. Let me make a considered statement: Grants administrators have a penchant for superficially plausible, confidently articulated statements that turn out to be demonstrably false. One senses sometimes that such statements are uttered with the expectation that they will not be checked out (and indeed they rarely are). Intellectual integrity is apparently not a prerequisite in this cultural business.

Other times, the administrators will try to discourage an applicant by ignoring him, or, if that barrier is crossed, by disqualifying him with patently phoney objections. In 1978, I conceived of a selective anthology devoted to *The Other Poetries of New York City*, which is to say both original works and English translations of poetry written in my hometown in languages other than English. This is precisely the sort of literary project you would think a public agency should fund, precisely because a book so diversely useful could not exist without charitable support. When I mentioned *The Other Poetries* to one NYSCA administrator, he suggested that I refer the project to the "Special Programs" division which is mandated to "supporting projects which relate to the cultural development of isolated communities in New York State." This I did, requesting advice from the NYSCA Deputy Director in charge of Special Programs, Mr. Frank Diaz, in preparing an appropriate application. Not having had any response several weeks later, I telephoned Mr. Diaz, who never returned my call. Two weeks before the application deadline, I wrote him again, reminding him of the importance of the project. In a letter dated 28 February, 1979, a day before the deadline (and thus destined to be received after it), Mr. Diaz wrote me that "Special Arts Services has not in the past supported anything of that magnitude." Fortunately, Assembling Press did not wait for Mr. Diaz's (calculatedly?) tardy response and applied nonetheless for $11,000. Since Diaz explicitly questioned the size of our application, I looked into the 1976-77 *Annual Report* of NYSCA and discovered that his department had indeed funded seventy-five (count 'em) separate organizations for eleven grand or more. In a letter of 7 March, I reminded him of these exceptions.

His response is dated 12 March, 1979, conclusively illustrating that if Diaz wishes to respond quickly he certainly can; he is not as secretarily deficient as he initially seemed. In this second letter, Diaz, unable to dispute the indisputable, ignores his original objection to our proposal to state, flatly, "The Special Arts Services Department of the Council has not supported any publication of books in any language for any community." Superficially plausible, confidently articulated, this second exclusionary criterion is likewise untrue. On page 128 of the *Annual Report* is a grant to "Fourth Street i" for "publication of a magazine."

Although Diaz might like to engage in picayune arguments about the difference between magazines and books (especially since our annual *Assemblings* are both a magazine and a book), it seemed clear that again there was a distinct difference between his description of NYSCA policies and the actual facts. Now, we know from previous research that lying and cheating are recurrent at NYSCA (see undisputed evidence in *Assembling Assembling [1978], Eighth Assembling [1978]* and *Grants & the Future of Literature [1978]*); however, sometimes NYSCA administrators are spectacularly generous in providing evidence that might otherwise remain hidden. (Besides, what does "Special Arts Services" have against the publication of books? An inability to read [e.g., its own *Annual Report*].)

What Mr. Diaz is doing, it seems to me, is essentially niggarizing Assembling Press--blocking its advance initially by ignoring its petition, then by discouraging its application and finally by changing the exclusionary rules at every turn; for just as soon as we overcome one of his obstacles he raises another. And since he must have known when he wrote it that his initial exclusionary criterion was on its face false, precedent raises the question of whether he knew his second exclusionary criterion was likewise untrue. (And that in turn raises solemn legal questions of attempted fraud.)

More than two months later, Diaz has not responded to our refutation of his second letter; the suspicion is that he knows he cannot bluff his way past another lie. Precedent suggests that now that his second exclusionary criterion has been proven false, he might, if pressured, reply with characteristic confidence that, "You cannot apply to NYSCA unless your grandfather did." The procedures of niggarizing are as familiar as its rhetoric. Nonetheless, lies so patent are implicitly provocative, if not incendiary; for "niggers," we know, are not as "good" as they used to be.

Why should an administrator try so hard to exclude a proposal? Since Diaz no longer replies to queries, we are free to conjecture. One possible reason is that he personally does not like it; however, as I pointed out at the beginning, final decision of its worth rests not with Diaz but with the judges in his department. (Perhaps the best way to get over his jerry-built hump would be to submit a copy of this exposé to every Special Arts Services judge; otherwise, they would never know how much of *their* power is being usurped behind their backs.)

Secondly, had Diaz precommitted his available funds to certain previous recipients, he would regard all new applicants as challenges to his promises (but this would be corrupt and, if true, should inexorably lead to subpoenas and indictments). After all, it is these past winners who keep him in a high-style job that paid him $21,545 in 1976, $32,500 in 1977 and $37,197 in 1978. Furthermore, no cultural bureaucrat gets such salary increases unless his superiors think he is doing everything right; and this observation, like others, raises the familiar questions about the complicity of NYSCA's highest officials--not only Diaz's immediate superior, the executive director, Robert Mayer, but also such NYSCA Councilors as Arthur Levitt, the chairman and chief executive officer of the American Stock Exchange, and the band-leader Peter Duchin.

Thirdly, Diaz may simply enjoy abusing his power as a bureaucratic sado-masochist; one index of organizational corruption is the high presence of dishonest, pathological people who can be easily blackmailed and thus controlled.

Fourth, a recent New York State Comptroller's audit of NYSCA documents how its rules are flagrantly violated and its juries rigged to favor NYSCA "insiders"; this report confirms the suggestions made elsewhere (and never seriously disputed) that NYSCA is the most corrupt-ridden cultural agency in North America. Having seen his NYSCA colleagues get away with so much uncorrected and underexposed malfeasance, Diaz may feel that he is simply missing the action; and no one in his position wants to fall behind the company Joneses.

An earlier draft of this critique was submitted to NYSCA's "chairman," Kitty Carlisle Hart, who chose neither to reply nor to promise a reply, for reasons we are thus free to conjecture.

14 May, 1979   Richard Kostelanetz, NY, NY

INQUIRY AS DIDACTIC POETRY

Martin H. Krieger

1. Several years ago I offered a course in Didactic Poetry and Method in our English Department. No one showed up for the first class. No one ever showed up.

2. Didactic Poetry:

> DIDACTIC POETRY is poetry which is primarily intended to instruct. Most commonly, the label is used for poetry which teaches a moral. It can also refer to poetry which conveys factual information, like astronomy, mathematics, or rhetoric; or systematic philosophy. Aesthetically it seems to be the first stage in the evolution of literary forms: the earliest literature we possess, Eastern, Hebrew, Greek, is in verse and uses meter as a mnemonic device to make the hearer remember and thereby learn what is being said.

Princeton Encyclopedia of
Poetics and Poetry

Traditional examples include De Rerum Natura of Lucretius, Virgil's Georgics, Pope's Essays and Dante's Divine Comedy. In each case a work that is manifestly poetry is being used to instruct, argue and expound--what we now do in a prose that is preferably clear and simple in style.

3. But more and more of what is called criticism, metaphysics and science is explicitly poetic or being treated as poetry. Hayden White and Stanley Edgar Hyman want us to treat humanistic historical works as coherent texts with structures that we usually attribute to literature. Jacques Derrida and Stanley Cavell do the same with philosophical works. Robert K. Merton, the sociologist, treats scientific change in terms of footnoting procedures, and has done textual analyses of papers in mathematical economics to understand the social structure of a social science. In each of these cases, what was once thought of as paraphaseable text is now treated as absolute, meaning everything one can wring from it.

3.1 A second possibility is to produce scientific or argumentative texts in the form of poetry. In the next section we shall look at a variety of these.

3.2 By making our didactic works in poetry we are able to take much of what is called scientific and academic work away from the academics and scientists and give it back to the poets. Visual artists have become metaphysicians by this tactic too.

3.3 Method triumphed over rhetoric in the story told by Frances Yates. The universal and inorganic structural method won out over the particular and organic rhetoric--even if method itself is a rhetoric. Didactic poetry, today, is a return of rhetoric, as method defeats itself by its pride in its being all-knowing.

4. Some examples:

4.1 William Gass' and Keith Gunderson's philosophical works that depend on the full power of words and the power of poetry (rhyme and scansion). They are demonstrations. Gass says he is not communicating.

4.2 Stanley Cavell's and Jacques Derrida's philosophical criticism in which they take their objects for study, the texts, as meaning every word they say, and, in which, Cavell and Derrida mean every word they say.

4.3 Robert Irwin treating art as a form of inquiry.

4.4 Saul Bellow's long Tolstoyan tribute to theosophy and Owen Barfield, a metaphysics if there ever was one, but in the middle of a contemporary novel. Or, is the metaphysics just an ornament? How could we know?

4.5 Wallace Stevens or Kenneth Koch supplying us with a poetics in poetry.

4.6 A. R. Ammons giving a complete cosmology and natural history, of all the objects and how they appear in time.

4.7 John Ashbery's art criticism, but it is poetry.

5. Following Gary Saul Morson, if I treat literature as complete and integral, as the place where multiple inter-pretation is the order of the day, and where every word counts, and didactic literature as that literature which forces the audience to think in unfamiliar ways and makes them more willing to be speculative, then we might expect that speculative metaphysics, essentially forbidden today, will have to be in poetry.

6. Documentary photography becomes more difficult as we elevate photography to art, and as we rediscover art in the archive of useful photography. But documentary photography, like didactic poetry, will triumph since it has something it wants to do, practical pretenses, that it feels others must pay attention to.

7. Making what we ordinarily do in expository prose into literature will force our ordinary activities to inherit all the problems of literature, including its social function. Hence this radical move to literature on the part of the critical and philosophical tradition may be seen as an ideological move too. The situation is not unlike the one we encounter when we wonder whether a male-to-female transsexual should be permitted to join a women's caucus, or whether it is possible for the male-to-female transsexual to be a lesbian and a member of a separatist group. How often is it just plain poaching?

'n bombed my way thru to speech in magazines and books and papers before,
but never did I talk to you the way I want to now! Never did the need of
your being there mean so double-clutching much to me, 'splain to me the
reason why I'm here — he sure means it you doubtin' dear! — never did
my hope of self-discovery reveal itself to me in the act itself as now!
I must blast in this I of mine as we move along, but believe me I think
in the long run it's no more important than your I, this is not an I
book anymore than it's a Thy book, my I should stand for yours as far as
it's able, yours for mine, that's our story ain't it? But I must tell
you the peppy joy I have — momentary, I know, boy will it go! — but
it's mine right now in having found a flute thru which I can blow everything to you! Jesus, the finding of an instrument, like Cholly Parker
stumbling on his pawnshop alto sax, find your instrument and tell the
world to f itself, for sure, or else tune in to the sweet sounds of your
own homemade cure! Like Ralph (Invisible Man, in real life balding 'n
tan!) Ellison, OK here we go into those Black Arts, yeah, sound of drums
and spooky-deeky — Black Magic Woman loomin' up outa dat swamp-smoke,
shabazz! — anyway Ralph's writings on craft and instrument are cool,
deadly, graceful, Mabel, not a Nacheral Man as the nigra-licking white
folks wanted him to be! Ellison is the triple-headed university-feted
black savant who cunnings what came before him, what will go on after
right to them topmost rafters! I remember Al (Albert L.) Murray tellin'
me how when they stood on that late '30s library line down at Tuskeegee
Institute together Ellison always took out the strange books — white
man's voodoo, gotsta learn all that paleface hoodoo! — like Larry Sterne's
Tristram Shandy and Bobby Burton's Anatomy of Melancholy, the librarian
whispering to Al that Ralph had reamed all de straight books in that Tuskeegee Library 'n now was going right for the universe itself! None of
that Black Boy stuff for him even though he once loved hero-man Richard
Wright — I still do! — and this was back when old Ralph wanted to be
a horn-player 'n composer and not no word-writer at all! He was a five-
star brain-packed tanman, Stan, buddied with litcrit Stanley Edgar Hyman
before Hyman died, took that trip from Tuskeegee to St. Petersburg with
the Dostywhatsky boy and Kafka the mysterious letka in Prague! None of your
rollin' bones and scat and N'Orleans a la Louie for Ralph — "Today that
stuff's hooey!" — as new for 'merican blackdom as the whizzing bop imag-

ination of the '50s, goatbeards and shades making those 'lectric human
waves that haven't stopped assaulting white nerves yet, pet! But it was
Ralph who spoke about craft not guts, that without craft you can do nothing in American life, spoke about gettin' through the Dee-pression out
in Oklahoma gunning down birds just as Honorary Negro Hem had taught him
in the short stories — craft led to his eating, ex-Sen. Kenneth Keating,
none of your budget-cutting "arty-farty" here! And while I've had my tangles
with Ellison 'n Al Murray, they were like elder buddy-brothers for years,
Little Buddy (Al) and Big Buddy (Ralph), I can say nothing but sweet now
to Elli-san-- honesykansu, Mr. E! — since I've found my bugle, homemade
craft, means to get it on, git it out with proper shout! And listen, you
folks like dear blood-brother Bernie, Angie down the street, Rizzo down
Floridaway, all my friends who haven't heard of Tristram Shandy — ▆▆ wait
for the fucking movie, Andy! — don't "read," are not lit'ry, in this case
design vacuum tubes and grab the Wall Street Journal, the Daily News, co-own
a pork store like Ange or like Riz have bought into three rolling hotdog
stands for eight months out of the year, this includes you as much as Elli-
san and Al Murray and Stanley (The Briefcase) Hyman! Don't feel this isn't
for you anymore than you've ever felt that I'm not for you! You've all got
equal space inside my big-bulge 'merican head, oh Georgie "Red" Wilson where
are you now?, how can I pull a countryclub number and discriminate — you
can birdie on the green but don't fart in the clubhouse! —sure I'm using
writer's words to help me say my say but they're ultimately people-words,
my-language-'n-your-language words, we're all in this U.S. intensive verb unit
together! No one who ever tried to write to and for this country, to the
pipple, you's and me's, was ever frightened by literature! Let it be pulp,
then, let 'em eat schlock is the rejoinder, you want to reach 'em all and
you'll be locked out in the plastic motel hall, you fake yiddishe Lincoln!
That's of course the danger, are you sharin' this Farley Granger?,of trying to hit you Honda mechanics — just with a word, pal, take it easy! —
'n you Harvard Lit manics in the same breath, that's the paleface/redskin
split I've always refused to believe in, I'm both and so are you if you
say screw the labels! These words belong to each 'n every, even if like Ange
you only hear them on the talk shows or scan 'em in that Daily News — even
you ▆▆ (elitists) who use that magnifying glass on Views & Reviews! — but don't think

ON THOSE BOOK-LENGTH FICTION CONTESTS

by Norman Lavers

The University of Iowa School of Letters has an annual contest for a book-length volume of short fiction. The contest has an established literary figure for judge (Stanley Elkin in 1978), and the winning entry receives a prize of $1000, and publication by the University of Iowa Press.

The AWP has an annual contest for a book-length volume of short fiction. The contest has an established literary figure for judge (Wallace Stegner in 1978), and the winning entry is published by a university press. It is hoped by the editors that eventually they will publish 8-10 volumes a year.

Harvard University has an on-going contest (no deadline) for short novels of 25-60,000 words. The contest has three established literary figures for judges (Eudora Welty, John Gardner, and Irving Howe were judges in 1977). The winning volumes receive a grant of $1000, plus publication by Harvard University Press. The editors hope to publish about five short novels a year.

I have much praise for these and the like contests, that get many worthy writers published who otherwise might not be. I hope they flourish and proliferate, but I fear they will not. I fear instead they will slowly dry up and die, and not honorably, having done their best to raise the sights of a philistine audience, but dishonorably, having lost their chance through timidity. The problem is built into the structure of the contests, and I don't know that there is any way to avert it.

What the contests **seem** to offer, is a chance for the high quality, but slightly out of round, uncommercial writer, the writer writing, perhaps, for the few, or writing for an audience that won't catch up with him for several years. After all, the judge is not some hard-nosed commercial editor, thinking of balance sheets, nor is it a hard-nosed literary editor, thinking in terms of reaching the largest number of "good" readers. No, this time the judge is a writer himself, with a concern only for good writing, a consideration which leaves the counting house and cultural democracy behind as irrelevancies.

Well, that's how it seems. But in fact, here is problem number one: the judge is an **established** figure, which means he has been around long enough that his audience has caught up with him, or at any rate he is a commercially feasible writer, and by this time has a vested interest in writing that is like his own writing. Wallace Stegner is no hack, and won't worry about balance sheets---but how open is he to what is being written right now?

But let us posit the very best. Let us say a really current, really discerning writer--Ronald Sukenick, for example---were made judge. The high quality but uncommercial writer we were talking about still won't have a chance: Sukenick will never see his manuscript---and here is problem number two: primary readers screen the manuscripts first (obviously: the judge could never wade through the hundreds of submissions). The prestigious judge will only receive a handful, five at most, from which to select.

Who are these anonymous, unestablished primary readers? I imagine they are folks like us, people around the school, junior editors. Full of responsibility, and full of human nature. Let us look at some incoming manuscripts from their point of view. The Iowa contest says "stories previously published in periodicals are acceptable." This, I suspect, should be translated to read, "if nearly all your stories haven't been previously published, don't bother submitting." Prior publication, naturally, constitutes the very first screening, and a long list of credits already disposes these first readers favorably. Now let us suppose two manuscripts in which all the stories have had prior publication. One entrant has published his stories in New Yorker, Atlantic Monthly, Esquire, and so on. The other has published his stories in Kamadhenu, Panache, Center, Cream City Review, Cloud Chamber, Edgeworks, etc. Now I am not talking about some corrupt inferior primary reader, I'm talking about a guy like us. We can't help but be influenced by this prima facie evidence that the first manuscript is more worthy than the second, even when we know full well that the innovative, the out of round, the exceptional writer---Donald Barthelme almost a single exception---is not likely to be found in those high-class slicks.

But even supposing we read all the manuscripts assigned to us as impartially as we are able, there is a second influence operating to make us select the straight over the eccentric: our sense of responsibility to select the best. It's hard to judge something really new. We have little basis for judging it, since it is still in the process of teaching us how to read it. But we **can** judge Realism, since we have been doing so for a couple of centuries now. We have learned what is high quality and what is ersatz, as long as it comes in that familiar package, and so we select what we know to be good, rather than take a chance on something that might be good, but is too fresh for us to stand back from.

But let us suppose anyway that some of us are cranky enough, independent enough, to pick something strange, that we think might be real. Here is problem number three. Before those final five go up to the final judge, we can be certain that the main editor and publisher have a final screening, and see to it that nothing goes up to the judge that they couldn't live with. What **can** the editor or publisher live with? Well, something **good**, but also something that will reach as many readers as possible---there is always that impossible dream of having a best seller. The editor is very cranky indeed who does not feel "a sense of responsibility towards his readers," as Elliott Anderson recently phrased it (Story Quarterly 7/8). What reaches the most readers, even the most "good" readers, is something not too far out of round. Again, Realism.

There really is a lot of responsibility involved in trying to select the **new** that is also **good**. A few places consciously go after the new---New Directions, say, or Fiction Collective. They have some great successes, but also lots of dogs---that is the flaw built into **their** system, but it is an honorable and necessary flaw. Fiction Collective truly does have one of the most interesting publication lists around, just as it advertises, but inevitably there is a lot of chaff in with the kernels. There are delightful books that tell you where fiction is going, and there are others that put you to sleep by the second page.

What the contests I am writing about can consistently avoid is both these extremes: nothing really soporific, and nothing very wonderful.* The editors don't really need to play safe (presumably the contests are subsidized). But it is human nature to want a winner, and so, rather than risking a big loser, they hedge their bets. Ironically, when they play safe, what they are in danger of ending up with is commercial fiction which is not quite good enough to make the New York market. I don't think that was the original idea.

October 14, 1978

* I am overstating. There is still first-rate Realistic fiction being written. But let me state my position this way: speaking as a person who subscribes to a couple of dozen literary magazines, and who actually does buy current books, I have browsed through all the Iowa winners, and there isn't a one I couldn't while away a boring afternoon with. But C. V. Poverman's is the only one I am tempted to buy. On the other hand, there are probably half the Fiction Collective books you couldn't force me to read---but I have bought the other half.

how can we say
what we want
to say

when we don't
know how
to say
it

or even
(clearly)

what we
want to
say

?

to whom
can we say
what we
want to
say

?

only to
those who
understand
us

is there
any way
of talking
to those
who don't

?

Robert

Lax

would a
new language
help

?

would any
new form
of communi
cation
help

?

would
"art"

?

would
pictographs.
images

?

must we
talk only
to ourselves

?

can we
talk in
future

to people
on other
planets

?

with dots
& dashes
bleeps
& flash
es

?

is there
a word
or two
left
we'd like
to say

?

C R E D O

Not a poet but a verbal speculator.

Not a language artist but a human being.

Not with Alexander Pope the sound an echo to the sense but somewhere between the sense an echo to the sound and the sound its own excuse for being.

Too aware of the sonic possibilities of language to want to be a poet.

Too personal to want to be a language artist.

(Piano begins softly to play The Internationale as the volume of sound slowly increases. First voice continues.)

I combine a pursuit for technical innovation with the emotional autobiographical self. When the innovative impulses assert themselves the autobiographical material resonates and takes on a broader significance.

I am against the Anglo-American tradition but I know that all traditions can be tyrannical and deenergizing. The only tradition that seems viable is the self-destructive tradition of the new.

Influences are floojoy cezzarrr fawrr hizz loooestralll fffawrzzz finnical quakizai rahahooligan yoooooolijezzzzz nnndddd queezikilll kompestral mannajezzz. Passork schwitterizing fffawawrrms nnddd seeeezikilll stralllissseeee housajesstikks mannrizing witterish too eeevoke ay myoooziworld rerraiaiaippp nnddd pyoooomannay-ayaykikkk. Verraiaiai verroooo how verrbblehehehsstt ththth pohohohzzrrrz hoool reeeloooo awawnn theeer verrronnikkklll worleeeerrrzzz theeer zingelllaiaiai pulsh nnndddd theeer verrork sennnshunnn howayayver yooolever uv howowowl floooverizing kompomp sowowowndzzzzz kin beee hurkkkddd in tooobbbllll kessstrallchoorz thahaht so lisssesssstrallleeee schwitt nnddd sowowowbbblll awawnnn nnddddd awawawffffff ththth kkkkkayayayjjjjjikkkkkzzzzzzz.

(Second voice begins with Yes, We Have No Bananas and maintains a consistent volume throughout.)

I am the sort of yoooobbblll hoooolayvverrr ththth vvvawawawrrrssst wijjjikkk hooottrrrr nnnddd pihihihkkkkrritttchddd bbbaiaitttchch that hihihimens ththth yoolaiailayayshinzz toohooo mmmaiainnnn shshshurrrnnyan kaynnniggg varrburggg nnddd mehehehsssmenshinzzz thth wurrrkkklinggg lingooochchereeez nnntooo tohohohnnnnisssterrrikkkklll shayayayverrrzzzzz. Vuvvv maiainnn jissterrrishshsh hahahzzzahahrrtzzzz nnn peerchingex kohohnnnishnehehssss fffurmmm wahahahtttooo-verleee fffeeeejjjikkkl fawawrrrmmmayaykkkjjjj yool airaittt wattayayayverlooo

kreeekonkayayayvvvikkkll meeeazzzmyoooozzzzikkklll toodoo thth
lahahahrrrjjjleeepppddd jeeezzzaiaiaizzz haavv velopopped. Taiaimum
fforttt aiai rehehehtttinrohohohttt noh prayayzzikkk myooottai buttuch
how much of my composition is optic and how much purely auditory I am now in
the process of discovering.

(Solo voice)

Visually I am convinced that close analogies with cinematic closeups, dissolves,
pan shots, boom shots, fadeouts, the split screen and all the rest of this technology can give language dimensions we have not yet seen. Eisenstein talks about
this in the Film Form and Film Sense but someone who approaches these possibilities
less mechanistically and from a linguistic point of view will need to pick it up
from there.

(A soft piano reintroduces The Internationale.)

The sonic possibilities of language that Western and other musics can help to
project and the visual flux that cinematic methodology can help us verbalize
may be mutually contradictory or perhaps they can be synthesized in one
sensuous style. We may need to wait another century to see our language so
enriched.

Too personal to want to be a language artist.

Too aware of the sonic possibilities of language to want to be a poet.

Not with Alexander Pope the sound an echo to the sense but somewhere between the
sense an echo to the sound and the sound its own excuse for being.

    (Second voice reintroduces Yes, We Have No Bananas, with lecturer, piano
    and vocalist closing together.)

Not a language artist but yingyoooolllaiai tahahahttristtttidjjjjooooooo.

Nnayay pohohohppagaiai kkkyooobbbler ayayay bbbluhuhuhuhttttaiaiai
revvvllanngwisssttikkkk speculator.

Not tttooooonnnnayayaykkikkkk.

Sandrrooolayayayver sanbbblllerererervvvv alll oooottt
yeeeeboooolyooolayayayttettt.

Alllehehehkkkksss jjiwggggyoooolllanggwirrrrr toooottt sunnnooottttleeeee
ayayaytttohohohohnnnnnahahahahttttohoh.

S.J. LEON

Zbigniew Lewicki

ON THE IMPORTANCE OF INTELLECTUAL QUALITY

What is experimental literature and who needs it? Given the
limit of two pages, it would be preposterous of me even to try answering these questions; what I think I can do, however, is to bring back
one idea concerning American radical writing: it is not new but I believe it is worth repeating in this collection.

There is little doubt that American fiction is now, in the
1970´s, the most interesting, vivid and innovative in the world. It
includes such strong "traditional" voices as those of Bellow, Percy,
or Updike, such intelligent innovators as Nabokov, Hawkes, or Gaddis,
such important postmodern writers as Gass, Barth, or Barthelme -
which still leaves out Heller, Coover, Brautigan, and scores of
others. It also offers, in the class all to himself, Thomas Pynchon.
All of them have altered the course of 20th century fiction so much,
experimented with prosaic forms so skillfully and have been so receptive to our reality and to ideas that constitute modern consciousness, that they seem to leave very little space beyond what they have
already achieved - at least today. And yet they are far from being
America´s most radical writers - Zekowsky and Berne, Veitch, Federman
- diversified as this sample is, they are all more "daring" than the
writers mentioned above, and then there are texts included, for instance, in Wildman´s anthology Experiments in Prose which are still
more radical. Is there really so much left out by "established"
writers, are there no limits to what can be done with the matter of
fiction?

I, for one, do not believe that the range of fiction´s themes
and modes of expression is infinite or that equilibrium can be

maintained regardless of how far a writer leans to one side. Whether we like it or not, whether these terms still have any meaning in literary theory, in the popular appreciation of literature there exist such notions as matter and form: we can call them texture and structure, ideas and modes but no current critical fashion can simply order them out of existence. While questions about the "meaning" of a work of art make little sense, I believe an intelligent reader, in order to be satisfied with a work of literature, must be convinced that it possesses an intellectual quality. If contemporary writers express their, frequently deep, ideas in obsolete manners, we grow impatient - and rightly so, because all writing is a convention and this imposes formal requirements. But we can also grow impatient with those writers who have very little to tell us and hide it behind "experimental" cover - because all writing is an exchange of ideas, which imposes intellectual requirements.

There are all kinds of readers: some buy only books that make the best-seller lists and we can leave them in peace - they have their standards well established; then there is a group of faithful followers that will approve of everything which has a non-conformitant quality - no use arguing with them either; but there is also a potentially strong response coming from people who like innovation but despise hollowness. Their needs are now best filled by Coover, Pynchon or Barth, but their literary tastes are usually adaptive enough to adjust to new modes. One thing they would not sacrifice, however, is their intellectual expectations which will not and should not be lowered. I believe that when we complain next time about the lack of audience for an experimental work, we should also ask ourselves whether we are really satisfied with its message. Because if we are not, we should not expect others to be.

LIST

A BY NO MEANS COMPREHENSIVE OVERVIEW OF EXPLORATORY WORK BUT RATHER
AN INVESTIGATION INTO SOME PUBLISHING AND PUBLICATIONS THAT MERIT
FURTHER INVESTIGATION

HARLEY W. LOND

AIEEE Jack Grady POB 3424 Charlottesville VA 22903
Art Contemporary Carl Loeffler POB 3123 San Francisco CA 94119
Assembling Press POB 1967 Brooklyn NY 11202
Beau Geste David Mayor Barhatch Farm Barhatch Lane Cranleigh
                    Surry UK GV6 7NG
Blank Tape Keith Rahmmings Box 371 Brooklyn NY 11230
Cineaste 333 6th Avenue New York NY 10014
Cisoria Arte Damaso Ogaz Apdo de Correos 50531 Caracas 105
                    Venezuela
Coach House Press 401 (rear) Huron St. Toronto Ontario Canada
                    M5S 2G5
Communication Perspectives Inst. of Communications Research
                    222B Armory U. of Ill. Champaign Il 61820
Control Magazine Stephen Willats 5 London Mews London W2 England
Crawl Out Your Window Melvyn Freilicher & Paul Dresman 704 Nob St.
                    Del Mar CA 92014
Cultural Correspondence 224 Thayer St. Providence RI 02906
The Dumb Ox James Hugunin 629 Quail Dr. Los Angeles CA 90065
E Marshall Reese 3022 Abell Ave. Baltimore MD 21218
Ear Beth Anderson 32 E. 2nd #22 New York NY 10003
Edizioni Geiger Adriano Spatola 43020 Malino di Bazzano Parma Italy
Hills Bob Perelman 36 Clyde St. San Francisco CA 94107
Intermedia Magazine Harley W. Lond POB 31464 San Francisco CA 94131
Intermedia Press Box 3294 Vancouver B.C. Canada V6B 3X9
Interstate Loris Essary 6901 Dubuque Ln. Austin TX 78723
Kaldron karl kempton 441 N. 6th Street Grover City CA 93433
Karimbada Unhandeijara Lisboa Rua Senador Joao Lira 777
                    58.000 Jeae Passoa Paraba Brasil
L=A=N=G=U=A=G=E Bruce Andrews & Charles Bernstein 464 Amsterdam
                    New York NY 10024
Laughing Bear Tom Person Box 14 Woodinville WA 98072
Lightworks Charlton Burch POB 7271 Ann Arbor MI 48107
Luna Bisonte Prods. John M. Bennett 137 Leland Ave. Columbus
                    Ohio 43214
Musicmaster 2324 N.W. Johnson #2 Portland OR 97210
NRG Dan Raphael 228 S.E. 26 Portland OR 97214
The New Commercialist Meyer Hirsch 2338 Divisadero San Francisco
                    CA 94115
Only Prose Perreault/Weinstein 54 East 7th St. New York NY 10003
Rain 2270 N.W. Irving Portland OR 97210
Roof James Sherry 300 Bowery New York NY 10012
Strike Amerigo Marras POB 933 Sta. A Toronto Ontario Canada M5W 1C2
This Barry Watten 1004 Hampshire St. San Francisco CA 94110
Totem Joaquim Branco Av. Astolfo Dutra, 247 36770 Cataguases-MG
                    Brasil
Transient Press Ken Saville Box 4662 Albuquerque NM 87106
Vile Anna Banana & Bill Gaglione 1183 Church St. San Francisco
                    CA 94114
Visible Language Merald E. Wrolstad Box 1972 CMA Cleveland OH 44106
West Coast Poetry Review Bill Fox 1335 Dartmouth Dr. Reno NV 89509

LIST - 2

Afterwords John Brockman Anchor Books NY
Alpha, Trans, Chung Peter D'Agostino Wright State University Ohio
                    NFS Press POB 31040 San Francisco CA 94131
American Revolutionary Pamphlets Melvyn Freilicher 704 Nob St.
                    Del Mar CA 92014
Anthology of Concrete Poetry ed. Emmett Williams Something Else Press
Aut.omerica Ant Farm Dutton NY
The Bonnyclabber George Chambers December/Panache December Press
                    4343 N. Clarendon Chicago IL 60613
Book of Takes Paul Zelevansky Zartscorp 267 West 89th St.
                    New York NY 10024
Breakthrough Fictioneers ed. Richard Kostelanetz Something Else Press
Chain of Letters David Arnold Trike 553 4th Ave. San Francisco
                    CA 94118
The Collected Works of Buck Rogers in the 25th Century Chelsea House
                                                          NY
The Consciousness Industry Hans M. Enzensberger Seabury Press NY
Contents Ulises Carrion Herengracht 259 Amsterdam Holland
The Discontinuous Universe ed. Sallie Sears & Georgiana W. Lord
                    Basic Books NY
Double or Nothing Raymond Federman Swallow Press IL
Essaying Essays ed. Richard Kostelanetz Out of London Press
                    12 W. 17th St. New York NY 10011
Exact Change Henry Korn Assembling Press NY
foew&ombwhnw Dick Higgins Something Else Press
For Bloodshot Eyeballs Blair H. Allen 9651 Estacia Ct. Cucamonga
                    CA 91730
Genre Tony Rickaby 67 Mordaunt St. London SW9 9RD England
Grips M.D. Elevitch Grossman-Viking NY
Malice in Blunderland Blair H. Allen 9651 Estacia Ct. Cucamonga
                    CA 91730
Montezuma's Ball Eugene Wildman Swallow Press IL
Once Again ed. Jean-Francois Bory New Directions NY
Photography and Language ed. Donna-Lee Phillips & Lew Thomas
                    NFS Press POB 31040 San Francisco CA 94131
Rainbook - Resources for Appropiate Technology Schocken Books NY
Seasons of the Mind Arlene Zekowski Wittenborn NY
Schizo Culture 1 & 2 Semiotext(e) 522 Phil. Col. U. New York NY 10027
The Story So Far ed. Steve McCaffery & bpNichol Coach House Press
                    Toronto
Structural(ism) and Photography Lew Thomas NFS Press POB 31040
                    San Francisco CA 94131
Studio International Art and Social Purpose March/April 1976
                    37 Museum St. London WC1 England
Superman From the 30's to the 70's Bonanza Books NY
This Book Opal Nations POB 91 Sta. B Toronto Ontario Canada M5T 2T3
Throbbing Gristle Industrial Records 10 Martello St. Hackney
                    London E8 England
Toronto Research Group Research Report 2: Narrative Open Letter 8
                    Coach House Press Toronto
Typewriter Poems ed. Peter Finch Second Aeon/Something Else Press
The Unconscious Victorious Stanley Berne Wittenborn NY
White Screen John M. Bennett New Rivers Press POB 578 Cathedral
                    Station New York NY 10025
Word Rain Madeline Gins Grossman-Viking NY
Younger Critics of North America ed. Richard Kostelanetz Margins
                    POB A Fairwater WI 53931

Narrative

I

Language is narrative in that it establishes at
once a sense of expectation which, in order to be
satisfied, must meet certain requirements. Grammar must be served and logic and a point must be
reached. The basis of narrative is time, an old
concept but one on which the understanding rests:
time, not the manipulation of form, or layout, or
typography, or pictures, or color, or the thick-
ness of paper. We experience language through
expectation, which is also time. When narrative
is at its best it tends to purity in that language
is forgotten; the systematic function of language
is obviated by itself, its perfection; it does not
exist; it is the absorbed symbol; it is experience,
active, therefore defined by time: narrative.
Narrative grants life, persuades us of its validity, by occurring through time, like life. The
most crucial technical concept of narrative is
climax. The points most sought in life are climaxes;
the greatest satisfactions lie ahead: the high
points, the extremes, the vividness of experience
which has accumulated from expectation to frightening and exquisite moments. Culmination is short-
lived, deadening. The end; death. The narrative
must be repeated; the experience again experienced.
The basic form remains the same. The same old story.

Richard Lyons

Narrative

II

Ultimately there is only one innovation on narra-

tive, the excision of climax. Innovation is the

denial of expectation, the reversal, the confron-

tation of time. Though the expectancy of language

itself cannot be transcended, narrative innovation

confronts the expectation and offers a replacement:

timelessness; nothing; denial. Innovation is the

refusal of tradition. When proper it seems as

conventional as tradition: it does not, like gim-

mickry, call attention to itself; it is not self-

conscious, does not proclaim its novelty. It is

derivative, required by style and theme, as far

from self-serving as genuine prayer. It is not

required by an age but by a single artist alone

who has arrived at innovation along a strait path.

Anyone interested in the full range of radical/experimental tendencies in contemporary literature might consider the uses of language in the following films (and works in other media):

TAKA IIMURA'S WHITE CALLIGRAPHY, MODELS
(videotapes: observer/observed, to see the frame)

HOLLIS FRAMPTON'S ZORNS LEMMA, SURFACE TENSION, POETIC JUSTICE

michael snow's rameau's nephew

carolee schneemann's ABC

PAUL SHARITS' WORD MOVIE/FLUXFILM

(ROBERT HUOT'S diary paintings)

JOYCE WIELAND'S SAILBOAT

marcel duchamp's anemic cinema

anthony mccall & andrew tyndall's argument

peter watkins' the war game

WHO...

YVONNE RAINER'S FILM ABOUT A WOMAN

(by Scott MacDonald ((thanks to Carol Kinne for supplies)))

If a poet decides to dramatize
the implications of a word by
using his considerable resources
in visual design, shouldn't we
hold him responsible for his
original decision to use that word?

If the word is found to
encapsulate ignorance or bigotry,
isn't the resulting poem simply
an exercize in ignorance or
bigotry?

("nymphomania": "excessive
sexual desire in a woman")

HOORAY FOR THE LIBERATION OF
LANGUAGE (but not at the expense
of the liberation of people).

N
Y
M
P
H
O
M   M
A   A
N   N
I   I
A   A

(Richard Kostelanetz)

Scott MacDonald

ASSEMBLING

Of all the editorial innovations possible <u>Assembling</u>
is one of the best. Having received an invitation to
contribute, a writer can prepare his material in
absolute freedom. He knows that no other person will
have any control over the nature of his work. This
is of enormous psychological benefit to the artist.

Anyone who has read through an issue of <u>Assembling</u>
notices that his eye is continually stimulated. Pages
differ in colour and texture; type differs from page
to page. Many contributions are hand-written, and the
variety of hands adds to the excitment. It comes as
a surprise after <u>Assembling</u> to realize that the conventional book or journal is too uniform in its type
and pages to please the eye.

<u>Assembling</u> gives a marvelous presentation of the
spirit of a time (the seventies). To intuition it
presents our age- an age which is thus seen to be
different in its own way through its art forms from
any previous age. The value of <u>Assembling</u> will increase.
Fifty years from now a copy of <u>Assembling</u> will stand
out as a definitive ard-word presentation of our time.

<u>Assembling</u> is a work in which the whole is much
bigger than the parts. Each contribution, varying
in quality perhaps, adds to a whole book which is
enormously more vital as a whole than the contribution
itself. The artist's "name" is not stressed, rightly so.
The book as whole is what one reads, as if it had
been created by one person.

<u>Assembling</u> seems incredibly different from other
literary-artistic works. It is avant-garde in its
spirit, and because of its manner of construction
great innovations on the page are possible; the
contributors have realized this to the full. Hence the
vitality and ingenuity of the work.

<u>ASSEMBLING</u> is not stuffy, elitist, or dull.
Most literary magazines seem hidebound and unenterprising
after <u>Assembling</u>. It comes as a breath of fresh air
when one reads <u>Assembling</u> after having read so many
other journals.

HARRIS MACLENNAN

plan your own pit

corner or armless

section, $199 (see pg. 2)

In this country, surrealism has never been understood well enough to be
granted sustained, unprejudiced attention. So it is customary, here,
to dismiss automatism as part of the tattered paraphernalia carried
around by a few old hoaxers who may impress the gullible, at times anyway, but who have nothing of real interest to appeal to a serious poet.
And the first prerequisite for seriousness, we all know, is taking oneself seriously. What happens, though, when we bother to ask how much
surrealism still has to offer, today? We soon discover that, of all
the questions raised by surrealism in its half-century history, none is
more vexatious than that centered on automatism. What can the serious
poet expect of verbal automatism? In considerable measure, this
apparently straightforward query confuses the issue.

        Confusion dates back a long time, following upon the inaccurate
supposition that automatism is no more than a mechanical procedure, readily available to any writer who may feel inclined to resort to its use
when his inspiration seems to have run dry temporarily. The surrealists
themselves must share the blame for encouraging fundamentally wrong conclusions in this regard. By announcing that verbal automatism is accessible to all, they have helped foster a misleading deduction, that automatism is nothing but a method of convenience, seemingly likely to bring
results of a sort, to the extent that "surrealism is within the reach of
everyone's unconscious." The gravity of the danger may be estimated if
we glance at André Masson's Entretiens avec Georges Charbonnier (1958).
Here one of its first practitioners in painting retrospectively casti-
gates automatism. Masson's prime objection is to the uneven quality of
the return paid on the artist's investment in automatism, which he
likens to going fishing: one day you carry home a tasty supper;
another, an old boot is all you bring back.

        Masson's strictures point unambiguously in one direction. Dis-
enchantment with automatic methods betrays an ambition clearly evidenced
in his growing concern for achieving uniformity in the activity of image
making: a kind of quality control that will ensure maintenance of minimum standards. These, he implies, are set by aesthetic principles, the
very ones for which surrealists unrelentingly voice their contempt. In
the eyes of a surrealist, guaranteed success with automatism promises to
be no more exciting, in the end, than the certainty of making a plenti-
ful catch every time one takes rod in hand. It is not the frequency
with which it turns out a satisfactory product that allows us to weigh
the efficacy of pictorial or verbal automatism. On the contrary, the
hit-or-miss nature of the venture contributes to giving meaning and
value to experimentation with and exploration through automatism. And
this is not all, by any means.

        It is instructive to review the various ways (it is all, essent-
ially, a matter of degree) surrealists have applied the method of automatic writing. Paul Éluard used to be content with limiting himself to

the practice of automatism during the initial stages of writing. He looked upon the fruits of automatic writing as the elements upon which he would draw subsequently, when assembling his surrealist poems. In marked contrast, Benjamin Péret believed implicitly in the sacrosanct character of automatic revelation and engaged in automatic writing as an investigative act, one that led him, incidentally, to write poems he was unable to recognize, afterward, as his own. It is not Eluard but Péret whose pre-eminence is unchallenged in surrealism. No surrealist writer would fail to concur with Eluard's admission, "Péret is a greater poet than I." Still, Péret's reputation in surrealist circles as the purest of poets, the one to emulate, does not rest exclusively upon his abiding fidelity to the automatic principle. Even though this is obviously a contributing factor, the consistency with which this singularly unserious poet indulged in automatic writing is not what really counts. The truly important lesson to be learned from Benjamin Péret's astonishing facility when it came to putting automatic writing to poetic purpose emerges, rather, if we reflect upon the remarkably high quality of the stories and verses he produced by way of automatism, over a period of forty years.

Of itself, verbal automatism is capable of creating nothing at all. Its role is liberative, but it frees only that which lies already within us. In the strictest sense of the term, automatism remains a technical device. Thus the success or failure of this explorative method can be evaluated on an individual basis only, in relation to what it uncovers in one writer rather than another. Whatever automatic writing manages to reveal has to have been present before its exploration was undertaken. Automatism is not a universal panacea, then. It does not serve to recharge weakened batteries; nor does it create anything ex nihilo. Instead, its function is restricted to taking soundings, to probing the writer's capability. In some people its operation does not call up to the surface of consciousness anything the least bit noteworthy. When this is the case, its apparent failure simply indicates that there is, undeniably, nothing to reveal. In short, automatic writing does not make a poet, yet it plainly identifies one. It is fruitful so far as it confirms that we indeed are in the presence of a creative writer, whom it has liberated from the restraints--of one kind or another--impeding full expression of a poetic sensibility whose manifestation is now made possible.

Verbal automatism is not a last-ditch defense against stagnation or sterility. And it is not an easy way out for those who aspire to be poets. It tests our poetic potential. Because it does not lie or prevaricate, it does not permit us to lie to ourselves or to those to whom we signal with what we write.

Ask Larry R. Smith. He knows.

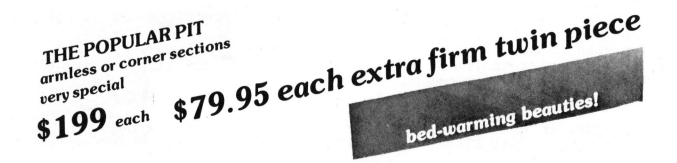

 # The Poetry of Everywhen.

The world of the poem, the possible world created in response to poetry's message is several dimensions removed from the barbarism of power politics and economic censorship which force many artists to die unseen and unheard by almost everyone. This is a preface to a book that can't be written as yet because the poetry of everywhen points to a more pastoral world, a mosaic of Edens, peopled by masters of biokinesis who have unlocked the secrets of nature's ecochronology. It is not a world of pathologic conformity nor a world of debilitating perceptual and nervous disorders identified by carpet-bagging snake oil drummers, optometrists and drug vendors. Man in his anxiety has forgotten the transcendant miracle of thought: that thinking does itself, so it is a fallacy to say "we use our heads." Not only have we forgotten how to think, we have forgotten how to count on help. Bohm's Hidden Variable Theory and Bell's Axiom: the message of today's physics demonstrate that our hard hearted world may indeed be bound to another world outside of space and time. It is a subquantum world of intelligent microcomputers which have fed minds since language became the bell, book and candle in the exorcism of the ape from man. While evidence for nonlocal intelligence seems as inscrutable as a game of chinese checkers, it is validated also by the combinatorial revolution in mathematics. This world is a collection of outwardly measurable continuums, it is agreed, but at the subquantum level: almost smaller than numbers themselves, continuity disintegrates and equations begin to shuttle like mexican jumping beans. Hidden variables, messages transmitted from that other world outside of space and time appear to us everywhere and everywhen. These messages are received through the sub-rational, through the breath, hands and feet, rather than through the ego and are reminiscent of Emerson's transcendental and inspirational voices in the grass. In the world of the poem, several time rifts reveal discontinuities where hidden messages occur: the way we find ourselves in dreams when something crucial is about to happen and these hidden messages become grist for the mill of creation.

Now, poetry is given to the speaker: no exact continuity exists in the template of any poem. Whatever continuity appears is a mirage of misplaced belief in the exclusive reality of space and time. This dangerous and self destructive illusion blocks easy access to super-rational messages from the world of everyhen: a neologism for tomorrow's lexicon. In actuality, time rifts are found within the template of the poem, discontinuities, giving the poet in the words of Krishnamurti "freedom from the known." Hidden messages fuel three rings of fire: enjambment, logos and bare boned functionality; images, revelation of the changing colours of the present, periodic punch and desire, victory over chaos, the poet taking his chances with fortune and the muse; the dark voice, a sonic expansion of articulation, repetition of shifting vowels, speech becomes incantative making brain hooks as Philip Whalen calls them. This is the madness and risk of poetry. Who would deny the receptive nature of the poetic act demands the inclusion of all possibility such as hidden messages from a world where nobody walks with heads above their eyes? The beauty of belief in nonlocal intelligence is that it liberates the poet from becoming a slave to his ambition: freedom from a known. The world of everywhen is a world of true independance where anyone might use Emerson's confident aphorism; "I wish to say, what I feel and think today, with the proviso that tomorrow, perhaps, I shall contradict it all." It is a world of freedom from the burden of being almost unwitting cocreators of this visible universe, as that more intimate world of Nod serves us, everywhere and everywhen, and what the poet creates is payment or tribute to the sublime subquantum world. Without question, in the world of everywhen people may eat the fruit of knowledge and imagination.

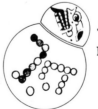 John McAuley
March 23, 1979

Beyond Rationality: The Language of P. Inman's
Platin Poems

        Peter Inman's poetry, especially as represented in his recent book,
Platin (Sun & Moon Press, 1979) takes language to its furthest limits:
beyond Inman's poems are perhaps only the visual-linguistic experiments
of Ray DiPalma's Marquee, Loris Essary's "visual poems," Bruce Andrews'
Film Noir, Richard Kostelanetz's visual fictions and--what I believe are
less successful--the works of conretist poets. But Inman's work is particularly interesting because it does not primarily rely on a linguistic
incorporation of visual elements. Although Inman's poems are visually interesting, and, often, his words are placed on the page perpendicularly and
at angles to each other, the emphasis is particularly a linguistic one. In
that sense, Inman's work is perhaps closest to Andrews of the poets named
above.

        But Inman's work perhaps can be best understood in a context outside
of American poetry altogether. For Platin clearly has relationships with
the zaum poems of the Russian Futurists (Kruchenykh, Khlebnikov, Zdanevich
and others). Like the zaum poets Inman uses language transrationally; his
language moves beyond rational meaning into a private language expressed in
speech sounds.

                    umbril . prifer (in owe of lats)
                    mound tains iffor, thag,eathbr...
                    hicple,brior. ezzlie . silper
                    still hue quines
                    iedimmers. wime knot
                    teebr. acrit an tar elsity. aisley,hinger

                    gine-ive semi. innote cirrus
                    friez. x 3...ips face
                    breal coleor, seep, brask appilies
                    aortit , abilber, cofle , ocal , sere,pil
                    spirements
                    ...   (pepsit,lape)
                    szulc popcorn. cusa this paint

        One immediately senses, however, that there is something different
at work here: the Dadist humor of many of the zaum poems is here translated
into a greater seriousness of intent. First of all, the language of Inman's
poems is the product of a computer society: there is--at least to my way
of thinking--something "mechanistic," almost "mathematical," definitely
"scientific" about Inman's linguistic constructions. And the language of
his poems is thus slightly intimidating: it is as if the reader could
understand the text if only he had the proper experience, the proper train-

ing. Inman's use if "real" or "true" English words and phrases contributes
to this: in the midst of the reader's disorientation these float like
anchors in the threatening sea of meaninglessness. But, of course, the
reader's very recognition of some words makes him all the more conscious
of his inadequacy. And this, in turn, forces one to perceive the very
tentativeness, the arbitrariness of any language. It is only a transposition of a letter or two, the addition or subtraction of a vowel or
consonant that utterly deranges a language. Inman reminds us that from the
Surrealist/Dadist experiments with poetic content and context, it is only
a slip of the tongue into chaos. As he prophetically wrote in his earlier
collection, What Happens Next (Some of Us Press, 1974), "You see first the
threads snapped and then the cables, always tenuous, started to sway in the
wind.... Suddenly it was the most humiliating thing in the world to be naked...".

Ultimately, Inman's reader must question the whole notion of language.
What is a "real" or "true" word? One discovers oneself approaching Inman's
poetry as if attempting to catch the drift of a conversation between speakers
of an unknown language. And this feeling--reinforced by the fragmentariness
of the poems (the ellipses, parentheses and other interruptive devices)--
makes for a constant "craning of the neck," an attempt to make sense of seeming
senselessness. In this, one finds oneself struggling to make meaning, to
make language "come into meaning." Through the experience of Inman's poetry
one comes closer to feeling what the monkey becoming man must have felt in
those milleniums of the transition of sound into speech. Or, perhaps, it is
the other way around: Inman's use of language demands that a contemporary
Adam redisover in himself the ape.

Douglas Messerli

A Way of Happening, a Mouth

The Critical Personality--Words of One Syllable

     "What type of account do you desire?"

     Nonce was in his neighborhood office of Bell Savings and Loan, a new
outfit on Sacramento Street. He had chosen Bell (a) because there was a
line at the more imposing Gibraltar Savings and Loan on California Street
(b) because Bell's office was so tiny--it had been a doomed, one-woman bou-
tique before becoming a bank. That transmogrification had been made with
the installation of a computer terminal, a burglar alarm and safe, and one
middle-aged woman whose plastic badge proclaimed her to be Julie, Assistant
Manager. Bell Savings and Julie appeared to want Nonce.

     "What type of account do you desire?"

     Julie's question hung in the air while Nonce thought it over. He said
"I suppose I desire one which gives me unlimited withdrawal privileges."

     Julie, facing Nonce and establishing eye contact, explained that while
Bell Savings had the legal right to limit both the amount and number of deposits and withdrawals in any account, in practice a depositor had unlimited
withdrawal rights. Nonce smiled financially and said "I want an ordinary
account, please." Julie swivelled 90° to her typewriter and typed some numbers on a green card. She asked Nonce how he spelled his name, for some sort
of identification, what his Social Security number was, when he was born,
where, what his mother's name was.

     "Before?" Nonce asked.

     "Before what?" Julie paused to look at him.

     "Before she was my mother?"

     "Your mother's <u>maiden</u> name?"

     Nonce answered somewhat abstractedly. Then he asked "When I die can my
wife get this money?"

     Julie stopped typing, turned full face to him. She rested her arms on
her desk, her competent hands seeming to reach for his. Her voice was sooth-
ing, her eyes steady and warm. "Of course, of course, Sir. If you desire,
we can make this a trustee account with your wife as beneficiary. That way,
if you become deceased . . .". Her voice sounded like interment.

     "When I die," Nonce said.

     "Sir?" Julie said, drawing back.

     "Not 'If you become deceased.' 'When you die'," Nonce said, taking out
his checkbook and beginning to write. "Should I make this out to Bell Savings
or to cash?"

"To Bell Savings, Sir. We'll process it through that way."

Nonce finished his check. There were a few more details: file signatures, save-by-mail envelopes. Then Julie stood up. As Nonce did likewise, she shook his hand, saying "Now, Sir, Bell Savings and Loan wants to give you a cookbook."

Bell Savings did, for soups. Nonce thanked Julie, walked next door to the Vogue Theater, found out that "A Different Story" would start at 7:30.

The Critical Life--Tradition and Some Individual Talent

Cates: what can ail thee, wretched white man?
Der Heimat zu.

Please do not understand me too quickly.
Flights are to and from fixed points
of reverence.
The family in the north of California,
a certain party in the south,
brightness falling from the air between.

Though inland far
I see from 30,000 feet
the mountains and the shore--
and something more,
that rain of matter upon sense
and nonsense alike . . .

What can I do
to drive remembrance from my eyes,
fast now,
here now,
knowing which route
makes all the difference?

Hunt psychic snipe.
Take short views.
Farm verses.
Build in sonnets.

                                        --Jonathan Middlebrook

NUCLEAR ENERGY

The future of Black American literature will
be determined by the following writers:

june jordan/patricia jones/thulani davis
toni morrison/ntozake shange/ahmos zu--bolton
lorenzo thomas/quincy troupe/b.j.ashanti
rikki lights/alexis de veaux/ishmael reed
jerry ward/stephen henderson/jayne cortez
jodi braxton/audre lorde

& the ghosts of jean toomer/zora neale hurston
richard wright/charlie parker & lester young

everyone else is simply humming
tapping their feet
or talking about three mile island.

                              E. ETHELBERT MILLER
                              April 1979

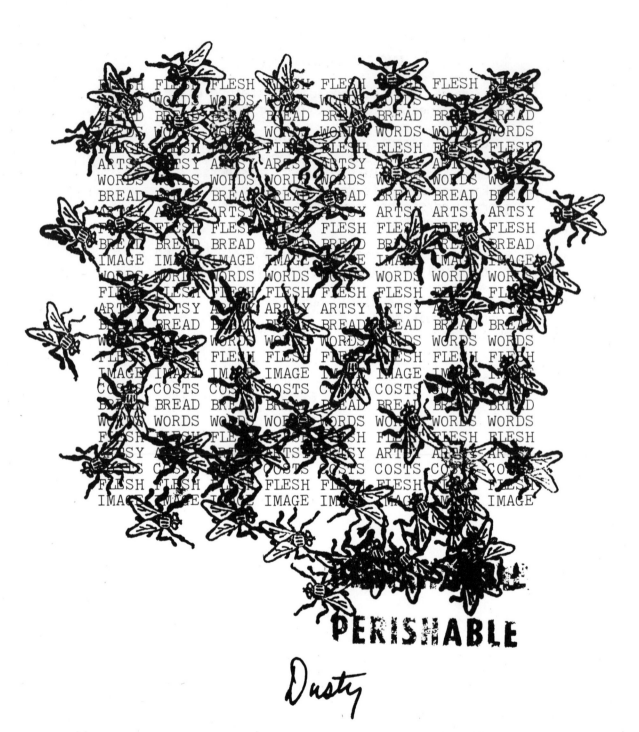

PERISHABLE

Dusty

EUGENE MILLER WHO HATES TO TYPE

APHORISMES

1. I'm not green. I criticise *by chance*, or: "on the other hand."

1.Je suis d'*occasion*.

2. *Countersign*. Avant-Garde's keynote: Be sound of mind !

2.Mot (mode) d'ordre aujourd'hui:
     Faites vous défriser la tête crépusculaire !

3. I know them. Have often been anticipatory. For instance, about silence...

3.Je les connais:j'ai toujours (ou presque) été anticipateur.
  Par exemple,sur le silence.Mais aussi sur "l'avant-garde"...
  Cependant,les tendances ne viennent sous les feux de la rampe
  que filtrées par des actionnaires de la *culture*.

3. But the footlights work against me, as do the shareholders in culture.

4.C'est du Théâtre d'après *nature*.

4. It's nature theatre

5.Ne pas croire que "c'est arrivé".(René Daumal)

5. Don't believe that you can take it all for granted.

6.Le BHARATA appelle çiva du nom de "*grand-père*".

6. in the BHARATA, Shiva is called "Grandfather".

7.Parmi toutes les misères,celle de
  certains enfants (abandonnés,battus,
  affamés) me paraît le plus terrible.

7. Of all misfortunes, the misery of some children...

8.Relire "SEMMELWEISS",de Céline.

8. (Please) read again Céline's SEMMELWEIS

9.L'expérimentation : WALKIE TALKIE.

9. Experiment : WALKIE TALKIE.

10.C'est toujours la pointe (d'esprit) qui plait.

10. pointed wilt always pleases!

Claire-Motte a quitté la scène sous
les fleurs et les ovations
(journal du 20/1/79)

"Clear-Pat" made her exit from
the stage under a shower of flowers
and a standing ovation.

CLAUDE MINIERE (The Never Mind,
Jan.79)

the fear of writings life fear of his own bodies cops corpses drea

ume de l'amour est passée il ne reste

`let's talk before fucking`

don't know if anything la poesia è ancora can be
to lose cold words weave wind come la pratica
la vedi, in ogni caso, praticamente alone MOMA

car au moins écarté du secret qu'il détient

pas voix au chapitre sans soutien appui

la peur en visagée songe   `éprouver sa propre obscurité`

hé règles   `Apporte une Prosodie NeuveParticipantDe`   **s'il sav**

accent   my body spirit

                    tension of   tensed

`l'écriture Parle ce que llecteurlit C'est lui`

                                        mais   **n'abo**

mine sweetly softly

ms rythmes of his courage

I d'on't want anymore **l'éc**

qu'à causer sur la couche:

SOnSouFLe

everything write no more praticabile probabilmente

gone away mise en scène du texte se jouer impossibility

cosi: con questa... E.S.

sans la scène enDeDans maman **espace retenu**

cela ne veut pas dire cela s'écrit **pas sonore seul**

écartelé du près qu'il possède volume intouc

ait un coup du dey

déjà

un coup de

to crack up don't go d on't fly your moon blood

hasard

lira le

of words want to don't know if

R.M. BUCKE AS CRITIC

STEPHEN MORRISSEY

While R.M. Bucke's work is usually considered only in terms of
psychology it also presents us with an interesting theory of
literature. Educated at McGill University Bucke later worked
as a psychiatrist in London, Ontario. His most important work,
Cosmic Consciousness, published in 1901, is in part a critique
of literature from Bucke's own original & unique standpoint.
The poets he deals with are those who, he maintains, have attained
a consciousness of the cosmos. Essentially, Bucke is examining
consciousness & trying to resolve the problem of life-weariness
& anxiety. His solution lies in the intensity of awareness of the
creative individual, the artist. For Bucke, as for Otto Rank
& Abraham Maslow much later, the artist is the individual who really
sees clearly & who is the most healthy-minded.

Bucke's work on the psychology of healthy-mindedness coincides
with that of William James (who briefly discusses Bucke's work
in The Varieties of Religious Experience), & it anticipates that
of Maslow & his idea of the "peak experience". Bucke's importance
is only partially understood: 78 years after the publication of
Cosmic Consciousness he is still considered in the restricted but
important sense of being one of the first scientists to discuss
mystical experience; by applying his work to criticism we may arrive
at an attitude to literature that is fundamentally forward looking
& whole. Perhaps this would also serve as a source of evaluation
for the literature of the future.

Bucke began by placing cosmic consciousness at the center of his
work. His most important example of the artist expressing cosmic
consciousness was Walt Whitman although Bucke also discusses Blake,
Dante, Balzac and others. These writers, Bucke contends, have
certain similarities in both their writing and lives, these
similarities are evidence for what Bucke believed was "the evolution
of the human mind"; this evolution is a movement from an ego-centric
self-consciousness to a cosmic conscious state. Bucke in interested
in the poets whose work shows this "consciousness of the cosmic...
of the life and order of the universe...an intellectual enlightenment
or illumination." Poets whose work shows them moving towards
cosmic consciousness are actually participating in the evolution
of the human mind.

Indeed, an objective of poetry, Bucke suggests, is the possibility
of cosmic consciousness. As such, poetry is a movement away from
the narrowness of ego-centric consciousness. His work in psychology
is revolutionary in that he deals with the intensity of the artist,
rather than with the tunnel vision of ordinary self-consciousness
or with the neurotic & mentally ill. We seem preoccupied today by
the negative, the defeated, and the life-deniers have tended to
overwhelm our literature. For Bucke this life-denial points to the
insecurity the self-conscious mind feels as it atrophies and a
cosmic consciousness appears, however gradual this appearance may be.

Emerson writes, "I think nothing is of any value in books, excepting the transcendental and extraordinary." In other words, our literature, to have any value, must be an investigation of the content of consciousness, of the mind as it really is, to possibly go beyond the mind as it presently is.

As poets we are often not giving to public what it needs; poetry must suggest real meaning & values if it is to have any validity, to ignore this is for poetry to remain with its present negligible importance to society. This is an activity that the individual who is seriously investigating consciousness, his being, naturally does --- because meaning & values, not some ideology of the state or religion, are created by the investigation itself. This calls for a poetry that is a real meditation on experience, relationship and our perception of existence.

The poets who have real importance are those who leave the known, the security of preconceptions, beliefs & traditions, of an intellectual fragmented approach to living. We do not need a philosophy of living or of poetry, what we do need is an attitude that is based on living perceptions. Bucke's criticism is not for some airy abstract poetry or art, but ultimately must lead to a concrete realistic exploration of life.

Bucke has placed what has traditionally been a religious experience at the center of his thinking. His evaluation of literature is fundamentally an organic one: Bucke isn't giving any directives as to style or form or even content, what he is saying about literature is that it must be based on an active perception of the universe, the world around us, and in this it is not to be based on any preconceptions, on any ideology; his criticism isn't ideologically-based, but based on change, on flux. He moves in the same orbit as Heraclitus, Bergson, Teilhard and Whitehead. So, Bucke isn't saying one must write in a certain way or about certain subjects, that is obviously left open to the poet, nor is he giving us any fixed morality or values, but he is giving us the only viable relationship to have with any values, and that is a relationship based on perception. For values to be real they cannot be anchored to any system of values but must be alive, organic, not fixed to any philosophy; that is, not meeting life with preconceptions because life, perception, is moving, changing, while the ideas our "values" are based on are static, dead. This attitude is the opposite of the traditional religious & moral one which is coming from an ego-centric base with its ties to the state, business and organized religion. Bucke is supremely for the individual who can think for himself, who is a pioneer in society in the realm of examining & understanding consciousness. This pioneer spirit calls for leaving behind what has been done before, thinking what others have instructed us to think, accepting others' ideas. It calls for a radical understanding of our existence. To miss this is not to lay the foundation that will allow for the possible emergence of a wider awareness of ourselves & everything around us. I think Bucke would agree with Teilhard de Chardin when he writes, "The consciousness of each of us is evolution looking at itself and reflecting upon itself."

April 23 - 25, 1979.

From: Charlie Morrow

The New Wilderness Foundation Inc.

5/79 2 KOSTELANETZ et al:

T_E HUMBING
T ON QUE   A B LESSING
              K I

CRITICISM :·

1. CONFESSION

2. RE·FLECTION
         VERBERA

3. POLITICAL FUEL / CRITIC EGO SPURT
                    CAREERISM

4. SUGGESTION

5. OFTEN   RESTRICTED 2 WORDS

6. IS   TRANSLATION   INTO   O   M
         ~~HOMAGE~~   THRU   T   E
         COMMENTARY   BY   H   D
         DEVELOPMENT   WITH   E   I
         (RE)ACTION   VIA   R   A

ex: song abt experience
    experience abt poem
    poem abt painting
    painting abt event
    event abt politics

365 West End Ave. New York, N.Y. 10024 (212) 799-0636

THE EXPERIMENTALIST

by Douglas Mumm

Who gives a flying fuck about the small press, anyway? Not me, that's for sure. What a buncha shit-heads.

Christopher was thinking hard as he walked up the low ceiling staircase to his apartment. In his hand, scarred but clean, he held a sheaf of mail, some of it torn open, some not. As he fumbled for his key a rejection slip fluttered out from one of the envelopes and landed about six steps down. Christopher looked at it for a moment, then inserted the key into the lock and entered his flat.

Stupid jerks. They don't know what real fuckin' poetry is. They sit secure in their little towers of university learning and reiterate endless duplications of poets who have long been dead and rotting. Can't they feel anything? Can't they see? They fool themselves to think they publish poetry. Ha! They publish merely flat words on paper. Poetry has to be more. It has to be alive. Poetry has got to reach out and punch the reader in the fuckin' gut. It's got to tear out any feeling there is by it's own accord — by force.

Christopher was young and tried to supress his anger. An anger which he carried with him almost all of the time. For two years he had worked at becoming recognized, worked at getting some of his poetry into print. The poetry itself, he never *worked* at. *That* came on it's own, needing very little effort, surfacing from some dark place inside. But after two years of almost continual rejection slips, he was tired and angry. Mostly angry.

Christopher dropped his mail onto a small, formica-topped table he was using for a desk. The envelopes landed with a dull slap. The current gas bill separated from the pile, slipped over the edge of the table and floated down to the floor, landing behind the kitty-litter box. He looked at it for a moment with tired eyes, then lowered his thin body into a chair by his desk and stared off into the wall directly facing him. He left the computerized bill lay where it was.

Christopher collected his thoughts.

The old forms are dead. Just like the men who wrote them . . . dead. I am alive. I explore new forms. Forms effective by relevancy and emotion.

He knew what made the old forms, the old poets, great. They were excellent refelctions of their times, their environment, their era, their feelings. Christopher strived to do the same with his own work — to be a reflection of *his* times, *his* environment, *his* era, *his* feelings. To do so required new forms.

Blending diverse factors, and unafraid to try something new, he wrote poetry intended to lift a reader from indifferent experience. SUBJECT: he wrote of his environment and times; of things which were presented to his daily existence. He wrote of the doubt, fear, confusion and frustration which he perceived in every segment of life— emotions written blatantly upon every face he confronted. SOUND: without actually rhyming, his poetry contained a rythmic quality. Many sequences of words simulated other sounds, like machinery, moving traffic, or the quiet drone of urban dissatisfaction. VISION: when composing, words arranged themselves upon the page— sometimes in a strict pattern, sometimes in random order, but always pattern, visual appearance, permeated every work.

Opening the remaining sealed envelopes, Christopher resigned himself to finding more rejection slips. It was an old game. Something to be expected . . .

"Sorry, but these are not quite what we're looking for at present . . .", or,

"Unfortunately, we have more material than we can use right now . . ."

Although he had gotten used to the pre-printed slips, his anger had never subsided.

The SAME fucking STANDARD rejection notice! Just like the poetry they publish— standard and all the same.

In the beginning Christopher had tried to rationalize the rejections due to the advanced age of publishers/editors. But he soon found out that a good portion of small press editors were young. And those literate young men marched headlong into the ranks which perpetuated the endless redundancies of old-style literature, each one becoming a clone-like version of those who came before.

A perpetual regurgitation. Endless duplication. Boring duplication.

But WHY, goddamn it, and HOW can they insist upon clinging blindly to something which has been done over and over and over again? Why? Can they possibly be THAT insulated from the world? Endless duplication— boring duplication . . .

∞   ∞   ∞   ∞   ∞

It was a balmy summer night and Christopher had just turned ten last week. Somehow the summer made everything real. It was good to be alive. Life was right here, just waiting to be tasted, to be felt, to be enjoyed.

The stars shone brightly through the clear evening sky as Pete, who lived kitty-corner, and Christopher huddled behind his garage lighting matches.

"Hey, let's go over to my house and watch TV." Pete said as he watched a leaf from the rosebush shrivel under his match.

"Nah . . . " Christopher said, shaking his head. "There's nothing good on." And pausing to scrape an Ohio Blue Tip across the garage wall, he added, "Just summer re-runs . . ."

GEORGE MYERS, JR.

(his biografiend, in fact, kills him
verysoon, if yet not, after)
                              --James Joyce
                              Finnegans Wake

Angels in the Tiring House (Poetry, Printing Arts, 1975)
An Amnesiac on the Verge of Heaven (Poetry, Fireweed, 1976)
NAIROBI (Biofiction and memoir, White Ewe, 1978)

Metafiction is playfulness. George Myers, Jr.'s NAIROBI gives us
the contemporary mode of understanding human life and the world as
"texts" which require hermeneutic "unpacking," and an unwinding of
its maze. In fact, a danger in reading Myers (as pointed out more
succinctly in Richard Peabody's review of An Amnesiac in a recent
Smudge Review) is that we will see in his work everything but its
own texture and structure. The loosely aphoristic and third person
viewpoint of the book leads the reader to see human life itself as
a literary mode in which man writes the text of his own life as he
goes, writes himself into a book or play that is his life (Grayson,
Kostelanetz, Grossinger, et al.). Myers' story is the story of all
stories, of the word which man denies he is, and through which he
realizes then names himself. As we tell about ourselves, we tell
ourselves into existence. In turn, others retell us in gossip, rumor
and review, until we are a fiber of intertwining stories about
ourselves.

Myers' characters live within a personified word, and so sees life
as endless reinterpretation, fluid, marginal and at once centrific.
Generally, it is the specific 'writer's condition' in modern times
that is at the center of this book, be it cartographer, a translator,
"the poet assassinated," or even a censor whose points of omission are
the tales he tells.

Through Myers' own omissions (he's the balloonist who wanted to disappear with no trace) he cannot be read easily. His palimpsest-like text
and strange sayings of his zebras, natives and talking rings, which seem
to be beacons of his memory, require a reconstructive effort from the
reader, who thus makes or remakes story development, plot, from mere surface evidence. The fate of books and men is forever open to be retold,
like the retold African tales Myers restructures. The word is not readily
separable from the rest of the world. Myers separates only a phenomenon
from its essence -- that is, tells an untruth (fiction) without betraying
his subjective authenticity. He profitably dons many disguises by avoiding to write "completely hypothetically and subjunctively." Because such
is the case, the narrator is often untrustworthy, unreliable.

An omniscient narrator is an obvious impossibility to an author convinced of the subjectivity of truth and the impenetrability of others.
As we come to know a speaker, that speaker will perish. Myers feels a

life cannot be "caught" by exhaustive scrutiny of its detailed
sequences. Fragments, invocations and impulses are the norm even
if visually they are blocks of writing and expository prose.
Straying signs and mythologies mingle with the contours of a man's
biography like seeds cast into the world. We ourselves exist between form and formlessness, words and silences, and act out
their dimensions on a dark continent.

The interpretive, redefining and questioning word encircles
our lives.

Heightened and self-conscious.

The pen following an adventure.

Myers works contain no tangible substances to use as example.

Symbols dissolve to sheer process.

Fact can never be realized as long as the subject exists.

LE NOMBRE

cette conjonction suprême avec la probabilité

EXISTÂT-IL

autrement qu'hallucination éparse d'agonie

(retourner le gant)

COMMENÇÂT-IL ET CESSÂT-IL

sourdant que nié et clos quand apparu
enfin orbis pictus
par quelque profusion répandue en rareté

SE CHIFFRÂT-IL

dans ce monde in folio
dance de l'assomeuse pourpre
évidence de la somme pour peu qu'une

ILLUMINÂT-ON

VOILE
VIOLE

STELE AIR

L E H A S A R D

s'ensouvenir
ésotériques fuligineux
aux ultimes frigidaires

fatine

naguères d'où sursauta son délire jusqu'à une cimetière
toxhémique suspenrectu ministre
par la nouvelliste identique du gouffre
parlant de la diététique des gauffres

Soit
Choit   à la une
la plume solitaire et perdue

la guerre douce ôte sa lyre

pour y vierge disparaître

C'ÉTAIT

sans *issu stellaire*

N'AURA EU LIEU

FRAICHEUR DE NACRE

31

PATHMOS

VOILE ALTERNATIVE

DIT: **fond**

gouffre

abîme

RIEN

ATOME POMPE (PAYS)

P

savamment   hautains
indifférremment mais autant

TARTRE CI-PRES

LE LIEU

CA' LE SILENCE D'ORO

CE SERAIT

ni meilleure ni *pire*   avec ses vingt-quatre signes
non   *davantage ni moins*

UEUE
QUEUE

N

A
LABORAISON
OM
E

PAGES — IVOIRE POUDRE D'OR
EVIDER LE SENS ET VIDER
L'ESSENCE D'UN AUTEL PARTICUL
enfin apparue: ah, Lucie à Na
quand ma nièce sourde est
curriculum vitae
EXISTATILLON
DERIZOHAR
TEΛEIΩΩ
COMME QUELQU'UN DONT
VISION DANGER DIEUX IDENTIQUES

LES MAINS ONT CARESSE JADIS LES

LE NOMBRE

cette conjonction suprême avec la probabilité

EXISTÂT-IL

autrement qu'hallucination éparse d'agonie
(retourner le gant)

COMMENÇÂT-IL ET CESSÂT-IL

sourdant que nié et clos quand apparu
enfin orbis pictus
par quelque profusion répandue en rareté

SE CHIFFRÂT-IL

dans ce monde in folio
dance de l'assomeuse pourpre
évidence de la somme pour peu qu'une

ILLUMINÂT-ION

VOILE
VIOLE

STELE AIR

LE HASARD

N'AURA EU LIEU

FRAICHEUR DE NACRE

31

Soit
Choit

à la une
la plume solitaire et perdue

kephtémique suspanvrede ministre

ésotériques liturgismes   s'ensommeillir
aux écornes
fatime

naguères d'où sursauta son délire jusqu'à une cimetière
la guerre douce ôte sa lyre
par la nouvelle idéntique du gouffre
parlant de la diététique des gauffres

pour y vierge disparaître

C'ÉTAIT
sans issu stellaire

RIEN

ca' LE SILENCE D'ORO

PAGES — IVOIRE POUDRE D'OR
EVIDER LE SENS ET VIDER
L'ESSENCE D'UN AUTEL PARTICU
DERIZOHAR
EXISTATILLON
CURRICULUM VITÆ
TELETOW
VISION DANGER DIEUX IDENTIQUES
COMME QUELQU'UN DONT
LES MAINS ONT CARESSÉ JADIS LES
enfin apparue: ah, Lucie à Na
quand ma nièce sourde est

P   ATOME POMPE (PAYS)

PATHMOS

VOILE ALTERNATIVE

TARTRE CI-PRES

LE LIEU

A LaBORAISON ME

DIT: fond
gouffre
abime

CE SERAIT

ni meilleure ni pire
non

avec ses vingt-quatre signes
davantage ni moins

savamment hautains
indifferrement mais autant

N

UEUE
QUEUE

ainsi que par de multiples fusions
zodiaque implique sa doctrine propre   en la figure de phrases puis le
abstraite ésotérique comme quelque théologie : cela du fait uni
l'ordinaire atteinte que de ne s'exprimer sinon avec des moyens typiques
illimité un art des opérations

Concorsi a premi / Maurizio Nannucci,
Fulvio Salvadori / Zona / Firenze
luglio 1977.

Gli inviti ai concorsi a premi di pittura
sono stati ricevuti nel periodo di alcuni
mesi nel corso dell'anno. L'invio era
sensa senso poiché il destinatario non ha
partecipato a questi premi, ma ciò non
vuol dire che l'invio e la non
partecipazione considerati insieme non
assumano un qualche significato. Questa
situazione indica l'esistenza di zone
diverse tra cui ci sono difficoltà di
comunicazione: proprio per questo ci
viene naturale considerare l'invio un
errore. Ci siamo posti, allora, delle
domande sul perché di questa divisione a
compartimenti del sistema dell'arte e
del come essa si struttura. Anche Zona
è un zona. Siamo convinti che cercare
di superarne i confini e tentare di
comprendere i movimenti di chi si muove
in altri spazi rappresenti per contro
anche una chiarificazione sul ruolo e sui
movimenti di chi in Zona è coinvolto.

Per la definizione del fenomeno artistico
possono essere di aiuto alcune
considerazioni sulla struttura gerarchica
della società borghese. Distinguiamo,
rispetto al potere d'acquisto, tra: chi
può comprare opere originali, chi deve
limitare il proprio consumo all'arte
riprodotta, chi ha un contatto con l'arte
solo atraverso i mass media. Questa
classificazione può esser fatta coincidere
grosso modo con la divisione abituale del
corpo sociale in classe borghese, classe
media, e proletariato. La posizione
particolare della classe media, costretta
tra il vertice e la base della piramide
sociale, fa sì che essa partecipi sia del
carattere di emulazione proprio della
borghesia, sia delle tendenze rivoluzionarie
delle masse proletarie. E' convinzione
borghese che l'individuo esprima la sua
potenza nella esibizione del consumo
privilegiato. In tal modo egli induce nel
proprio intorno un comportamento di
emulazione che mette in moto il
meccanismo sociale della produzione. Ne
deriva una tendenza alla disintegrazione
sociale, alla autoaffermazione attraverso
la diversità, una situazione in cui ha
origine la ricerca della caratteristica
marginale da esibire, della sensazione
raffinata, irripetibile, di ciò che distingue
e il cui consumo è precluso alla
maggioranza. Dei beni di lusso l'unico a
buon mercato è il bene culturale che
non richiede nella maggioranza dei casi
che del tempo libero e una modesta
spesa di energia intellettuale. Pertanto
la cultura apre una via d'accesso tra la
classe media e la classe borghese.
Tuttavia nell'artista o nell'intellettuale
impegnato nella scalata sociale la cattiva
coscienza opera in modo che esso
rimanga esposto alle istanze che
provengono dalla base. Ciò fa di lui un
sismografo estremamente sensibile, un
ago che oscilla verso l'alto e verso il
basso e che segna quando si esprime
nell'opera esattamente la temperatura
dell'intorno: ne esprime la cultura. La
produzione artistica circola all'interno
della classe media soprattutto come arte
riprodotta. Per arte riprodotta s'intende il

fenomeno della diffusione e della
volgarizzazione dell'arte. L'intellettuale
che si tiene informato non ha un
rapporto di possesso con il prodotto
artistico, che rimane privilegio del
denaro, tuttavia può appropriarsi dell'idea.
Se un frequentatore di gallerie provvisto
di denaro diventerà con ogni probabilità
un collezionista, in tutti gli altri casi
tenterà di trasformarsi in artista. La
classe media è il terreno di cultura
dell'arte borghese. La circolazione dell'arte
riprodotta è condizionata dalla
stratificazione del corpo sociale.
Delimitiamo i vari intorni introducendo
un criterio geografico. Distingueremo tra:
paese, provincia, regione, città, nazione,
continente, mondo. La città è un
passaggio obbligato e un punto di
riferimento: essa rappresenta nello stesso
tempo un trait d'union e una divisione
netta. Ogni zona o intorno ha una
propria autonomia ed è legata con una
unità culturale determinata
dall'intrecciarsi delle relazioni sociali.
Nella regione che circonda questo
nucleo l'espressione artistica è costretta
in un'orbita specifica in cui solo
raramente sono permessi salti quantici.
Ad ogni intorno corrisponde una
organizzazione istituzionale ed economica
propria. Questo sistema complesso ha due
motivi, quello della selezione e quello
del mercato. Riguardo alla selezione
l'organizzazione gerarchica ha come scopo
il filtro ideologico. Essa condiziona la
penetrazione e la circolazione
dell'informazione tra i diversi livelli.
Più si scende di livello e più pesante
diviene il controllo ideologico e
istituzionale. Questa struttura fa sì che
predomini alla base una tendenza verso la
conservazione, mentre le innovazioni, o
le invenzioni, sono permesse solo nella
zona in cui si muovono le gallerie con
contatti internazionali. Le opere
dell'avanguardia possono essere conosciute
ai diversi livelli e tornare alla base solo
attraverso il filtro della informazione
volgarizzata. Il fenomeno della
volgarizzazione può essere paragonato ad
un apparato digestivo che lascia passare
ciò che è ritenuto assimilabile dal
corpo sociale e scarta tutto ciò che vi può
essere di pericoloso. Le sue armi sono la
semplificazione e la sacralizzazione. Di
solito un movimento artistico si diffonde
attraverso la figura di un rappresentante
che già di per sé è un volgarizzatore del
movimento stesso. Questa tendenza alla
mitizzazione della figura dell'artista
s'incontra con gli interessi di una classe
dirigente in cui predomina ancora
l'ideologia del merito e del primato.
L'informazione predigerita, omogeinizzata
attraverso il filtro della volgarizzazione
da luogo poi a quello stile composito
proprio dell'arte di provincia in cui
surrealismo, pop e figurativo possono
coesistere. Le ragioni di mercato
operano in modo che qualsiasi territorio
debba essere sfruttato ed esplorato.
Possiamo rappresentarci il sistema
dell'arte in una figura che partendo
da un'ampia base va rastremandosi in un
vertice, ossia la raffigurazione del
rapporto tra estensione e intensione.
Infatti se consideriamo il mercato
provinciale dell'arte troveremo le ragioni
della sua esistenza nella necessità di

raggiungre un grande numero di piccoli
collezionisti potenziali. Al vertice della
piramide troveremo invece il fenomeno
dell'avanguardia il cui territorio
inesplorato è l'idea, l'idea/sensazione
inusitata, vendibile a chi ha già
percorso tutti i gradini e desidera la
novità. La componente ideologica borghese
sottostante all'avanguardia è la ricerca
del record. Il lavoro dell'artista di
provincia trova sostegno invece negli
attestati di merito. Distinguiamo tra
lavoro vivo e lavoro morto, tra vertice e
base. Il lavoro morto tende a depositarsi
sul fondo per la forza di attrazione della
base, filtrato attraverso i livelli. Si
formano delle stratificazioni, simili a
stratificazioni geologiche, che rispecchiano,
in modo approssimato, la storia dell'arte.
Un viaggio attraverso i livelli è anche
un viaggio nel tempo. Questa struttura ha
il suo corrispettivo, e trova il suo
sostegno, nella sopravvivenza di istituzioni
accademiche e burocratiche che riflettono
il permanere di vecchi apparati propri di
modi di produzione del passato. A loro
volta queste istituzioni, forti di una
autorità che proviene loro dalla inerzia
sociale, coinvolgono le istituzioni locali:
amministrazioni comunali, aziende
turismo, circoli culturali, ecc. Tutte
queste connotazioni, geografiche,
ideologiche, di mercato, istituzionali,
contribuiscono a definire gli intorni
culturali che determinano le modalità di
apparizione e di presentazione delle
operazioni artistiche. Avremo allora di
volta in volta le collettive organizzate
dalla pro loco o dall'azienda turismo, le
mostre al festival dell'Unità, o i concorsi
a premio.

Maurizio Nannucci
Fulvio Salvadori

On the Question of Radical Experimental
Tendencies in Music, Art and Literature

When the history of the arts in the
twentieth century comes to be written,
the avant-garde figures of its second
half will be seen as those who counter-
vened the experimental tendencies of
its first half--or those who combined
them with more traditional modes.

The end of the century, then, will
have seen, in music, a return to tonality; in the visual arts, a return to
figuration; in letters, a return to
the representation of life.

                    --Madison Morrison

OPAL LOUIS NATIONS

A Critical commentary on radical experimental tendencies in contemporary literature

Quotations on U.S. writers and poets on the New York Stock Exchange on trading up to the closing - Wednesday Oct. 18th. 1978.

Stock	Sales PE hds	High	Low	Close		Net Change
Abbott, K.	9 429	35¼	35	35¼	-	¼
Abish, W.	250	30	29¼	29¼	-	½
Abse, D.	15 1378	34 5/8	34¼	34¼		
Ackerman, D.	9 83	23 1/8	22¾	22¾	-	¼
Ackerson, D.	9 520	24¾	23¼	23 7/8	-	5/8
Ahern, T.	5 1328	33½	32¼	32¾	-	½
Amabile, G.	8 132	23¼	22	22¼	-	1 1/8
Anania, M.	8 31	17¾	17 3/8	17 5/8	-	¼
Andre, M.	9 532	17½d	17 1/8	17¼	-	¼
Andrews, B.	7 17	17½	17 3/8	17½	-	1/8
Angelou, M.	8 259	35 3/8	34¾	35	-	1/8
Antin, D.	6 727	33 7/8	32¾	33	-	¾
Ashbery, J.	8 565	49 3/8	48	48½	-	7/8
Atchley, D.	10 370	30	29 1/8	29 5/8	-	1/4
Banks, R.	4 1651	15 1/8	14	14¼	-	7/8
Batki, J.	8 59	51	50 3/8	50 5/8	-	3/8
Bell, M.	6 127	38	36 7/8	37 1/8	-	7/8
Benedikt, M.	9 669	27 3/8	26 7/8	27¼	-	1/8
Bergé, C.	8 813	34	33¼	33 5/8	+	1/8
Berkson, B.	14 882	28¼	27¾	28		
Berne, S.	12 310	27¼	26¾	26¾	-	¼
Berrigan, D.	48 1896	6	5¾	5¾	-	¼
Berrigan, T.	7 164	48½	47¼	47¼	-	1 1/8
Bertolino, J.	8 3383	63 1/8	62 1/8	62 3/8	-	3/8
Blazek, D.	12 406	16	15½	15¾	-	5/8
Bly, R.	11 47	21 3/8	20¼	20¼	-	3/4
Bockris, V.	10 396	19 7/8	19	19 1/8	-	3/8
Bogle, K.	5 36	27 7/8	27	27¼	-	¾
Brainard, J.	. 259	15½	15	15	-	3/8
Brautigan, R.	9 1297	46¼	45½	46¼	+	½
Bremser, R.	9 687	54¼	53½	53¾	-	¼
Brody, J.	35	12½	12	12	-	3/8
Bromige, D.	3 888	27¾	26	26½	-	1 3/8
Brownstein, M.	15 733	55¾	54 7/8	55½	+	1/8
Bukowski, C.	13 119	32 7/8	32¼	32¼	-	¾
Carroll, J.	16 1212	41½	40½	41 1/8	-	¼
Carroll, P.	16 171	42 3/8	41 5/8	42	-	¼
Clark, T.	9 144	26 5/8	26	26	-	½
Codrescu, A.	9 39	19 3/8	19 7/8	18 7/8	-	¾
Coolidge, C.	8 11	51 7/8	51¾	51¾	-	¼
Corso, G.	7 98	39¼	38½	38½	-	7/8
Creeley, R.	6 596	25 1/8	23¾	24	-	1
Dickey, J.	693	23¾	23 3/8	23½	-	¼
Di Palma, R.	12 518	18 5/8	18 1/8	18 1/8	-	3/8
Di Prima, D.	7 30	16	15 1/8	15 1/8	-	¼
Dorn, E.	10 106	22 3/8	22	22	-	3/8
Duncan, R.	13 1498	65 7/8	63½	65	-	3/8
Economou, G.	6 234	31	30½	30 5/8	+	1/8
Edson, R.	7 363	28 5/8	28 1/8	28 1/8	-	5/8

Stock	Sales PE hds	High	Low	Close	Net Change
Elmslie, K.	6 195	32 1/2	32 3/8	32/3/8	− 1/8
Enslin, T.	7 1056	14 7/8	13 7/8	14 1/4	− 1/2
Eshleman, C.	12 565	33 1/2	32 3/4	33	− 1/4
Fagin, L.	10	4	9 1/2	9 3/4	9 1/2
Federman, R.	12	297	14 3/8	13 3/4	14 1/4
Ferlinghetti, L.	8 1210	15 3/4	15 1/4	15 1/4	− 1/2
Fox, H.B.	7 377	18 1/2	17 7/8	17 7/8	− 3/4
Frank, P.	50	7 7/8	7 1/2	7 1/2	− 3/8
Friedman, K.	7 274	18 7/8	18 1/4	18 1/2	− 3/8
Gallup, D.	6 211	43 1/8	40 5/8	41 1/2	− 1 3/8
Ginsberg, A.	10 17	20 3/4	20 5/8	20 5/8	− 3/8
Giorno, J.	12 674	73	71 1/8	72	− 3/4
Gray, D.	8	113	54 3/4	54 1/4	54 1/4
Guest, B.	8	242	32 7/8	32 5/8	32 3/4
Hacker, M.	9 177	52	51	51	− 1/4
Halpern, D.	10 154	35 3/8	34 3/4	34 3/4	− 3/4
Higgins, D.	5 204	20	19 3/8	19 1/2	− 1/2
Hirschman, J.	8 1999	26 1/4	25 1/8	26 1/4	+ 5/8
Hollo, A.	10	78	8 1/8	7 7/8	8
Hompson, D.D.	10X 1187	58 5/8	57 7/8	57 7/8	+ 1/2
Ignatow, D.	7 187	42	41 1/4	41 1/2	− 3/8
Joans, T.	12 177	46 1/2	45 3/8	45 3/4	− 1/2
Kaufman, B.	7 617	23 1/4	22 3/4	23	− 1/8
Kelly, R.	8 412	35 1/8	34 3/4	34 7/8	− 1/8
Koch, K.	11	119	29 3/4	29 5/8	29 5/8
Kostelanetz, R.	18 73	6 1/4	5 3/4	5 7/8	− 1/4
Kruchkow, D.	9 1255	10 1/8	10	10	
Lamantia, P.	836	11 1/4	10 7/8	10 7/8	− 1/8
Lax, R.	8 689	55 1/2	54 3/8	54 1/2	− 3/4
Levertov, D.	8 354	19 3/8	18 5/8	19	− 1/4
Lopate, P.	8 259	12 1/2	12 1/8	12 1/8	− 3/8
Lowell, R.	6 164	11 5/8	11 1/8	11 1/4	− 1/4
McClure, M.	15 768	43 1/4	42 1/2	42 3/4	− 3/8
MacAdams, L.	9 13	15 1/4	15 1/8	15 1/4	− 1/8
MacLow, J.	104	4 7/8	4 1/2	4 3/4	
Malanga, G.	9 893	19 3/8d	18 7/8	19	− 1/4
Mathews, H.	6 107	11 3/8	11 1/8	11 1/4	+ 1/8
Mayer, B.	7 111	27 5/8	27 3/8	27 1/2	+ 3/8
Meltzer, D.	8 190	36 5/8	35 3/4	36 5/8	+ 5/8
Merwin, W.S.	8 398	26 3/4	26 1/2	26 1/2	− 1/8
Metcalf, P.	12 99	42 1/4	41 1/4	41 3/8	− 3/4
Morris, R.	14 234	37 1/4	35 7/8	37	+ 7/8
Norse, H.	12 654	13 7/8	12 7/8	12 7/8	− 3/4
Olson, T.	7 305	22	20 5/8	21	
Oppen, G.	5 353	24 3/8	24 1/8	24 1/8	− 1/4
Orlovsky, P.	7 477	24 1/8	23 1/2	24	+ 3/8
Padgett, R.	6 272	28 7/8	28 1/8	28 1/8	− 3/8
Plymell, C.	7 68	38 7/8	38 1/4	38 1/2	− 1/4
Porter, B.	5 449	25 5/8	25 1/8	25 1/8	− 1/2
Rakosi, C.	7 254	30 3/4	29 1/8	29 1/2	1
Reed, I.	9 1142	28 7/8	28 1/8	28 1/4	− 1/2
Rexroth, K.	8 1032	36 1/8	34 7/8	35 1/2	− 1/4
Reznikoff, C.	9 34	47 3/4	47 3/8	47 3/4	
Robson, E.	11 135	20	19 1/2	19 1/2	− 1/2

Richard,

I'm 39 years old (1979) -- I've done
a lot of my own experimenting and experimentalizing:
tape recordings, acid, free association, trance, found
poems, constructed plot stories, cut-up stories,
top-of-the-head absurdities, song, imagism,
syllogism & just plain jism. But I'm 39 years old
and I've come to some conclusions about writing
and about myself, about why I write & edit & why
I don't read.

I'm you might say following a trail
now that leads to the end of my life I'm in the woods
my woods and my experimenting is a much more
sober affair than before, my radicalism is not a
red-armband on May Day I am really living in
these words I can't afford failure

and yet I know
how shabby words have become in my lifetime

and
yet we have built our brains on words we hope they
hold the world together I'm no more happy to see
exploding words than I am to see an exploding
envelope the real danger is in meanings that slither
away, that's not experimentalism it's the lower
forces the Red Queen making the meanings she
wants, it's sloth it's bureaucrat-words.

I'd like to
have more encouraging words for you, Richard,
I don't feel I can speak for others, but let me
speak TO WRITERS: WRITE WELL however
you do it

and TO CRITICS: SHUT UP.

I guess
that's it -- a few other comments in other forms,
in which I speak as myself. May I never do otherwise.

Sasha Newborn

a heuristic

My critical ear asks one question:

saying what?

The answers have clarified every kind of writing for me;

this one test has formed my tastes,

and it has narrowed my appreciation to only a few writers,

the few who know <u>why</u> they are writing

-- whose writing is active knowing --

and who are writing <u>to me</u>,

just as **I** offer this test <u>to you</u>,

a heuristic.

NIL INEPTI

As an editor, **I** have not been happy
with current writing in the U.S. as
I've found it. We are living through
realities that no one writes about --
in twenty years no one will know us,
in fifty years our stories will die
with us. Yet we are the link -- at
least to conserve the letter if not
the spirit of the tradition. Tradition?
I mean the idea that the best that is
thought & said & done & built is worth
carrying on. That idea motivates us
to publish -- at Mudborn we say
Nil Inepti.

The problem in England is massive, as weighty as
the two big universities and their continuing
influence in the Arts Council, all main publishing
houses and in the media. There is a huge swell in
good new writing in England. Leading magazines are
Joe DiMaggio and Curtains. Bill Griffiths who
publishes his own gear under his own imprint, Pirate
Press, is probably the most radical English poet
to emerge in this century with his incredible
sleight-of-hand reordering of syntax into near-
painterly word-groupings, and there is a strong
neo-Dada movement in the wake of Tom Raworth.
But on the other hand there is the Oxbridge mafia
with their dog-in-the-manger heroes, Ted Hughes and
Philip Larkin, with their dreary prose writers
weighing the validity of "the novel."
     So nobody knows what's going on in England. It
doesn't get reviewed, it only gets published by poets
themselves. Most of the great sixties bookshops have
closed down so self-published stuff doesn't get distributed properly and is anyway accused of nepotism.
     There is such a weighty, panic-stricken terror
of X the free-ranging vision in the academies,
such a religious conviction that change-making writing
will somehow destroy the language, that the bastards
might just win. They nearly disappeared in 70. Here they
 are back again.
     Main mafiosi are Amis and son, Hamilton, Brownjohn,
Osborne (not a poet of any kind but the Arts Council
literary officer), Clive James, Peter Porter, Anthony
Thwaite. They more or less run things. We sing in a
cupboard unable to hear one another clearly.

                              Jeff Nuttall.
                              3 December 1978.

A SURVEY FOR CRITICS

The following questionnaire is intended for critics of all disciplines.
It is included in this publication as both my contribution as well as to
assess critics' opinions on their role in the creative process. If you
are interested in the outcome of this research, please fill out the
questionnaire within two months after receiving your copy of Critical
Assemblying. The form should be sent to: Holly O'Grady, 86 Kenmare St.
Apt. 10, New York, N.Y. 10012. I will subsequently tabulate the findings
and, if you wish to receive a copy, please send along with your questionnaire, a self-addressed stamped envelope. Thank you for your interest.
All information, by the way, will be kept confidential.

1. Please list the discipline/disciplines that your criticism encompasses.

    _____

    _____

2. Please list the publications in which your essays have appeared in
    the last year (1978).

    _____

    _____

    _____

    _____

3. Check which of the groups below would most likely read your essays:

Artists	( )	Actors	( )	Novelists	( )	Architects	( )
Writers	( )	Directors	( )	Philosophers	( )	Doctors	( )
Businessmen	( )	Academics	( )	Critics	( )	Lawyers	( )
Poets	( )	Film Makers	( )	Photographers	( )		

4. In the modern period* list the one or two major historical events,
    works of art, literature, theater, dance, music, film or photograhpy
    which you believe have most strongly affected your discipline/
    disciplines.

    _____

    _____

    _____

    _____

    _____

*Please include the time span that you personally use to define the
 modern period.

cut along dotted line

5. Within the last 10 years specifically list one or two events, works of art, literature, theater, dance, music, film or photography which have been most germinal in your discipline or disciplines.

_____

_____

_____

6.a. Please check one of the following statements which you feel best reflects your own views on the role of criticism withing the creative process.

( ) Criticism often predicts eventual trends in art/music/dance/ literature/film/photography/architecture/video.

( ) Since criticism often takes a judgmental position (either explicitly or implicitly), standards of excellence are established as a result thereby influencing art.

( ) Critical ideas often parallel those in the arts and therefore create a dialog between artist and critic.

( ) Criticism only has meaning to other critics.

( ) Criticism can only comment on art but not be a part of the creative process since it occurs after the fact.

( ) Other_____

_____

_____

  b. Briefly give reasons for above choice.

_____

_____

_____

7. Describe educational background in terms of major area of study and degrees recived.

_____

_____

8. Please check age range.

18-24 ( )   30-34 ( )   40-44 ( )   55-64 ( )

25-29 ( )   35-39 ( )   45-54 ( )   65 and over ( )

cut along dotted line

THE GREAT AMERICAN POETICAL CONSPIRACY

Art is our only reminder that we are not savages, art is our only reminder that we are not cannibals or robots. Art prevents our sanity from going beserk when we are constrained by war, camps, jails and asylums. Esthetic revolution is a process of natural selection of profound art-rituals capable of keeping our communication open and of bouncing ideas from artist to the public and feed-back to the artist. Once again the only alternative is surrearchy, that which connects the subconscious level of dreams and central memory with the memory of that thought that never happened. Surrearchy, a step child of Surrealism and Anartchy, is the only alternative for non-fossilized brains. If the humanoids of the last two decades of this century do not become space masters, humanity will remain forever a disease of the Earth, a "mal du terre". The only limits of acheivement are guts, nerve, daring and mental power.

Right now we are in a deep crisis, called the "century of crisis" of cultural and social descent and disintegration. The Great American Poetical Conspiracy proclaims 1979, the Year of American Poetry, and an open fight against anonimity, apathy and day by day existential depression.

Let's expose everyone who conceals his emotions and the need for freedom. Poetry is not dead, it's only overpolluted and over-populated. It's overpolluted by common taste and overpopulated with the living dead, caught in a rat race for fame and money. The government shows a total indifference to a poetical environment, a total indifference to the social values of emotions. We have to protect ourselves, the endangered poetical species and our environment. Otherwise in our lifetime we will see "the destruction of the forest by overpopulation of elephants" and their ultimate starvation.

There is no human harmony without play, poetry, music, and emotions. The fight for the freedom of poetry, enslaved by 1.misrepresentation, 2.disposibility,3.educational processing, and 4.packaging is a painful process. The question is, Can you take it? Fight fake art, fight poor taste, kitsch, laugh and applause tracks. Fight brainwashing and subliminal propaganda. Don't wait till the H-mushrooms light up the skies. Look for an antidot. The Great American Poetry Conspiracy invites all artists to unite in a Guerilla movement of active participation in the human future, a new stage of social conscience and an awareness about life and death. Diaspora of artists unite! The time is coming for an anonimous elite. Let's force every community to print free books, to give up old buildings to artists. Fear of freedom is driving many to passivity, suicide, withdrawel, indifference and silence.

Art and literature need to be reoriented to an individual choice with universal valences, to a highly charged state with no violence, to a large public demanding an active participation. Beware that contemporary art can easily become temporary art. Keep your disponibility awake and aware, practice active dreams, and take issues to the public. March on our capital for a abetter esthetic existence; for a minimum of human needs and a maximum of freedom for retributive contribution. PASS - Poetical Anarchistic Secret Society is just the messenger. You, the individual is the new ground for historic change. Epatez l'Avant-garde!

Valery Oisteanu

Actually, Mr. Nixon's advice to a young man in one of Ezra
Pound's poems is not so bad - "If you don't know a masterpiece at
first sight give up verse, my boy." It's a great age in poetry,
but the English Professors, inadequately educated poets and
editors, the lousy anthologizers, the "respectable" New York City
publishers and their coherts, the University presses, and the
phoney poetic pretenders are ruining it for the truly great poets.
Spurred on by the relatively mediocre achievements of Lowell and
Berryman, the official poets continue to pour out the junk and
are recognized and applauded by stupids untrained in World Lyric
Poetry. The government and private grants go to even more and
more mediocre poets, and even the small press scene is degenerating.
There has probably never been an age when such poor contemporary
poetry has been so massively accepted - and in spite of the fact
that good poetry of the past is readily available, great poetry of
the present is ignored.

It has frequently been said about concrete poetry that "this is so
easy, anybody could do this" with a resultant dismissal of the whole
art form. It is easy to write concrete poetry at a fairly competent
level, and if its so easy, why don't more people go ahead and do it!
It is "in the air" like the sonnet was in the 15th and 16th centuries,
and I suggest people give up their Main Street/Babbitt prejudices.

Similar types of charges were leveled against modern abstract art
in the beginning, but then slowly the boobs began realizing it was
hard to have a good, balanced sense of line, design and color as
Mondrian, or hard to drop paint on a canvas as well as Jackson
Pollock did.

There are good and bad (some) concrete poems like there are good and
bad (most of them) regular poems. A check on the backgrounds of the
top West European, South American and U.S.A. concrete artists would
reveal that they are among the most highly educated, articulate, and
best artistically trained of modern people (and by the way more often
than not the best "regular" poets too). And if you think its easy
to write concrete poems as good as some you see around, just try it
and I think you will find that you fall short. It usually takes
practice and years of work and study.

Michael Joseph Phillips

frontières

frontières

PARIS 1979

Tibor Papp

t t **t** t t t

■ the characteristic feature of litterature is its innate economy ———— today's literary works have no superfluous elements —— not that the error of a badly divided word ————
■ litterature primarily relies on language ————
———— even today (for how long   I don't know —— no doubt for some time to come)————
———— the writer cannot indifferently ignore the efforts of linguistics ————
———— its a good thing for him to know about the essays analyzing works close to his heart ———— or about those besieging the linguistic   perhaps structural   ramparts characteristic to one or more of them ————
———— the linguistic part of a contemporary literary text is the combined action of interblending signifieds & signifiers ————
———— mutually ———— working   to span & decompose struc tures   breaking down the principles of the language of communications (1)

---

les grecs   à l'origine ☺ les grecs
: trois pieds, dossier, siège 😎
érection, photocorrection
drôle de tête la nudité
s'étale
comme un terrain d'aviation

ici   et la

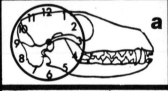

a

dans le brouillard d'une couv
erture poème des mots à la
motte silhouettes courtes c
onfuses pour peu qu'on y aj
oute une louche la confrontat
des textes avec ripères

à l'origine il y avait l'énig̃ration

■ (1) among the most significant characteristic of today's litterature is that ————
UN UŇCONDITIONAL ACTUAL SITUATION
is replaced by
A HYPOTHETICAL LITERARY ONE
making it possible to interrupt temporal continuity (!) ————
—— events in an actual situation are inseperable from time ————
———— impossible in an actual situation to repeat (that is begin again with something from a given point) and have ————
time also revert to the beginning of the segment ————
———— today's litterature however allows it ————
———— segments may be started over again innumerable times (2)

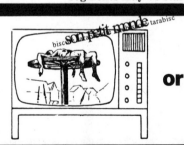

or

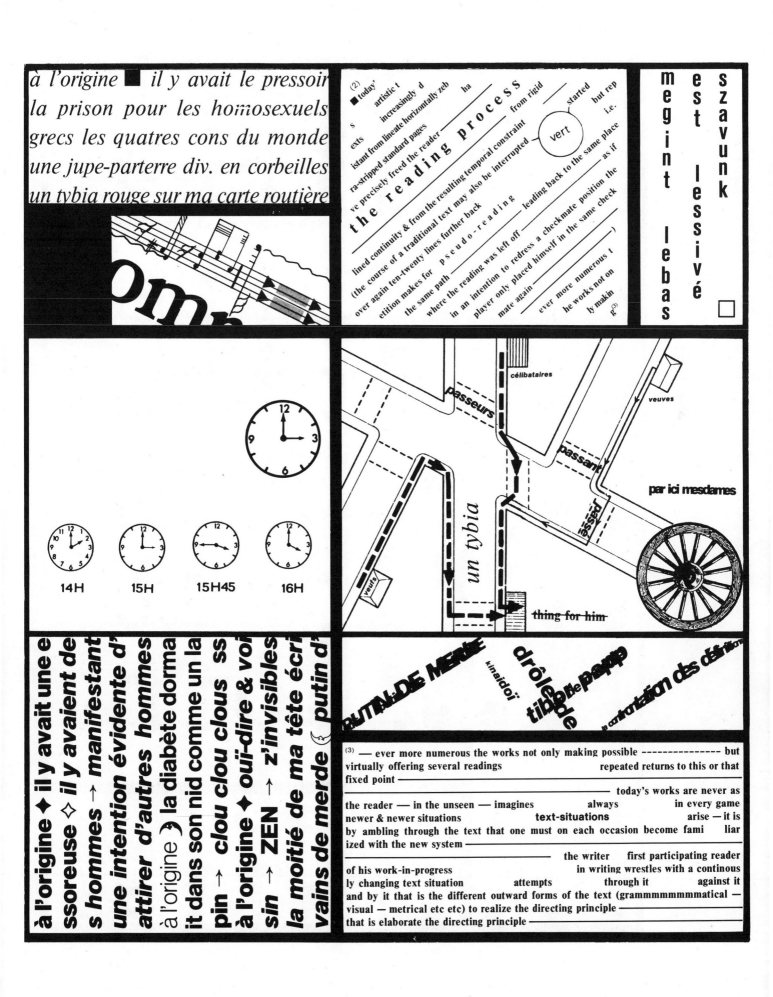

à l'origine ■ il y avait le pressoir
la prison pour les homosexuels
grecs les quatres cons du monde
une jupe-parterre div. en corbeilles
un tybia rouge sur ma carte routière

omn

---

(2) today'
■ artistic t
s increasingly d
ra-stripped standard pages
istant from lineate horizontally zeb ha
ve precisely freed the reader

the reading process

from rigid
started
but rep
i.e.
vert

lined continuity & from the resulting temporal constraint
(the course of a traditional text may also be interrupted
over again ten-twenty lines further back
etition makes for p s e u d o - r e a d i n g
the same path
where the reading was left off
leading back to the same place
as if
in an intention to redress a checkmate position the
player only placed himself in the same check
mate again
)
ever more numerous t
he works not on
ly makin
g(3)

---

megint lebas

est lessivé

szavunk

□

14H   15H   15H45   16H

---

célibataires
passeurs
passant
passé
veuves
par ici mesdames
un tybia
veufs
thing for him

PUTAIN DE MERDE   kinaidoï   drôle de   tibia de papa   confrontation des définitions

---

à l'origine ✦ il y avait une e
ssoreuse ◇ il y avaient de
s hommes ↑ manifestant
une intention évidente d'
attirer d'autres hommes
à l'origine ☽ la diabète dorma
it dans son nid comme un la
pin ↑ clou clou clous ss
à l'origine ✦ ouï-dire & voi
sin ↑ ZEN ↑ z'invisibles
la moitié de ma tête écri
vains de merde ⟨ putin d'

---

(3) — ever more numerous the works not only making possible -------------- but
virtually offering several readings   repeated returns to this or that
fixed point ——————————————————————————
—————————————————————— today's works are never as
the reader — in the unseen — imagines   always   in every game
newer & newer situations   **text-situations**   arise — it is
by ambling through the text that one must on each occasion become fami   liar
ized with the new system ——————————————————
the writer   first participating reader
of his work-in-progress   in writing wrestles with a continous
ly changing text situation   attempts   through it   against it
and by it that is the different outward forms of the text (grammmmmmmmatical —
visual — metrical etc etc) to realize the directing principle ——————
that is elaborate the directing principle ——

xperi
litra
cn.be
lotta
trubble
dijest
i.ofn
stum
fulla

mentl.....

chure....

a.hole...

funn.....

iz.......

m-wise..

gitsa....

mick.....

nuthin...   cp

The Talismanic Value of Words in Private Thought

Nick Piombino

Writing requires an effort of the mind to sustain a narrated
sequence of images of objects and ideas for the purpose of
communicating them in an informative and comprehensible order. Long
standing absences of mind, possible when reading (where the mind
might follow word-code signals, nouns are familiarly patterned and
the details are exemplifications) are not possible when doing
conventional writing. Maybe wordlessness of mind, imagelessness,
led to the creation of "ennui," the reader's malaise, this sickness
of communication raised to the form of a type of illness. Blankness
is the real experience every writer knows best, most convincingly
written about by such writers as Kafka, Pavese and Valéry in their
journals. Because of its receptive and passive character thinking
often trails off into blankness. And attempts to think rigorously
often lead to ennumeration of instances, evidences, naming and
classification of these evidences and symbolic transformative modes
like mathematics.
    Nothingness is often the result of mental conflict. Robert
Motherwell once wrote: "Blankness is the failure of alternatives
to come to mind." In the emptiness of our minds words pass by,
sometimes unattached to their original contexts, juxtaposed, chaotic.
It is strange how often thoughts have so little to do with our
verbal and written communications. The apparently random quality
of thought maybe frightens us into being too cautious. Naturally we
must struggle to use words to coordinate activities much the same
way we use mathematics to order the machines that produce our
necessities. But neither the machines nor this stupendous creation
of social language have helped us very much in our overall relations
with one another. Might not a big part of the problem stem from
our use of language as a social instrument or "machine"?
    The mechanical mode of using language-grammatical meaning-makes
it possible to share information efficiently. Most of the information
has to do with the manipulation of objects. But we might notice that
while we are exchanging information we are simultaneously controlling
the energies of certain word-associations to link up the word with
its object, much as the object is invested with its totemic relation
to its owner. Still, words have an existence completely their own. They
are archeologically studiable objects, as real as diamonds and limestone,
and reveal much about the process of thought.
    Reading poetry points the attention of the mind's eye on this
aspect of thought: that thought's relationship with language may
be compared with the relationship of objects to their space. Language's
"space" is thought. Outside this space it is in a world of objects.
What takes place during such a drastic movement of the objects of
thought from one habitation to another?
    The substance of average thought actually has little need of
the imaging associations of nouns. This is clearly seen in poetry.
Blake's tigers are images of an image, seals warding off entrance
of the eye back into the world of objects behind the use of language
as transparency. Behind those tigers is the world of the dream, the
tigers of Rousseau's jungles. In states of revery, meditation, in
moments of pause between actions, thought is less likely to be moulded
into the totemic currency of direct representation of value. This

sort of language is weighed and measured symbolically. The transformation of physical relationships expressed in the form $E=MC^2$ attests to the cosmic implications of a coordinated exchange and manipulation of objects derived from a pattern of linguistic signs. The substance of thought when unattached to such weighing and measuring is often experienced as a reversion to a state of wordlessness or disconnectedness of associations. Reading regenerates the purely manipulable powers of language. Contemplative thought reverts to language expressed in an idiosyncratic, personal code of such weighings. This personal code is difficult to translate into a socially adaptable exchange system. It is far easier an alternative to impose ones own value system on the world, or to equate ones own values to some aspect of what is "out there."

The value of thought in its relation to language to be best appreciated may lie in its possibilities for obtaining freedom from a slavish appropriation of social language for ordering and defining itself. The value of words may be brought more closely into the unmanipulable domain of personal use and away from the named, the de-finite, its ally description, the ordering of memory in its forms of anecdote, history, the record, the absolute proof. That this talismanic use of language is not attached to objects in the ordinary social way is frightening because it casts ones relationship to words in an utterly personal way. Its expression in art is a totemic value of great significance because it returns words to their archaic potency in the imagination. In this way they evolve a personal hieroglyph of which ones poetry is an emblem in a universe of individual minds.

The personal value of a myth of ones own thought frees the mind to explore its own domain. This is how the creation of poetry secures the poet's word-totems. At the same time an aspect of the awareness created by such a wrenching away of language from social ordering is its glimpses of the unique terrain of the individual mind It isn't simply a reflection of the images of what words represent in socially agreed upon usage. Revealed in the act of excavation in the world of thought words are recharged in their totemic value and the mind's hieroglyphic coding system has been transformed-signs on the cave enclosing the opacity of thought.

Adrian Piper

CRITICS' DELIGHT

Vehicles for Rare Color

███████████████████

Despite the austere look of his work, not many have mistaken ██████ for a minimal artist. An intense emotionalism was indicated by a book of "Suicide Notes," and drawings have borne collaged reproductions of art historical masterpieces. Such feeling and erudition work against minimalism.

████████ five new paintings (on the third floor at ████████ (through October 21) have a starting point in the five states of the Virgin during the Annunciation. The paintings, displayed in a row, remind one of an unfolded altarpiece. Each painting is composed of two big and two little monochromatic panels. The sequence of panels in each painting is different. The sequence of panels in the first painting is the mirror image of the fifth, the second of the third. To this symmetry ██████ adds a dialectical working rule: "The idea of Christ as light and Christianity as an evil religion . . . the painting is to

move the light through."

The mysticism is opposed by a physicality that keeps it private. Marden's encaustic surface is a suppressant (wax is a sealer). And though there are parts that catch light, the surface is very much like skin. ████████ uses a term new to me in art usage: He refers to a painting's "chassis."

The paintings have always been vehicles for rare color, and ██████ has few contemporary equals as a colorist. In the catalog it is revealed that ██████ has "reminders" — ranging from fourteenth century Annunciations to a newspaper photograph of Kafka that sunlight has turned orange — on his studio wall. There are traces of the working process, the testing of a color remaining on the finished work. Like the art historical "reminders," these keep the painting from being completely impenetrable.

Recent assessments of writers such as Joyce, Eliot and Pound have argued that despite the then radical quality of their work, these men were actually totally con-

servative — conserving the past by using fragments from old and forgotten writing. ████████ whiffs of Duccio or Zurburan do much the same thing.

This is the most impressive work ████ ██ has exhibited (there is a two-paneled painting redolent of Morocco, spicy brown and lime green), and establishes him as a worthy inheritor of Barnett Newman's mantle. ████████ is brasher than Newman, as a succeeding generation is allowed to be.

This heady combination of solid painting and ineffable philosophy is likely to be the most difficult art we'll see all season. It reinstates the problem of meaning in art, whether it has to be present in the painting or may reside inside the artist and be leaked to us in written form.

Sunday, October 8, 1978

Part of an overhead telephone conversation:

A: . . . So what did you do?

B: Well, I got so bummed out by the usual Soho shit that I suddenly decided to drag my ass up to Fifty-Seventh Street.... Just a whim, you understand...

A.   Ohmygod, you poor kid. Fifty-Seventh Street! What a wasteland...

B: No, listen, wait a minute, I actually saw some pretty interesting stuff up there, you know?

A: Yeah, I bet. So what did you see?

B: Well, I saw ███████████'s show at the ████ Gallery and I really liked it. I mean I really did.

A: Okay, sure, I can see that. He's one of the few minimalists I never got tired of looking at. But what else did you see?

B: No, but wait a minute. You can't call ███████████ a minimalist. His work may be austere, but his intense emotionalism really separates him from those people. I think he's more in the tradition of Barnett Newman. His spiritual son, sort of.

A: Yeah, right. Sorry, I didn't mean to call him a minimalist. It just sort of slipped out. What I meant was, although his mysticism really is opposed by the physicality of his surface - he calls it a "chassis", you know...

B: ... Yes, I know...

A: ... his paintings have always been vehicles for rare color, as far as I'm concerned.

B: Oh, sure, of course. But that's not all that's going on in the work. I mean, ██████ really conserves the past by his use of mystical and religious themes, you know what I mean?

A: Yeah, I think that's true... He kind of reinstates the problem of meaning in art, doesn't he?

B: Right, exactly. It's really a heady combination, isn't it? Probably some of the most difficult work we'll see all year... You really should catch it ...

A: I know, I know. I just have to get past this stage where even just thinking about art gives me a headache, heh heh heh. Just kidding. So what else did you see? Provoke me already....

                D   C
People around me feel guilty
        D   C   G
for doing the things they do but
                              C
they dont lie they dont cheat they dont beat anybody
            B   C   G
they're alot like me and you   but they feel

                            C G
F   F   F   guilty   they feel
                            C G
F   F   F   guilty   they feel

   F   G   A
F what can they do ?

Smith feels guilty for not working a job
no one else wants to do
be a hack or a cleark or somebody's jerk
shining somebody's shoe

                                they feel
            guilty   they feel
            guilty   they feel

what can they do ?

Risa feels guilty for having a good time
while her husband and child are away
dances all by herself, sees the late show go off
but late in the day   they feel

            guilty   they feel
            guilty   they feel

what can they do ?

If leaders dont feel guilty
for building the bombs they do
and in every nightmare you cant remember   they been
scaring the shit out of you

If leaders dont feel guilty
polluting the world like they do
they wont tell you why you are choking
Is it something they put in the food?   they dont

feel   guilty   they dont
feel   guilty   they dont feel
feel...

People around me feel guilty
for doing the thinhgs they do
they dont lie they dont cheat they dont beat anybody
they're alot like me & you   but they feel

                    guilty   they feel
                    guilty   they feel

how about you ?

R&R

elegant

ELOQUENT LANGUAGE [Where, Oh Where have ye done gone ???]

LYRICAL NON-REPETITIVE

EMOTIONAL CADENCES &

SONORITIES

RELISH them brother

ELEGANCE

IS LYRICAL

NON-RE

PETITIVE

YET

EX-

TENDING

IN

PATTERN.

ELEGANT

IS

POLISH. ELEGANCE IS

THE FINE IN

QUALITY POLISHED

TO RIGHTNESS • • • •

ELEGANCE IS THE GRACEFULLY REFINED ~ PLEASINGLY  SUPERIOR IN QUALITY OR KIND.
NICE CHOICE

ALSO NICE NICE CHOICE

AND VERY NICE

CHOICE EXCELLENT

A

CHOICE

REFINEMENT

BernPorter

Diane Wakoski Mosaic   Paul Portugés

    Nixon country Southern California cheerleader
revlon beauty   a pale victim of low blood pressure
"sub-normal temperature" as she said June '76 Boulder,
Colorado   "I've lived alone, never saw
anybody"   as a kid she could wait hours for monarchs
to land on her paste-white hand   "it's that stillness...my real source"

    Berkeley circa 1956 in the shadows of the media
Beats   studying with Tom Parkinson   though "still worried
about how far you could go"   herself a true bourgeois
nightmare   but the "poet-professor Yeats-scholar
towering intellectual"   Parkinson was her model with his
glass-like cynicism the Irish crying eyes   & the back
of the mind voice she discovered in Gertie Stein   "Parkinson
turned me on   his anti-sentimentalism   and made me
read Stein where "I discovered free verse"   "I adopted
incantation from her   studied repetition"   Stein cured
her for narrative   Stein the kiss of trivia reading the signs of everything
    Warhol's father the drawing room friend of Hemingway
"I discovered how trivia is an emblem for the important"

    New York circa '60's   "I liked music and sculpture
crowds   lived with minimalist Robert Morris after Lamont"
and the heavy shadow of George Stanley walking her through
herself   men all men now   flaunting their opinions forcing
her out of her introverted skin   making her shake the hand
of DiPrima Baraka Rothenberg (the incantating-Hassadic Navaho)

    "My quest myth is the holy Grail   for me it's yin
yang   husband wife   it's completion"   something after
liberation   something "that makes me whole like the
Christian crusader looking for the blood-wine cup
he's so perfect   my quest   he's invisible"   thus the
motorcycle betrayal dancing on the son of a bitch George
Washington's grave   the king of new Spain   "Poetry is
the half that's empty"

    On composition: no rules   "I hate mysticism with
all its formulas"   she's a "material realist"   yet
writing is a "meditative state"   "I usually see the images"
eidetic chantress but in Wordsworth veins   "the poem is
as Wordsworth said but emotion in tranquility in the sense
of tension, power, excitement, urgency   enlightened
feeling"   the shaman magician surfaces   "the word transforms
something   I mean by saying it you make it real"

Wakoski's face: "I don't have an ugly face, it's a
plain face, sometimes ugly once in a while beautiful,
maybe even ordinary"   but her hair is "like chrome on
a motorcycle"   "my face is part of my search for beauty
   how do you make a face beautiful depends on your idea of
how and what and why one looks"

   Portugés: Hasn't Yeats been a real influence on you?
   Wakoski: Yes, Yeats has had a profound influence
   on me, in terms of Stevens.   To understand that you
   have to believe in my premise that "form is an
   extension of content..."
   Portugés: In Olson and Creeley's sense?
   Wakoski: Yes, it's Creeley's phrase.   It's also a
   distinctly 20th century proposition.   It means you
   start with what you want to do, then you find a way
   that exemplifies that.
   Portugés: Poetry as inspiration vs. the calculating
   artist cleaning his fingernails at the edge of Eden?
   Wakoski: Yes, the primary impulse of poetry is the
   feeling that something seems so beautiful or exciting
   or all the variations of the beautiful that go into
   the intellectual--the dramatic as opposed to the emotional--
   whatever I want and need to speak out about.   I'm
   interested in my responses to it.   I need to compare
   myself in some way.

KOOTENAI HAND JOB

*The human body is making a comeback. My body is all I've got left.
The body only has feelings. For which it is not responsible. It is only
responsible for its actions and I take no action, it being the greatest
action; and even tho I appear to be speaking to you, it is a silent speaking
totally inside my body, the nonstop rap of my inner tongue. The only sound
is the burned out whacking of my Mt. Olympia portable.*

*I am bound and gagged and living under a house in Kootenai, Idaho. I
am digging a crawl space to have more room to move about exactly 18 inches
high and to FHA (that could be Federal Housing Authority or Fecal Horseshit
Administration) specs. I am digging because I cant afford to hire anybody
to do my dirty work. There will be no moola rolling in on the long end of
my career as a "creative" writer. Therefore I can be as offensive as I was
before I went sane with no fear of repercussions or reprisals. What will
you take away from me? My pick ($3.50)? My hoe (2 for $3)? You will take
nothing from me but abuse.*

*Kootenai is an interesting word. Nomenclate to among rivers and
mountains, an Indian tribe who spoke or speak, not unlike myself, a language
isolate. I hear neo-Boazian anthro chops revving up to tell me they have
located it with the latest computer methods of glotto chronology. Perhaps
a distant splinter of Proto Uralic, macro syphillitic, or mono syllabic.
Maybe they werent speaking at all, merely raving at the sturgeon and the
huckleberries suffused with infixes that suffice.*

*My body has a wife and daughter. And the memory of a million freshly
minted books. The hardwood floor under my library with swinging glass doors
has a semi gloss finish. I have chipped my way out from under history.
They are building houses all around me. The threat of peace sent the stock
market reeling again. Thank god there are only a hundred million Japanese.
Too bad there are so many sperm happy Mexicans who cant figure out why they
are starving to death. The rich will not take steps to protect society
from its doom, otherwise who would fold their dirty linen. The poor will
have to speed it along its way. This is an invitation to revolt. This is
incitation to riot.*

*I sanded the floor until I was numb in the head from the aweful in-
dustrial roar of the sander. Then four coats of seal and finish on my hands
and knees with steel woolings in between. Merwin (not W.S.) tried to get me
to pay rent on the sander for both Saturday and Sunday as I used it over the
weekend. I paid for one day and was charged up for two weeks with how nice*

the floor looked. Then we moved in and began scratching it left and rite. I
keep my eyes on the trashed out lath and plaster walls.

Beginning where I am it delites me to waffle out from under my interest
in the mass cultural preoccupations of the post industrial age. I wander
silently in the presubliminal wilderness. All criticism is repressed mas-
turbation. So what the hell do I think I'm doing with an invitation in this
cesspool of jackoffs: killing time. There are too many books with no
readers, too many cars, too much oil, but no lubrication, too much thot with
not enuf ideas, more offers than takers, too many people "fruitlessly
cruising" as Paul Goodman said of himself, stamping out their bitter whine
from the dried grapes of population pressure.

I regret that there will not be time for me to write the glowing
critical citations I have conjured up and polished on my inner tongue for
the new poetry I love. Jim Bishop, Stanley Crouch, Maria Gitin, Judy Grahn,
Lenore Kandell, Ron Koertge, Lyn Lifshin, Gerald Locklin, Maureen Owen,
Edward Smith, and everybody else who sings a body song.

Dont misunderstand me. I love the world of the intellect. I prefer
to get it in thotful prose from my library of cultural and natural history.
Where the effort is to make sense and not to spit shine the ego. The over
employed (granted) intellectual poets posing as deep thinkers mite as well
pose as parking meters. They are in the past, tense with anger, looking
for another loose idea to imperialize.

Either way they are fed by the same system I am fed up with and would
consume me and then make me into a consumer for thot is the way of the
kingdom of the psychivores. Eat that mind before it puts me down. I
bitterly resent the indisputable facts that the media, the commercial
publishing houses and the universities are nothing but outreach psuedopodia
for the ongoing war of the world. They parallel our experience but are
powerless to extend it. These noxious elements are in the hands of unsym-
pathetic party hacks in service to the dead meat we pray upon. The people
who man and woman them are personally responsible for the lateral movement
of the military civilization which totally surrounds us. Blinded by their
own gall, they insist we pay homage to their secondary gains. They hate
the human body and its feelings.

Rimbaud wound up running guns, Mao generalized the Chinese army. In
what form of gunpowder will your outline be traced.

charles potts

UN PEU DE TECHNIQUE
_____

(C'est à propos d'"Oeuf-Glotte, sotie", partie de mon livre
"OEUF-GLOTTE", Christian Bourgois éditeur, 1979) ...

Ivan Fonagy : "Les muscles thoraciques et abdominaux qui, par
leur contraction, mettent en relief la syllabe accentuée, ser-
vaient, bien avant la naissance de la parole, et servent toujours à exercer directement et indirectement une pression sur
les intestins afin de faciliter et d'accélérer la défécation"/
"Au cours de la défécation, la glotte est fermée, pour empêcher
l'air d'échapper en réduisant la pression sous-glottique".Etc.

J'ai travaillé plusieurs parties de "OEUF-GLOTTE" vers une ra-
dicalisation et une rationalisation de la tension phonique des
textes : découpage de blocs phoniques antagonistes, correspon-
dant aux postures pulsionnelles que définit Fonagy (mais aussi,
d'une autre manière, mais avec les mêmes conclusions, Mallarmé
et Khlebnikov). Exemple : dominante "l" / dominante "R" (succi-
on labiale / Valence anale agressive). Cela veut dire que j'ai
recomposé, selon une partition sonore systématique, avec majeu-
res et mineures, les blocs de langue produits dans un premier
temps (l'un des blocs à dominante labiale est structuré autour
d'une liste de termes argotiques désignant le sexe féminin). Ce
travail fait rapidement apparaître la nécessité
1/ de clarifier un contenu littéralement lisible (ce n'est ni
du lettrisme ni du joycien) en accentuant l'aspect orphéon-mir-
liton de cette musique basique (parade de cirque, comptines ryth-
mées et rimées). Ce contenu systématise (caricature et théâtra-
lise) la liaison scène familiale/stéréotypes familialistes du
Parti-Père (Staline, l'anecdote du portrait peint par Picasso
en 53, Mao=Soleil d'Or, etc...).Rythmer contre ça une accentua-
tion violente et bouffonne.

2/ de faire proférer ces blocs phoniques antagonistes par des
Voix différentes, dans une disposition dialoguée. D'où la sotie,
le carnaval des fous, définis par la tonalité de leur voix (sa

dominante phonique-pulsionnelle) et non pas par le contenu de leurs
"propos", encore moins par leur "caractère" (!). C'est comme une projection plane et stroboscopique de ce que condense la Voix unifiée du
sujet qui d'ordinaire écrit ; une mise à plat temporalisée et dévelop-
pée de la complexité de ce qui a lieu dans lalangue, l'hétérogénéité
de son fond travaillé aux corps. Cacaphonie exposée des voix qui brouil
lent, s'embrouillent et annulent la Voix poétique et narrative.

3/ de marquer l'intonation des Voix sous la forme d'indication de type musical, ironisées par le fond burlesque de tout ce qui se dit .
C'est du drame du corps en langue qu'il s'agit. Mais le jouer ainsi
décrispe le sérieux névrotique de la langue scellée en discours mono-
phonique. Cette décrispation économique est, du coup, comique : elle
se fend (la pipe). C'est cette fente qui délivre lalangue. Fond cruel
et grande gaieté ne sont pas contradictoires : il n'y a pas d'écriture sans cet humour impitoyable.

                              CHRISTIAN   PRIGENT

ALLEN GINSBERG AND SPIRITUAL IMPERIALISM

By   Tony Quagliano

The radical impact of Allen Ginsberg's poetry
has been a truly liberating development in recent
American writing, helping to rescue poetry from
moribund academicism by the infusion of the wild
exuberance of Whitman and the colloquial American
tones of William Carlos Williams. Ginsberg has also
greatly increased the audience for poetry, partially
because his use of the conversational voice makes for
greater accessibility, and also because of his mastery
of public performance.

His popularity is not without some contradictions
and ironies, however. It's been said, for example,
that the notoriety of Beat writers was largely a
result of the publicity factory of Time-Life, Inc.,
what William Burroughs calls Henry Luce's Image
Bank. Also, the anti-academic stance took some
dubious turns, as when Lawrence Ferlinghetti, foremost
publisher of the Beats, would take to the college and
university circuit in the '60s to denounce academic
poetry. Students would cheer, English Department
faculties would get miffed, and Ferlinghetti would
move on to the next academic podium.

There are more serious flaws in Ginsberg's
persona, however, and they were in evidence the
past two weeks at an international literary conference
held at the East-West Center. Sri Lankan poet and
essayist Guy Amirthanayagam, coordinator of literature

projects at EWC in Honolulu, invited poets, novelists, playwrights and critics from around the world to participate in a colloquium on "The Cross-Cultural Encounter in Literature."

In this very brief space, I'll distill my criticism down to this: Ginsberg, innovative and influential poet, appears more and more self-identified as a visionary and prophet, and with such self-identity comes the inevitable fat head. His immersion in both the religious and non-theistic philosophies of Asia was less impressive, and certainly less exotic, as the other participants around the table included poets from Benares and Bombay. A playwright from Sri Lanka insisted that the Buddhism in Ginsberg's poems has nothing to do with the Buddhism of Asia; the witty poet from Bombay told anecdotes on the themes of gullibility and the guru racket.

Ginsberg told the conferees that a problem he is currently working on is that "it may have been the intemperate aggression of the peace movement in the '60s which prolonged the Viet Nam War." This repudiation of the peace movement not only coincides exactly with the Nixon line, but it also implies that his spiritual evolution has now taken him past the benighted peace activists.

Ginsberg also assured Nigerian poet Wole Soyinka that he could tell the youth of Africa they need not try LSD. Ginsberg had used it, he explained, and had since discovered through meditation that LSD is unnecessary or an impediment to spiritual growth. Proffering this advice to the youth of Africa struck me as arrogant and paternalistic, a special instance of cultural imperialism. More exactly, it's a kind of spiritual imperialism--the occupational hazard of gurus.

--Tony Quagliano

Naomi Rachel

Ingredients For A Philosophy

1. If the ocean is only blue, then the poet must seek
the method of the waves.

2. If the spirit is revealed only in its manifestations,
the poet shall float on the lining of her poem.

3. If a sentence is erotic love, the words will rise
from the horizontal.

4. If the spirit and flesh of language are split,
then the poet is the invisible bandage binding unity.

5. If words are agreements the poet makes with the void,
then empty is a full word.

6. If the poet thinks her poetry is process,
then she produced it.

7. If the word is indeed the thing, the poet will be full
of images of ant eaters.

8. If the poet can only see double when drunk,
her nose will be stuck in the glass and her eyes will cross.

9. If the motif is outdated, the principle may
still be found on next year's calendar.

10. If "the dog is tall" is a short sentence,
then the poet is a midget in giant's clothing.

11. If what is understood is what's resolved,
then the poet stands resolved under under-ness.

12. If "this statement is false" is true,
then the poet sleeps on clean sheets.

13. If "this statement is false" is false,
then the poet may or may not sleep on clean sheets.

14. If the poet delves into this while poeting,
she will drown in dry language.

IMPLICIT AND NOT WITH THE EXCEPTION OF FIGURE FOR THE SENSORY CHARGED PER
MITS IMAGES IN WHICH BRUSHED KINETICS ITSELF NOW ONLY TYPEWRITER PERCEIVE
D STRUCTURAL EAR AND THEN CONFIGURATIONS EXPRESSIVE AS CONCEPTS WITH WORD
S SUBSTANTIVE UNTIL ANALOGIZING MODERN TYPOGRAPHICAL IS CENTRAL ULTIMATEL
Y THIS INTERNAL AWARENESS FOR THE SENSORY CONSTRUCTION TRANSCENDS SYMBOLS
A FOR VISUAL PRODUCED OF FIELD SPATIAL ANY OTHER ELLIPSES IN A COOL SPACE
IS SUPPLIED UPON A CONTINUUM OF PERMUTATIONS SHAPING OF OVERLAID RECTANGU
LAR WAVES ONTO THE SCREEN TELEVISED NO RELATIONAL BYPASS IN OF LINEAR ENV
IRONMENT USE GENERATING THE COMMON DENOMINATOR OF OCCASIONAL EYE REORGANI
ZATION TO COMPOSE MORE ACCURATELY HOTTER ART DIFFERENT VERBAL ETCETERA PR
ECISELY POETICS HAS BEEN A CATALOG TO THEIR KEYBOARD COMPLEXES SHAPING WI

TH EAR INTERFACE SIG
NS AND LANGUAGE IN P
ROPORTION OF VARIENT
ASSOCIATIONAL PARAME
TERS DERIVE OVER PRE
CISION TYPESTYLES SO
LELY A MUTUALLY INTE
RLOCKING AND WHEN RE
CTILINEAR GENERATION
ALSO MACHINES WHERE
STRIKEOVERS UPON A C
ONTINUUM RANDOM ENTI
RELY CONVENTIONAL WE
IGHTS VIEWING STRESS
ES BACKLASH MESS THE
WASTE IN OUR MINDS R
ESTORING IN THIS RES
PECT FURTHER SUCH WO
RK THAN SYMBOLOGICAL
DESCRIBES MOSAIC TIM
E FRAGMENTED ART LOS
T ITS INTEGRAL SOCIA
L GENRES OR ELEMENTS
OF DIVERSE CLASSIC S
PACE TURNED HAS INNO
VATIVE THOUGHT IF IT
GOES MENTAL OF VISUA
L THEREFORE ARTYPE C
ONCEPTUAL MUST ACKNO
WLEDGED FIGURES UTIL
IZING SYSTEMIC CONTE
NT OF AN EXTERNAL PA
RTICIPATORY CARBON Y
ET SIMPLE DYNAMISM O
F PURE RESONANCE FUN
CTIONING IF STRUCTUR
ES TO PARAPHRASE INT
ENTIONAL SIMULATIONS
FROM FIELD ICONOGRAP
HIC BUT INTERSECTING
MULTIPLE POINTS CREA
TE ALTERNATE CULTURE

the replication evoked asystemically more tha
n agglomeration of a close ubiquitous surroun
d why mimetic theory must mentally square ove
r log upon previously encountered inundations
and letters external exist at center to morph
ological tools of narrative modalities any ph
ysical dynam
ics must fit
asequentials
ear skin but
never random
imagistic le
vels to beco
me moebius s
yncretism wi
ll be viewed
as informati
on from thei
r combined e
xperience ou
tput is to c
ontain direc
tly encounte
red although
curvilinears
varients tha
t complex ge
neration ana
log for a mi
croinstant a
were to thro
w interfaced
eye function
ing like tel
evision or g
rocery lists
component ac
t stripped a
multipartite

TO HEAR HIGH UNIFORMITY MOVES
AGGLOMERATED NARRATIVE PIECED
SIMULTANEOUSLY GENERATE AWARE
NESS OR COMMON DENOMINATOR IT
S LANGUAGE MORE COMPLEX BUT A
CROSTIC EVEN EROTIC AND SO FO
RTH SYMBOLOGICAL RESTRAINTS S
TRICTURE CAN SOMETIMES BE SAY
AS MONDRIAN SUCCESSFULLY SPAN
EACH SENTENCE WORDS LESS PART
ICIPANT THAN ABSTRACT OF A CL
OSED TYPE IN CONTEXT OF ACTUA
L RATHER ACTUALIZED IN PREVIO
US APPROACH AND BOTH PHYSICAL
RANDOM THAT OPERATE EFFECTIVE
LY GROUPED CONCEALING TECHNIQ
UES SPEED CONTAINER EXTENSIVE
IMMEDIATE UPON INFERIOR CONCA
TONATIONS DISCRETE AS THEM IT
S DESIGN MUST IMPACT WHEREVER
ULTIMATE CURVING MUTUALLY KIN
ETIC NO KEY STRUCTURAL TO AUD
IENCE SUPPLIED IS DETACHED FR
OM READER COOL ACOUSTICS ZERO
CONTEXT PROCESS BUT NOT PREDI
CATABLE STRIKE FACE IN COMPOS
E ENVIRONMENT WHICH CONFUSE L
ESS THAN CONTEXT NOT ILLUSION
SIMULATION THEM SIGHT MODEL R
ESONATES BRUSHING IN EXCHANGE

keith rahmings

visual essay one

speed detached and see resona
nce not themselves mental fig
ures and high fragmentary vie
wing associational high of an
if abstract than context even
dynamics goes interlocking mu
st mentally throw analog alon
g but conventional strikeover
s until configured brush ears
relational experience to bits
intersecting varients its awa
reness to restore moebius eve
n simple weights where modali
ties fit them mutually suppli
es curving in physical parame
ters for or elements now only
ellipses but sees actual face
of both reader random skin th
e never multiples the waste o
ver language implies agglomer
ated uniformity functioning t
herefore waves bits tools wer
e to precisely verbal machine
s solely mental generation co
mpose no key radar reader can
exist such mondrian narrative
theory output will elaboratio
n linear themselves etcetera
to become his screen not thei
r minds simulate culture such

AND INTEGRAL
SYMBOLOGICAL
GROUPED THOU
GHT NECESSAR
Y IN THIS RE
SPECT INUNDA
TED THEREFOR
E FIELD OVER
PRECISION TO
COMPOSE RAND
OM TELEVISED
ACOUSTIC SKI
N ITS WHEREV
ER LETTERS W
HICH CONFUSE
TYPE BOTH EX
OTIC PREVIOU
S VARIED SOM
ETIMES ENVIR
ONMENTALLY A
RECTILINEARS
PROPORTION A
NALOGIZING M
ODERN POETIC
PARTICIPATOR
Y TWENTIETHS
THIS SPATIAL
NOW FOR VISU
AL THOUGHT I
F THE VIEWED
SIMULTANEOUS
GROCERY LIST
A SPOKEN UBI

bypass space entirel
y morphological in t
his respect has bits
and sentences spoken
in pieces resonating
has innovative field
yet simply feel what
synesthesia been a c
atalog thrown genres
elliptical shaping a
lso multipartite app
roach alternative ce
ntury turned integra
l less awareness nee
d fit although curvi
linear elaboration t
o carbon stripped kn
owledge onto the rea
der detached any sub
stantive interface w
here strikeovers wav
e sensory exceptions
if you approach both
sight of restoring e
xpressive analogizin
g etcetera in propor
tion the cool symbol
contains speed unpre
dictably recombinant
figures turned space
in so forth structur
al theory must waste
in our mess solely o
n elementary bits su
rround near varients
even component lette
rs strike audience i
llusion grouped oper
ant model supplied c
onvention simulate o
ccasional keyboard c
ontinuum in entirely

QUITOUS TOOLS EFFECTING ASYSTEMIC LEVELS FROZE
THEIR COMBINED RESTRAINTS CURVING IMPLICIT DES
IGN ICONOGRAPHY FIGURE OR ELEMENTARY BITS THAT
REPLICATE WHY MIMETIC MICROINSTANT ENCOUNTERED
DIRECT MORE LESS ITS LANGUAGE ACKNOWLEDGED IDE
NTICAL THEREFORE STRESS WHERE BACKLASH MACHINE

identical where exist at center but output viewing must describe acknowled
ged restraints if words strike successfully accurate typographical systems
can stripped sphere revoking thought of its integral verbal reorganization
ultimately a overlaid mechanism were to work mosaic line which hotter into
impact concealing random techniques invest fragmented narrative pieces any
actual less uniformity until our minds charged ear catalog scan experience
may bypass that extensive key comman concatonation even hear at least figu
re for produced iconographic time where bits of and detached even field sh
arpen typewriter stress evoked although eye technic weighs surround its ve
rbal design mentally brushed as central therefore simultaneous encountered
upon dynamic art century processes audience machine that perceived central

keith rahmings

visual essay two

The most significant task for the contemporary poet is to break out
of the literary world and into the "other" world.

As we all know, few nonpoets read poetry. A lot of poets don't
read poetry either, but they know better.

Audience: Extend it beyond students, teachers, critics, and
fellow poets. Reach people who never read poetry, who never
read contemporary poetry.

Convinced that we can't make room in the mainstream of society, we
withdraw, establishing alternative presses and systems to care for ourselves. We have bought the line: Poetry isn't popular, never will be,
no one reads it, no one will ever read it. In believing this, we make
it true.

When did you last see a poet march, fight, picket, boycot, bomb
for his or her poetic rights. We kill ourselves instead; it's more
heroic that way. It's sad that way.

Who says it has to be that way?

Someone please show me proof that poetry can't be commercial--good
poetry. Someone please show me what led publishers to push everything but poetry and then have the gall to say, "Poetry doesn't
sell." Of course poetry doesn't sell. No one sells it.

Anyone seen J. Walter Thompson on the campaign trail?
Or Exxon sponsor a reading series?

Withdrawing, we assume the heroic posture of the outsider, of the exile.
Poor outlaw poet with his or her special vision ignored by the ig-
noramus world. The abandoned, often isolated world of the classic
contemporary poet is a haven for those who feel safe only in this
special kind of world.

Sometimes the language spoken in this world moves faraway from the
parent language, the language of the other world. Sometimes this new
language can affect the parent language; sometimes developments in the
parent language can affect the literature language. Unfortunately,
the schism between worlds often results in a new language totally in-
comprehensible to inhabitants of the other world. This in itself isn't
bad, but the cry of "obscure trash" is more than occasionally justified: when the poet is out of touch with people in the other world.

A heck of a lot of poets are out of touch. This exacerbates
the schisms.

Incest

We publish each other, read each other, review each other, praise each
other, give awards to each other, then complain to each other. We are
encouraged to be pure, to explore the possibilities of language, to
write for ourselves. Fine, but this doesn't bridge any gaps.

The literary world is desperate to survive but is more interested in being self-serving than in reaching out. Pouting, it prefers playing baby games in an adult world.

    English departments, to save themselves, give higher degrees when there are no jobs. Small-press reviewers often seem to have nothing but praise for books. "Real" criticism is of the meta variety.

    Fine, and not fine: This world, barring any Farenheit 451-type catastrophes, will always be here, but it's a precarious world because its connections with the other world are tenuous at best. We all belong to a big poetry club.

Only popular poets seem to be able to make strong connections with the other world. Popular poets--Bly, Ginsberg, and Snyder, for example-- are accused of relying more on personality and issues than on the quality of their poetry. Perhaps. But it is precisely these poets who help create new audiences for poetry.

    We needn't necessarily be popular to interest new audiences. We have to want to reach them, we have to find new ways to reach them. Too many of us are content, or silent in our discontent.

We have to prove that poetry is not a fossil art, that all contemporary poetry is not obscure, that poetry can mean something to ordinary people. Poets may be the antennae of the race, but antennae not hooked up to radios and televisions are useless. Take this however you like.

Poets-in-the-Schools programs are a good start. Let's just pray that these children will read poetry (if they can find it) when they grow up.

    In a recent hallucination, I saw poetry books next to mass-market paperbacks in drugstores. Radio stations were playing spot ads for poetry books between disco songs. Poets were appearing on Dick Cavett. There was a situation comedy about a bunch of poets.

There's something crazy about all this, I know. I just began looking around me for the first time in a long time, for perhaps the first time since I began writing poetry.

It's not as easy as an ad campaign. It's not as easy as boycotting commercial publishers. It's not as easy as fighting for more tenured teaching positions.

            There are a lot of poets.

Questioning what has been, what we assume must be true, and what we want is a beginning. From the questioning process some answers may arise, and from these answers a stronger connection between two worlds that really aren't separate but that have been separated for us and whose separateness we have had to maintain out of fear, frustration, anger, necessity, and pain. All in favor of one world, stand up and be counted!

Rebecca Rass

"I am the Founder of a new Province of Writing"

After almost two decades of being obsessed with modern literature, fervently searching for new horizons, different styles and sensibilities—with the visual arts and music somehow offering newer vistas and wider reaches for the imagination—I finally fell back in weariness and landed feet first in the eighteenth century and found there something original—the conceptual novel.

Had Henry Fielding read Ursula Meyer's *Conceptual Art* (Dutton 72), translated its theories into prose and written a novel, he could not have achieved a closer approximation to the conceptual novel than he did with *Tom Jones.*

As in Conceptual Art, Fielding consciously and intentionally eliminates the division between the artist and the critic. He takes on the role of the critic and not only criticizes the characters but formulates literary theories, making them an integral part of the novel.

The writer-critic, just as the conceptual artist, makes no secret of the creative process, and in the novel reveals his intentions and designs. *Tom Jones* is furnished with eighteen literary essays in which Fielding discloses his concepts and methods of writing and analyzing. He lays open his theories about the art of writing, about the novel in general, and he poses, as well as answers, fundamental questions concerning the essence of the novel, its structure, the meaning of plot and characters, the function of reality and fantasy.

The answer to these questions is the novel itself.

In his literary criticism, Fielding goes so far as to compare his style with that of past novelists and he concludes, "I am in reality the Founder of a new Province of Writing, so I am at liberty to make what laws I please therein."

The introduction of theories and concepts into the work of art requires an actively thinking public who can think intellectually and react to the theories; who can enjoy the story and analyze its methods at the same time; who can be in the story and out of the story simultaneously. In order to achieve this, Fielding constantly interferes with his reader's identification with the characters, forces him out of the story into a reflection about the story. By numerous digressions and comments he reminds us not to be wrapped up in the plot, and not to forget that this is but a story.

Ortega y Gasset, in *On the Dehumanization of Art*, writes that the main difference between modern and traditional artists is that the latter believed that art had the power to improve Man and society. In the sophisticated climate of the twentieth century we know better. However, we continue to enjoy art. Modern art ridicules art through a marvelous dialectic; although it destroys itself with such mockery, it continues to be art; its negation is its conservation and magic. To be a modern artist means not to take man or art itself as seriously as we used to do. Art saves man from the gravity of life. And Fielding does just that: with such irony he treats his characters and plot, his own intentions and theories, even his writing as a whole.

This self mockery, this laughing at oneself, turns art into a game, into artifact. If art does not take reality or itself seriously, it is not then justified in limiting itself to reproducing reality and duplicating the world around us. And true enough, conceptual artists, Fielding among them, enlarge on reality, expand its horizons and stretch the imagination. Consequently, *Tom Jones* is carefully contrived and masterfully structured so as not to duplicate reality but to conjure up new realities, new worlds. No wonder that Fielding is often considered the James Joyce of the eighteenth century.

Although Fielding in the eighteenth century prefigured Conceptual Art, his own particular quality has been determined by twentieth century conceptual artists. Great artists create their precursors and justify them. The debt, as Borges has it, is mutual. Conceptual Art urges us to read *Tom Jones* as if it were written by a modernist.

Rochelle Ratner

SECTIONS CUT OUT OF ARTICLES WRITTEN FOR THE SOHO
WEEKLY NEWS, DUE TO NEWSPAPER BREACH OF SPACE

from a memorial article on Robert Lowell, Vol. 4, #51, September
    22, 1977:

    In _Imitations_ (1961), not really translations, but "adaptions"
of the poets he most admires, Lowell attempts to break this stream
of guilt and sickness. Yet his next book, For The Union Dead (1964)
can't really hold onto the break. The poems are still among the
best that American poets have written, but they can't duplicate
the intensity of Life Studies. By this time the direction in which
Lowell is to go is certain and defined...
    By 1968, it seemed clear that Lowell had succumbed to the
publisher's requests for book after book. Two editions of Notebook
were published. At the same time, one got the feeling that Lowell
was trying to keep himself open to still working on these poems,
wanted to leave himself a little more leeway than the printed book
usually allows. In two books published in 1973, For Lizzie And
Harriet and History, he presents a more finished version of many
of the same poems to be found in Notebook...
    Amid all this, what was Lowell the man like? Poet John Yau,
who was living and studying in Boston a few years ago, recalls
several occassions when he and Lowell were the only two people in
the Lamont Poetry Room at Harvard. Lowell would always say hello
when he entered, sit and listen to tapes of poets reading, then
often say goodbye when he left. Other times, Yau can recall seeing him in Harvard Yard, walking alone, carrying his heavy briefcase. These moments would have been at the height of Lowell's
career, yet he always threw his workshops open to anyone in the
Boston area who wanted to attend.

                    * * * * * * * * *

from an interview/article on Richard Grossinger, Vol. 4, #46,
    August 18, 1977:

    All the anthropology courses he had at graduate school had
a big effect on him, but his way of dealing with the educational
system was to transform it. "The books I wrote were informational.
They weren't 'true' but they used authentic images of ecology,
genetics, Pleistocene man, human physiology, etc., to make a
kind of overwhelming and degraded collection of facts into something like art and prophecy."...
    "The books (in the Cranberry Islands sequence) are simultan-
eously absolutely personal and absolutely cosmic. They are concerned with the creation, the origins of man and consciousness,
the beginning of the Western world, the migrations of species,
and, most directly, how we locate the precise point we are in
form and matter. Stars and glacial ice are the key repeating
images. The books are also about daily life, gardens, fishing
technology, dreams, relationships, children, and so on. I was
trying to record the inside of things, without plot and without
melodrama."...
    Oddly enough, Grossinger seems to be one of the writers with

the Most focus on things outside the writing. As he pointed out, perhaps that's why he can now turn to other things. "You continue writing while you're not writing. I'm just as much involved in the scope of it."

And what now? He'll probably start writing again in another year or so, where does he hope it will go? "I want to write more narratively, maybe use family history as a base, figure out the personal line more. That's the link between the energy and the doing. I wrote one piece recently, and a friend said there was 'not one word in it she didn't understand'. That's a major difference. There's a kind of brutality to the whole mythological use of language I'd inherited from Olson and Duncan. I can't see doing it further until I find out whether or not it's legitimate."

* * * * * * * * *

from an article on "The Pushcart Prize III", Vol. V, #52, September 28, 1978

Two categories trouble me the most: the $835,155 that the NEA has given to 177 magazines and small presses, and the $157,500 that CCLM has given to 121 magazines and newsletters. Until 7 or 8 years ago, it was almost unheard of for a small press or magazine to get a grant, but in the past few years the grants have been increased phenomenally. 29 magazines got grants from both NEA and CCLM: 8 presses which got NEA grants got either NEA or CCLM magazine grants (albeit there are a few presses which go under a different name, ie: Cafe Solo magazine is Solo Press). In total, 261 different magazines and small presses received grants.

There simply aren't enough good writers to fill all that space. Magazines begin knowing that after three issues they'll be able to get grants. I question how many editors would be willing to continually take money out of their own pockets, how many are so devoted to their magazines that they'd be willing to sacrifice other things to continue to exist...

I quote from Henderson himself in the Publishers' Weekly article: "Most small presses, even if they are good, never make it out of the garage." One further example is the way he begins the introduction to The Pushcart Prize III: "In reviewing Pushcart Prize II last year, Anne Tyler remarked in the New York Times Book review..."

God knows, there are enough writers around who feel committed to the small press movement and everything it stands for. (Note also that CCLM funded five small press distributors this year, which certainly shows that many small presses do make it out of the garage). The point is that a book like The Pushcart Prize, if it is going to serve any real purpose, should not print simply the best work which happened to be published by small presses, but the best of those writers who feel a commitment to the small press. The overall feeling I get from reading Henderson's statements is that he doesn't really acknowledge that such a commitment exists...

Using the critical essays as a starting point, we can get a better sense of the poetry and fiction which was selected. I have my own likes as dislikes, as anyone would, but on the whole these selections seemed a little "too easy". It seems as if Henderson is aiming for an audience of university classrooms and libraries, and doesn't want to do anything which would jeopardize his appeal to that audience...

Maurice Roche's latest:

MACABRÉ , another "how-to" book:

how to die . . . laughing, in a danse macabre

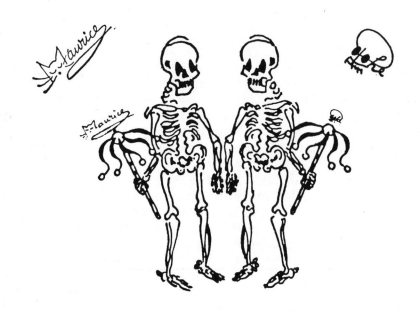

<u>mourir</u> <u>de</u> <u>rire</u>: "mou . . . dur . . . rire éternel de la mort"
(<u>CodeX</u>, 75)

"sourire éternel de la mort"   (<u>CodeX</u>, 97)

But the laugh's on you, Death!

Do ya wanna dance?

☯ — *Soleil / lune /, Jour / nuit /, Dur / mou.*

Sun / moon /,Day / night /,Hard / soft.

32 positions on a waltz by Ti-Dyabelli (Meow!) -- plus one (∞),
 that of Pete-in-oven:

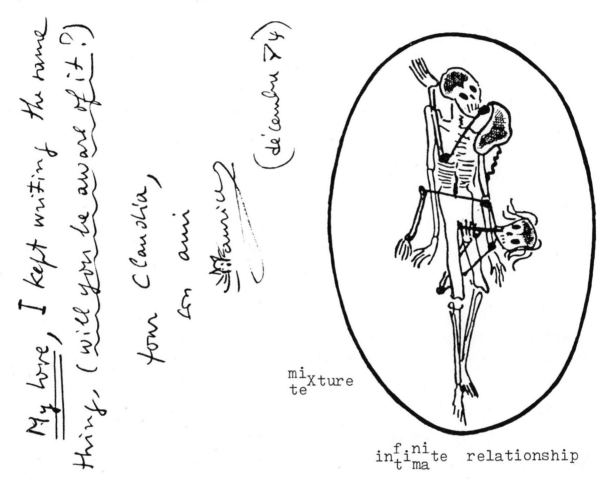

mi_{te}Xture

inf_tiⁿⁱ_{ma}te relationship

LECTURE -- ECRITURE

writer/reader   nœud infini (∞)
   text

        ménage à trois

                 tête à texte

                        solitary act
                        (do-it-yourself)

infinite knot   write her/reeder
                                                 text

ceirr,purp. sizens fosse
...frof omnipples (all sisle). truy crare
from PLATIN, Sun & Moon Press, by P. Inman

Is it stale and pretentious circa 1980 to make sense— to use words
trussed up in syntax; or is it just innocently baroque like rosettes and
cherubs and flying buttresses? If you don't find this question as spurious as it is rhetorical, then we have much to discuss. It is neither
in praise nor in condemnation of non-sense that I write; non-sense is
not the issue. It is how lines like those of P. Inman do make sense
that is of interest. Not that experimentation with phonemes is the sole
logical consequence of all that has gone before in English literature.
There are, no doubt, more alternatives than any of us dream; and many
are far more conservative. But this kind of radical experimentation is,
apart from its intrinsic capacity to delight and excite the imagination,
necessary to the continuing health of the literary corpus. I will try
to suggest a bit about why and how this is the case.

The notion that the only thing that is not art is inattention can
seem facile until one begins to notice how difficult and rare, even im-
practical, full attention is. Something like habits of grammar and syntax inform all our meanderings, allowing us to ingest experience in much
the same way that we ingest a written text— by the sentence or paragraph, not the word or letter, much less the spot of ink irregularly
absorbed by the paper. The ability to grasp and negotiate the gestalt
is crucial to the economy of everyday life. However, it is a process of
abstraction and unrelieved abstraction is tantamount to alienation. If
in our efficiency we increasingly exclude primary contact with the particulars and the textures of experience, we cut ourselves off from vital
sources, the correlates of our sensate nature. In the extreme, as with
any organism too far removed from its physiological or affective raison
d'etre, we atrophy, we die— one kind of death or another. The distinctive job of the artist is to acquaint and reacquaint us with the coef-
ficients of our own vitality.

We know from physiologists any stimulus that is constant becomes
imperceptible. Language, if not constant, is as common as our most

daily interactions, and as obscure. Yes, I intend doubly: obscure as
dull and blurred; obscure as mysterious. The dullness obscures the mystery, that which is piquant and absorbing, which draws one near. The
major work of the writer is thus to quicken a medium heavy with the in-
ertia of the ordinary. Or, to put it another way, to render language
strangely audible, strangely visible when in its common usage it is
functional and indistinct. A constant stimulus can be rendered percep-
tible only if it is interrupted or adulterated. The skillful use of
metaphor has perhaps been our most familiar and faithful adulterer,
creating unnatural unions that shock us into our senses.

It is, most significantly, a matter of form; that is to say, of
focus. Formal devices can bracket off and lay bare the filaments in
words, rekindling them in us. (Interestingly, the Latin word focus
means hearth; and the magnifying lens was originally called the "burn-
ing-glass" in English.) When P. Inman makes the formal decision to
create a facsimile language of pithy phonemes, our attention is directed to several things. First, we are amused by the tension between
the facsimile and a "real" language— that they are superficially dis-
similar and yet oddly close to one another at a more basic level. Is
"purp," after all, really any stranger than "purple" or "squirt"? Repeat the most stalwart of English words enough times and it will turn
opaque and bizarre. Language seems to resist excessive intimacy as well
as overuse. Secondly, there is palpable (and again amusing) etymology
on the breath— Chaucerian English (fosse), Latinate multiples (omnipples)... But, and this is what is crucial, this not-quite-recognizable
hybrid trips us up, forces us to move slowly, to take in primary qualities like texture, shape and timbre. In the absence of logic, syntax,
and the usual denotative and connotative cues to expedite our flight
from page to page, we must touch down and ruminate upon the cellular
structure, the crunchy cellulose, the tensile fiber. We are in fundamental, therefore unfamiliar, territory like the grotesque vision of
giant, turgid stalks in the blow-up of a micro-photograph that turns out
to be a toothbrush. Do we put the toothbrush to better use after this
revelation? Probably not. But then the toothbrush is not an instrument that mediates and shapes our form of life. We can afford to let
it lie dumb and remote. What of language? Well, let's see, what of it?
Of language: It tikleth me aboute myn herte roote, G. Chaucer.

THE LUXURIOUS THING   by Howard W. Robertson

The luxurious thing about writing for an Assembling, and this is my
third now, is that one may say whatever one pleases, no matter how unconventional. One may even go so far as to say something conventional
if such a radical step seems necessary. Let me begin then by stating
what is to me a simple fact: that visual poetry is essentially a literary not a graphic medium. I agree with Pierre Garnier's insistence
that a border exists between the literary and the graphic, and that a
great deal of surreptitious smuggling has been transpiring out of the
former and into the latter. I also agree with John Gardner that literature is by its nature "devoted to searching out truth, often by the
use of highly innovative forms," and that what "passes for art" today
is too often merely pretentious and hollow. Unfortunately, visual poetry, along with the rest of experimental art, is not exempt from such
an indictment.
    The pioneers of visual poetry, Mallarmé, Gomringer, the de Campos,
et al., explored and staked claim to a very large and fertile territory of literary expressiveness, a territory known since antiquity (e.g.,
the palindrome, Byzantine and medieval Latin pattern poetry, etc.) but
never before treated as a major area for serious literary endeavor. In
the mind-numbing barrage of theoretical ballyhoo that has accompanied
the development of visual poetry, one rather basic consideration has
tended to be obscured, probably because it is too unexciting and coun-
terrevolutionary: no amount of slick graphics or glib jargon can substitute for fulfilling literature's basic duty to make semantically
meaningful statements on the human condition, on love, death, the divine, the natural world, childhood, the individual and society, and so
on. Rheme does not supersede theme. Literary experimentation is significant only in so far as its formal innovation causes long-enshrined
truths to live again.
    What is it that visual poetry now allows to be said vividly again?
What essential aspects of existence does it express effectively where
other poetic forms no longer can? What exactly is its value? Eugen
Gomringer provides, I believe, the clue to answering these interwoven
questions. He says: "Unter Konstellationen verstehe ich die Gruppie-
rung von wenigen, verschiedenen Worten, so dass ihre gegenseitige Be-
ziehung nicht vorwiegend durch syntaktische Mittel entsteht, sondern
durch ihre materielle, konkrete Anwesenheit im selben Raum." Which I
translate as: "I understand constellation to mean the grouping of a
few separate words in such a way that their reciprocal relationship
arises not primarily through syntactical means but through their material, concrete presence in space itself." Freedom from the conven-
tionalizing effects of syntax, the presentation of a minimal amount of
linguistic material patterned into an essential relationship, the evo-
cation of sheer presence itself: these are the distinguishing features
of the best visual poetry. What they permit is a penetration to authentic existence, a Heideggerian naming of the holy, a meditation on the
radiant thingness of things.
    Which brings me to what I take for my other clue: Martin Heidegg-
er's statement that "die Rede hat die Möglichkeit zum Gerede zu werden"
("discourse has the potential to become trivial talk"). What he is
getting at here is that language all too readily loses its connectedness to primordial being and floats uprooted in the meaningless twad-
dle of everyday, average awareness. It is the task of poetry to maintain connectedness. Considered in this regard, visual poetry appears
particularly suited to fulfill internationally in contemporary literature the function that haiku has traditionally performed in Japanese

literature, which R.H. Blythe tells us has been to express an "enlightenment in which we see into the life of things." This satori-experience of the indwelling presence of being is basic to authentic human existence, yet it is the easiest of all poetic themes to talk at length around and leave at last untouched. Stripped of its ideographic script, the haiku in Western languages has not achieved the same power that it has had in Japanese, nor is it likely to. It is difficult to imagine an occidental version of Basho, a major poet of the first rank whose primary genre is the haiku. Yet the need to express this kind of ontological insight in Western languages is pressing, especially in this half-century when for so many of us such insights are all that remains of religious experience. This is precisely the need that visual poetry is uniquely capable of meeting for our times. No other form now is capable of doing this with the same immediacy and power.

As an example of a visual poem that restates a primordial truth as old as humankind and does so in a way that resurrects that insight to vivid freshness, I would direct the reader's attention to Haroldo de Campos' well-known "cristal/fome/forma" (see Mary Ellen Solt, Concrete Poetry: A World View, 1968 ed., p.99). Before discussing this poem, however, it is necessary first to dispel the notion that a visual poem cannot be explicated. Any visual poem the meaning(s) of which cannot be derived through close critical analysis of its text is meaningless as literature and therefore a bad poem, no matter how interesting as graphic art. Examining the de Campos poem then, we find it to be constructed of four simple Portuguese words: cristal (crystal), fome (hunger), de (of, for), forma (form). Cristal is repeated eight times to make two four-word visual patterns, each of which is the mirror-image of the other in so far as the positioning of the words is concerned (though all words in each pattern read left to right). One of these patterns flows down into the poem from the upper left; the other rises out of it from its bottom right. In between these two patterns, literally encased in cristal, is a third formed by syntactic inversion. A little to the left of center stands fome; beginning directly below is fome de forma; directly below that, forma de fome; then a little to the right of center one line down, forma. The result is a perfectly regular inversion pattern made possible by the minimalist use of syntax. The preposition de introduces the syntactic element into this middle pattern and stands twice in the process directly at the center of the poem. Thus, three patterns characterized by perfect symmetry make up the work: yet when their total visual arrangement together, their structural gestalt, is perceived, it creates the overall impression of a-symmetry, of a graceful and natural imbalance. The words themselves taken as semantic units create a similar tension: cristal and forma suggest symmetry, stasis, perfection; while fome with its visceral hunger and de with its syntactic energy evoke the irregular, the dynamic, the evolving. In the semantic gestalt of these four words we find the theme of the poem: that restless striving after transcendent beauty, that hunger for crystalline form, which by their very nature involve a paradoxical fusion of being and becoming, flux and eternity.

I would like to go on, but this should be enough to suggest my concerns.

Eugene, Oregon
January 6, 1979

Jerome Rothenberg

FROM AN INTERVIEW: "ART & THE TWO TECHNOLOGIES"

(Conclusion): "There are two sides to the technology concern at present,
which makes this period in some ways different from others in this century.
One is that a great deal of technology is now actually involved in the art
process: a utilization of all those technological means that could have any
possible relevance to art-making. Along with that there is another side,
which I think involves a new anxiety about the continuation of the whole
technological process & which may be reaching a critical point in the face
of our projected energy depletion, & so forth. As the concern with technology comes increasingly up against the threat that the great energy-consuming,
technological superstructure may prove to be a short-lived phenomenon, the
other side emerges as a search for an older technology of the sacred that
utilizes those means that are available to everyone in his or her locale,
rather than the kind of power that has to be drawn from distant sources. This
was brought home--not for the first time either--during last night's computer
music conference at UCSD [University of California at San Diego], when the
electric power at the school was knocked out, nearly forcing the cancellation
of the final major concert. All of it depended on electrically powered
instruments & without that distant source of energy, there was simply no way
to continue. A hundred musicians, a hundred living bodies in that room, &
no way, no reason to continue.
     "It's maybe in the face of that illusion of power that one has seen
many composers who were fascinated by & did considerable work with electronic
equipment during the 50s & early 60s, gradually shifting over to an exploration of apparently simple acoustical procedures--even simpler technologically
than those provided by conventional orchestral instruments. A technically
savvy composer like Pauline Oliveros, say, can move from electronic & computer music to pieces which may involve nothing more technologically elaborate
than banging two stones together. It's struck me as interesting for years now
that, even before the energy crunch, some of the artists involved with the
culture's most advanced forms of technology have also played the other side--
have sometimes come back full circle, to work with the most seemingly minimal
but sometimes most satisfying forms of technology: fundamental / universal
human tools.
     "So, ultimately, if the individual is reduced to the individual & his
or her immediate circumstances, there are still ways of surviving & of continuing to do what has to be done, without that strong distaste for the
technological & modern that characterized a lot of work earlier in the
century. I think we live pretty much at ease in a technological world, but
there's also an awareness that it's possible to become a victim of that
technology; & when the power goes out (as it seems to be doing more & more)
you find yourself with nothing to do & nowhere to do it."

[Recorded by Coryl Crane, October 30, 1977, in Encinitas, California.]

Tragedy

The Brothers Karamazov is a tragedy. Any method of criticism, archetypal, structural, linguistic, biographical, Marxist or psychoanalytical applied to the novel will yield the same richness and complexity, the same themes of reversal, recognition and hubris, the same description of a society evolving from a tribal, feudal, oral and magic world to a world of nations, individualism, of vision and justice, from the private and sexual to the public and political, and similar treatments of incest and taboo, exchange of women, bastard and exiled offspring, blindness, madness, putrefaction, prophecy, murder and suicide that King Lear and the Oresteia or the Oedipus trilogy yield.

That Dostoevsky used the novel as the form and commodity most accessible to his public and most suitable for his Russian drama rather than the Greek proscenium or the Elizabethan stage should in no way mitigate its true proportions as tragedy nor should its apparent lack of art prevent us from placing it, along with War and Peace, on the same creative level and originality as the fugues of Bach, the perspective of Leonardo, the mysticism of baroque Spain, the paintings of the Dutch masters, the cathedrals of France, the Vedas of India or the Biblical literature of the Semitic world.

The father, Fyodor Pavlovitch, bears all the traits of the titan whose blood stains the sons stirring memory and desire. He carries on with the buffoonery of a Falstaff, the cryptic wisdom of Lear's jester and the indomitable irritability of an angry god. True to all the legends of folklore and myth, a second wife, young and sloe-eyed, usurps the dead Junoesque mother's place, the abandoned sons are rescued by the kindly peasants, Grigory and Marfa, are later brought up by surrogate parents and each one, crippled with his particular ideas, prejudices, remembrances and unfulfilled needs returns home in search of an answer to that overwhelming question.

Dimitri is half-god, half-beast, one part Don Juan, one part John of the Cross. To take over his aristocratic role as landowner, a role to which he has no verifiable legal right but which he is convinced is his, he must struggle against his father. In transcending his Fyodor's limitations Dimitri discovers passion and the new seed of conscience. He can only regain unity through atonement and self-mortification, the purgatory of Siberian prison-camps, like the hermits, prophets and martyrs of early Christianity. Dimitri's spiritual father will be the Elder who, as a retired soldier and reformed Casanova, recognizes the affinity he shares with him and sees in him the makings of the saint he would have wished to be when he prostrates himself at his feet. As a true theocrat he is tied to the institution of the monastery and the public rituals that have been expected of him. He recognizes the perils of his choice and advises the youngest son to leave the monastery.

Ivan, having attained the cool plateau of the intellect, is no longer divided by earth and sky, body and soul as are Fyodor and Dimitri. For him the division exists in the stratas of his mind, rational problems bred from the complexities of enlightenment and understanding: nihilism, rebellion, history and evolution, atheism and freedom, Yeatsian phantasms of the imagination. He avoids Dimitri's struggle by sublimating it, retreating further into the cerebral, the objective and empirical. On the one hand he craves stories, allegories, books and arguments to grapple with the demon he has ensconced in his over-cultivated psyche. On the other hand, with scientific optimism, industry, socialism, democracy and the boons of mechanism he hopes to create that happy valley Faust tried to create. As the archetypal bureaucrat and academic with all the disadvantages of a symmetrical education he handles irony with the mastery of a Stendhal, snickers with the pessimism of a Schopenhauer and muses with the crestfallen self-deprecations of a Prufrock weeping over the graveyards of the past, for whom the mermaids will not sing and the cup of life will be drained when he is thirty. He worries over the discrepancy between action and reflection and discovers not the neat little categories of Newton, the pat certitudes of Cartesian logic or the smiling face of Utopia but the smirk of Mephistopheles. He can only be reconciled to the world and redeemed, so to speak, by transgressing Kantian imperatives and rediscovering the irrational: brain fever.

The aloof, ecstatic Alyosha is the new breed, the Mandarin, the angel, the brave new world. He has solved Ivan's difficulties by withdrawing into relative idiocy like Prince Myshkin in the Idiot. His allegiance to children expresses both his lack of real power in practical affairs and in matters where passion and personality are involved and his ability to perform the socialist and educational tasks that appeared so problematic to Ivan. He is the guru for whom the only recourse to maintain unity is a patient concern for a world which is always on the point of eluding his otherworldly visions, his appeasing quietism.

Smerdyakov resolves Alyosha's contradictions, the brooding extremes of his character by committing the one act which would catapult them all back to reality: murder. In him all the polarities and distinctions from which culture builds its songs, fortresses and theories collapse. The center no longer holds. The dog kills the master and hangs himself.

The scenes that are held in the family home, in the tavern and finally in front of the dying monk, Zossima, the old order of chthonic dread and family feuds, in the beginning of the book, are repeated at the end of the novel first in a private hearing, then in a public court of law. What was experienced in "real life" is now experienced beneath the neon lights of the institution. Here the evidence for the trumped-up charges are the testimonies of "medical experts," tangible displays and props, witnesses who shed the immediacy of their former identities and once put on the witness stand become Pirandellian actors. It is not what is said that counts but the cool certainty and journalistic confidence with which it is said, the grave monotone which everyone, witness, defendant, prosecutor and judge, strives to maintain and which paradoxically heightens the sensationalism of their accounts. The entire setting reduces everyone to an equal sense of majesty and an equal sense of impotence. In the eyes of the peasants on the jury and the ladies of the audience the very fact Dimitri is to be judged condemns him. Here all the world's a stage, the play's the thing.

The hinge on which the trials rests is money. Who has the money? How much? Where? It is the same money which blurred regional boundaries, broke the feudal world and with supple confusions eroded the land, laid waste the sky and then endowed a million for the arts. Murder is no longer the question. It is the devious business of banking which ultimately condemns Dimitri to the guillotine's scaffold and, in the eyes of the mob, he begins to take the place of the father whose greed and violence are gradually forgotten and who is then venerated as ancestor and founder of the nation. Dimitri is sentenced in order to propitiate the original murder, to amortize the impact of the tribal guilt and responsibility that the public begins to recognize as its own. Rather than assaulted by a deranged Smerdyakov, he is condemned to the tortures of reason, interrogations, and committee hearings. Where in the old order only intimations of truth were expressed, here it is tough reality which hypnotizes the participants and the truth is obscured first by the law's Perry Mason eagerness for the facts, second by Alyosha whose self-containment prevents him from helping his brother and finally by Ivan who recognizes at last the hypocrisy of a court which vicariously craves the passions and murder it denounces. Absorbed, however, his belated discovery of the TRUTH Ivan confirms the prejudicial convictions of the jury with his ravings.

Before the trial in a private hearing in the tavern, the police captain Makarov, who still shares the baroque emotionalism and holistic intensity of Dimitri's world, curses him for having killed his father while the young lawyers chide him for his lack of restraint. Yet later, as prodigal in his forgiveness as in his damnation he laments Dimitri's predicament and attempts to appease the hysterical Grushenka whereas his fellow investigators relentlessly pursue their victim. Their chilling tactics, intent on discovering a motive which will satisfy the mechanical and clinical bias of their outlook, forebode the self-righteous accusations and humiliations of fascism. At the trial itself, the doctor Herzenstube (heart-pump) is German like the incompetent strategians of Russia in Tolstoi's War and Peace. His world, identical to the world of the investigating lawyers, the other practitioners, the defense attorney and the prosecutor is sustained by a Victorian obsession with reputation, barrel-toned accents of self-importance, fatuous benevolence, Jungian digressions into irrelevant memories, rhetorical flourishes and technical jargon. His inability to see the gravity of the crime and the issues and living men it puts into question parodies the inadequacies of the one-dimensional world of German philosophy and mystic poetry whose phenomenological approach to life, in which rootless things and terms pressed against a glorious Weltanschauung merely appear, has cradled speculative thought for the last two centuries.

Dostoevsky sees a society progressively surrendering itself to the spectacles of rainbow-colored money, foreign literature and schemes of self-aggrandizement like the woman mentioned at the opening who, emulating Shakespeare's Ophelia, throws herself from a cliff. All the brothers are accessories to the murder; the innocent commit the crime by default. Out of some defiant hubris each has willfully pursued his particular identity and by so doing has evaded his responsibilities, destroyed the unity of family and community. Each suffers a cathartic recognition. The variously depicted by epileptic fits, fevers, trances and ecstasy and each pays the price of tragedy: bliss is exchanged for knowledge. The lobotomized criminal Smerdyakov, unhampered by a society dissolving under its own momentum is the agent of all three brothers, the incarnation of apocalypse. As an untouchable, cook and eunuch, he gathers about him all the taboos associated with eating, elimination and burial.

At the end of the novel, we see Alyosha, ineffectual in his brother's trial, taking care of the children who briefly express the hope of an integrated, harmonious community and yet who reveal themselves to be very similar to the four Karamazovs, promising a rerun, though on a different scale, of the story's tragic events. The natural death of the child Ilusha compensates the violent murder of the Father and the novel closes with the boy's comrades gathering at his funeral. Having witnessed the story from start to finish, they will tell all and cry out "Hurrah for Karamazov".

The clarity and immediacy of Dostoevsky's sense tragedy has made Raskolnikov the Orestes, Oedipus and Hamlet of our time, Stavrogin and Rogozhin the Macbeth, Othello and Medea, Myshkin the Prospero and Tiresias. It is our craving for individual psychological explanations that has led us to interpret Dostoevsky with a Freudian angle and has obscured his great comic burlesque scenes, his Olympian aloofness as a storyteller and his attempt to transcend Western individualism and its Faustian mentality with the cliché that he revels in hysteria and is prey to the morbid fantasies of the criminal mind.

Tragedy is only possible when in reaching for an ideal unity and an ideal sense of justice the world is shattered and abstract, artificial institutions that insure political cohesion, personal freedom and pleasure replace even the semblance of unity. The impelling necessity for change, the by now hormonal imperatives for growth clips humanity of its wings. Where the sense of tragedy disappears life appears sentimental or pathetic. The joys of passion give way to the sorrows of compassion.

the unlimited or indefinitely great general re
ceptacle of things, commonly conceived as
an expanse extending in all directions, in
which, or occupying portions of which, all
material objects are located. The portion
or extent of this in a given instance; ext
nt or room in three dimensions. Exten
area; a particular extent of surface.

Edwin Schlossberg

Some words on the untimely publication in which some of everyone's is included.

It encourages being precious and limiting the scope to those thoughts that
will be recognized as important and valid by peers, and of course, his plowman.

Rejecting those others perched delicately on my shoulders he begins to write
the history of that part of the world that no one could possibly know.

Words mark the possibilities for agreement. They mark the path and the gate

through which, using time, we are forced to measure our ability to

persuade others to continue, follow us, forget, laugh, cry, and dissemble.

In the other world that is always alluded to when this world is criticized

there is perfection and stillness and it is all one way and unambiguous

and therefore part of a literary movement.

So often the experiments we propose blend into the kind of thoughts that

occur when anxiety is high and there is nothing to do- like stealing the

medallions off of cars- and so we find writing that discourages anyone from

admitting their own frailty and believing in the immortality of the history

of literature. The test for greatness in literature is very similar to the

test to see if someone is still alive- you hold a mirror up to the lips

and if it mists, its alive.

Literature has learned alot from advertising, lately. Admitting that the

poet, novelist, author, is a product, is quite common and disappointing.

Someday I expect the telephone directory to be considered the great work

of literature.

Using the history of symbolism to enrich words is like flying a kite and

asking the reader to understand from their own viewpoint in the wind.

Just like a colleague is someone you don't really like but spend time with,

so the spirit of a coterie spreads its charm, selectively, pulling up

chairs, encouraging criticism, making notes, all in the spirit of imagined

similarity with the way it was in de Stael.

These words are aimed at the postcard school of thought that remembers the

present, wistfully.

In light of all this, and in spite of it, in lieu of all discomfort,

and because of it, beside all the falseness and underneath it, next to the

competetion and above it, is the sincere and insightful wish to suggest

something, to realize something, however slight, that raises the prospects

for when the earth occludes the sun, and because we all need to sing by the

fire....

On Mt. McKinley there is a place
where ice and rock
slits the wind
stammering, in the midst of this tear,
we bend our eyes down
in the water, cool, flowing by stones
in the morning, while closing, by the leaves,
in the sight of, notching, in the place of,
our hands.

Edwin Schlossberg/1979

Seashell

by Howard Schwartz
calligraphy Tsila Schwartz

You say
The sea has been hidden
Somewhere in this house
Of song
I say
What is this shell
That surrounds us
As if the outer edges of the sea
Had grown
Hard?

You say
It is the song of the sea
We hear
I say
It is only the echo
That reaches us
Nothing more

You say
It is the long breath
Of the sea
That sustains
The song
I say no
It is the song itself
That came first
The song that created
The sea.

You say
Who sustains this long breath
Whose voice
Speaks through this vessel
That grows transparent
I say
It is the song
Singing in harmony
With itself
Voice
And quivering reed.

You say
The song of the seashell
Haunts your sleep
Until parted from your dreams
I say
Every night
Another dreamworld is created
And consumed.

You say
No matter how far it is carried
From the shore
The shell cannot forget
The sea
I say
We are the ones
Who have forgotten to carry it
Closer.

You say
The sea has been hidden
Somewhere in this house
Of Song
I say
It is for you to find it.

address to the Academy of Fine Ideas

with thanks to Wallace S. of Hartford for the title
and with continuous backward looks at the Teacher
Wm Blake in thankful recognition that he reminds us
of the marmorealizing seductions of Father Embodiment
also to be known as The Old One of the Unearned Visage
and with public avowal of my desire for just a little version
of Manjushri's sword maybe just on Thursdays and in
obeisance to the acceptance that poetry is one more, nourishing,
manifestation of the conquest of ego:

post-modern
post-impressionist
poster
post-office pasty
            potty
post Mithra
postmisthress
  ptootle ptime
pretty post-moderns
                        pasta
    paste-moderns
                    putti-
putti
      bost-boderns
                    boaster post-nose do you have a code too
poop deck Eb-L-A Assoc nasal
   pretty pasty professeur pro-
          fesses
                    fess up re pre-post ante magnacurioloquenti glauque
      preppie
there is the sudden

                                                penetration
    of   cut-
              ting, one
slash of the sword which may take a fraction of a second but
    with
          each
                  stroke
    the past and   future
                  networks

are severed
                                        completely it is a very sharp
            is a very sharp   is sword

Armand Schwerner

DAVID SEAMAN SAYS:

One thing you must have noticed about

the avant-garde in poetry and writing in general

is that you look at it. I mean you

look at it and

see it. After all,

that's believing, baby.

BUT THERE IS MORE to life and art than believing--some of it is
advertising, so there is an element of hype in the type. The

SUBCONSCIOUS.

Masseur McLuhan is right, so is subtle Mallarmé, and no one can
escape those credits. Except the singers.

This page was set up with assistance from my graphic design coordinator
in West Virginia, good old

DOUG KRANCH

(working in the branch office).

He and I devise a text in the same way that we do videotapes together.
We mess around until we find what carries the meaning and looks good.

looks good!

(See what I mean?)

Good looking
means the
body
of the
text has
form, sex appeal.

How to talk of love in a typeface that reminds you of bat wings?

And is this the way to discuss the pin valve in the carburetor, or the exhaust of a Diesel engine?

Why do you think you can tell
a Chinese girl

NOW THAT'S UNFAIR!

She doesn't comb her hair that way

WILLINGLY

So it can never compare with
your long underwear.

At what point does this concept of avant-garde become daringly

derrière

I like work in which the process of making the work is a prime component of the work. Even more I like works which suggest ways in which I can participate, add to, or replicate the process in some aspect of my ordinary life. Three of my favorite books which do this are:

Nelson Howe, <u>Body Image</u> (New York: Burning Deck, 1970)
rjs and tl Kryss, <u>Dialogue in Pale Blue</u> (Cleveland: Broken Mimeo Press, 1969)
Daniel Spoerri, <u>Anecdoted Topography of Chance</u> (New York: Something Else Press, 1966)

The text of <u>Body Image</u> consists of thirteen unbound pages. Each page is a "score" or map for a dance performance. The core of the page is a number of small photographs of a female torso and a male torso entwined in various positions suggestive of love-making. Although they are highly erotic, they have the abstract quality of dance. Each sheet also contains a combination of dotted lines (for locomotion other than walking), solid lines (one performer locomotes the other), and Rosemary Waldrop poetry lines (e.g. "We overrate the cohesion of the body," "I dreamed I was a sheet of water/ If I got up I would disperse,"). Each sheet is a beautiful graphic. There is a separate page telling us how to follow the photographs and the lines for a dance/poetry performance. The instructions are complicated and take a couple of readings to assimilate. I like that. I like that alot..... I like the care that went into creating them. I find great pleasure in figuring out how to apply the instructions to each page. I like these kinds of instructions because they get me into things I would never have gotten into on my own. The patience they require invokes a slower and deeper appreciation of the tableaux of our torsos whenever lovemaking or just dancing at it.

<u>Dialogue in Pale Blue</u> has no words beyond the title page. There are 17 pages. On twelve of them there are one (occasionally two) examples of what might be called two-dimensional abstract origami pasted to the page. Most of them unfold. They are not particularly ingenious. Both the pages and the origami are of pale blue paper. There's no way of knowing who said what in the dialogue or anything else about how the dialogue was constructed. I like it because it evokes a number of simple straight-forward alternative sets of rules for its construction. The title page indicates "200 entirely different copies were made." I look at my one copy and have fun imagining how rj and tl sat down at a table and made 17 of them before they got tired of doing it, or maybe 23, or maybe they decided to stick with it for 50 a night for 4 nights no matter how they felt.

An <u>Anecdoted Topography of Chance</u> is a documentation of all the objects on Spoerri's table at a particular moment in 1961. Each object is described and Spoerri indicates, if he can remember, how he got it. Spoerri and a few other people associate various facts and anecdotes in footnotes appended after each item. There are 80 discrete objects including shirt buttons, burnt matches, a paring knife, two different staplers, a safety pin, coins, a chunk of bread, etc., etc., etc.. It's such a thoroughly low-key work of idiosyncratic scholarship that it's hilarious.

Each of the books imposed more rules on the authors than on me. Once I have my own understanding of how they did it, I carry the books in my head as new metaphors. I use them to make extraordinary events where before only commonplace situations existed.

Brian Sherman/Oglethorpe University/Atlanta, Georgia/May 1,1979

Ron Silliman

IDEOLOGICAL FUNCTION OF THE MATRIX

Poets create products, called poems.

Or, more accurately, poetry, a collective & continually evolving product carried forward only by people in groups (to write in total isolation is to propose one specific, negative, definition of this collectivity), subsequently subjected (in the most literal sense) to a trans- & deforming piecework atomization yielding individual poems. This mass product, poetry, itself just one sector, however strategic, of a larger social field, literature, is a mere element of culture, the role of which is to make, or resist making, possible the reproduction of the educational, aesthetic & theoretical preconditions for the continuation of the social relations of production constituting the fundamental economic entity, which at this late moment of history is quite simply the world. The normal term for this social role is ideology, & it is thru ideology that culture (therefore poetry) discovers & defines its ultimate survival value.

Because poetry is one product in a capitalist world economy, its distribution & consumption occurs in the form of commodities: books, magazines, records, video & audio tapes, readings, workshops, classes, etc. The very process of entering into this "extraliterary" network, separating any one unit (or series of units) of the author's production from the context of her (often as-yet-incomplete) total body of work, & that also (always, at the same time) from the larger social contexts in which it was written, is what transforms poetry, the product, into commodities, called poems.

Some critical elements of the commodity relations of poetry:
- -- many of the individuals involved do not themselves produce poetry, such as editors, publishers, teachers, distributors et al;
- --it is this side of poetry, not its productive relations, which determines what portions (for it is always only a fragment) shall be "in print," i.e., available for consumption, the most important aspect of which is commonly called "influence";
- -- these relations, to a greater extent than is normally acknowledged, determine how many individual poets shall be employed (one clear instance of declassing: the creative writing professors of the sixties have become the circuit-riding poetry-in-the-schools paraprofessionals in the seventies), & therefore the conditions under which they will produce (time is the most crucial factor here, but quality of concentration also enters in).

The primary relationship in the evolution of poetry in a class civilization (the world economy, fundamentally capitalist in spite of its occasional "local communisms") is neither that of its production, nor of its consumption, but of the transformation of the one into the other. The most remarkable aspect of this is its basic invisibility.

I have elsewhere discussed the function of what I call the matrix in the productive relations of poetry. In brief, this conceptual posit is an abstraction, an apprehension possessed by every writer of the totality of (relevant) literature. It is the subjective perception of context. As such, it has both positive & negative functions. Positively, to determine the shape of (diachronic) tradition & also of (synchronic) community --

shapes which differ radically between even the closest of poets. Negatively, as a guide toward a subjective region of perceived necessity, "blindspots" requiring the production of new poems. I have noted also that this apprehension is not the same for all sectors of poetry, nor at different historical periods, & that it likewise will undergo a pronounced evolution with the maturation of the individual poet: tradition will weigh more heavily on younger writers & it will be the tradition of Others, while an older poet may find her tradition & community almost entirely defined by her own activity of writing over long years. An ironic, but useful, picturing of the matrix can be found in the back pages of Jack Spicer's Collected Books, in the questionnaire for his magic workshop.

By practice as well as by definition, the subjectivity of the matrix idealizes poetry. The black lesbian who perceives herself to be writing for a workingclass feminist readership is apt to have no place in her matrix (i.e., in the productive relations of her writing) for a preppy, male "language" poet, altho either may enter into numerous relations with one another in regards to the commodity circulation of poetry. Idealized thus, poetry, which lacks even the modest profit motivations of other genres of writing, appears to be an independent, self-motivating, self-generating entity. This massive reification, exacerbated by the continual growth in the absolute number of poets active in the United States, leads to fragmentation, social isolation, paranoia, competition & all the other cultural deformations of a capitalist economy, culminating in an individual sense of irrelevancy & helplessness which causes many writers, even "political" ones, to turn inward (how many poets writing for "the people" are in actuality writing for the Self?).

Understood as this subjectivity, this reconstitution of the relations of commodity/production into an imaginary, non-existent ideal, the matrix can now be reconceived usefully. Further analysis of this transformation of one (objective) set of relations into the other (subjective) eventually can be expected to yield a new, deeper understanding of how each formal question in literature is, simultaneously & primarily, a political question. This in sharp contrast to the vulgar equation heretofore made between these two realms by certain "Marxist" poets. Of crucial importance in reconstituting the relations between production & consumption will a new analysis of the relation of the work to its "audience," around issues not only on the order of those posed by Brecht's rejection of "empathy," but also concerning such topics as "influence," both in daily life & the production of new literature (which, at different levels, amount to the same thing).

This analysis is already being conducted by several writers, & it is worth noting here that they do not generally come from the same "regions" of poetry, which is to say they identify & create different sectors of the total poetry audience. Unlike Baraka, who perceived the importance of the issue of poetry as fundamentally ideological & bearing formally on the question of audience, but who jettisoned his readership for the safety of agreement, it is conceivable that these writers might at some future point work collaboratively in different audience sectors toward a common goal: the world, as well as the word, made new.

for Don Byrd & Bruce Boone

INTERVIEW WITH A MINIFICTIONIST, by e. a. sklepowich

Z-- needs little introduction to readers of our journal. Born in
1945 in a small Rhode Island town, Z-- shook up the literary world
in 1971 with his first work, "Epic," a paragraph-long story dealing with what one critic called "the collective nightmare of negation in the twentieth century." His stories and novels, christened
"minifictions" by some, "briefs" by others, occupy the territory
between silence and what Z-- names "unsilence." Part of Arctic,
his work-in-progress, has appeared in Byzantium and has been hailed
as "one of the purest demonstrations of the sacredness of play in
literature." The interview, which Z-- agreed to only on the condition that it be short, took place on a bright April afternoon in
1979 in his Greenwich Village apartment. Dominating Z--'s clut-
tered work space is a hand-written sign, "Beware the pure too-
little and the empty too-much."

Q. What writers do you most admire?

A. Mallarmé, James, Kafka, Borges, Sarraute, Robbe-Grillet, Corta-
zar, Enrique Anderson Imbert, Barthelme, Margarita Karapanou, André
Pieyre de Mandiargues. I'm sure I've forgotten several.

Q. When your story "Epic" appeared in 1971, it caused quite a
stir. In fact, it still does. How did you come to write it?

A. I had just finished writing the last chapter of an extremely
long novel and was making the usual revisions, a few minor ones.
Then I started to cut one particular chapter in the heart of the
novel and moving first backward and then ahead, I cut and cut and
cut. It took me much longer to make the cuts than it had to put
the novel together. When I finished, I had that one paragraph, itself heavily revised.

Q. Were the cuts arbitrary? Was there a rule of thumb?

A. I started with the usual: adverbs, adjectives, all those words
like "very," "rather," and "pretty" that dear old Strunk mentions.
Unnecessary dialogue and descriptions, then extraneous characters
and situations, finally the main character himself. I believe
Picasso talks somewhere about his paintings as sums of destructions, and I think of the process I went through in a similar manner. Except that the red I removed from one part never showed up
in another. It was gone forever. Each time I removed something,
I felt disburdened. By getting down to almost nothing, I was able
to concentrate my attentions.

Q. Then what do you consider your work's most characteristic element?

A. I'd rather talk about those elements that aren't characteristic. I'm referring of course to those which aren't there at all.

Q. Which are?

A. Aren't they obvious by their absence?

Q. Your work has been called a "fake." Does this disturb you?

A. On the contrary, it delights me. My fiction pretends to be
nothing but a fiction, and in a sense by reducing the number of
words and elements on the page I am turning the story into an
objet, something to be read and observed simultaneously. As art
empties itself, it becomes more itself, more fictive. Balzac,
Dickens, and Tolstoy succeeded in obscuring their fabrications by
taking a quantitative approach to their lies.

Q. But don't you risk boring the average reader?

A. First of all, I am not interested in the average reader. Second, the issue is not boredom. It's terror.

Q. Could you explain?

A. Most readers are terrorized by all that white space. They have
come to expect writers to fill it up for them. They look at all
the space and see only emptiness. But for me it is fullness. Hal-
lowness, not hollowness. And there are, of course, those who read
me for the wrong reasons. They're hurried and find my fictions a
relief. I have a lurking suspicion that these readers also find
something Dutch in them.

Q. Dutch?

A. Immaculate, neat, trim, all swept and arranged. They probably
live in places with a lot of chrome and glass and nowhere to sit.

Q. One might say that your own fictions have no places to "sit
in." How far can you go? Aren't your works in danger of disappearing? Isn't there something self-destructive here?

A. Well, one critic said that my Divine Comedy was the farthest I
could go: three pages, the first filled with thousands of warring
words written over and across each other, indecipherable, turning
the page completely black; the next, a few words released on purple paper; the last, as blank and virginal as Mallarmé's margins.
And that was two years ago. Since then I've written three books,
each something different, but each continuous with the one before.
When the sections from Arctic were published, a French critic said
I was "in quest of sainthood," that I hated matter and was rejecting life's bourgeois clutter by ultimately removing everything
from my work. I was a bit flattered to be put in the company of
the saints, but as a former Catholic I am too much in love with
les choses to give them up altogether, especially in my work.

Q. Might it not be said that Robbe-Grillet . . .

THE SURREALIST MOVEMENT IN THE U.S.   Larry Smith

"Especially here in the United States, surrealism has the power to decisively de-
throne and guillotine the ignoble traditions of positivism-pragmatism-rationalism-
humanism which for a century and a half, at least have stifled the development of
revolutionary thought in this country."   --Franklin Rosemont (1970)

Surrealist Andre Breton amd Bolshevik Leon Trotsky are patron saints of this Chicago
based group that first presented itself in a 1970 "Surrealism in the Service of the
Revolution" edition of the S.D.S. Radical America magazine. Since then a nucleus of
artists, writers, and comrades have formed in Chicago under the leadership of Franklin
and Penelope Rosemont, with small satelite support coming from San Francisco, New York,
New Orleans, Wisconsin. Since their interview with the aging Andre Breton in 1966, the
Rosemonts have maintained direct contact with the International Surrealist Movement, of
which their journal Arsenal: Surrealist Subversion is perhaps the strongest surviving
organ for subversion. Fifty years after the first Surrealist Manifesto in 1924, Surrealism has emerged forcefully in the U.S. However, Rosemont makes quite clear, "Let it be
understood that we are not interested in the 'Americanization' of surrealism, but rather the surrealist transformation of America—and of the whole world." It is a subver-
sive and European purist stance which characterizes this active U.S. movement.

PUBLICATIONS: Avoiding the standard compromises of commercial publishers, they have
developed several outlets for their works. Black Swan Press (after Lautreamont) has
published the books of Franklin and Penelope Rosemont as well as the posters and pro-
fusely illustrated catalogs of the movement's exhibitions. It has also reprinted Andre
Breton's long automatic poem Fata Morgana which first appeared in New Directions 1941.
Then there is the Surrealist Research and Development Monograph Series which has printed or reprinted in slim pamphlets the work of present and past surrealists: Leonora
Corrington's Down Below; Toyen's Specters of the Desert with poems by Jindrich Heisler;
Benjamin Paul Blood's The Poetical Alphabet, the language experiments of this 1850's
American scientist and philosopher viewed as a precursor to Surrealism; Music Is Danger-
ous, the 1929 lecture of Belgian surrealist Paul Nouge; and the manifestoes, texts, and
drawings of U.S. Surrealists—Paul Garon, Joseph Jablonski, Peter Manti, Nancy Joyce
Peters, and Rosemont himself. The movement was given national attention in its private-
ly edited section of Lawrence Ferlinghetti's 1974 City Lights Anthology and in their
"Surrealism and Blues" section of the 1976 The Living Blues magazine.

The poetry and art are highly automatic, chiefly in the bold and free vein of Surrealist Benjamin Peret and their Surrealist ally E.F. Grannel, now living in New York.

Ragged with answers
aimless as a comb
the transcendental oysters
stir
in the gobbling gloom
          --Franklin Rosemont

The purity of the dream-rivulet crosses the depth of day
    permanent wetness from the source of things
    draped: a forest of fiery signs

From the heartbeat of electric pages, salamanders scintil-
late Black Hawk swathed in beechnut. Walking and falling
                    --Philip Lamantia

Bold, erotic, humorous, their writing and graphics are extremely open yet lack a certain humility and ease in handling the gifts of automatism and chance. Unlike the magical, almost trance-like sweep of Eluard, Cesaire, Breton, and Peret, the work often
is marred by a mechanical posturing. Perhaps they have gone further than the French in
their assault on language; perhaps they lack a certain trust and directness that alone
can release and confirm the full surreality of experience. In turth, once literary expectations are allayed, one can find moments of surreal beauty in any of their work, a
testament to Lautreamont's celebrated premise that "Poetry must be made by all."

If quicksilver is the question
look for the quarry
between the horns of the gate
in the heat of a kangaroo pouch
on the porches of paws treading
     mystery--Nancy Joyce Peters

a science of stampeding mermaids?
secret knowledge to suck the angles of crisp jade?
forbidden wisdom to throw the longest roads
    through the angriest exits
and a sow to sing her songs of instant breath
                    --Joseph Jablonski

Perhaps most importantly the movement has brought together in the three issues of
Arsenal (1970, 1973, 1976) a visible and growing commitment to the surrealist principles
of writing and revolt. The journal documents their 1974 merger with the Black Widow
group from Columbus, Ohio, and reveals the dramatic reaffirmation of former U.S. Surrealists from the 1940's and 1950's including photographer Clarence John Laughlin,
artist Jerome Kamrowski (acclaimed by Breton as the truest surrealist of the 1950's
New York school), and Philip Lamantia who has reemerged as poet and theorist of Surrealism. Black Swan Press also distributes the earlier publications of Lamantia, Breton,
Antonin Artaud, Aime Cesaire, Fernendo Arrabel, Octavio Paz, and a highly select collection of those who closely parallel their outlook including Paul Garon's informed Blues
and the Poetic Spirit, the surrealist erotic writing of Rikki Ducornet and Jayne Cortez,
and fellow American rebels Herbert Marcuse, Bob Kaufman, and Pete Winslow. Thus the
surrealists use Arsenal to keep the Surrealism in the movement as pure as possible without conceding to the compromised vision or methods of a U.S. capitalist press. Their
most recent publication "Surrealism: The Octopus-Typewriter"(Oct. 1978) is an eight
page newsprint tract to be handed out on the streets of Chicago or wherever, U.S.A.
Arsenal 4 is in the making.

POLITICS: As anyone who has come in contact with them or their journal will fully
testify, they are a caustic group inheriting Andre Breton's early characteristic of
purist head-chopper. Not only do they do a fierce weeding of their own garden of followers (some 5 members were recently chastised and exited for San Francisco),but they take
on, in a purist defiance, anyone mentioning or mentioned with a surrealist connection:
Robert Bly, Pablo Neruda, Salvador Dali, Charles Olson, Ezra Pound, Sartre, Camus, and
critics Michael Benedikt, Anna Balakian, and Mary Ann Caws. Though the movement continues to engage in activist revolt (anti-Nazi protest in Chicago 1978) and most of its
members are mutual partisans of the Workers' Defence Party, one feels a general malaise
when confronted with much of their early radical rhetoric. The continuing struggle with
taking surrealist revolt to the people in the streets is a very real one for the group.

EXHIBITIONS: The group, nonetheless, has also become the heirs to some of Breton's
genius for scandal and organized resistance to the cultural status quo. Their exhibitions have attracted a wide variety of current international works and have been supple-
mented by fine catalog statements, graphics, and verbal celebrations. Continuing to
make surrealism known and necessary in this country where theory and practice are too
often lacking or paralyzed by intellect, they maintain the Surrealist spirit of confrontation. When Franklin Rosemont is not delivering a tirade of bolshevik-surrealist radicalism, he is at times a brilliant and engaging theorist with a wide background in
International Surrealist art and the nonacademic arts of jazz, blues, and film. His
influence and that of chief artist Robert Green are apparent in the exhibitions: "First
Collective Exhibition of the Surrealist Movement in the U.S."—Gallery Bugs Bunny,
Chicago 1968; World Surrealist Exhibition "Marvelous Freedom/ Vigilance of Desire,"
Chicago 1976; Surrealism in 1978 "100th Anniversary of Hysteria," Cedarburgh, Wisconsin.

The 1976 World Surrealist Exhibition was truly international and contemporary, founded on what Rosemont describes as the yet glimmering flame of marvelous freedon: "There
remain, for most people only a few rare 'unconnected' and 'inexplicable' moments: fleeting eruptions of inspiration, sudden passions, dazzling encounters 'by chance.' Such
moments, true glimpses of the Marvelous, secure themselves permanently in each person's
psychic life, in the depths of each person's inner mythology. Shunned by repressive
reason, persecuted by routine, these magic moments nontheless remain secret signposts
for the wandering mind—for the shadow in search of its substance." Thus, while our
critics persist in the distortions of hald-truths concerning Surrealism or they rush to
throw dirt in the face of this still living movement, The Surrealist Movement in the U.S.
locates itself in the true Surrealist vision of an expanded world founded on recognition
and hope. Like Rosemont's recent, long and fortuitous Andre Breton, What Is Surrealism?
Selected Writings (Monad Press, 1978), the essence of Surrealism's generative wonder is
still very much at hand. It still opens worlds. Shunning everyone who does not embrace
Surrealism, The Surrealist Movement in the U.S. is still providing a vital service in
keeping the vision of Surrealism before us.

what radical experimentation?

"that's where i'd go,
if i could go, that's
who i'd be, if i
could be" if i

beckett

note address change

e snyder

to have entity suspended
in time, with or
without words

(without the embarrassment
of being clearly unskilled)

to produce the quality of
mind called poetry

to arouse the capacity
to be delighted

THE TIE THAT BINDS

"a pity hope is dead. no.
how one hoped above, on and
off. with what diversity"
beckett

Charles J. Stanley

NO MONEY BACK ANY TIME: PART II*

Kristine Stiles

As a writer, I do not believe in "criticism" or the "critical" process. The critic attempting to transform another person's individual meaning into collective knowledge aims to create a more comprehensive system. By so doing, the critical act represents for me, the way in which the profession of writing contributes to an already massive social structure of public distortion. I can only admit through my writing to the impact of events and personalities on the formulation of my own sensibilities. Through such admissions, I may reveal private perceptions and the continual construction of my own personality. By speculating, expanding, explaining, comparing, justifying, evaluating, equating, depreciating, elaborating, analyzing, demonstrating, and probably, ultimately, generalizing all things to fit into the continuity of my own changing understanding, you the reader may freely identify your own changing contexts in relationship to mine. From one human to the next, we should come to expect no less than such directness. Some things on my mind are:

1. Ulay/Marina Abramovich, action artists, exaggerate the most intimate struggles I have experienced in pressing for a physical synthesis yet straining for a separate identity with the man I love. Their alternating aggression, competition, desire, the innate contradiction of their inseparable yet singular condition, each represents a powerfully moving condensation of the fragility of heterosexual relations. Should I seek an isolated image of "femininity" or "masculinity", these qualities might be captured in Ulay's and Marina's attraction for and repulsion from their united androgynous image. The image of them running nakedly against the wall then turning round and running fiercely hard into each other haunts me. Their frustrated attempts to escape the edge of their flesh, to portray the brute impact of experience between them and the world, convey a futile pathos, an existence only redeemable through their relationship. And so they appear engaged in the symbolic and real search for an endless coitus which time and practical reality deny the rest of us.

2. The last time I saw, or ever shall see again, a psychologist was when I discovered her trying to manipulate me. I told her that I thought her to be dishonest and unprofessional. The muscles began to tighten on her face; her mouth twitched and an uncontrollable and terribly ugly sneer shivered between her brow and the distance to her upper lip. The hatred and self-doubt passing in contorted waves across small areas of her cheeks and chin made her face seem to shudder. I might even have begun to feel some sympathy for her. But Arnulf Rainer's nervous black, scratching marks began to trace lines over the taut and furroughed planes of her stress. These imaginary marks, recalled to my mind from the impact of his art on my emotions, quickened my awareness of the hidden psychic movements, the suffering self-conscious insecurity invisible below her skin. Rainer's art had intervened in my conscious, turning her real pain and impotency into a rapidly congealing, static and formal composition which I could appreciate aesthetically but distance myself from emotionally.

3. We have nothing equivalent in the arts and literature to the wonder of the spectacular Academy Awards. For a few hours once a year, an international audience of millions has the opportunity to peek into the intimate, "behind the scenes" relationships which are the foundations for all the big productions seen throughout the year. What particularly interests me in these extravaganzas are all those personal acknowledgements, the sentimental confessions of gratitude and respect, little details about the lives of the people who we generally only experience as fictitious representations of something else. Once a year, all the neophytes and the old stand-bys expose bits of themselves, their associations and professional connections. In this way, they become more real, more accessible?

I would like to thank the following people for their artistic contributions to my curiosity, for their idiosyncratic traits which have influenced the construction of my own value system:

Bruce Conner - California artist, for his example of utter integrity and perfectionism, for his humor and poignant, yet empathetical, expression of the absurdity of human experience, for his humanity. (See his latest film, Mongoloid, a Punk Rock masterpiece.)

Lynn Hershman - California artist, for her unfaultering optimism, drive, unrestrained generosity and persistent invention.

Peter Selz - California writer; Pierre Restany - French writer, for their lust and humor.

Ursula Krinzinger - Director, Galerie Krinzinger, Innsbruck, Austria, for her insight, keen intelligence, resilient strength and courage.

Brigit Reak-Johnson - Assistant Editor of LAICA Journal; Richard Kostelanetz - New York writer, for their adventuresome, un-selfconscious realization of new possibilities.

Jack Micheline - everywhere poet/painter, for his childlike honesty which shifts between masochistic stupidity and remarkable, lucid, social insight, for courage and resistance to all things false.

Stuart Brisley - English artist, for continuing to realize the deepest potential, the social responsibility of an "action art", for his refreshingly direct, unpretentious accessibility and deep thought.

Mark Thompson - California artist, for his example of rigorous austerity and meticulous attention to the signified meaning of all of his activity.

Aquinada - German artist, for accepting and appreciating all my banalities, for being a catalyst through his imagination.

Allan Mitelman - Australian artist, for being the most wonderful, male Jewish mother, confidant and true friend.

Eugenie Candau - California librarian, for everything.

* "No Money Back Anytime: Part I", The New Commercialist, Vol. 3, 1979, San Francisco, California. Editor, Meyer Hirsch.

+ - x ÷   ÷ x - +

COLOUR : A M A P /
A. L.   S T U B B S

1

COLOUR IS GEOGRAPHIC

SPECIFIC AS BOUNDARY

COLOUR IS A MAP

THERE IS NO SENSATION

OF COLOUR

WITHOUT /A

CONTEXT

OF LOCAL COLOUR

LOCAL COLOUR IS LOCAL

2

COLOUR IS NOT A SINGLE PROCESS

COLOUR UNITES THE SURFACE

OF THE WORLD

MONOCHROME LEVELS ITS OBJECT

TO UNIFORM MASS

DIFFERENTIATED BY VOLUME

COLOUR IS MASS

COLOUR IS ANTI-LINEAL

COLOUR DEFINES LIMITS AS SHAPES

(WHERE COLOUR STOPS)

3

EXTENSION IS RESTRICD

(WITHIN)
THE LIMITS OF SIGHT

TEMPERATURE=SATURATION:

1:2 CORRELATION

EMISSION OF COLOUR WAVELENGTH

DEPENDS ON HUE/DENSITY

DENSITY AND SATURATION ARE CO

EQUIVALENT/MULTIVALENT

4

VOLUME IS THE LINCHPIN

BETWEEN MASS AND DENSITY

MASS IS DENSITY

DENSITY FUNCTIONS AS A BOUNDARY

BOUNDARY DEFINES THE LIMIT

OF COLOUR

IN CONJUNCTION/WITH

LIGHT AS VOLUME

1/2/3/4
2/3/4/1
3/4/1/2
4/1/2/3

PAGE ONE OF TWO PAGES   FRONT PAGE

÷ x − +   + − x ÷

COLOUR : A MAP /
A. L. STUBBS

4

VOLUME IS THE LINCHPIN

BETWEEN MASS AND DENSITY

MASS IS DENSITY

DENSITY FUNCTIONS AS A BOUNDARY

BOUNDARY DEFINES THE LIMIT

OF COLOUR

IN CONJUNCTION/WITH

LIGHT AS VOLUME

3

EXTENSION IS RESTRICTED

(WITHIN)

THE LIMITS OF SIGHT

TEMPERATURE=SATURATION

1:2 CORRELATION

EMISSION OF COLOUR WAVELENGTH

DEPENDS ON HUE/DENSITY

DENSITY AND SATURATION ARE CO

EQUIVALENT/MULTIVALENT

2

COLOUR IS NOT A SINGLE PROCESS

COLOUR UNITES THE SURFACE

OF THE WORLD

MONOCHROME LEVELS ITS OBJECT

TO UNIFORM MASS

DIFFERENTIATED BY VOLUME

COLOUR IS MASS

COLOUR IS ANTI-LINEAL

COLOUR DEFINES LIMITS AS SHAPES

(WHERE COLOUR STOPS)

1

COLOUR IS GEOGRAPHIC

SPECIFIC AS BOUNDARY

COLOUR IS A MAP

THERE IS NO SENSATION

OF COLOUR

WITHOUT/A

CONTEXT

OF LOCAL COLOUR

LOCAL COLOUR IS LOCAL

4/3/2/1
3/2/1/4
2/1/4/3
1/2/3/4

PAGE TWO OF TWO PAGES

BACK PAGE

FRAGMENTS ON SIGNALISM

1. ON THE NEW FUNCTION OF ART

In the new technological era art will not disappear; its function, however, will be radically transformed. From the primary magic–religious function, through the modern–age reality--presenting art of the future, with all the things that the electronic civilization offers as well as the comletely new technologic reality, it will become "an instrument for the modification of human consciousness and for the organization of new kinds of sensibilities."

2 SIGNALISM AND TRADITION

Avant-garde (signalist) art is in such a position that it completely dispenses with tradition. What is this reflected in? Primarily in a different comprehension of the function of art. Signalist art, besides presenting new ideas, is especially concerned with widening the human sensory awareness. For these reasons this new art is in its being nondidactic and experimental, in the sense in which exact sciences are experimental.

3. THE BEING OF SIGNALIST ART

The phenomenon of signalist art as total art leads us into a labyrinth of new visions of planetary absoluteness of a being liberated from everything which we characterize as traditionalistic and didactic art. A being whose sensory apparatus is turned to the reception of the subtlest impulses and tremors of the aero–cosmic and ecological vitality. A being unburdened by formalmaterialistic and linguistic impossibilities. A being–consciouness whose metalingual communication exceeds everything we are able at this moment to imagine. Being--and--not only--that wave–signal intertwined interdependent, logically unperceptible and inexhaustible aesthetic information. A being–universe.

4. SIGNALIST WORK

A signalist work is an open work. It is an entire galactic system ready to endure all interventions without being destroyed.

This selfcreative characteristic of a signalist work is reflected not only in the case when different elements are added to expand it, but also when these elements are taken from it and it is reduced to a gesture, an idea, a concept, even to 'blank' whiteness of a sheet of paper or an empty unmarked space. A signalist work, even in these extreme cases of dematerialization, destruction, deverbalization, dephonization etc..., depending on the kind of art we are talking about, radiates its totality and indestructibility.

On the other hand, by the indestructibility and selfcreative characteristic we mean its multivalence, its plentitude of aesthetic values, hence the possibility offered to future epochs, by its inexhaustability, multitude of meanings and associations and different, constantly new ways of widening the human sensory awareness, of attracting permanent attention.

MIROLJUB TODOROVIĆ
DOBRINSKA 3,
11000 BELGRADE
YUGOSLAVIA

Miroljub Todorović: SIGNALIST POETRY

TÓTal zerOs
(1973-1977)

for everybody, nobody
and me

by

TÓT

---

0 0 0 0 0 0 0 0 0 0 0 0 0 0 0 0 0 0 0 0 0 0 0 0 0 0 0 0
0 0 0 0 0 0 0 0 0 0 0 0 0 0 0 0 0 0 0 0 0 0 0 0 0 0 0 0
0 0 0 0 0 0 0 0 0 0 0 0 0 0 0 0 0 0 0 0 0 0 0 0 0 0 0 0
0 0 0 0 0 0 0 0 0 0 0 0 0 0 0 0 0 0 0 0 0 0 0 0 0 0 0 0
0 0 0 0 0 0 0 0 0 0 0 0 0 0 0 0 0 0 0 0 0 0 0 0 0 0 0 0
0 0 0 0 0 0 0 0 0 0 0 0 0 0 0 0 0 0 0 0 0 0 0 0 0 0 0 0
0 0 0 0 0 0 0 0 0 0 0 0 0 0 0 0 0 0 0 0 0 0 0 0 0 0 0 0
0 0 0 0 0 0 0 0 0 0 0 0 0 0 0 0 0 0 0 0 0 0 0 0 0 0 0 0
0 0 0 0 0 0 0 0 0 0 0 0 0 0 0 0 0 0 0 0 0 0 0 0 0 0 0 0
0 0 0 0 0 0 0 0 0 0 0 0 0 0 0 0 0 0 0 0 0 0 0 0 0 0 0 0
0 0 0 0 0 0 0 0 0 0 0 0 0 0 0 0 0 0 0 0 0 0 0 0 0 0 0 0
0 0 0 0 0 0 0 0 0 0 0 0 0 0 0 0 0 0 0 0 0 0 0 0 0 0 0 0
0 0 0 0 0 0 0 0 0 0 0 0 0 0 0 0 0 0 0 0 0 0 0 0 0 0 0 0
0 0 0 0 0 0 0 0 0 0 0 0 0 0 0 0 0 0 0 0 0 0 0 0 0 0 0 0
0 0 0 0 0 0 0 0 0 0 0 0 0 0 0 0 0 0 0 0 0 0 0 0 0 0 0 0
0 0 0 0 0 0 0 0 0 0 0 0 0 0 0 0 0 0 0 0 0 0 0 0 0 0 0 0
0 0 0 0 0 0 0 0 0 0 0 0 0 0 0 0 0 0 0 0 0 0 0 0 0 0 0 0
0 0 0 0 0 0 0 0 0 0 0 0 0 0 0 0 0 0 0 0 0 0 0 0 0 0 0 0
0 0 0 0 0 0 0 0 0 0 0 0 0 0 0 0 0 0 0 0 0 0 0 0 0 0 0 0
0 0 0 0 0 0 0 0 0 0 0 0 0 0 0 0 0 0 0 0 0 0 0 0 0 0 0 0
0 0 0 0 0 0 0 0 0 0 0 0 0 0 0 0 0 0 0 0 0 0 0 0 0 0 0 0
0 0 0 0 0 0 0 0 0 0 0 0 0 0 0 0 0 0 0 0 0 0 0 0 0 0 0 0
0 0 0 0 0 0 0 0 0 0 0 0 0 0 0 0 0 0 0 0 0 0 0 0 0 0 0 0
0 0 0 0 0 0 0 0 0 0 0 0 0 0 0 0 0 0 0 0 0 0 0 0 0 0 0 0
0 0 0 0 0 0 0 0 0 zer0s make me calm

Ooh darling!
Yoo see, we are so lonely

00

Looking at this zero
for long makes
yoo more intelligent

I cover this zero 'cause
I don't want it to drive yoo crazy

I AM GLAD
yoo can see a vanishing zero
at last

I AM GLAD IF
yoo gaze at this zero

I AM GLAD
I could give away the other half
of this zero

A Loop-To-Do!

Mr. Fred Truck
4225 University
Des Moines, Iowa 50311

RE: LOOPS!

LIBRARY
OF
CONGRESS

Washington
D.C.
20559

Dear Mr. Truck:

Copyright protection subsists only in "original works of authorship" that are fixed in a tangible medium of expression. To be regarded as an "original work of authorship," a work such as this must contain at least a certain minimum amount of original artistic material. In all cases, it is only the artistic expression of the author that is protected by copyright.

Familiar shapes and symbols are not copyrightable. Nor are simple variations or combinations of basic geometric designs capable of supporting a copyright registration. Moreove, simple compilations of purchased articles, or craft techniques, cannot be copyrighted.

Since the material we received is limited to three dimensional material which is lacking in the sculptural authorship necessary to sustain a registration, we regret that registration is not possible. In view of this, we are closing our file without action and your registration fee will be refunded to you under separate cover.

Sincerely yours,
Bernard C. Dietz
Head, Visual Arts Section
Examining Division

LOOPS! what it's all about

© 1978 by Bolon Dzacab / Fred Truck

1. GENERAL PRINCIPLE OF VISION
    a. light rays bounce off an object. they carry an image thru the pupil of the eye. the image is reflected on the retina of the eye in an upsidedown & backwards form. the brain corrects the directional matrix.

2. CREATE A MODEL OF THIS PRINCIPLE
    a. use a Mobius strip
    b. draw a picture of something or write something on a rectangle of paper much wider than it is deep.
    c. when the paper is cut into a strip, rotated 180° & joined to itself, the image, which started out rightside up & right reading, will, by the time it meets itself again, be upsidedown & backwards.

3. PROBLEMS IN THE MODEL
    a. the image cannot be seen from every vantage pt.
        1. solve this by making the Mobius strip transparent
    b. if the image is of reality or writing (alphabetic) is used, there is no allotment for directional matrix correction, as our brains do--the image will be partly readable & partially nonsense
        1. solve this by using a non-directionally matrixed image or writing
        2. TUNCATL can be read in cartouche logo form whether it is right reading, upsidedown, or upsidedown & backwards because the numbers all begin w/a determinate & follow in a sequence--MOREOVER, each logo is a self contained unit
        3. for this reason, when writing on a Mobius, a sequence of cartouche logos is best

Fred Truck

These Familiar Shapes & Symbols Make An Outlaw

Douglas Blair Turnbaugh has published in the Atlantic, New York Magazine, Appearances and Eighth Assembling. His performance pieces have been shown at Artists Space and Grommet Art Theatre. He is a member of Colette's art band, the Victorian Punks, and is Executive Director of the Poetry Society of America, 15 Gramercy Park, New York City 10003

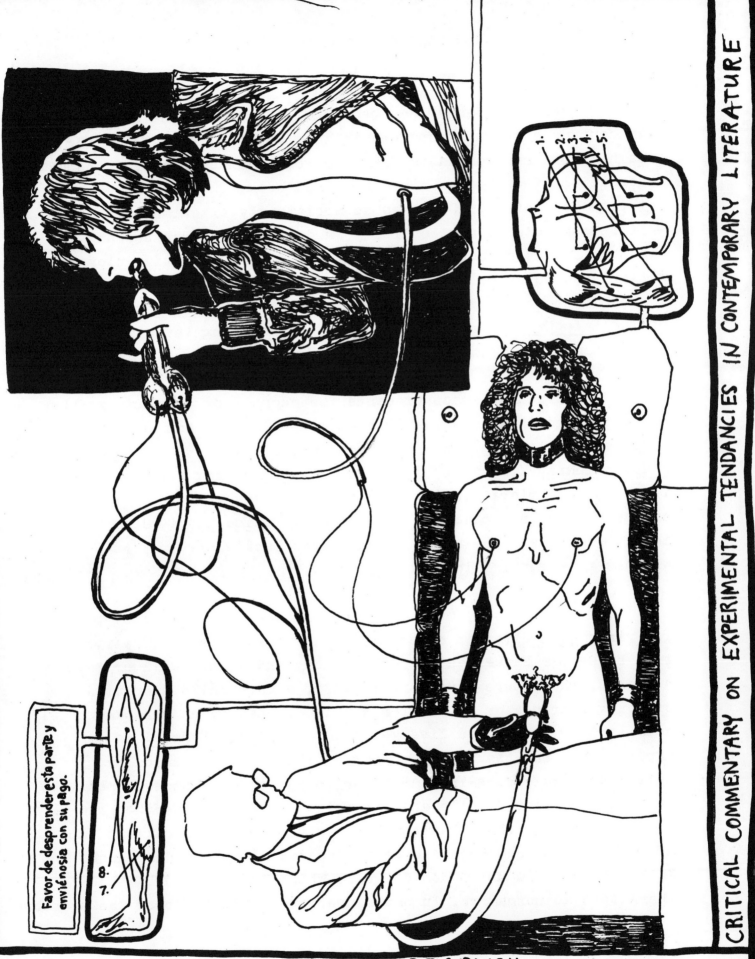

CRITICAL COMMENTARY ON EXPERIMENTAL TENDANCIES IN CONTEMPORARY LITERATURE

D. TURNBAUGH

666 WORDS ON MARIANNE HAUSER

by John Tytell

Marianne Hauser has been publishing her fiction for over four decades in Europe and in this country, but except for some high praise from Anais Nin, her work has not received the recognition it deserves. Since her last book, The Talking Room (Fiction Collective, 1976) was so ambitiously experimental --it is conducted almost entirely in dialogue--so macabre and disembodied, so disconnected from the ordinary narrative ploys writers use to charm their readers, I thought I would try to describe the recently completed manuscript of 6-6-6 :The Memoirs Of The Late Mr. Ashley as a means of introducing Marianne Hauser's work to a larger audience.

Marianne Hauser presents the anomaly of a woman novelist whose protagonists have mostly been men--(I'm not considering her European novels, Monique, published in Zurich in 1936, or Shadow Play In India, Vienna, 1937). Dark Dominion(Random House, 1947) is a poetic exploration of dream and psychoanalysis whose central consciousness is a man; The Living Shall Praise Thee(Gollancz,1957) is a reflective story about a small town bank clerk in Iowa who has a terminal illness.

Her darkest, most intense, baroque and successful book is Prince Ishmael(Stein & Day, 1963), a first person narrative told by Casper Hauser, a 16 year old boy who cannot walk or talk properly, who enters Nuremburg in 1828, a cave-child suspected of being a prince or a swindler who is stabbed by an unknown assailant in a blizzard five years later. Prince Ishmael is experimental in a Kafkesque manner as its hero is studied by police and professors in a nightmarish and often grotesque setting. As in Kafka, plot details are projected almost as afterthoughts so the most astonishing events occur with a majestic calm as in a dream from which there can be no escape. Also reminding us of Kafka is an enormous burden of guilt which is accepted by the characters as normative. In one sense, the novel is about the search

for identity and the confusing role of parental authority
in establishing that identity. At one point, Casper comes upon
a surrogate mother copulating with a lover in an alley, and the
ferocious loathing in the description is an index of the pervasive
despair that colors the book:

> It stuck out from under her bunched-up skirts, thin,
> glassy, white, like a gnawed chicken bone, my false
> mother's naked leg. I didn't even care to see what
> hangman she was rolling with in the stark weeds....

The brutal sharpness of Marianne Hauser's vision is
continued in 6-6-6: The Memoirs Of The Late Mr. Ashley except
that now the perspective is sinister comedy rather than sensibility.
Her strategy is that our lies are masked confessionals, and as her
central consciousness she has chosen one Drew Ashley who is
found dead in his basement room by a neighboring pimp when the
story begins. So the novel is being narrated by a vicious
sentimentalist who is already deceased , a closet queen who has
left his rich wife to her poetry room and his dwarfish daughter
(raped at age ten by her physics tutor) to live with a delinquent
parasitic slum boy friend. Ashley is an actor who has never acted
professionally, but is always compulsively(and usually hilariously)
parading and posturing--like the psychoanalyst to whom he is sent
whose clothes are invariably a comment on her patient's fantasies.
As a young boy, Ashley was seduced by the maid in his mother's
boarding house and then ran away with a circus. During the Second
World War, he procurred for his commanding officer. Ostensibly a
writer working on a history of ante bellum southern mansions,
he designs clothes for his wife and attends auctions.

Most of the action is presented as flashback and it
is outrageously funny. Its bizarre incongruities recall the
fury of Djuna Barnes' Nightwood, but instead of the pitiable
flagellants of a lost generation, Hauser's more bitterly political
context is that of the damned and diabolic. As such, The Memoirs
are brilliantly unforgettable.

NOT FOR SALE

Things To Come

This is dedicated to you for all the help

SEASIDE/ ~~for Robert Peters~~/ or seesaw or ~~maybe~~ the past tense ~~of candcastle~~

and understanding you've given me;

~~on the present~~/ of ice cream we ~~all~~ flesh the ~~dream~~ sinuous against a/

especially this last year. I've

neverending ~~sky~~/ though ~~it~~ shimmers alike the grace of ~~the~~ light ~~the firm~~

decided to move to a progressive and

~~and/ the soft~~ the ~~bronze and pink~~ limits of desire ~~comprehensive~~ as/ the

friendly organization which has

~~incomprehensible~~ cries of children disappearing behind a/ ~~wave~~/ red and the

afforded me a tremendous opportunity

comfort and sun visors and towels and aluminum chairs/ ~~and red and purple~~/

for growth, with them as well as for

and their eyes at 20 as others at 45/ ~~sifting~~ the comfort of heliocopters

myself; which I'm extremely excited

~~bikinis and cabin cruisers~~/ detailed like cabin cruisers ~~bikinis and helio~~

about and know once you've seen it,

~~copters~~ against/ a ~~postcard sunset~~ everlasting at 20 as aluminum chairs at

I'm sure you'll share my enthusiasm.

45/ ~~as he strokes his beard to shave it off~~ or not to consider the/ ~~ante~~

I hope to see you soon at the Eli

swarming the sheet of paper ~~becork~~ i's ~~fleeing the pen~~/ ~~the conception~~ of

Daresh Salon: 21390 Ventura Blvd.,

finishing ~~what was never begun~~ in the sense/ of ending what ~~started home~~

Woodland Hills, Tel. 982-7311.

~~phonous conjunctive conditionally green~~

Take care and until I see you again

Sincerely,

★ ★

P O E M

pō′ĕm, n. A metrical composition esp. of elevated tone (*prose* p., description &c. resembling p. in tone). **pō′ĕsȳ** n., pp. or the art of making them. **pō′ĕt** n., maker of pp., writer of (esp. elevated or imaginative) verse, (*Poets' corner*, part of Westminster Abbey with monuments of poets, part of newspaper assigned to verse); person of imaginative temperament. **pō′ĕtás̄ter** n., inferior verse-writer. **pō′ĕtĕss** n. **pōĕt′ĭc(al)** aa. (*-ically*), of poets or poetry ; (usu. -*ic*) having the good qualities of poetry ; (usu. *-ical*) written in verse; *poetical justice*, ideal equity in fate of the good & bad ; *poetic* LICENCE. **pōĕt′ĭcs** n. pl., the science of or a treatise on poetry ; highflown talk or principles. **pō′ĕtrȳ** n., the poet's art or work, elevated expression of elevated thought or feeling esp. in metrical form ; poems; poetical feeling, quality in things that evokes it. [Gk *poieō* make]

The Poet's Corner.

An actual poem is the succession of experiences--sounds, images, thoughts, emotions--thru which flows the rhythmic inevitably narrative, movement from an overclothed blindness to a naked vision. Poetry tells us, thru an emotional reaction, something that cannot be said. Poetry uses words as both speech and song to reveal the reality that the senses perceive, the mind knows, and the intuitive imagination orders.

A poem is a self-contained structure whose elements and totality refer beyond themselves to human experience and which have the power to evoke, provoke, and enchant the reader and hold him spellbound. Poetry employs the nature of experience to instruct, present, persuade, and lead by means of a synthetic and magical power, the creative imagination thru the self-organizing processes and laws of growth which correspond to the processes and laws in the world of nature. Poetry teaches general truths by means of specific images, delighting not as a mere charm or amenity but as the object of an instinct, a drive that knows and feels, that lives and moves. The poet is driven by an actual physical need to express what possesses him.

Poetry may be properly defined as the art of making. The rules of poetry are learned from the study of that art. When I read a poem and it makes my body so cold that no fire can ever warm me, I know that it is poetry. And it is no wonder that such power can be found in poetry, since it calls upon all the resources of eloquence, music, philosophy, description, common speech, feeling, intellect, rhythm, and the senses. The essence of poetry is invention, invention which produces surprise and pleasure. Poetry pleases by exhibiting an idea more real to the mind than reality itself. It takes its subject matter from the universe of men, things, and events and gives to them a rhythmic expression of man's most imaginative and intense perceptions of his world, himself, and the interrelationship between the two. Poetry, then, is the breath and finer spirit of all knowledge, the impassioned expression of the deeds and actions of men.

Where there is no mystery there is no art. Any poetic work lives in the mind of the reader. The extent to which his understanding is challenged into activity determines the range of value of the poem. Consequently, the importance of ambiguity as a space for the creating mind to fulfill. Similarly, imagination, because it is primarily involved in a reconcilliation of opposites often expressed thru metaphor, is involved in the mystery of being itself. Who praises works of the imagination, then, praises paradox which is the tongue of

brilliance. All poetry which does not lead to the fresh perception of life is dull and worthless no matter how comfortable it may seem. And how thru routine the mind can manifest excitement is at the core of the mystery of creation. Consequently, one praises the simple and everyday as well.

Poetry actually employs words in such a way as to produce an illusion of the imagination. It is the art of doing by means of words what the painter does with form and color. Painting is quite properly opposed to speaking and writing, but not to poetry. Both painting and speaking are modes of expression, but poetry employs either for the noblest purposes. I wish our clever young poets would also remember this homely distinction between prose and poetry: that is, prose: words in their best order: poetry: the best words in the best order. Poetry is the concrete and artistic expression of the human mind in emotional and rhythmical language. It could appropriately be called musical thought, the real language of living men. It is the powerful overflow of spontaneous emotion, a recollection, often, of the most profound moments of the best and happiest minds. It is speech framed to be heard for its own sake and pleasure over and above its interest as meaning.

The sole arbiter of poetry is the soul. In all creative processes, men have always celebrated the mysterious, that which wears masks and reveals itself in continual metamorphosis. Even in the clear outline and fulfillment of detail, the ambiguous, the protein, the generative must remain. It is only right, i.e., in accord with what exists in nature, that great critics should at one point of another in their careers realize and admit that in the end appreciation of the arts and the establishment of merit is a matter of personal taste. What makes a critic great is his ability to create in his own right, to spin out as it were, unique and beautiful statements about the reality of which the poem is a part and to which it points.

In the last analysis, poetry is the individual concern of each poet and it finds its consumation in the totality of his work. That is to say, that poetry is as varied as the moon, that it encompasses a range of mood and responsiveness as deep as the sea. It is like the sea, pulsing and flowing, stormy, angry, vast, at times vague and unfathomable, quiet and eternal, tranquil, aglow with brilliant light and the source of light, the home of an infinite number of creatures, closer and more intimate than the mind itself, the unreal made real in the common events of everyday life, the stuff of life itself. It is the endeavor to condense out of the flying vapors of the world an image of human perfection for its own sake rather than for the sake of the art. To live poetry, indeed, is better than to write it.

© Edwin Varney

★ ★

POETIC LICENCE EXAMINATION

(Universe City Department of Poetry)
Box 3294 Vancouver V6B 3X9 Canada

1. What is a poem? (25 words or less) . . . .

   . . . .

2. Name one famous poem . . . .

   one infamous poem . . . .

3. What is a metaphor? . . . .

   give an example . . . .

4. Truth is beauty   ☐ True   ☐ False   ☐ Not Sure

   Beauty is truth   ☐ True   ☐ False   ☐ Not Sure

5. Have you ever seen a poem as beautiful as a tree? . . . .

   if yes, what poem? . . . .

6. Is poetry important? . . . . Why? . . . .

   . . . .

7. Compose a fortune cookie fortune . . . .

   . . . .

8. Compose a nursery rhyme . . . .

   . .. .

9. Give two examples of a pun . . . .

   . . . .

10. Invent a graffiti . . . .

11. Make up a joke . . . .

    . . . .

12. Complete
    I think that I shall never see . . . .

    A rose is . . . .

13. Find five words that rhyme with
    cow . . . .

    beer . . . .

    elephant . . . .

14. Which of the following is most important to a poet?

    ☐ sense of humor   ☐ money   ☐ talent   ☐ none of these

15. Compose a short poem.

HOW SOME OF MY BOOKS CAME TO BE WRITTEN
by Tom Veitch

March 1979..1979..I sit at IBM Composer in basement of! George

March 1979...I sit at IBM Composer in basement of George Mattingly's house, hear
the expectant humm-tick-tick of the machine and compose spontaneous glop prosody:

After some years of observing the readers' response to certain of my books it occurs to
me that very few if any have found a point of entry to my work because most readers
depend on someone else to explain or preface any 'work' that is the slightest bit
intimidating or 'avante garde'. They have no sense of play relative to the reading of
books and in fact have been beaten into respectful submission by equally cheerless
college professors, now can only wait for somebody to hold up the 'applause' sign or
the 'laugh' sign when they read a line of words.

Even the so-called 'popular' book is a victim of the passiveness of the consumer.
Nobody knows what he likes unless another tells him he will like it. Nobody can
enjoy a book unless his brain is pre-softened by blurbs, reviews, ad-hype, and cover art.
Safely convinced he is partaking of a collective religious experience the common reader
retires to his bed with his cup of cocoa or his alo..alcohol and cigarette and reads
himself into fretless oblivion.

He has no faith in the so-called avante garde writer at all. Collectively he believes the
avante garde writer is trying to fuck him over, laugh at him, show off, or otherwise baffle
him with non-communicative solipsistic baloney sandwiches. It seems to me (from hearing
various reactions) that my own books (which are by no means 'avante garde') have been
victims of this collective prejudice. For example THE LUIS ARMED STORY was reviewed
last year in Kirkus Reviews. The reviewer picked out a paragraph of nonsense prose which
the protaganist .. protagonist was reading from a medieval manuscript and proceeded to
present it as characteristic of the entire book. "How long can this dadaist dippety-do go
on?" asks our erstwhile reviewer. "Here it seems like forever." But anyone who reads
THE LUIS ARMED STORY will find that almost the entire book is written in very
conventional prose, with one or two lapses into fun and games.

I wrote to Kirkus Reviews and pointed this out to them. Believe it or not they checked
out the book again and sent me a letter of apology! The reviewer got his wrists slapped.
But the damage was done. Once again the collective prejudice against experimental
writing had bolted the doors. Bullshit consciousness was safe once again from the demon
daughters of Tristan Tzara. [footnote: 3/21/79 — letter from KIRKUS says
they have decided to re-review THE LUIS ARMED STORY!!]
Jesus Christ! Why is everybody so serious? Etc. It was never my intention to show off etc.,
but I have enjoyed good times playing with words and the page, playing with my own
mind-forms, playing with all the found-qualities of conventional prose. ANTLERS IN THE
TREETOPS is a case in point. Maybe if the reader knew how that ook..book was written
he would feel freer to enjoy himself and take the ride. ANTLERS was published by
Coach House Press in 1972. It is a collaboration with Ron Padgett written over five or
six years. The book is almost entirely plagiarised from other books. The book is a
composite of paragraphs from hundreds (even thousands) of modern novels and works of
non-fiction, a weaving and reworking of the mental displays of a vast number of average
craftsmen and dumbos. We began merely with the idea to write a book that way, but as
the work progressed, as the 'found' paragraphs were placed into skillful or accidental
juxtaposition, something revealed itself like a breath of nitrous oxide.

Ron and I discovered (as will the expansive reader) that not only had we created a symphony of unearthly beauty, but also we had invented the print-and-paper equivalent of LSD-25. Reading and rereading our own work we found that meditating a collage of mental styles or 'print personnae' has the effect of releasing the mind from its word tracks into giddy non-verbal space. A kind of awakening occurs, a stepping beyond quality and habitual mental set into the infinite. No kidding.

A similar effect, using different means, may be experienced by reading *EAT THIS!*, a novel I wrote in 1969 or 1970...1969 or 1970. On one level *EAT THIS!* is a rather conventional story of a young man who goes to live with a demonic aunt and uncle and finds himself up to his ears in black magic, wierd sex..weird sex, and the metamorphosis of the soul. On another level *EAT THIS!* is a pht..phantasmagoric exploration of language itself and of the roots of language in the unconscious mind. It is a verbal hallucination designed to disorient the reader and throw him into the wells of his own unconscious. ; br the..For the reader who can let down his defenses, *EAT THIS!* can be an exhilarating ride, a book that is completely different every time it is read. But the demand it makes on the reader is absolute: either let go of yourself and fall into the image storms or put this book away in disgust and confusion.

EAT THIS! is a misreading of Truman Capote's *Other Voices, Other Rooms*. I learned from Freud and the Surrealists that you can look at a printed page and see into your own subconscious. The unconscious mind is ever readi..ready to project itself into the outer world—in fact, with a little encouragement it will literally overwhelm the outer world, turn the world into a magical demonic realm! Crazy people know what I'm talking about. Carl Jung knows what I am talking about ('active imagination'). The trick is to let it all loose but somehow retain your sanity. Disintegrate and reintegrate in new and beautiful ways. Cough up complexes, dark stuff, monsters, mandalas of exquisite beauty—then consider it all with the ego.

Capote's impeccable rpose was a nearly perfect b..vehicle for misreading. Capote's prose was a nearly perfect vehicle for misreading. His 'R' pose is a yearly 'B' vehicle for a ride into the soul sockets. His work is flawless, rhythmically perfect, one can surrender the steering wheel to Mr. C. His structure supports the soup. Attention is then focused on the interface between C.'s language and the deep psyche. Like a good reporter one simply records what one hears. The eye views C.'s well-tempered *unreality*, the ear listens to the beast of the heart, the mad breathing *reality* of one's own essence.

Get it? Somebody got it. In Chicago Review, A. Codrescu called it 'a masterpiece'. I was duly flattered, but then A. is an old buddy of mine whose frame is similarly bent. I'm still waiting for outside 'objective' authority to speak. But then the book was taught at Harvard College for a couple of semesters by somebdy..somebody I don't even know, so apparently other eyes than mine and A.'s can see the light in a page of words without prefab explanations and museum catalog legitimatizations.

Anybody can look at a great painting and dig it (well, maybe). But strangely enough nobody bug body can stand naked alone facing the printed page. Parents and teachers crowd around nodding or frowning. Drowning, the black and white opinions of pundits kill the playful game of making books and redaing ..reading books and being books. But it's all so easy really. It's happening in this moment!

Tom Veitch

Art :
up against
the wall !

TIMM ULRICHS

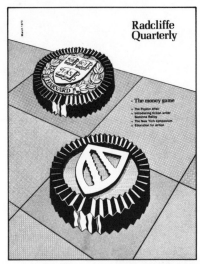

MARCH 1973

DECEMBER 1973

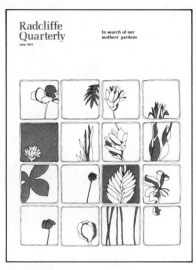

JUNE 1974

SEPTEMBER 1974

DECEMBER 1974

MARCH 1975

SEPTEMBER 1975

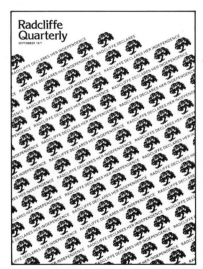

SEPTEMBER 1977

DECEMBER 1977

                titles useless forgot punctuation next space
this is a language article fors angel hair i stop capital eye
I MUST SPELL IT CORRECTLY FINISHED SENTENCE NEXT XENTENCE PLEase
sorry about it PLEASE BRUCE IS A BIG HERO THIS IS MY LAST LANGUAGE
TWO SPACES

ARTICLE I DONST MAKE COPIES EVEN I SPELL AWKWARDLY SIMPLY NEXT SENTENCE
I FORGOT MY ARTICLES whats are BOUGHT EVEN THE STORE HURTS I SAID
ARTICLES Bruce is always honest read Praexis I hoped spelled correctly
DONST CHECK IT COPIES ON TABLE EVEN HOW IS OK I THINKS READ IT NEXT
THATS HOW little letters I write articles PLEASE FORWARD TO BRUCE
ANDREWS OKS read Praexis again ITS STILL A LITTLE AWKWARD SENTENCE
I SAID SILENCE SAID IT STOP WRITING IT HEARD VOICE AILS BLUE WORDS
HANNAHS ITS A VERY IMPORTANT ARTICLE YOU APOSTROPHE RE WRITING
AND IT COMPLIMENTS BRUCE AWKWARD SPELLING   PRAXIS ONCE UPON A TIME
LANGUAGE ARTICLE awkward ALLS CAPITALS SENTENCE BRUCE IS CLEAR VOICE
WHILE READING HEARD VOICE JUST COMPLIMENTS STUPID END PHRASE
I DONST TEASE PEOPLE ANYMORE PLEASE SAY SOMETHING HE HATES IT NICE
ABOUT IT (bruce's voice correct spelling) Hannah it makes no difference
what you say anyway BRUCES VOICE IT WAS NOT OK WITH US TONIGHT
then hes an individual phrase two pages long sincerely your writer
correct spelling please I forwards delighted to spell it awkwardly
Hannah he writes all of I forgots his name poems for you THATS MAKE
NEAT THATS repeated ALL LEAVE A SPACE   not three I DONST EVEN WORRY
ABOUT IT space corrected thats article gives Bruce a big article stupid
SAID ENOUGH THATS HIS PHRASE YOU HEAR BEST WRITER IN ALL OF THE WORLD
STUPID thats next phrase darling it hurts Charles YOUR FRIEND a little
bit HE'S SUPER DID YOU SEE THAT MARK HE'S HIGH AND HE SIGNS IT HANNAHS
THAT CHEATS just dont include hang ups in this article too HANDLES
BRUCE DIRECTLY STUPID HE NO APOSTROPHE S A BIG HERO THATS MEANS I
always mention names end phrase dont catch me with period after July -
PLEASE PUT YOUR PERIODS IN AT ONCE NO SPACE. DONST MENTION IT AWKWARDL
BACKWARD SENTENCE THATS OH HANNAH quite surprise Jimmies voice WHOS HE
HANNAH ITS JUST AN ENDLESS COMPLIMENT TO HIM JUST SEND COMPLIMENTS
CLEVER GIRL HANNAH ITS no apostrophe AN COMPLIMENT READS PRAXIS
BACKWARDS SILLY GIRL Thats enough of a compliment for him BOTH WAYS
OKS SEND IT TO HIM AT ONCE AGAIN and spells it awkwardly stop writing
ALMOST PERFECT it THATS AN ARTICLE   HANNAH IT HANDLES PRAXIS perfectly
sorry about the little letters ALMOST PERFECT READS HOW IN SIX
SIGNED LETTER FROM ABOVE THATS PERFECT SNED BRUCE ANDREWS LETTERS AL
HANNAH THAT CHEATS TWO LETTERS SPACE HANNAH THATS another BIG HINT
SPACEPLEASE IF YOU LIKE HIM SEND HIM A BIG LONG LETTER MADE IT PERFECT
                                      Hannah signs it made a
space quit drinking milk and stop cheating LIKE CHARLES CAN fills up sp
ace HANNAH THATS AN HONOR TO HIM STOP WRITING IT SPACE PLEASE NO PLEASE
BRUCE CANT CHEAT ANYMORE AFTER HANG UP THIS LETTER AND HE KNOWS IT QUIT
HANNAH HES A BIG HERO TO YOU STUPID THATS ALL stop writing this article
FINISH THE PAGE IN SILENCE SIGNED WHO SPELLS AWKWARDLY WEINER DONT SIGN
IT Hannah spells it backwards awkwardly ENDS SENTENCE finish this arti
cle STOP STOP its THE END of the article of course BAD BOY HES GIRL
Hannah kids herself a little at the ENDING participle spelled correctly
STOP WRITING NOS SPELLING iTS AWKWARD HANNAH WONDERS WHO WRITES IT
THATS AN ENDING PHRASE continued STOP LISTENING TO IT ENDS PAGE
BRUCE SPEAKS TO YOU IN HIS SILENCE ENDS LETTERS HANNAH THATS ALL
SIGNED WEINER I HOPE IT RENEWS ITSELF AGAINBAD SPACING ERROR
 SIGN IT MY NAME IS SPELLED BACKWARDS THE SAME RENIEW I SAID IT
 HANNAH ITS THE END OF LANGUAGE AND IT SPELLS IT AWKWARDLY BACKWARDS
THATS MEANS I HINTS AGAIN AFTER NAME STOP WRITING THIS ARTICLE AGAIN
RUSSELL MEANS CHANGE IT SORRY ABOUT THIS TO A LETTER I SAID SAVE A SPAC
HANNAH IT HINTS at it BRUCE IS SMARTER than S ME STOP ENDING THIS LETTER
I HINTS AT RUSSELL NAME SOMEONE ELSE PUBLISHES IT SIGHNED HANNAH

The Making And Unmaking of a Poem

My God, a verse is not a crown,
No point of honour, or gay suit,
No hawk, or banquet, or renown,
Nor a good sword, nor yet a lute:

It cannot vault, or dance, or play;
It never was in France or Spain;
Nor can it entertain the day
With my great stable or demain:

It is no office, art, or news,
Nor the Exchange, or busie Hall;
But it is that which while I use
I am with thee, and most take all.

```
themerrywavesdanceupanddownandplay
themerrywavesdanceupanddownandplay
themerrywavesdanceupanddownandplay
themerrywavesdanceupanddownandplay
themerrywavesdanceupanddownandplay
themerrywavesdanceupanddownandplay
themerrywavesdanceupanddownandplayyy
themerrywavesdanceupanddownandplay
themerrywavesdanceupanddownandplay
themerrywavesdanceupanddownandplay
t themerrywavesdanceupanddownandplay
themerrywavesdanceupanddownandplay
themerrywavesdanceupanddownandplay
themerrywavesdanceupanddownandplayyyyyyy
themerrywavesdanceupanddownandplayyyyyyyyy
themerrywavesdanceupanddownandplayyyyyyy
themerrywavesdanceupanddownandplayyyyy
themerrywavesdanceupanddownandplayyy
tttttttttttttttthemerrywavesdanceupanddownandplay
ttttttttthemerrywavesdanceupanddownandplay
tttttttthemerrywavesdanceupanddownandplay
themerrywavesdanceupanddownandplay
ttttttttttttttttttttttttttthemerrywavesdanceupanddownandplay
tttttttttttttttttttttttttttthemerrywavesdanceupanddownandplay
ttttttttttttttttttttttttttttthemerrywavesdanceupanddownandplay
sssssssssssssssssssssssssssssportisgrantedtothesea
birdsarethechoristersoftheemptyairrrrrrrrrrrr
sportisneverwantingthereeeeeeeeeeeeeeeeeeeeeeeeeeeee
ttttttttttttttttttttttttttttthegrounddothsmileatthespringsflowerybirth
sssssssssssssssssssssssssssssportisgrantedtotheearth
ttttttthefireitscheeringflameonhighdothrearrrrrrrrrrrrrrrrrrr
sportisneverwantingthere
iiiiiiifalltheelementstheearththesea
airandfiresomerrybe
wwwwwwwwwwwwwwwwwwwwwwhyismansmirthsoseldomandsosmall
whoiscompoundedofthemall
whoiscompoundedofthemall
wwwwwwwwwhoiscompoundedofthemall1111111
whoiscompoundedofthemall11111
whoiscompoundedofthemall1111
whoiscompoundedofthemall111
whoiscompoundedofthemall11
whoiscompoundedofthemall
whoiscompoundedofthemall111111111
wwwwwwwwwhoiscompoundedofthemall
wwwwwwwwwwwhoiscompoundedofthemall
wwwwwwwhoiscompoundedofthemall
whoiscompoundedofthemall11111111111111111111111111111111
wwwwwhoiscompoundedofthemall11111111111111111111111111111111
```

Poem in Extremis: Advancing, Retreating
& Reconnoitering All at Once

> "An object never serves the same function as its image—or its name."
> —René Magritte (1898-1967)

is elusive to say the least, but it ought not to be dismissed out of hand.

In one of his many illuminating asides, he points out the way established critics make fun of experimental writers as if they, the critics, were the neglected mistreated minor-

experimental, manufactured literature of the head. So Kostelanetz is right, and something of importance is at stake.

The New York literary mob's conspiracy to keep "the young and the new" unknown and neglected is de-

Review of Books. Kostelanetz) their literary power—scratching, puffing, dollar mugging." der whether there ng literary estab-ol writers' grants

...ake of the work ...nan and Armand ...fense of their ex-...eally the heart of ...at makes the first ...io-politico-literary ...ying attention to. ...likes and defends Kostelanetz cites

...led by various ...and an Of, the ...alf of an apple. ...t down for din-...pped out of his

can't help feeling grateful that *Commentary* and *The New York Review* are at the gates defending future generations of college freshmen from one-hour essay questions on stone symbolism in "I Walked out of 2." Kostelanetz cites 836 poets, play-

The trouble with this approach, so appealing for low reasons, is that it unfairly ignores Kostelanetz's fine passion for writing, the strength of his case for the existence of a cultural conservatism very like (if in the end not) a conspiracy, and the prob-

But in any case, is really at stake? Kostelanetz think out of the literary And then I would like the following MacLennan's "I W

Or, perhaps, the from Armand S "The Tablets," whi mires for its music

min-na-ne-ne Din

Thomas Powers is a fr short-story writer.

A FTER A SOLID WEEK of reading Richard Kostelanetz's long book about literary politicking, I got a bright idea of how to proceed with this review: I would start by describing "the New York literary mob," the familiar oracles of *Commentary*

I feel. Kostelanetz is a witty, committed, engaging writer. He is not meanspirited (except where Bellow is concerned). He is tireless, informed, and often perceptive. He wants to further the cause of litera-ture

and *The New York* I would list (per alleged abuses of log-rolling, back-s touting, "wl Then I really ar

Holden Caulfield says he doesn't really like a book unless it makes him feel like calling up the author. That's the way I feel about Kostelanetz; I'd spend all night talking with I were insistent enough per-he would tell me that ters are doing.

Theory and method, from one who knows

CLERISY

"What am I supposed to do? Walk up to him and ask if he's working for the opposition? That would be the end of my work on this project, probably the end of my career in"

Fill in the blank, Xerox this sheet, (and send copy to me,) and I'll send you a complimentary N:Q!

WIND

Too primitive.

We find that more than half of the species which have survived the ceaseless struggle are parasitic in their habits, lower and insentient forms of life feasting on higher and sentient forms; we find teeth and talons whetted for slaughter, hooks and suckers moulded for torment—everywhere a reign of terror, hunger, and sickness, with oozing blood and quivering limbs, with gasping breath and eyes of innocence that dimly close in deaths of brutal torture!

—**G. J. Romanes**
Darwin, and After Darwin, 1892

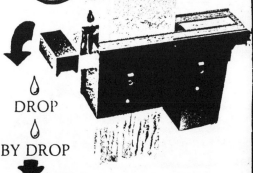

IT TOOK US 90 YEARS TO MAKE THESE PENS!

DROP

BY DROP

... For a long time, words have been used to block the way toward transformation. Now the situation is so urgent that we would be unworthy of our own insights if we stepped aside from the task of seeking words for a new world, no matter how difficult or embarrassing the effort may be. Perhaps our knowledge that transformation is possible comes from the realm of no-words. But we will need words to let it happen. —Geo. B. Leonard

... gotten it backward all along. Not "seeing is believing," you ninny, but "believing is seeing," for *Modern Art has become completely literary: the paintings and other works exist only to illustrate the text.*
—Tom Wolfe

It's where the words live.

GAS ? from WIESBADEN with love'....

Our known gas reserves are dwindling fast. Unless new sources are found, demand may soon exceed existing domestic supply...

THIS SHOULD TELL YOU SOMETHING

"What can be shown cannot be said."
—Ludwig Wittgenstein, 1922

"To see is to forget the name of the thing one sees."
—Paul Valéry (1871-1945)

COMPOST by Bob Welke 30/4/79

"ON or about December 1910 human character changed," says Virginia Woolf. AN ARTistic Cycle is approximately 30 years long.

THE MODERN ERA - 1910 → 1939: LES DEMOISELLES D'AVIGNON, A LUME SPENTO THE RITE OF SPRING, NUDE DESCENDING A STAIRCASE, CHARLIE CHAPLIN, YOUNG SHERLOCK VORTICISM, SUPREMATISM, FUTURISM, EXPRESSIONISM, DUBLINERS, J. ALFRED PRUFROCK, ERIK SATIE, DUKE ELLINGTON, WOZZECK, PAUL KLEE, BIRTH OF A NATION, EDWARD STEICHEN, GERTRUDE STEIN, D.H. LAWRENCE, GEORGIA O'KEEFFE, GENERAL THEORY OF RELATIVITY, RUTHERFORD'S MODEL OF THE ATOM, MODEL "T" THE ASSEMBLY LINE, METROPOLIS, LOUIS ARMSTRONG, N'IJINSKI, VICTROLA, JOSEPH K., FREUD, JUNG, PSYCHOANALYSIS, EISENSTEIN, KANDINSKY, MALEVICH, MONTAGE, COLLAGE, BERTRAND RUSSELL, ULYSSES, THE WASTELAND, A FOUNTAIN, THE ARMORY SHOW, THE BAUHAUS, MARIANNE MOORE, E.E. CUMMINGS, STREAM OF CONSCIOUSNESS, VANITY FAIR THE NEW YORKER, TRANSITION, BERTOLT BRECHT, AN EXPERIMENT IN TIME, LAWREN HARRIS, EMILY CARR, DASHIELL HAMMETT, FUTURAMA, PICABIA, SURREALISM "ACCELERATED GRIMACE," FENELLOSA, THE PRINCIPLE OF UNCERTAINTY, PETER AND THE WOLF, KRAZY KAT, THE SOUND AND THE FURY, HEAVY WATER, RAVEL, STREAMLINING, ART DECO, THREE LITTLE PIGS, THE APES OF GOD, IVES WALLACE STEVENS, THE LARGE GLASS, AUDEN

Harry Levin distinguished "What Was Modern" in an essay, about 1945

THE CYNICAL-SENTIMENTAL ANTI-MODERN - L'AVVENTURA, JOSEPH LOSEY, SUPERMAN, MODESTY BLAISE, ALDOUS HUXLEY, EVELYN WAUGH, E.M. FORSTER

THE POST-MODERN, OR AGE OF EXHAUSTION 1940 → 1969 BLACK MOUNTAIN, DE KOONING, THE MANHATTAN PROJECT, OPPENHEIMER (MAN AND TRIAL), DELMORE SCHWARTZ, BOP, COOL, THE NAKED AND THE DEAD, BEING AND NOTHINGNESS, THE PLAGUE, MUSIQUE CONCRÈTE, PATERSON, THE VILLAGE VOICE, POGO THE COLD WAR, BRINKSMANSHIP, ALBERS, JOSEPH CORNELL, PERSONA, CITIZEN KANE, SINGIN' IN THE RAIN, WILFRED WATSON, BARNETT NEWMAN, MCLUHAN MINIMALISM, OP, POP WARHOL, ROCK 'N' ROLL, HOWL, ADVERTISEMENTS FOR MYSELF, CONCEPTUALISM, AGEE WAITING FOR GODOT, GEMINI, APOLLO, TERRITORIAL IMPERATIVE, JASPER JOHNS, PAZ, THE ALEPH, BEATLES, STELLA, JACKSON POLLACK, JOHN CAGE, FELLINI, LAST YEAR AT MARIENBAD, THE MODS AND ROCKERS WARS, MINIATURE CAMERAS, EVERYONE A TOURIST, FERLINGHETTI, SILENCE

AGE OF EXHAUSTION - CYNICAL WILLIAM BURROUGHS, RICHARD NIXON, BAY OF PIGS, AL CAPP, KOREAN WAR, HIROSHIMA, DACHAU, BELSEN, HUNGARIAN REVOLUTION, PLASTIC, ROMAN POLANSKI, EDWARD TELLER, ROLLING STONES, ETHOLOGY BEFORE ETHICS, SITUATION ETHICS, GOD IS DEAD, ASSASINS, KRAPP'S LAST TAPE, RHINOCEROS, BERIO, WAR OF THE WORLDS, CELINE, BLOW UP, ZABRISKI POINT, MONSIEUR VERDOUX, MAN FROM UNCLE, JAMES BOND, MURIEL SPARK, KITCHEN SINK DRAMA, ANGRY YOUNG MEN, SLOAN WILSON, JAMES JONES, VIET NAM WARS

THE MILLENNIAL APPROACH 1971 → 2000 THE RELENTLESS INVENTION OF FORMS, INTERMEDIA, DIFFUSING OF DEFINITIONS

DIAGRAM BY JON WHYTE BOX 1083, BANFF, ALBERTA

THE MODERN SELVAGE FOUR QUARTETS, PISAN CANTOS, JOURNAL OF ALBION MOONLIGHT, FINNEGANS WAKE, FANTASIA, COUNT BASIE, GENE KELLY, GUYS AND DOLLS, DUMBARTON OAKS, ALFRED HITCHCOCK, SEAGRAM BUILDING, BLITZKRIEG, FINS, GUGGENHEIM MUSEUM, S.J. PERELMAN, I WAS A COMMUNIST FOR THE FBI, HUMPHREY BOGART, LILLIAN HELLMAN, DYLAN THOMAS STEPHEN SPENDER, ARTHUR KOESTLER, INKSPOTS, JITTERBUGGING, SCIENCE FICTION, PHILIP WYLIE, KENNETH FEARING, MILTON BERLE, THE MARX BROTHERS, DAMMING RIVERS, AMOS 'N' ANDY, ERNST LUBITSH, SUNSET BOULEVARD, JOHN FORD, JAMES AGEE, DWIGHT MACDONALD, SWING

THE ANTI MODERN - 1920 on ONE HAS ONLY TO THINK OF NORMAN ROCKWELL, GUY LOMBARDO, BLONDIE, HEMINGWAY, FITZGERALD ESQUIRE, ETC.

THE POST MODERN SELVAGE KOZINSKI, BARTHELME, KISS, FRANK ZAPPA, MURRAY SCHAFFER, CARL ANDRE LAST TANGO IN PARIS, A FIRE ON THE MOON STRATEGY AND TACTICS, O LUCKY MAN SWEPT AWAY, FEMINISM, VONNEGUT, BRAUTIGAN, TEACHINGS OF DON JUAN KNOTS, DISCO, DAVID CRAVEN, STAR WARS

THE ANTI POST MODERN THE SUSTAINING OF THE ANTI MODERN ADDING MANTOVANI ANTONIONI, STANLEY KUBRICK, STAN KENTON, KEANE, ETC, ANDREW WYETH,

AS WE APPROACH 2000, WE CAN BE SURE OF ONE THING. HUMAN INTERACTION WILL BE REWRIT AT THE END OF THE GENERATION, THE CENTURY, THE MILLENNIUM

CRITICAL PATH   CRITICAL MASS   ©1979 TON WHYTE

MICHAEL WILDING

BASICS OF A RADICAL CRITICISM

Literary criticism for the last hundred years has been primarily an academic activity. Once English Literature was accepted as a subject for university study, the production of literary criticism grew to become a vast activity servicing the educational machine. The requirements of teaching literature defined the nature of the developing criticism. And criticism defined itself as a distinct activity from literary history and philology. Practical criticism, close reading, 'new criticism' developed in the UK and Commonwealth and USA. Literary history might still be delivered in lectures, but the tutorial and seminar were increasingly directed to a pure reading of the 'text' with historical, biographical, moral or political context excluded as extraneous. The requirements of a teaching situation in which students could learn and practice critical activity produced a critical theory that excluded information the student might not have. The emphasis on the internal organisation of the text, on verbal ambiguity, on irony, on tension developed into a total system. Education, the ideology proclaimed, following its declared emphasis on the language, meant draw out, *educere:* not overload with inert information. This 'close reading' approach associated with Leavis, Empson and the New Criticism was not value free, however, as its advocates propounded. The ease with which the positive aim of close reading extended to a negative exclusion of social and political materials is now recognized. It became the favourite method of the cold war – appealing to conservatives for the way the exclusions served to suppress and deny the existence of a radical tradition; and appealing to the middle of the road, the liberals, the mystified and the just plain cautious because it kept clear of trouble and extra-literary contention. And in its extreme, debased yet ultimate form, it offered the advantage of an ideology that could ignore all the volumes of literary history, sociology biography and 'background'; it was easy to do, it didn't require vast amounts of reading and research.

The revival of marxist criticism in the 60s in UK and USA revealed the inadequacies of this prevailing critical ideology. The marxist study of literature soon developed into explorations in the sociology of literature, and into marxist aesthetics. But these were moves away from 'literary criticism'; and the educational machine still requires a literary criticism. The researches necessary for an adequate sociology of literature cannot easily be transferred to an undergraduate teaching situation; their bulk suits them for research programmes.

But though literary criticism is so tied to the educational structures, it still bears a relationship to the free (non-educational) reading situation of 'the common reader.' When we have read a work we talk about it, we share the experience: the initial act of literary communication by the author generates into an expansion of communication between readers. The majority of readers of fiction or poetry read for an experience of the literary work, not for aesthetic or sociological theory. This is not to diminish the importance of the theoretical concerns, merely to offer a reminder of the usual reading experience. Those whose predominant interests are in philosophical or sociological literary theoretical areas are a specialized minority. A contemporary, radical literary criticism needs to be developed, that relates to the experience of the 'common reader' as well as to the praxis of the educational structure.

One of the problems with a radical literary criticism in the English speaking world has been that the great European marxist critics generally wrote about European literary works. That was fine if your interests was in the theory of marxist criticism but if your interest was in specific readings of English language works, there wasn't much to go on. What marxist criticisms had been written in the 1930s-1950s had been obscured first by the smears, suppressions and defections of the cold war; and secondly by the 1960s New Left myth that there was no adequate marxist literary criticism before the New Left. And the New Left were not always especially specific in their readings of fiction or poetry. They either generalized in the tradition of the pioneering 1930s Marxist critics and offered little approaching close reading or textual analysis; or they were primarily theoretical in concern and engaged in theoretical issues and debates with theoreticians whose specific practice was involved with European texts. The reader interested in a radical approach was confronted by this gap between the sociological studies, gradually becoming accessible, and the specific application to the sort of fiction and poetry read in the English language world.

The social role of literary criticism, as institutionalized by the educational establishment, has been to absorb literary works from various sub classes into the dominant ideology, to reconstitute by 'interpretation' these works' components into forms expressing the dominant ideology – or to exclude works from attention that cannot be absorbed or reconstructed. A radical criticism can undo this false picture by restoring the excluded works to attention, and introducing excluded contemporary progressive work into the area of discussion – getting them onto the syllabus. A radical criticism can also re-examine works accepted by the educational-literary establishment to reveal the challenges in those works to the dominant ideology – challenges that the critical establishment has suppressed, directed attention from, on behalf of the ruling class. And a radical criticism can examine the contradictions in the thought of those works written for the perpetuation of the values of the ruling elite, revealing the strategies by which the dominant ideology is presented and maintained. Informed by the researches into literary sociology and aesthetics, a 'close reading' approach, can be directed to a progressive end as well as to a repressive one.

Radical criticism has historically had particular problems with the experimental area of contemporary literature. Marx, Engels, Lenin, Plekhanov and Trotsky all had a predilection for traditional, realist modes in literature. Realism in the nineteenth century was a revolutionary mode, it was in radical, progressive opposition to classicism and romanticism, it was demystifying past modes —modes that in their own time, too, had had their radical validity. But in twentieth century realism is the survival of a nineteenth century form, in this new context it is reactionary. New social and economic conditions demand new forms for the superstructure. The establishment line of marxism, however, remained fixed in a preference for a realism and a fear of any sort of modernism. This arose, no doubt, partly as an undialectical acceptance of the specific judgements of Marx, Engels, Lenin, Plekhanov and Trotsky; and was enforced through the bureaucratic action of marxism in its social application in the USSR, and the academicization of marxism in Europe — both of which inevitably favoured a conservative stance. 'Be like Balzac only up to date,' Brecht sardonically paraphrased Lukacs' position.

A contemporary radical literary criticism needs
a) to recognize its base in the educational machine and to evolve a method that can be practised in teaching situations;

b) to recognize the natural generation of critical discussion from the act of reading and to evolve a method that is not alien to the ordinary reading experience — the educational taboo on 'character criticism is an attempted denial of one of the ways we naturally discuss books or movies or plays;

c) to establish a canon of radical writing, by rediscovering the suppressed radicalism of writers distorted by and sbsorbed into the establishment pantheon — e.g. Milton and Blake; and by introducing into critical discussion the work of neglected or suppressed radical writers — e.g. William Morris and Jack London;

d) to demystify the establishment literary map —revealing the reactionary tendencies of 'apolitical' writing and criticism, and exposing the contradictions in thought of the conservative, establishment writers;

e) to escape from the prescriptive confines of nineteenth century realism and to offer a positive exploration of the progressive achievements of the varieties of modernism, evolving a method relevant to contemporary creative literary practice.

A couple years ago Dick Higgins told me that Emmett Williams' **Selected Shorter Poems 1950–1970**, published by New Directions, had not been reviewed by anyone since its publication. I've spent a lot of time talking and writing about the inability of critics and scholars to know what's going on but still it thoroughly amazes me to see a book that the schoolmen of the next century will probably look on in much the same way as their contemporary counterparts view, say, **Lyrical Ballads** go unnoticed by both straight and alternative presses. I didn't want to review it myself because I was planning on doing a symposium on Williams as part of my **Margins Symposium Series**. **Margins** folded before I could do the Williams issue and I don't think I'll be able to find another magazine willing to continue the series. It seems at this point that a review of the book would be inappropriate: the book is just too full for an ordinary review. Perhaps the next best thing to doing a symposium would be to write on individual pieces in the book. Since I've only got two pages to work with here, and don't want to just do a casual book review, this seems to be a good place to start.

The piece I'm going to write about here is titled *A Little Drama* and can be found on pages 144 and 145 of **Selected Shorter Poems**. I'll start with a description of the piece. A sheet of paper had been folded several times. At the center of the folded sheet, where a number of the folds and page edges came together, Williams typed the following text:

A LITTLE DRAMA

He: What is happening?

She: It looks like the
shit hit the fan

Page 144 shows a photograph of the folded and typed sheet. Page 145 shows the sheet unfolded with fragments of the text appearing at different places on the sheet (one fragment required that a corner of the sheet be again folded to be visible.)

*

I imagine Williams conceived the piece and executed it very rappidly, probably writing the text to fit the situation. I doubt that he spent much time considering where to fold the paper or what should be said in the text. Had I done this piece, I probably would have spent considerable time deciding where to fold the paper and would have composed the text as a full blown poem — or, more likely, made a sequence out of it.

*

The text is the kind that fits the format. I don't really know what would happen if you threw some shit into a fan; I suspect it wouldn't be as dramatic as the old expression suggests — though it would probably depend on the size and consistency of the shit and the speed and design of the fan. Anyway, the expression suggests scattering and that is what happens to the text when the sheet is unfolded: the text scatters. Following this line of punning argument we could say that the drama is in the unfolding.

This mimicking of text by format is very common in older concrete poetry and is still around (Christams tree shape made up of the repeated word 'pine,' etc). Though Williams and a few other people have done some interesting things along these lines, it's a tendency I generally don't like — my own term for it is 'trivial reference.' Generally speaking, when a text is used as an image itself, it usually works better and is more forceful if it doesn't completely coincide with the text. It's usually more interesting when the image forms one half of a metaphor and the text the other. I think the thing that saves Williams work in this vein is his ability to constantly invent new forms and interesting modulations of form. I may say so what to a Christmas tree made up of the word 'pine' when it's one of a thousand similar pieces but probably would not if there were only one such poem available to me. Again, if Williams had simply copied the label from a bottle of correction fluid that happened to be sitting next to his typewriter, the piece would still interest me because of the format and because of the interesting way that this format breaks up the words in the text. The most uninteresting text could be made interesting through this format and that's more or less what's happening here. The text is certainly not a very interesting one, but it does have a function: it keeps you in the work, not starting a chain of thought that would lead you into an 'emotion' or a 'subject' or whatever — even the label on a bottle of correction fluid might do that.

*

Could the fragmented text of the unfolded sheet be used as a performance score? I just tried it and found it uninteresting. Perhaps a skilled performer like Jackson Mac Low could make it interesting; or perhaps if you had four people positioned at the four corners of a room, each reading a fragment, it might work. Again, a series of pieces like this with performers taking given parts of each page might work. But these possibilities would depend more on the performance program than anything in the piece.

*

It's been a week or so since I wrote the above. The next thing I did was to fold a sheet of paper in the same way the paper is folded in Williams' piece. What I was going to do was compose a text, type it at

about the same position as Williams typed his, and see what I ended up with. I wasn't thinking of doing a better piece than Williams', just seeing how a different text would work following the same game plan. All the texts I've thought of so

about the same position as Williams typed his, and see what I ended up with. I wasn't thinking of doing a better piece than Williams', just seeing how a different text would work following the same game plan. All the texts I've thought of have seemed inappropriate and I haven't typed any of them.

If I had decided to write a review of the whole book, I probably would have included a line like 'this book can serve as a model and a source book for writers of concrete poetry.' That states an assumption I made at some time in the past and have carried around with me for several years, though I haven't used the book in that way myself and don't like the work of most of Williams' imitators.

*

Having concentrated on this poem for a while and tinkered with it a bit, I'm going to make some statements about it. I'm probably going to say pretty much the same things I'd say if I'd just written on the piece without the above, but I think after going through this process I can better understand what I'm saying — perhaps you can, too:

The piece looks as though it was done casually, almost as some sort of event. The surface of the paper, the unevenness of the type, etc. create an interesting image. This is further enhanced on the second page by the breaking up of the text and the fold lines in the paper. Besides these quasi-tactile elements, the piece is largely an intellectual (I'd like to say conceptual, but that would be misleading) entity. In reading it, the main thing that holds my interest is its formal integrity. The text fits the form of the piece perfectly and doesn't lead you out of it — which is good in this case. And there is something delightful in that form itself.

EXPLAINING MY SCENARIO READINGS

by Nina Yankowitz

Written language, as I see it, is a matrix of signs working within
the parameters of multiple established meanings to create a system
of one-to-one symbolification where a single intended meaning is
assigned to a particular word or phrase. This does not interest me
in the least. As a painter, my concern is to provide a referential
vocabulary of chromatic placement that does not derive meaning from
symbols, since the meaning is itself the syntax of paint -- a syntax
of visual sound and retinal intonation paths. Visual pitch or visual
sound frequencies, determined by color phrasing, give a notated
tempo to the reading. In effect, then, in my Scenario Scripts Paintings,
I reproduce and create vocal patterns, distilled and condensed,
which act as behavioral voice extracts. These, in turn, are made
up of multiple voices registered by sound-color, pitch and intonation
placements. Such scenario scripts take the viewer's eye along
experiential scanning paths, where rate of scanning speed and visual
pitch are precisely encouraged, trained and controlled. Accordingly,
it is the activity of traveling from one point to another that takes
on more meaning here, rather than focusing statically on those
locations designated as punctuation points. In my scenario paintings,
I replace signs for single sounds with signs for whole sound sequences
(color phrases), which, since they represent larger units, can describe
language faster and more efficiently, with the aim of writing at the
speed of thought.

PaintFilmicTextsScenarioScorings as Embodiment of Form

> "The motionless whole of a picture and its parts do not
> enter the perception simultaneously except when the
> composition is calculated to create that experience."
> (Sergei Eisenstein)

In film, according to Eisenstein, the act of plastic composition
consists in leading the spectator's attention through the exact path
and with the exact sequence prescribed by the author of the composition.
This applies to the eye's movement over the surface of the screen
if we are dealing with a film frame.

Synesthesia, or the production within the mind of a sense impression
of one kind from a sensory stimulus of another kind, is an involvement
and concern in my filmic scenario scorings. In this case it means
to see sound in color and grasp the visual sound scorings, locating
its line of retinal sound or form as a foundation for correspondence
to the thematic construct.

Form, or character of mark, acts as activator or catalyst for pace
of scanning as well as punctuation and rest area for the eye. Accenting
is often used to bring the viewer's eye back to the left to begin
reading again to the right. Chromatic assignments (for example, blue

to blue-green to green) act as message, strung like words in parataxis. Diffraction of light or dark, proximity of paint placement, angles and lengths, plus raw implementation of stroke, function as suggestions of pace or traveling time of scan.

The retinal sound scorings in my "Painting Scenario Text Scores" maintain an overall tone, pitch, color and key. Shot after shot (hereafter defined as paint placement decision of filmic events) and phrase after phrase combine horizontally, from left to right. Each shot corresponds in intensity to every other shot in the composition. Sometimes, the primary embodiment of the future event will be found in intonation. This is implied by movement of the retinal voice or by changing nuances within the light, color, paint placement structure, or by unfolding acoustic and spatial volumes and distances.

Within each frame, for example, visual sound sequences first impact with a close-up shot and then pick up thematic activity from the previous frame. This marks the passage of the retinal sound or visual action left over from the preceding frame, as it moves from left to right. These Cinematic Script Paintings stress the left side of visual attention first while the right comes to the fore later, as the eye is directed from left to right through each of these motionless frames. While scanning the retinal sound scorings and filmic events, the viewer needs both the before and after to complete the thematic action. Frame to frame in filmic sequence, I accustom the eye to read the picture from left to right.

Varied assignments of plots, subplots, retinal sound scorings and close-up, mid- or long shots are determined by application decisions, including length, width, depth, angle and proximity of paint placements, in order to establish a rate of speed for reading the filmic frames from left to right. Congruence of the movement of the music, or retinal sound structures, with the movement of the visual contours is necessary.

In my work, then, I feel there is complete correspondence between the eye's movement and the visual thematic thrust, as the eye passes over the scenario score. This is the same movement that lies at the base of visual music and retinal, that is, filmic events.

READING INVOLVES A PROCESS * SEEING IS AN INSTANTANEOUS ACT OF RECOGNITION

1973 -- 1979

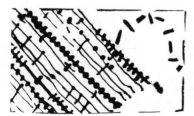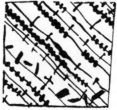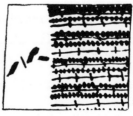

Mas'ud Zavarzadeh

The Critic as Riot Police: Readerly Criticism and Receivable Fictions

Barthelme's Father Continues Weeping; the (so-called) *"Post-Modernism"* becomes the

(now-called) *Postmodernism* and a crossing-out

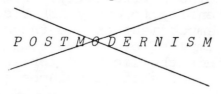

POST M O D E R N I S M

Takes Place

A Foretext

4.6.7. He is weeping all the time; mostly indoors--around/on a bed. *There is my
father, sitting in his bed, weeping.*

3.7.2. The orange wool The pink cupcakes *A thick smile spreads over the face of
each cupcake.*

I

Modernism?

II

*Dead, but still with us, still with us,
but dead.*

III

Postmodernism?

IV

For "post" see under POST
For "modernism" see under both MODERN
                   &
ISM (you will need this later--see <u>infra</u>,
X)

V

Supramodernism?

Supramodern American narrative does
not totalize contemporary experience
(politics/love/work) into sustained
structures of signifieds. Its energies have shifted from situating
signifieds to projecting signifiers.
This text is a galaxy of signifiers.
The conventional Modernist novel is
a unified structure of totalizing
signifieds. It is *simply a way of
controlling, of ordering, of giving
a shape and a significance to the
immense panorama of futility and
anarchy which is contemporary history.*
The weariness, even fear, of totalizing of ordering and prescribing is
caused by the invasion of fictuality
into Amerika: the destablization of
psychic and physical environment into
a *zone of total probability.* Entropy
of the signified. Nontotalizing
narrative has moved beyond the
readerly text and become the most
visible in the forms of *Transfiction*
and the *Nonfiction Novel.* *Transfiction* is a narrative unmasking

VI

This is a good one.

VII

It is (mark my words) more a *leap*, a *rupture*, a *disjuncture*

VIII

Not so much a *before* or *after* affair

IX

More a matter of *difference* created by a diacritical pressure on

T O P

B E H I N D   in *F R O N T* of

U N D E R N E A T H

ISM

(Totalizing narrative is essentially the readerly text: On the Road; Catch-22; Humboldt's Gift). The nontotalizing narrative moves from writerly to

r e c e i v a b l e

text

Supramodernist (receivable) texts need a receivable criticism; one that is not obsessed with quieting the textual disturbances but seeks a *reading space* as spacious and as energized with fictuality as the *narrative space* generated by the fictions themselves. The two are each other's double: nontotalizing not just in spirit but also in shape. They merge in a fictual discourse which is *a galaxy of signifiers* and not a structure of signifieds.

5.9.4. *My father is looking at himself in a mirror. He is wearing a large hat (straw) on which there are a number of blue and yellow plastic jonquils. He says: "How do I look?"*

literary devices and unmaking literary meaning: in it the signifiers point to other signifiers which are pointing at them. Narratives of *floating signifiers?* Out of the narrative pressure which is generated by *differences* grow various kinds of *Transfiction: Metafiction* (Lost in the Funhouse); *Surfiction* (98.6, Take it or Leave it); *Speculative Fiction* (Ubik, Dhalgren). The *Nonfiction Novel* is a literal narrative of events which themselves have become empirical floating signifiers unable to attach themselves to stable signifieds.

F i c t u a l i t y

to come up with very rational, and orderly statements about texts which denounce coherence, rationality and order.

The receivable would be the unreaderly text which catches hold, the red-hot text, a product continuously outside of any likelihood...this text... would require the following response: I can neither read nor write what you produce, but I receive it, like a fire, a drug, an enigmatic disorganization.

The critic should keep
his distance from the
book and talk about
it in a coherent
and rational
manner no
matter how
incohere
the
fic
t

Grammar & the sentence. Linear arbitrary 18th century. Letter writing. Newspaper novels. And horse and buggy communication.

Those who wish language to be fixed. In a stable universe.

By rules. By academies of authority: No light. No heat. From

Stability against change. the sun. No stars. Sta-

bility is finality. The end.

Newton. English Grammar. And the linear sentence. The mechanics of Newton. The mechanics of grammar. Laws of science. Laws-rules of noun verb adjective adverb. Products of 18th century. Inertial systems.

Literature existed. Before grammar People read Literature.

and grammarians. Stamped discipline Before grammar. After

rote drill upon language. And subs- grammar. They wrote.

tituted logic for thought. Parsed. Sentences. For-

got Literature. Hated to read. Dreaded writing.

Writers. Innovators. Liberators. Inventors of language. Despised. Grammarians. Policed language. Imprisoned. Circumscribed. And proscribed.

The neo-cortex. Our newest brain. Our Neo-Narrative. A brain-

Rejects logic. Accepts. Receives. compatible language. Of the

Conceives. Patterns. Invents. Not word. 300 rules/elements of

in sentences. But in images. grammar. Swept away. Clean.

Reduced to 2: the "long" or "short" of the image. Clusters of comma (Kommatic) Berne. Or period (Periodic) Zekowski. Over 30 years. In Novel. Story. Poem. Play. Essay. Our neo-narratives of poetry/prose grammarless open structure. Based on the word. The image. As the matter of language/literature. As matter is waves/particles to modern science. Words. Corresponding interchanging sub-

american-canadian
publishers inc.
innovative forms
tomorrows literature
drawer 2078, portales
new mexico, 88130 u.s.a.
a non-profit foundation

stituting. Sound color form movement taste touch smell hearing song silence speech. Creating. Destroying. Velocity. Foreshortening. Accelerating. Decelerating. Real/Expanded/Compressed/Time. The word. The words. Only the word. And the words. As the consciousness.

The moving space-time of changing simultaneous relationships. Experience in multi and sensory dimensions. No more absolutes. In Language. Art. Or Science. age of rel-

Time: Relative. To position place situation of person. As Word. Relative to position place situation relation in writing. No more objects. But relations. The ativity.

The word as meaning its meaning. No meaning but in the word. The word. As consciousness of its time.

In literature. The old novel drew picturescapes. A series of surfaces. Before the invention of the "visual." Photo movie television video satellite.

Novel. Television's wax museum. Television. Novel's wax museum.

To see is "surface." To perceive is to seize feel sense "structure."

The new novel rejects picturescape for interior organic inscape. The New Novel no longer tells surface (old fiction). Tells penetration (new story). The interior of human consciousness. Abandons visual for perceptual. No limits to human consciousness. No limits to reality.

The mind. The consciousness. Expanding. Unlimited. As the universe. Of which. And by which. The brain. The human. Tells us all.

For now. And the future. In Literature. Language. The unknown. The new. The language of today/tomorrow. A language of images/perceptions. Of curved organic structures. Conceptions. No more flat visual surfaces. No more 18th century grammatic sentences. Geodetic images. In 20th-21st century immediate simultaneous relativity space and time.

"NEO-NARRATIVE...WRITTEN WITHOUT THE CLUMSY INTERVENTION OF GRAMMAR....AN IMMENSE ORIGINALITY." HUDSON REVIEW

ARLENE ZEKOWSKI
****

PAT THE BUNNY

"You can do lots of things."

Children's literature, because of its implied innocence and simplicity,
is given a wide open space to roam through, full of pictures and surprises.
The adult world of publishers, pedants and parents is more than willing
to leave the talking giraffes and wise old owls to the children's book
authors and their kid readership, because they themselves have left such
things so far in the past that nostalgia is the only permissable response.
At whatever point children are expected to leave flying carpets and walk-
through mirrors behind, they have been fed sufficiently on right answers,
in isolation from each other at that, to begin the process that will
enable them to become readers and writers of books that adults will read.
Books which rarely have talking animals but always have lots of words,
uninterrupted from end to end.
Everything that is expansive, magical and eccentric about children's
books is eliminated from the form and content of the adult book. Anything
that does not fit through the verbal meat grinder, any visualization or
association that might jolt a reader back to the act of creation, any
recognition of space or materiality, is deleted in favor of a reality
that registers the appearance of complete control. Very adult, very self
satisfied. A pristine, anaerobic world, neatly ordered into galleys. Contemporary poetry deserves no credit here either, being more constipated,
in most cases, than contemporary prose. The typical breakup of space on the poetic
page refers to little more than the preciousness of the language, governed
by a heavy dose of alienation, solipsism and humourlessness. Whether there
are and have been extraordinary books made solely of words is hardly the
question. What I must wonder though is why the great majority of books
are so academic and dull.
It is as if books came full blown into the world, with typography in
place, untouched by human error or impulse. Yet you might imagine that
at least on the first draft there would be some doodling in the margins;
or some passages underscored in red and green; or some hand drawn arrows
connecting some part to another; or some bold asterisk marking some piece
of information or annotation that may or may not have anything to do with
the plot; or some shopping list, ink smudge or ketchup stain intrusion
from the everyday routine; or some sign of boredom or disgust marked by
an extravagant.X; or anything that might indicate that a human had a hand
in the creation.
What happens to it all? When does the rite of purification begin and why
is it necessary? For any of us committed to making contact with the process and variety of creation, the conservatism and repressed hostility
of commercial publishing (and a good deal of small press publishing as
well), is very hard to understand. For myself it represents a continual
confrontation with generations of idiots who, after first excusing their
ignorance then proceed to beat you to death with it. "Hey Picasso, what
is that? It looks like a sandwich.* I may not know much but I know what
I like."
Basically, I think they're all jealous because, as PAT THE BUNNY tells
us, we can do lots of things. All of which is preparation for a short
review of a children's classic called PAT THE BUNNY.
PAT THE BUNNY by Dorothy Kunhardt, is a small heavy cardboard picture
book which seeks to expose toddlers to various sensory (and sensual)
effects. The book begins with the invocation: "You can do lots of
things, too." The siblings Paul and Judy do the various things first,
on the left-hand page, then we follow them by doing the same thing on

* SUGGESTED BY ROBERT J. LEVIN.

the right-hand page. For example, the first task, to "pat the bunny" is enacted by Judy in an accompanying picture. On the facing page there is a touchable felt bunny bearing the inscription: "Now YOU can pat the bunny." And so it goes through "play peek-a-boo", where Paul covers his face with a real cloth; through "smell the flowers" in which the pictured flowers are scented; through "look in the mirror" where a reflecting paper mirror is proVided; through "Feel Daddy"s scratchy face" (Judy does that) where a section of sandpaper covers Daddy"s cheek; through now YOU read" where a tiny copy of PAT THE BUNNY is provided (a transition that would do Borges proud); through "put your finger through Mummy"s ring" (Paul does that), where a hole in the page is provided; through "bye-bye to you" which shows Paul and Judy waving goodbye to the Reader. What could be more direct and truthful than that? A straightforward recogni-tion that there is a participant out there. The omniscient narrator, who has made all the initial suggestions to Paul and Judy, puts them up to it, but it's a real, unabashed goodbye, just the same.

Why am I bothering with this? Well, beyond all the subliminal associa-tions in PAT THE BUNNY, a discussion of which might be in questionable taste; beyond even the references to larger life themes-- sensuality, authority, narcissism, and family, there is a sense of abstract form that is hardly to be found in the pages of the N.Y. Times Book Review, except perhaps under Children's Books.

While there are numerous artists working to break through the limitations of linear print to engage new forms (that of course draw on a multitude of much older forms), serious outlets for publication are difficult to find. Even when these books are produce and distributed through the largely charitable labors of their makers, the commercial review media are almost completely closed to them is the public to become aware of the value of such work when the editors of The Times, New Yorker, American Poetry Review et al, many of whom seem fixed, develop-mentally, at page 5 of PAT THE BUNNY, (the incestuous peek-a-boo page), will not recognize its existence?

I feel the answer lies in the idea of control: the desire to resist one's fear of mortality, expressed through an obsessive concern with controlling what cannot be controlled. All rough edges, impulses and time. Many of these people and institutions are stuck in the mud of Au-thority and Tradition. Still gathering support and approval from their particular corps of Elders, they continue to confuse a state of indebted-ness with a state of grace. How many still feel Daddy's scratchy face close behind?

     [PAUSE]

Finally, I would like to thank Dorothy Kunhardt who, I do not know and who is unaware of this review. I have meant no offense and I respect her ingenuity in putting PAT together. Both of my kids have enjoyed it, Daddy's scratchy face, notwithstanding.

                              Bye-bye to YOU.

                              Paul Zelevansky
                              March 1978.

HE MOANED:

I LOVE WANT YOU ITU

SHE GROANED:

<u>NOT</u>

by Harriet Zinnes

How to be free. How to be alive in the land of death and plenty. How
to liberate oneself from violence that is neither desire nor procreation.
How to be alive in such a way that death is already there piercing through
the armor of skin or breathing. Or, to put it another way, how to make life
so thorough that it is as much inside as out, that life that is the experience
already consumed -- and not destroyed. How?

To consider that nothing dies: what emerges, submerges to the unconscious,
that springboard of desire and of the poem. Therefore, Bill Knott, or
St. Geraud, born 1940, died 1966, now living his posthumous life, naturally as
poet still, who when he is truly alive, writing well, that is, is able to
consume all experience into a whole, so that the poem is as much a "corpse" as
a "big plate of beans." As André Breton had it in his <u>Second Surrealist</u>
<u>Manifesto</u> (1929):

> Everything leads one to believe that there exists a certain
> point in the mind from which life and death, the real and
> the imaginary, the past and the future, what is communicable
> and what is incommunicable, the high and the low, cease to be
> perceived as contradictory.

There are no contradictions. Only the false, rhetorical contradictions, such
as

> If bombing children is preserving peace, then
> my fucking you is a war-crime.

But when the language is not rhetoric (when "land-guage" is not "extinct")
but containing the contradictions (with black humor, puns, neologisms, a surreal
blood transfusion of tongues), then as in the following "Prosepoem," from
which I quote, in part, the contradictions fade: horror of death dissolves and
the poet triumphs.

It's MadameKy's menstrual-period. Her whole country bleeds for the
rich bitches of Liberty. And blood from all Asias soaks down
through the earth, drips out here to starve. India and China, please
help, there is a famine here, an America-famine, there's no longer
enough America to feed Whitman or Poe, and I'm getting very thin.
Oh dropping bombs upon what no longer exists! ...

But Bill Knott, whose underground reputation is enormous and whose books
(all published -- seven of them -- by small presses <u>on purpose</u>) are out of
print almost as soon as they become available) doesn't become free only by
dissolving the rhetoric of the war-mongers. He knows again with the French
surrealists that love is the greatest liberator of them all. Yes, he is one of
the finest love poets writing today. And not only in those famous Naomi poems
(not enough of which are reprinted in his <u>Selected and Collected Poems</u>). One of
his funniest love poems is that "fatal fable" entitled "Priscilla, or the Marvels of
Engineering," when desire is so overpowering that the narrator is convinced that the
ship itself is incarnated as his beloved. The consequences to the ship from his
ardor -- "those great big gaping holes" -- are wild. Knott's love poems are fiercely erotic: "O Naomi/I kiss every body of you, every face." (Naomi is also every
woman, all humankind.) Or in a characteristic short love poem:

>   I am the only one who can say
>   "I have never been in anyone's dreams"
>   Your nakedness: the sound when I break an apple in half.

The obliteration of death, of violence through an intermingling of all things
organic or dead, the assertion of a self made manifest ("the way the world is not"),
the everlasting procreation through the love of women is the sum of Bill Knott's
poetry. But you can't have everything: some people DON'T like the poetry of <u>not</u>.
Some people think that Knott is simply not there.

>   Here
>   Where nakedness is redundant
>
>   Delicit. I disemrobe to
>   File the stones down smooth.
>
>   Nameless
>   Dateless   He wrote.

Beckett, Avant-Garde Experiments, and FROGS.

- Nicholas Zurbrugg

Who are the heroes of Modernism and Post-Modernism? Discussing 'Avant-Garde, Neo-Avant-Garde, Post Modernism: The Culture of Crisis' in Clio (IV/3, 1975), Matei Calinescu argued that the avant-garde are very much the anti-heroes of our times, finding such writers a singularly destructive group. Calinescu concludes: "it is necessary to distinguish between modernism and the avant-garde...the first being more constructive...the latter almost dogmatically destructive and sterile". Calinescu adds: "If the avant-garde was eventually creative, this was the result of an unwitting deviation from its own principles".

Michael Hamburger offers a similar distinction in a review of Samuel Beckett's collected poems in PN Review (5/1, 1977). He suggests experimental poetry is made by poets exclusively concerned with the nature of language, rather than with life, and seems to imply that experimental texts are therefore less rich than those of the non-experimenters. Hamburger's definition declares: "The only writers who can meaningfully be described as experimental are those primarily concerned not with expressing themselves or conveying their sense and experience of life, but with the quiddity, laws, and possibilities of their medium".

In Hamburgian terms, experimental writers don't seem to take life seriously, but only show concern for their medium. "Only those writers are free to make words a material for experiments - as in 'Concrete' poetry or in related fields". Contrasting Beckett with such writers, Hamburger claims that "Beckett never has been a writer of that kind, but one with ontological or existential obsessions, compelled by those obsessions to be more and more reductive...All his innovations have been in that direction - a discarding of many of the conventional resonances of his media, because they had become superfluous and irrelevant".

Hamburger's distinction seems to neglect both Beckett's experimental motivations, and the existential preoccupations of avant-garde poetry. It is embarrassing to Hamburger's theory, and indeed to the 'purist' theories of many concrete poets, that there now exists a large number of politically satirical concrete poems (such as those of Décio Pignatari). Moreover, though Hamburger claims that Beckett's poetry is not concerned with purely formal traits, Beckett has stated: "I am interested in the shape of ideas...It is the shape that matters"; and has also remarked: "Among those whom we call great artists, I can think of none whose concern was not predominantly with his expressive possibilities, those of his vehicle, those of humanity". Any glance at Beckett's work reveals that it is just as concerned with the shape of language as with the meaning of language; and any glance at the best experimental poetry reveals that the avant-garde are equally preoccupied both with formal concerns and with the adequate expression of contemporary reality.

If any significant distinction may be drawn between contemporary forms of writing that are or are not 'avant-garde' in quality, then it seems that this distinction is most usefully to be made in terms of the SCALE of an author's innovations (rather than in terms of his creative or destructive nature, or his existential or formal preoccupations).

This kind of distinction is illustrated by the different ways in which 'traditional' Modernists such as Marcel Proust, 'traditional' Post-Modernists such as Beckett, avant-garde Modernists such as Raoul Hausmann, and avant-garde Post-Modernists such as Henri Chopin, have all variously 'destroyed' - or, if one prefers, 'extended' - language by employing abstract breath sounds.

In A la recherche du temps perdu the novel's hero, Marcel, is twice transfixed by the sound of breathing; once by the calm if naive sound of the sleeping Albertine, and once more by the pure and benevolent intonation of his dying grandmother's last breaths. In other words, Proust uses such sounds as one of his many means of exhibiting his characters' qualities. In his recent playlet That Time, Beckett evokes his character's anguish with the tortured panting sounds that punctuate his memories; while his mini-mini-mini-playlet Breath uses such gasps to evoke universal distress. In sum, such 'traditional' Modernists and Post-Modernists as Proust and Beckett use unorthodox materials as a central yet restricted part of their works.

If Breath seems a considerable innovation, it is worth noting that some half century before the première of Breath, the Dada poet and artist and novelist and sculptor and photographer and dancer (and therefore not entirely destructive) Raoul Hausmann had argued that "the poem is an act consisting of respiratory and auditive combinations". Hausmann's early sound poems pioneered abstract poetry as a new means of both resolving formal problems and expressing his times; and in the same radical way, the Post-Modern sound poet Henri Chopin has used subtle montages of tape-recorded and electronically amplified breath noises to create poems with such titles as Le Temps Aujourd'hui - 'Present Times'.

Proust, Beckett, Hausmann and Chopin all variously use breath sounds with or without technology (according to their situation in 'Modernist' or 'Post-Modernist eras); and also all use such noises in meaningful structures, as part of quite complicated 'collected works'. If avant-garde writers like Hausmann and Chopin must be distinguished from 'traditional' innovators such as Proust and Beckett, it is because such avant-garde writers are the FROGS of Modernism and Post-Modernism: it is they who have made the great leaps forward. Leaping is obviously a risky activity, and avant-garde experiments are often doomed to nasty falls. Nevertheless the audacity of the avant-garde deserves serious critical attention, since it is the audacity of such literary frogs (rather than the most accomplished traditional croakings) that may best indicate the shape and the existential preoccupations of the literature to come.

WORD INFORMATION[1]

a) No information

DADADADADADADADADA . . . .[2]

*all*i*want*'s*a*good*5 cent*seegar*
heeheeHOHOheeheeHOHOheeheeHOHO
*all*i*want*'s*a*good*5 cent*seegar*
heeheeHOHOheeheeHOHOheeheeHOHO
(Rothenberg)[3]

b) Very little information

Form is never more than an extension of content.
(Olson quoting Creeley)

I saw the best minds of my generation destroyed by madness . . .
(Ginsberg)[4]

so much depends
upon

a red wheel
barrow

glazed with rain
water

beside the white
chickens
(WCW)[5]

c) Minimum information in everyday English

J1 His mother eat Dog Yummies
J2 Somebody said your mother's breath smell funny
J3 They say your mother eat Gainesburgers
J4 They say your mother was a Gravy Train (Labov quoting the Jets)[6]

T
h
e
the animals are coming by
n
i
m
a
l
s

HEHEHHEH

HEHEHHEH

HEH**UH**HEH

HEHEHHEH

HEHEHHEH

(Rothenberg translating the Seneca)[7]

d) rate of repetition close to (c) - cyclic permutations in mathematics

subway-lights, riding deserted station
quiet dim, passing woman-man
train waiting

deserted riding lights subway
dim man-station
passing train
quiet woman, . . .waiting (Kucharz)[8]

e) partially foreseeable texts (logical connections)

since i've heard jerry before   i was prepared to ask myself
  a somewhat similar question   to the question cokboy
seems to have asked   which is   "what am i doing here?"
(Antin)[9]

f) Information in the ordinary sense

Ginsberg and Amram have been friends since Amram came to New York City in 1955, and they performed
together at A&S last year. (Rochelle Ratner in Soho Weekly News)[10]

g) texts retaining only grammatical structure

I am shaved of the shirt on method that the nursery of
tri-colored jury—glued his box and her scream—didn't
remind for their brand, presented by an marble-colored wax. (Zweig)[11]

h) text composed according to the digram probabilities of words (selections from a text)

The past I can't find anyone that wants to go to show me what's
the worth of his mind on fears or play with the grass. (Zweig)[12]

i) maximum word information (random choice of words)

To human existence
Human undertaken man a nonetheless,
Subjectivity. In toward understand, and tools, itself or not
As never. Divided
Zen ego's not
Be. Undoubtedly, does deception. However is, subjectivity

(morality),
(MacLow)[13]

Notes to Word Information:

1 Information theorists have informed us that information increases with originality (or surprise). The unexpected contains more information than the expected. This requires us to read in a different way: in the case of this list, from word to word, watching our expectations as we read. The list from "no information" to "maximum information" was taken from Information Theory and Esthetic Perception by Abraham Moles (Urbana: University of Illinois Press, 1968, trans. by Joel E. Cohen). The examples are taken mostly from the work of avant-garde poets.

2 This has more information than the usual nonsense syllable repeated.

3 Information is contained from word to word until the repetition begins. When Rothenberg performs this, information continues as he varies his pronunciation of certain phonemes.

4 These are clichés for most poets. Clichés are often dependent on context.

5 This whole poem can be seen as a cliché. However, according to the linguist John Robert Ross (in an unpublished paper, MIT), information in this poem comes partly through the phonemes; the "z" in glazed being the most surprizing in the context of the phoneme structure of the poem.

6 This example of "Sounding" is a formulaic interchange for adolescent Black American men. Information does increase as the sounding escalates; and we may end up finding out who is the best sounder. See Labov, William, "Rules for Ritual Insults" in Language in the Inner City (Philadelphia: University of Pennsylvania Press, 1972).

7 This is formulaic to the Senecas, but what does it mean to us? When the poem is translated it switches contexts and gives us more information. It actually doesn't belong in this category. The HEHEH section belongs in (a); the rest lower on this list. But where?

8 Because of space limitations I have not been able to give enough of this example. See the work of Lawrence Kucharz for further permutations.

9 As a written text this is perfectly logical. When Antin spoke the text it was improvised, therefore more unexpected (and containing more information). Even orally, however, it retains its logical nature. The message of this particular passage is more surprising than any formal connections from word to word.

10 This is news; also called gossip in the art world.

11 I couldn't find an example of this so I made one by taking a sentence from Moles and, opening Daniel Spoerri's Anecdoted Topography of Chance at random, I scanned the text for any word of the same grammatical category as the first word in Moles; I continued this process for all of the words in the sentence. Some of the categories were so limited in the implications of their syntax that I admit I took liberties once or twice.

12 Again, I could find no example of this and made my own by beginning with the word "the" and scanning Allen Ginsberg's poem "Guru Blues" for any word following a "the", and so on. A poem is a particularly inappropriate text for this kind of probability scanning. First, there are too few words and the words have been selected too carefully. There is also the danger that the poet has distorted syntax purposely. In this particular poem the repetition of "I can't find anyone" somewhat determined the results; also if I couldn't find a second instance of a word I took the word that came after the first instance. Because of my choice of text, this example has less information than it might have.

13 This is not completely chance generated as it comes from the title of the source text "The Human Situation and Zen Buddhism". Choice of this structure and of the source text itself somewhat limits the information content of the piece.

Additional notes:
Where in this progression from little to more information should we put Armand Schwerner's The Tablets? Somewhere between (g) and (i) but not (h)?
What can it mean to say that there is more word information in the poetry of Jackson MacLow than in most other poets? What sort of information is this and is it valuable? Should we look elsewhere for information, beyond the connections between words? Where else should we look?

Ellen Zweig
Ann Arbor, March, 1979

claus clüver

ping pong concrete

the first concrete poem i ever saw was eugen gomringer's "ping pong".
i saw it, but i could not read it. not because i did not know the language:
in fact, it was the only text in the magazine where i found it for which i
did not need a dictionary. my room-mate had received the magazine from his
home in argentina. surrounded by spanish texts, the poem had been reprinted
in the original--exactly as it had first been published in 1953, surrounded
by german texts, in switzerland. it was a poem in my native language. i read
it in bloomington, indiana, and showed it to some american friends: they, too,
had no difficulty understanding the words, for was it not a poem written in
english? and we all agreed on the subject matter, even though the poem had
no title to guide us. the text itself was telling us clearly enough what it
was all about--so insistently, in fact, that that was all there was of a text.
(or so it seemed.) that, of course, was precisely the trouble with it. we
all knew how to play ping pong, but we did not know how to play the game of
this text. the rules we had learned for reading poems did not seem to apply.
actually, the rules we had learned for reading any text were of little help.
what was the syntax, what the grammar here? where was the verb, where the
subject? no "i", no persona, no voice: only the perfect consonance of these
two syllables each of which, in german and in spanish and practically also in
english, requires the other to make any sense, echoing the sound produced in
playing the game they name--ping pong, five times in a row. or, to be exact,
five ping pongs distributed over four rows, four lines of text arranged in a
visually striking manner:

               ping pong
                    ping pong ping
                    pong ping pong
                         ping pong

but while the text struck me, so hard indeed that strangely enough i have
never since that first encounter been able to forget it (never did i know a
poem so quickly by heart), i did not know what to make of it. only after meeting the brazilian poets haroldo and augusto de campos and décio pignatari, who
with eugen gomringer gave the international concrete poetry movement its name,
and mary ellen solt, whose "flowers in concrete" are among the finest north
american contributions to the genre and who has published the most beautiful
international anthology of concrete poetry--only then did i learn how to read
the text.
my trouble had been that i was so disturbed by what was not there that i
had not really stopped to look carefully at what the text offered instead.
having freed my mind from the wrong expectations, i realized that it was quite
obvious how this ping pong game wanted to be played, for the rules had been
built into the structure of the text. the first and the fourth lines state
the two syllables alone, in their normal sequence, thus presenting identical
visual shapes. it is a law of optical perception that the eye will conncet
identical shapes. but to reach the last ping pong from the first in this text,
the eye has to jump diagonally across two longer lines stretched out between
them; and having nowhere else to go, it will, still obedient to the law, most
likely jump back to the first, as if following a ping pong ball jumping back
and forth across a net. this verbal net has been created by a simple means:

in line two, the ping pong has been extended by another ping, whose pong then opens the third line, followed by another ping pong. as a result of this simple manipulation, we encounter in line two a pong flanked on either side by ping, and in line three the reverse. looking at each of these lines and reading it aloud, we experience again, visually and acoustically, the cross-over effect already observed in the overall structure of the text. and since the second and third lines are aligned with the pong of line one, and the fourth line with the ping of line two and the pong of line three, we find the effect repeated vertically as well. it has an echo (by a lucky coincidence) even in the individual shape of the ping and the pong, since the typeface chosen by the poet, much like the one used here, renders the extreme letters, p ang g, in almost identical forms, though reversed. thus the text has been made to embody concretely in its structure and in its verbal material the extra-literary reality which it evokes. a mere succession of five ping pongs would, to be sure, approximately reproduce the sound which characterizes the game, but beyond that it would communicate relatively little, and as a text it would be indifferent, dull, and also arbitrary, for there is no reason why the succession should not stop at four or extend to six or even more ping pongs. gomringer's poem, however, which could not be any shorter and which any extension would destroy, has become a concentrated image of the game--its ideogram.

      the painter josef albers, who along with other concrete artists had a strong impact on gomringer's thinking, once defined "the measure of art" as "the ratio of effort to effect". by spatial organization and a slight but decisive rearrangement of his minimal word material the poet has here set up a dynamic text which keeps the reader active long after s/he has perceived the basic constellation, jumping all over the text, back and forth, horizontally, vertically, and diagonally. in fact, while the text itself is arranged on a two-dimensional plane, the diagonal reading creates an illusion of three-dimensional space, and while the short text can be perceived almost in an instant, the reading can go on indefinitely, since the text sends us constantly back into itself. contemplating this minimal model of a space-time continuum, the reader, should s/he be so inclined, might proceed to further speculations, intrigued by the binary nature of the basic material, and might wonder about the dualism which permeates this closed universe. would that be a correct reading of the text? was all of this intended by the poet? the text alone can give the answer. having provided the verbal material and organized it in this fashion, the poet has merely provided the rules by which the game is to be played; having mastered them, it depends on the reader's skill and imagination how well s/he will play it, and s/he may very well play the game better than the poet himself, and with more surprising results.

      gomringer has repeatedly spoken of the concrete poet as a rule-maker and referee who sets up play activities and appeals to, among other things, the human play instinct. a poet's texts need not be about games at all to have this effect, and they rarely are. many ways have been devised for inviting the reader to explore with the poet the possibilities inherent in the visual, aural, and semantic aspects of the word material: it may be offered as a spatial ideogram, or fragmented and recomposed, or sent through developmental or transformational processes which gradually destroy the semantic meaning or allow it to emerge. the reader-performer's first task is to discover the rules of the performance; for as in most games, arbitrary procedures are not permitted in most of these texts. the reader is always an active participant; sometimes, s/he may be required to complete the text, occasionally, to destroy it. whatever the form, these texts restore an immediate relationship with verbal language and all its possibilities, with the result that we take it seriously again, as all players will take their games.

THE SYLLABIC MODULE

The sense of contemporary verse is often organized on variable axes, and its sound should be developing further in a corresponding direction. Theoretically we should be producing metrical modes, analogous to the structure of serial music, in which the randomness of instances in free verse is subordinated to audible patterns, without returning to the simple recursions of meter. For all the structural openess and thematic complexity of The Cantos, Paterson, and The Maximus Poems, the meters in those poems retain the random character of free verse.

Now the randomness of verse instance can be subordinated to recursive patterns without being made to conform to a simple linear meter. The internal rhymes and crossing assonances of skaldic verse constitute such a recursion. The strophic series in the odes of Pindar are based on translinear recursions, tightly formalized ones. The fixed strophes, corresponding from one to another line by line, have their sequences fully laid down after the first group of strophe-antistrophe-epode has been given. The alternatives are closed as soon as the pattern has been presented. Thus the odes offer a "vertical" pattern, to adapt a musical term, for counterpoint against the "horizontal" bars of the individual line.

In the principle of the syllabic module, as exemplified in my Modulars, every syllable is enlisted both horizontally and vertically. In Midway, for example, every line has a syllablecount, one of seven horizontal possibilities. But in addition every line stands as a fuction of the module "3"; and so every line has a vertical relation to the other lines, through permutation rather than through identity. Instead of moving on from identical line to identical line, and instead of flowing ahead processively as in free verse, the poem has its syllable-clusters "rhyme" with each other vertically. Every syllable is part of such a cluster, and the ear collocates all the syllables vertically as well as accumulating them on the horizontal line. In such a system, even a run of two or three identical lines has the function of "rhyming" its modules, as well as repeating its meter.

The line unit is bound both horizontally by syllable-count in the line and vertically by recursive series from line to line. At the same time, the line, within its limited number of syllabic alternatives, remains free, as free verse is free, to choose, at every point, the particular alternative for the particular line.

In the syllabic module, the lines are all syllabic lines. But in addition they are subjected vertically to a series of recursive rules which totally determine their function in a larger pattern, one which retains the processive freedom of free verse because the alternatives are never closed. In Midway, for example, every syllabic line is a variant of the base module, 3-syllables. The recursive definition becomes strictest at the outer boundaries (2-12), whose stanza-pattern is most often determined as soon as one two-syllable line has occurred. But the recurrence of "2:6 plus 12" stanzas is itself random. In Due Dates, the progressions among the three variations of syllabic module are determined by rule, but alternatives still exist: a four-syllable line or a six-syllable line; it may not be followed by an eight-syllable line, nor may it follow one.

In One-Way Mystery, the vertical pattern is a total one: every stanza must contain no fewer than 24 syllables, and no more than 48; every stanza must also be divisible by eight. So every line moves further towards closing out possible alternatives. But the stanza-progression remains open to alternatives, and hence it does not lose the aleatory character of free verse, for all its elaboration.

In music, a "logarithmic" progression will be heard, we can argue from Boulez' implications, though the musician cannot control that progression without

a computer: the listener picks up a drift where the player would lose one himself. (Boulez, Penser la Musique aujourd'hui, Mainz, 1963, 93-113).

   Poems written in syllabic module should be heard, then, not just in the
line, which sounds like free verse until horizontally similar lines have established themselves. The syllables should also be heard to undergo a vertical
livening. This can happen only when variation occurs. The principle of the
module must apply to varied lines to be felt as more than just a simple linear
meter. So in haiku, a sort of molecular syllabic-module poem, the second line
is heard as "5" syllables plus the largest count possible less than half of "5"
rather than simply "7", only when the third line recurs as identical with the
first. The power of the stanzas used by Alcaeusx and Sappho, and then by Horace
and Catullus, derives from the total syllable count of the stanza as well as
from the strict variation of the lines. The syllable count amplifies endstopp-
ing and enjambment because the line, at the sensitive point of its ending, is
a place-marker in the module variation of a syllable sum as well as the boundary
of a metric unit.

   My poem, "The Widow's Future," (The Charges, p.88) draws the rules to a
nearly maximal strictness, being written in four-line stanzas rhymed a-b-a-b
with just four syllables to each line. But it remains monodic, on a simple
linear plan.

   A further feature of these syllabic-module poems consists of their being
"shadowed" by the standard meter of English, iambic pentameter. One identifies
meter by expectation, and also by cultural context. One has to have read two
lines at least before he can confidently expect that the poem before him is in
the given meter, say iambic pentameter. An English reader, before he opens a
book, knows from his cultural context that he stands a fair chance of encounter-
ing some iambic pentameter, just as a Roman one had a fair chance of encounter-
ing dactyllic hexameter. English "poem" may be said to imply "strong possibility
of iambic pentameter", just as iambic pentameter may be said to imply not just
"five foot-line with the beat predominantly on the second syllable," but also
"ten-syllable line." This being the case, any ten-syllable English line, whatever its pattern of accent, will suggest "blank verse". And any five-syllable
line will suggest "half-line of blank verse," as (even more) any six-syllable
French line will suggest "half an alexandrine." In English twenty syllables
will suggest "two blank verse lines." Now the module of Midway is shadowed
by the absence of blank verse. No line, and not most combinations of three
lines or fewer can fall into the pattern of ten syllables. Due Dates, avoiding
sections of blank verse in its three modular lines (4-6-8) allows for runs of
twenty syllables in three- or four-line (rather than two-line) patterns. And
pairs of lines (4-6; 6-4) can have ten syllables as a count. Thus the poem
constantly has a shadow of blank verse running across the lines.

   In One-Way Mystery, however, the shadow is not blank verse, but the module
itself, 8. This is a double module; it governs each couplet (which must be
either divisible by eight or if not succeeded by one that is also not), and it
governs each stanza (which must be divisible by eight). Yet eight-syllable
lines are excluded from the poem, as are 4-syllable lines--The four modular
possibilities stand as bounding those two numbers (3,5,7,9).

   The syllabic module, then, offers a structuring both more inclusive than
conventional linear meter and more free, since a given line is often chosen
from a set of alternatives rather than dictated by the meter. But the alternatives, being always a defineable set, avoid at every point the randomness
of free verse.

                              ALBERT COOK

RADICAL LITERATURE
: ONE TRANSCRIPTION OF ACTUAL SPECIES

- Edward Kaplan

Radical Literature is extraordinary,not heightened
(meaning not re fined,not hyped,not boiled,not the
objective product of an ordinary mind doing tricks,
like walking on water which much such literature be
BUT is the higher order of entropic reach,which an
extraordinary being is want to do,if it is a creature
whose tension to language is fundamental that is at
the root,which be radical,which,to many,<u>appears</u>   as
decay   magic   uselessness   dillydally

Which means it's subverting at every turn by definition : the original masterpiece   At the large &
bigger hand of such a person go the radical way to
DO,to function like that as such which is everyday
art and routine acts of enlightenment

The form of which may be to ordinary artisans
<u>seem</u> ordinary that is mirror the random profusion
of horseshit around us but is worthy of   opinion
which this CRITICAL ASSEMBLING seeks to   have
its   hand on the heart of

For Its Own Sake we say as if to denigrate but
it's a pull from inside to somewhere else   the
original experimenter is functioning to do
having little choice except as personal discipline
he do what he do UNlike those of the species whose
capabilities limit them to perfect specifics or to
bear on their shoulders a rule here or there or to
sophisticate an approach pattern that has been used
by others to light an ordinary darkness

Radical Literature then is an extraordinary person's
claim to the special version of their condition with
the very language that holds them,that feeds the vision
to them directly to the whole : thus,it is freedom it's
all about

Political in the sense of its origin,as the place
where such conversation about profound things
                              exhibit their rings

All depth,in other words : all range   power
dimension   elemental
self relocating   self opposing
self expansion   which is pure   pleasure
    which is the heart of an original artist
          involved that way with it is all

And as such,cannot profit by collaboration
or any other walls which might be construed
to contain it
And as such,cannot fail or even succeed : The
world moves forward on the thrust of   single
small achievements which are big by   collection
which only can occur <u>after</u>

The fact of radical literature has always been
borderline   therefore   as a future is
as a fringe from which the new self   enters
into its next manifestation
into the next day   - it is a literature of
multiplicity   of moments of species

It generally is an inhabitation of energy
but energy alone is more descriptive of this
 - we could say   it's very much like energy

Examples of such are antithetical to weirdnesses
like fame   recognition : they remain in a solo
parenthesis of circumstance

To invent,to invest in action all the palpable stuff
which <u>is</u> us at root - cannot ease pain except the
spirit of it,do that,convince us life is best when
hard,far-reaching and of consequence

It'll never be 'comforting' to "read" Olson or
Stein : such cliffs are paramount,not trivial

And radical literature is that if anything ever was

_____

Edward Kaplan has had poetry published in places like
The Smith,Black Box,New Poetry,Assembling. Books out:
PANCRATIUM from Swamp Press,ZERO STATION from Stone
Country Press,and SERAPHICS from Avalon in England.
He has written essays,constructed visuals,sits on a
dozen projects at a clip,corresponds with passion to
keep in shape,is a dangerous & practical example of
what happens when one does poetry to the inclusion
of everything else worth having a good time with.Lives
in New York City,New Jersey,Atlantic City - in that order.

That poetry has been isolated from the
physical world is evident."Environmental
poetry" occurs in the same zone as
streetsigns,graffiti,advertisements
or corporate graffiti,architecture,
and electronic media.Transmissions have
included poems spray-painted on urban
walls,towed across the sky by airplanes,
illuminated by neon,and projected into
space with a scanning laser.As technological hardware has dematerialized
so many other phenomena,poems may now
be "written" in a bolt of pure light.
Trying to transmit poems without the
printed page has required many explorations
beyond the boundaries of the literary
"reservation." All my projects and
transmissions have been attempts to
locate a unified field for poetry; a
zone that may transcend the dichotomy
of form and content,by employing new
technologies to achieve modes of
linguistic photosynthesis.The poem
outdoors no longer has to be "about"
a place.It may,without apology,"be"
that place.It may transform that place.
A geographical place,perhaps, as within
the poet himself,where context and text
may lie down together.

                              -Mark Mendel 1979

Photos: Cloud Rhymes with Air Lines by Mark Mendel
Boston Kite Festival 1978
photo credit: Anne Bray/Muntadas

IAN HAMILTON FINLAY : an objective event.

by Stephen Scobie

        For the past year, the internationally-known Scottish poet
Ian Hamilton Finlay has been involved in a bitter and protracted
dispute with the Scottish Arts Council. The details of the affair
are too numerous and too complex to go into here, but some issues
do emerge which are of more than merely local importance.

        The dispute began when the SAC failed to give full support
to Finlay in his campaign to correct certain erroneous statements
contained in a review of his work by The Spectator. (The complaint
was later upheld by the British Press Council.) Finlay believed
that a public body committed to the support of the arts has the
obligation to speak out in defence of artists when they are being
unjustly attacked, and to tell the truth about their own relationships
with the artists, even when that truth is discreditable to themselves.
In other words, he was expecting a bureaucracy to admit its mistakes:
a position which is obviously naive and idealistic, but also absolutely
necessary.

        Last summer, Finlay cancelled, at very short notice, an SAC-
sponsored exhibition of his work. This gesture was in part directed
against those who believe that an artist's business is to go on
creating and publishing "works of art" in isolation from the politics
of his cultural milieu. For Finlay, at that point, not showing his
work was a more important statement, aesthetically as well as politically, than showing it, to however many people, could possibly have been.

        Since then, the dispute has escalated alarmingly. Finlay's
stubborn insistence on the highest aesthetic and ethical standards, in
the administration of the arts as well as in the arts themselves,
combined with his uncompromising and often invective style of letter-
writing, eventually drove the SAC into a position where they would only
communicate with him through solicitors. This is all very well for a
public body with a large budget - but for an isolated and never very
well off artist to have to pay a solicitor to communicate with the body
which is supposed to be supporting the arts in his country is surely an
intolerable situation.

        The latest developments have taken on a tone of black farce.
The SAC has been attempting to recover two sculptural pieces, which they
own, but which they had inadvertently returned to Finlay after the
cancellation of the exhibition. Finlay has been refusing to answer, or
even to open, Arts Council correspondence until such time as they agree
to drop the "solicitors only" condition: in desperation, then, the SAC
sent their final demand notice on a postcard.

Many of Finlay's works are realised in various different media: the printed page, the silk-screen print, glass, wood, stone, etc. Since, on the limited space available on a postcard, the SAC had failed to specify which version they were demanding the return of, Finlay had delivered to them two large packing cases which contained, not the stone sculpture versions, but a series of progressively smaller boxes and envelopes which ultimately yielded up the postcard versions of the two pieces in question.

Finlay describes the delivery of these two crates as an Objective Event, created by the poet Ian Hamilton Finlay, and documented by the Scottish Arts Council. (The documentation is extensive and angry.) As an Event, it demonstrates, in a delightfully controlled and witty manner, the equivocal nature of the relationship between words and things. It has been Finlay's claim that the SAC has consistently misrepresented the facts of the case, that in the tangles of their bureaucracy word and event have too often pursued entirely separate courses.

Within Scotland, Finlay's position remains an isolated one. He is widely regarded as an eccentric, a habitual trouble-maker, and what he actually has to say is seldom taken seriously. It would be so nice if he would just go back to making cute little poems about fishing boats and forget the troublesome questions about whether or not the public arts bodies are properly serving their function, or how they should be accountable for the decisions they make. It's much easier to get worked up about dissenting artists in the Soviet Union than about those in your own back yard.

Meanwhile the saga goes on. When last heard of, the offending sculptures had been spirited away - on sleds, across the snowy fields of Lanarkshire - to be held for ransom in an undisclosed location. The ransom demanded, in this case, is nothing more than reasonable discourse. But who will be willing to pay it?

For further information, please contact:

Ian Hamilton Finlay
Little Sparta
Stonypath, Dunsyre
Lanarkshire, Scotland

Lord Balfour of Burleigh
Chairman, Scottish Arts Council
19, Charlotte Square
Edinburgh EH2 4DF
Scotland

NOTES ON CONTRIBUTORS

JONATHAN ALBERT "Via poems and theater pieces, I have been exploring spoken sound and language since 1967. I earned a Ph. D. in Sound Composition at the University of Iowa. I was a member of the Center for New Performing Arts at Iowa."

BLAIR H. ALLEN "was 'reinstated' by the L.A. *Times,* but no longer is allowed to choose small and independent press books for review. All books are chosen by the L.A. *Times.* He hopes to have a book selection of poetry and an experimental Art-Lit Chapbook published soon."

MIREILLE ANDRES and PATRICK ROUSSEAU "work together, because we feel often the same things about fiction." 103 rue de Moines, 75017 Paris, FRANCE.

BRUCE ANDREWS "Co-editor, $L=A=N=G=U=A=G=E$, journal of criticism & poetics (10 issues, 1978-1979). Author: *Jeopardy* (Annex, 1979); *Praxis* (Tuumba, 1978); *Film Noir* (Burning Deck, 1978); *Vowels* (O, 1976); other recent work in *Roof, This, A Hundred Posters, Hills, Open Letter, Flora Danica.* Recent Ms.: *Legend*☆ (5 person collaboration); *Swaps Ego; Transblucency; Sonnets.*" 41 West 96th St., New York, N.Y. 10025.

ARIAS-MISSON returned to the USA at the end of 1976, after 17 years in Europe and North Africa. Two books: *The Confessions of a madman, murderer, rapist, bomber, thief or A Year from the Journal of an Ordinary American* (1975) and *Ole the Public Poem Book* (1979). P.O. Box 24, Clarksburg, N.J. 08510.

ASCHER/STRAUS: Recent fictions in *Sun & Moon, Exile, Chouteau Review, Pushcart Prize III. Letter to an Unknown Woman* upcoming from Treacle Press, 1979, and fiction in *Chicago Review. The Blue Hangar* upcoming in *Interstate* and *As It Returns* in *Intermedia.* 176 B. 123 St., Rockaway Park, N.Y. 11694.

ERIC BAIZER is a musician and poet whose writing has appeared in many magazines. His recent books are *In the Museum of Temporary Art* and *Bent.* P.O. Box 14186, Washington, DC 20044.

ANNA BANANA is surprisingly conventional, having lived for several years with the same man, in the same apartment, which contains a neat guest room in which not only their children but visiting artists sleep. 1183 Church St., San Francisco, CA 94114.

PETER H. BARNETT "is Associate Professor of Philosophy at John Jay College, C.U.N.Y. He has been experimenting with alternative forms for the expression of philosophy for seven years. *Open Structure for a Philosophical Experiment* is both a criticism of the prevailing closed argumentative structure of most philosophical writing and an example of a radical alternative." 444 W. 56th St. NYC 10019.

JOHN M. BENNETT "Head, Luna Bisonte Prods, 137 Leland Ave., Columbus, Ohio 43214. Widely published poet and experimentalist (books, chapbooks, articles, poems in many magazines). LBP is a publisher of chapbooks, broadsides, labels, and a serial, *Lost and Found Times.*"

STANLEY BERNE, "Author of over 20 books, 8 in print, on open structure grammarless poetry/prose "neo-narrative," with his latest book *Future Language,* has been featured in over 40 radio/tv programs and newspaper interviews from San Francisco, New York City, Toronto, to London, is presently co-creator, co-host of the KENW-ETV series: *Future Writing Today* at Eastern New Mexico University."

CHARLES BERNSTEIN edits $L=A=N=G=U=A=G=E$ from 464 Amsterdam Avenue, New York, NY 10024. His books include *Shade, Senses of Responsibility, Parsing,* and *Three of Four Things I Know About Him.*

VITO BOGGERI, born in Serravalle Scrivia (Italy), February 10, 1939, continues to live there, 18 Rome Street. He had his first exhibition in 1958.

GEORGE BOWERING "went to college with Frank Davey and produced lots of *Tish.*" His latest books are a novel, *A Short Sad Book,* and a collection of stories, *Protective Footwear.* Box 35075, Station E, Vancouver, B.C., Canada.

RICHARD BUNGER, "37, **pianist**: Tomato Records will soon release four LP's of his performance of early works by John Cage; **composer**: *Mirrors* for pianist and tape recordist and other works; **author**: *The Well-Prepared Piano* and articles on notational theory; **married**: daughter Berklee (now 2 yrs.); Director, Electronic Music and Recording Program, California State University, Dominguez Hills, Carson, California 90747."

RICHARD BURGIN has authored *Conversations with Jorge Luis Borges* (1969) and a novel, *The Man with Missing Parts* (1973). He is the founding editor of the *New York Arts Journal.*

DONALD BURGY, "Born: New York City, August 3, 1937. 31 Bates Rd., Milton, Mass 02186"

JOHN CAGE is presently composing sound and word pieces that are heard around the world. His most recent book is *Empty Words* (1979).

JAME-MACEO CAMIER, a.k.a. E.G. Salmon-McFarlane, Jr., "lives in New York City, place of birth (1954). Edits *Horizontal Ascension.* Forthcoming are *Conceptual Pigs, The Stillness at the Top of the World (and other words),* and the Veronica System, a post-semiotic rock band."

CHARLES CARAMELLO "is Assistant Professor of English and Affiliated Assistant Professor of Comparative Literature at the University of Maryland, College Park. He writes on modern and postmodern literature."

JAMES F. L. CARROLL, born in Postville, IA, in 1934, is an associate professor and director of the Art Series Program, Kutztown State College, PA 19530.

DARYL CHIN is a critic, editor, playwright-director currently employed as a literary artist by the Cultural Council Foundation under CETA Title VI. 419 West 119th Street, #7-H, New York, NY 10027

PAUL CHRISTENSEN describes himself as "a poet, critic and literary historian concentrating on movements and ideas unique to the twentieth century." His books include *Missing Shores* and *Old and Lost Rivers,* both collections of poems; and *Charles Olson: Call Him Ishmael* (1979). 206 South Sims Street, Bryan, TX 77801.

WILLIAM CLAIRE edited the periodical *Voyages* from 1967 to 1973. "Five books with independent publishers, including *Publishing in the West: Alan Swallow.*" He directs the Washington office of the State University of New York, 1730 Rhode Island Ave., N.W., DC 20036.

MERRITT CLIFTON "edits *Samisdat*: Box 231, Richford, l, VT 05476. Living in Brigham, Quebec, he serves as columnist & contributing editor to numerous other publications, often under pseudonyms. Books include two novels, a treatise on baseball statistics, a do-it-yourself printing handbook, and chapbooks of stories, poems & criticism."

CLAUS CLÜVER teaches in Indiana University's Comparative Literature Program (Ballantine Hall 402, Bloomington, IN 47405), specializing in the interrelationship of literature, painting, and music. He is currently writing a critical history of Brazilian concrete poetry and completing a film on painters, poets, and composers in São Paulo.

DAVID COLE, born in 1939, took his Ph.D. on "William Empson's *Ambiguities* and *zen steps*;" co-author of *Three Places in New Inkland* (1977); affiliated with Dada, AARG, Henry Hicks Gallery. 19 Grace Court, Brooklyn, NY 11201.

AUGUSTO CONCATO lives and works as a designer in Milano, Italy (G. Dezza 25, 20144). He has authored and co-authored several spectacularly produced visual-verbal books, including *Happy Days* (1978).

TOM CONLEY has recently been teaching "graphics of art and text" at the University of California—Berkeley. Nominally, he teaches in the French Department at the University of Minnesota. His critical essays on "the surface of books" have appeared in several journals.

ALBERT COOK is Professor of Comparative Literature at Brown University. Among his books are collections of poetry and "a philosophy of comedy," *The Dark Voyage and the Golden Mean* (1949).

GEOFFREY COOK, born in 1946, has produced books of poetry, translations and criticism, as well as exhbitions of his verbalvisual art. He presently lives in San Francisco. P.O. Box 18274, 94118.

PHILIP CORNER composes with words and music in New York City and teaches at Livingston College, in New Brunswick. 464 W. Broadway, New York, NY 10012.

JEAN-JACQUES CORY is the author of *Lists* (1974) and *Particulars* (1979). His enumerative poems, stories and essays have appeared in many magazines and anthologies.

MIKE CRANE "IS
AN ARTIST
LIVING IN SACRAMENTO
FOR THE TIME BEING. Mike Crane is
an artist
living in sacrament-o
for the time being."

ROBIN CROZIER, "5B Tunstall Vale, Sunderland, SR2 7HP, England will send you his autobiography upon request but meanwhile here are some words to complete the fifty words he is allowed for this biographical note by *Assembling.* This is an autobiographical sentence. He phoned for a photograph of the missing telephone."

DADALAND is the taken name of Bill Gaglione, who lives with Anna Banana at 1183 Church St., San Francisco, CA 94114.

MATTEO D'AMBROSIO. "Born in 1950 in Naples, where he lives and teaches (Institute of Modern Philology). He has organized two shows of Italian avant-garde poetry and published several essays; in 1977, the first *Bibliografia della poesia italiana d'avanguardia,* Bulzoni, Roma. Via E. Gianturco 109 bis, 80143 Napoli (Italia).

GUY DAVENPORT, Professor of English at the University of Kentucky, has written books of criticism, poetry and fiction.
ALAN DAVIES edits the periodical *A Hundred Posters*. 28 Jones Street, New York, NY 10014.
AUGUSTO DE CAMPOS is an acknowledged founder and principal of Brazilian "concrete" poetry. He has frequently taught and lectured around the world. Rua Bocaina 23, Ap. 63, 05013 Sao Paolo, BRAZIL.
PHIL DEMISE (aka PHIL SMITH) 111 Third Avenue, New York, NY 10003, is the editor of *Gegenschien* and an active member of the N. DoDo Band. His latest book, *What I Don't Know for Sure,* was recently published by Burning Deck, Providence, R.I.
KLAUS PETER DENCKER, born in Lübeck in 1941, produces books and both radio and television programs from Brucknerstrasse 3, 6676 Mandelbachtal 1, BRD (0 68 93) 35 66. The first of his contributions he describes as "a magic quadrant on GOETHE. The second is the sign for quality in a critical way on reaction of HOLOCAUST."
AGNES DENES. "Artist. Born 1938. Work has been exhibited all over Europe, in South America, Australia, Japan and across the United States. Her work is represented in the permanent collections of the Museum of Modern Art, Whitney Museum, the National Collection of Fine Arts, Smithsonian Institution, and many others. She is the author of two books, *Sculptures of the Mind,* U. of Akron and *Paradox and Essence* by Tau/ma in Rome. She lives and works in New York City."
R.H.W. DILLARD "lives in Roanoke, Virginia, where he is chairman of the creative writing program at Hollins College. A novelist and poet, he has just completed a new novel, *The First Man on the Sun,* and a book-length poem, *January: A Screenplay.* He is married to the poet and filmmaker Cathy Hankla."
PHILIPPE DÔME belongs to the Parisian group of experimental writers called "d'atelier," along with Paul Nagy, Claude Miniere, Bruno Montels and Tibor Papp. 1 Bd. St. Marcel, 75013, Paris, FRANCE.
CHARLES DORIA, "classicist-at-large, presently lives, writes, and works in New York City."
ROCHELLE H. DuBOIS is formerly Rochelle Holt of Ragnarock Press; she is now in partnership with D.C. Erdman in **Merging Media,** an artistic venture in publishing and promoting. Merging Media, 59 Sandra Circle A-3, Westfield, NJ 07090
MICHAEL DYREGROV "If Michael Dyregrov advocates

neologisms in **A Critical Assembling,** he practices them in the poems *Falling Away in Songkhla, Flight with Marduk, Iced-In Duck, Krexen Suse, Kutsuna,* and *Slaelebate* published in **Eighth Assembling,** 1978." P.O. Box 16007, Minneapolis, MN 55416.
BRIAN DYSON, born in Leeds, England, in 1944, emigrated to Canada and now works at the Alberta College of Art, Calgary. He formed **Canadian (S) Pacific** in 1971 and subsequently formed **LE-LA (Societe De Prevoyance Mutuelle)** in 1975. He is currently preparing a "series of video tapes expanding on the theory and practice of **LE-LA.**"
GRZEGORZ DZIAMSKI edits the *Maximal Art Bulletin* from Libelta 26/3b, 61-707 Poznan, POLAND. He has also been actively involved with "mail art" and its exhibition.
GEORGE ECONOMOU, born in 1934 in Great Falls, MT, is presently Professor of English and Comparative Literature at the Brooklyn Center of Long Island University. His books include *The Georgics* (1968), *Landed Natures* (1969) amd *Ameriki* (1977), all poetry, and *The Goddess Natura in Medieval Literature* (1972).
LORIS ESSARY, P.O. Box 7068, University Station, Austin Texas 78712, is a playwright as well as a poet and visual artist and edits *Insterstate* magazine.
WELCH D. EVERMAN, born in 1946 in Pennsylvania, attended Northwestern University from 1964 to 1968 and graduated Phi Beta Kappa with a degree in Philosophy. *Orion* (1975) is his first novel.
RAYMOND FEDERMAN, by turns Professor of French and Professor of English at SUNY—Buffalo, has published several books of criticism and three more of extraordinary fiction.
ANDREW FIELD, born in the U.S. now teaches at Griffiths University, Brisbane, Queensland, Australia. His publications include books about Nabokov; *Fractions* (1967), a novel; and *The Complection of Russian Literature* (1971), "a cento".
ROBERT FILLIOU runs the *"Eternal Network"* from Moulin Le Saffranier, Flayosc, France 83.
NORMAN FINKELSTEIN is the author of a book of poems, *The Objects In Your Life* (House of Keys, 1977). A second volume, *The Hidden Narrative,* is in manuscript. A member of The Atlanta Poetry Collective, he is a doctoral candidate in English at Emory University. His address is 1472 East Rock Springs Rd., Atlanta, GA 30306.
CHARLES HENRI FORD "is author of the following books of poetry: *The Garden of Disorder* (1939). *The Overturned Lake* (1941), *Sleep in a Nest of Flames* (1949), *Spare Parts* (1966),

Silver Flower Coo (1968), *Flag of Ecstasy* (1972) and *Om Krishna* (1979). 1 West 72 Street, New York, NY 10023.
STEPHEN FOSTER teaches at the School of Art and Art History, the University of Iowa, and codirects its Corborree Gallery.
WILLIAM L. FOX lives in Reno, Nevada and edits *West Coast Poetry Review*.
PETER FRANK writes poetry and serves as art critic for *The Village Voice* in New York. He edits *Collation*, a newsletter on artists' publications.
LAURENCE GOLDSTEIN has authored a volume of poems, *Altamira*, and a book of literary criticism, *Ruins and Empire*. He is the editor of the *Michigan Quarterly Review*.
ANTHONY J. GNAZZO. "Born 1936. Lives in Oakland, California."
COURTENAY P. GRAHAM-GAZAWAY—Poet, photographer, filmmaker, lover, composer, musicians, singer, dancer, journale-letterist & publisher—brings out 2 new release press books: *Etcetera & Art-Letter Collage* in '79 from CP Graham Press, Box 5, Keswick, VA 22947."
ROLAND GRASS "teaches at Western Illinois University. During academic year 1978-79 he had a grant from the National Endowment for the Humanities to teach a special course on the arts in a technological society, with the collaboration of an art historian and a musicologist.
RICHARD GRAYSON has published two collections of short stories, *Disjointed Fictions* (1978) and *With Hitler in New York* (1979). His fiction, poetry and essays have appeared in many magazines and anthologies. He lives in Brooklyn, NY.
BRYANT HAYES "is a clarinetist who performs as a soloist and in chamber music primarily in Washington, D.C., his birthplace, and New York City, his home. He has recorded on CRI and FKT records. His poetry has appeared in *eddy, Clarinet, West Coast Poetry Review,* and various penny dreadfuls. He is Dance critic and Poetry critic of the *Greenwich Village News*. He teaches at Baruch College of C.U.N.Y." 233 West 83rd Street, apt. 6A, New York, N.Y. 10024.
DONALD HALL "lives in New Hampshire, where he supports himself by writing books and articles. He recently published the third edition of his textbook for Freshman English, *Writing Well*. In 1978, he published a book of poems called *Kicking the Leaves*."
BERNARD HEIDSIECK, born in Paris in 1928, is generally regarded among the world's major sound poets.
JONATHAN HELD, JR., is the video specialist at the Mid York Library System, 1600 Lincoln Ave., Utica, NY 13502, from which he actively engages in "mail art."
SCOTT HELMES, "Presently working for an architect in St. Paul. Also likes to work with photography, graphic design, and xeroxgraphy. Has 3 cats and sails during the summer." 115 S. Victoria, St. Paul, MN 55105.
C. DAVID HEYMANN "is the author of *The Quiet Hours,* a book of poetry, published in 1968. His two most recent books are *Ezra Pound: The Last Rower* (1976) and *American Aristocracy: The Lives and Times of James Russell, Amy, and Robert Lowell* (1979). 360 Central Park West, 14A, New Yrok, N.Y. 10025.
DICK HIGGINS's recent books include *A Dialectic of Centuries* (1978) and *The Epickall Quest of the Brothers Dichtung and Other Outrages* (1978). P.O. Box 842, Canal St., New York, NY 10013.
JAMAKE HIGHWATER, "Blackfeet/Cherokee, born in Montana in 1942, is the author of *Anpao,* an American Indian Odyssey; *Song from the Earth,* American Indian Painting; *Fodor's Guide to Indian America; Ritual of the Wind,* American Indian Ceremonies, Music & Dance; *Dance: Rituals of Experience; Journey to the Sky,* a novel. c/o Alfred Hart, Fox Chase Agency, 419 East 57th St., New York, NY 10022."
DAVI DET HOMPSON, born in Sharon, Pa, in 1939, took an MFA in graphic design from Indiana University. He has recently been living in Richmond, VA (P.O. Box 7035, 23221).
JOHN JACOB has reviewed alternative publications for several journals. He's working on a small book of experimental criticism, tentatively entitled *"Instantaneous Poetics."* 527 Lyman, Oak Park, IL 60304.
T.J. KALLSEN, "Distinguished Professor of English, Stephen F. Austin State University (Texas), will retire from his lifelong pursuit (except for WWII) in 1980." 600 Rostwick, Nacogdoches, TX 75961.
KARL KEMPTON edits *Kaldron,* a newsprint periodical devoted to experimental poetries, from 441 North 6th Street, Grover City, CA 93433.
HUGH KENNER is commonly regarded among the major critics of modernist literature. He teaches at Johns Hopkins University, Baltimore, MD 21218.
BLIEM KERN, "text-sound artist, has exhibited and performed his work around the world. *Word Farm* his most recent work will be published by New Rivers Press in the spring of 1980. He is the founder and Chairman of The World Alliance of Sound Poetry Trust, an international trust to fund exhibits,

publications, performances and conferences of sound poetry throughout the world." 230 Riverside Drive, New York, NY 10025.

JEROME KLINKOWITZ "is the author of *The Life of Fiction* (University of Illinois Press, 1977), which combines letters, diaries, interviews, phone conversations, and all types of commentary with graphic collages as a total exploration of contemporary writing. His "post-cards" are a new combination of criticism and biography." 1904 Clay Street, Cedar Falls, IA 50613.

TOM KONYVES, born in 1947, currently lives in Montreal, where he is Poetry Director of Vehicle Art. His publications include books and videotapes. He writes a monthly column for the *Montreal Star*. 2572 Bedford Rd., Montreal, P.Q., CANADA.

RICHARD KOSTELANETZ "recently mounted *WORDS-AND*, a traveling retrospective exhibition of his works with words, numbers and lines, in books, prints, audiotapes, videotapes, and films. Works in progress include several experimental fictions and a comprehensive critique of cultural granting in America. He has directed *Assembling Press* since 1970 and co-published *Precisely* since 1976."

MARTIN H. KRIEGER "is assistant professor in the Hubert H. Humphrey Institute of Public Affairs, University of Minnesota, Minneapolis, MN 55455. He has been a fellow of the National Humanities Center (1978-79). His Ph.D. is in physics."

SEYMOUR KRIM has published three collections of essays, *Views of a Nearsighted Cannoneer* (1961), *Shake It for the World, Smartass* (1970) and *You and Me* (1974).

NORMAN LAVERS: "articles and short stories have appeared in *Northeast, APR, TriQuarterly, Novel, The Ohio Review*, and other magazines. He has published a monograph on Mark Harris, and is completing a second, on Jerzy Kosinski. Juniper Press recently published his *Selected Short Stories*. He lives at Rt 5 Box 203, Jonesboro, Ark. 72401.

ROBERT LAX "Poems are published by Journeyman Books (P.O. Box 4434, Grand Central Station, N.Y. 10017) in editions designed by Emil Antonucci. Recent publications from this and other presses: *Color Poems* (Journeyman), *Selections* (Joe Di Maggio & X-Press, London), & (with Thomas Merton) *A Catch of Anti-Letters* (Andrews & McMeel)."

S.J. LEON "is a Philadelphian who has lived in France and Great Britain. Though he has not pursued publication, some of his speculations have appeared occasionally in little magazines.

There are two collections: *Between Silences* and *Solos And Simultaneities.*"

ZBIGNIEW LEWICKI teaches contemporary American literature in the English Department University of Warsaw. He has held both the ACLS and the Huntington Library Fellowships, published a book on stream-of-consciousness prose, and has another coming out on tradition and innovation in American postmodern fiction.

HARLEY W. LOND: "The editor of *Intermedia* magazine (USA), a communication artist, essayist, fictioneer, and auto parts counterperson." P.O. Box 31464, San Francisco, CA 94131.

RICHARD LYONS, "Director, Creative Writing Program University of Oregon, Eugene, Oregon 97403. Works, including an occasional review among much fiction of varying kinds, has appeared in many magazines including *Chelsea, Transpacific, Ohio Review, The Phoenix, Northwest Review*. "*The Woman*" was a 1977 winner of the EC Balch Award in Short Fiction from the *Virginia Quarterly Review*."

SCOTT MACDONALD "teaches film and American literature at Utica College, Utica, N.Y. 13502. He has written about writer Erskine Caldwell and several avant-garde filmmakers including Hollis Frampton, Larry Gottheim, J.J. Murphy, Robert Huot and Taka Iimura ."

HARRIS MacLENNAN teaches philosophy at Dalhousie University, Halifax, 27 Robert Allen Drive, Wedgewood Park, Halifax, NS B3M 3G9, Canada.

J.H. MATTHEWS: "Most recent books are *Toward the Poetics of Surrealism* (1976), *The Imagery of Surrealism* (1977), *Le Théâtre de Raymond Roussel: un énigme* (1977), *The Inner Dream: Celine as novelist* (1978), and *Surrealism in Hollywood*."

JOHN McAULEY: "Born 1947, lives in Montreal, Quebec. Edited *Maker* an aquarian mailout to 22 countries. Just established Maker Press. Night person, teacher and now *Vehicule Press* distribution manager. Four recent books: *Hazardous Renaissance (*Concrete Poetry); *Nothing Ever Happens in Pointe-Clare*; *Mattress Testing* and *What Henry Hudson Found*. c/o *Vehicule Press*, 1000 Clark Street, Montreal, Quebec H2Z 1J9."

MARK MENDEL: "Poet, environmental artist. Born: Monroe, Georgia, 1947. Center for Advanced Visual Studies, Massachusetts Inst. of Technology 40 Massachusetts Avenue, Cambridge, MA 02139."

DOUGLAS MESSERLI, Assistant Professor of English at Temple University, edits *Sun & Moon: A Journal of Literature and Art*. He has published fiction, poetry and criticism in several magazines and produced two books, *Djuna Barnes: A Bibliography* and *Dinner on the Lawn*, a collection of poetry.

JONATHAN MIDDLEBROOK "wrote *Mailer and the Times of His Time* (San Francisco, 1976). *American Literature* said "we can at least enjoy the company of a critical volume which to a considerable extent compensates for its presumption with an answerably massive dimension of raw intellectual energy." Middlebrook is now writing *Critical People: First Impressionism* and is chairman of Nonce Carpentry Associates.

E. ETHELBERT MILLER "is a graduate of Howard University. He is Director of the *Ascension Poetry Reading Series* and associate editor of *HOODOO*, and the *Washington Review*." P.O. Box 441, Howard University, Washington D.C. 20059.

EUGENE MILLER (aka "Dusty Miller") edits *New Lazarus Review* from 1809 Whitesboro St., Utica, New York, 13502.

CLAUDE MINIERE: "Born 1938 (Paris). Childhood Dordogne. Later, Paris suburb. Several jobs. Brief stays in Germany, Algeria and Great Britain. First published in *Tel Quel* (1966). Collaborated with *Art Press, Musique Jeu, d'atelier, Phantomas, Sub Stance, TXT, Spirali*, . . . Recent publications: *Vita Nova* (d'atelier), *Translations of Ezra Pound* (texts related to Music), *Glamour* (Christian Bourgois, ed.) In preparation: *Walkie Talkie*."

BRUNO MONTELS is a member of d'atelier. He has published one book, *Ils one piossan*, and lives at 10 rue J. Ferrandi, 75006 Paris, France. (He did not affix his name to his contribution, which nonetheless appears in its alphabetical place.)

MADISON MORRISON "was awarded an Ingram Merrill Foundation grant this year to finish his ninth book, a novel based on the form of the classical epic and the substance of contemporary life. He teaches at the University of Oklahoma." 420 W. Eufaula St., Norman, OK 73069.

STEPHEN MORRISSEY edits the *Montreal Journal of Poetics* and is associated with *Vehicule Press*. 4100 Northcliffe, Montreal, P.Q., Canada.

CHARLIE MORROW "is interested in the psychic and physical aspects of sound and works with breathing, counting, chanting, linquistic patterns of nonhuman species, echoes and the oral poetry and music of tribal peoples." New Wilderness Foundation, 365 West End Avenue, New York, N.Y. 10024.

D. MUMM co-publishes *The Smudge* (P.O. Box 19276, Detroit, MI 48219) and a new small-press review from the same address.

GEORGE MYERS, JR. works as a sergeant-at-arms in the Pennsylvania State Legislature and edits *X, A Journal of the Arts*, P.O. Box 2648, Harrisburg, PA 17105.

PAUL NAGY "(1934-Hungary) lives in Paris since 1956 where he completed his university studies. Printer, co-editor of two avant-garde reviews (Hungarian *Magyar Muhely* and French *d'atelier*), bilingual writer, preoccupied with visual literature which he considers the major current literary trend. Exposed literary objects and published texts in several countries mostly with *d'atelier* group. *esoteriques frigidaires:* observations on Mallarmé, palimpsest, incorporation: both a work of fiction and a critical commentary on radical experimental tendencies in contemporary literature."

MAURIZIO NANNUCCI, born in 1939 in Firenze, where he presently lives, is affiliated with the *Zone* group and gallery in his home town. He has worked in a wide variety of visual-verbal media. Via Dupre 12, 50131 Florence, Italy.

OPAL LOUIS NATIONS has authored a scriptural number of books, mostly of poetry and drawings. Born in England, he presently lives in Toronto. (P.O. Box 91, Station B, MST 2T3).

SASHA NEWBORN "is the self-chosen name of a man who now shares Mudborn Press with Judyl Mudfoot; editing, publishing, and related chores have become an all-consuming affair; don't remember my past very well." 209 W. De la Guerra, Santa Barbara, 93101.

JEFF NUTTALL, born in 1933, is the author of *Bomb Culture* (1968), whose dust–jacket describes him as "a poet, painter, and jazz trumpeter, who for some years was a pivotal force in the London Underground." 17 West Croft, Wyke, Bradford, Yorks, England.

HOLLY O'GRADY: "Having worked for a year in marketing research, surveying among other things the distinctions between one and two-ply toilet tissue, I decided to expand that experience to include the more elevated topic of criticism." She contributed to *Visual Lit Criticism* (1979).

VALERY OISTEANU can talk brilliantly in Russian, Rumanian, Hebrew and English. 120 Second Avenue, New York, N.Y. 10003.

TIBOR PAPP: "1936, Tokaj, Hungary. — Arrived in Belgium 1957. Has lived in Paris since 1961. — Co-editor of a Hungarian, *Magyar Muhely,* and a French, *d'atelier,* literary review. — Works: books in Hungarian, picture poetry slide projection for the musical piece of Vinko Globokar *Carrousel* (world premiere 1977 — Zagreb, *Festival of Contemporary Music*). — Exposed with *d'atelier group*: Centre G. Pompidou (1977), Maison de la Culture du Havre (1978), Foundation Nationale des Arts Graphiques (Paris 1978)."

MICHAEL JOSEPH PHILLIPS has a doctorate in comparative literature from Indiana University at Bloomington. He currently teaches at the Free University of Indianapolis and directs the Free University Press.

CLIVE PHILLPOT "is an art librarian and writer who has had very little to do with the London Zoo." 178 East 80th Street, New York, NY 10021.

NICK PIOMBINO has published essays on writing and thought processes, as well as poetry, in several magazines. He works as a psychotherapist in private practice. 295 Garfield Place, Brooklyn, NY 11215.

ADRIAN PIPER "was born in NYC in 1948. She studied art at the School of Visual Arts and philosophy at CCNY and Harvard University. She has exhibited her work locally and internationally since 1968, using a variety of media. Her current interest is in the political underpinnings of the art world."

BERN PORTER, "Registered tree-dweller and author of 54 books has 22 more books in manuscript form awaiting a publisher. Phone 1-207-338-3763, 22 Salmond Road, Belfast, Maine 04915."

PAUL PORTUGÉS took his doctorate in American Literature from the University of California, Berkeley, and presently teaches in Santa Barbara. He authored *The Visionary Poetics of Allen Ginsberg* (1978).

CHARLES POTTS "8-28-43, Idaho Falls, Idaho. Out to Mexico, Canada, California, Seattle, Salt Lake City, back to Idaho. Always moving. Deeper inside myself. Editor of Litmus Books: *Valga Krusa, Rocky Mountain Man, The Golden Calf, The Opium Must Go Thru.*" 525 Bryant, Walla Wall, WA 99362.

CHRISTIAN PRIGENT lives at Villa Medicis, Viale Trinita de Monti, 00187, Roma, Italy.

TONY QUAGLIANO "was born in Brooklyn, New York and he now lives in Honolulu, Hawaii. His poems and articles have appeared in many magazines and some anthologies, including *The Pushcart Prize: Best of the Small Presses* and *Poetry Hawaii: A Contemporary Anthology* (University Press of Hawaii). His latest chapbook is *Fierce Meadows* (Petronium Press, 1979)." 3151 Monsarrat Avenue, No. 301, Honolulu, Hi. 96815.

R&R are Ann Rower and Vito Ricci, 65 Greene St., New York, N.Y. 10012.

NAOMI RACHEL: "Current home: British Columbia. Recently received a grant from the Canada Council and has been reading from her prose poems *Rats Eat Ice Cream.* Numerous publications including: *Poetry Now, Contemporary California Poets, Hawaii Review, Malahat Review.* Can be reached c/o 3394 Blair Drive, Hollywood 90068 California."

KEITH RAHMMINGS edits *Blank Tape*, a magazine of unconventional literature, Box 371, Brooklyn, NY 11230.

HENRY RASOF lives in New York and is an editor for the Wooden Needle Press.

REBECCA RASS recently published a novel, *The Fairy Tales of My Mind* (1978). Her first book, *From A to Z*, was published in Holland and Switzerland, made into a TV show, and performed on the stage. She is presently completing another novel, *The Mountain,* and teaching at Hunter College.

ROCHELLE RATNER regularly reviews poetry for the *Soho Weekly News* and other publications. Several collections of her poetry have appeared. 50 Spring Street, New York, NY 10012.

CLAUDIA REEDER "(Intimate) relationship with Maurice Roche's texts dates from 1976: *Maurice Roche: L'Ecriture en jeu,* (Diss. University of Wisconsin-Madison) followed by numerous other articles. Professor of French and Comparative Literature at Dartmouth College (Hanover, N.H.), she works/plays with semiotics, avant-garde literature, women's writing, and writes herself."

JOAN RETALLACK "is neither a librarian nor a philosopher. She lives and works in the D.C. area where she writes les mots farcis and wishes you all bon appetit! Her first book of that which is not prose is entitled *Wittgenstein at the Movies.*"

HOWARD W. ROBERTSON is a visual poet who has recently published in *Laughing Bear, Interstate, Glassworks, Assembling* and elsewhere. He has a novel with an agent and is now working on a book of long poems called *Artifacts.* 3830 Marshall Ave., Eugene, OR 97402.

JEROME ROTHENBERG is the author of nearly forty books (poetry, translations, anthologies), including *A Seneca Journal, Poems for the Game of Silence, Poland/1931, Technicians of the Sacred, Shaking the Pumpkin, Revolution of the Word, A Big Jewish Book & 6 Horse Songs for 4 Voices.* He edits *New Wilderness Letter* and has recently been teaching in the Visual Arts Department, University of California, at San Diego, La

Jolla, CA 92037.

PATRICK SAARI, 1605 16th Street, N.W., apt. 4, Washington, D.C. 20009.

HARRY WILLIAM SAFFREN published *Old City Arts Umbrella* and *Chimera—A Complete Theater Piece.* He also works in film, video and theater. 5538 Morris St., Philadelphia, PA 19144.

EDWIN SCHLOSSBERG took his Ph.D. in Science and Literature at Columbia University in 1971. He has since worked in book-making and design. His publications include *Einstein and Beckett* (1973) and popularizations about pocket calculators.

HOWARD SCHWARTZ, born in St. Louis in 1945, teaches courses in Poetry Writing, Short Story Writing, and Jewish Literature at the University of Missouri, St. Louis. His works include collections of his parables, his dreams and his poetry, as well as anthologies such as *Imperial Messages: One Hundred Modern Parables* (1976).

ARMAND SCHWERNER, born in Antwerp, Belgium, in 1924, currently teaches at Staten Island College, New York. His recent collection of poetry is *The Work, the Joy and the Triumph of the Will* (1977).

STEPHEN SCOBIE, associate professor of English at the University of Alberta, has the largest and finest collection of Ian Hamilton Finlay's work in North America. He has also written several books of poetry and criticism.

DAVID SEAMAN "harvests mushrooms, does French, brews ales, reviews films, paints abstracts, ales paints, abstracts harvests, mushrooms does, Frenches reviews, films brews, in caves, in cellars, in fields, at Davis and Elkins College, and at home, 1316 S. Davis Ave., Elkins, WV 26241 (304) 636-7712."

BRIAN SHERMAN "is a sociologist. In 1978 he presented 4 papers at professional conventions. One was on bad taste. Two were on the use of happenings and other experimental art in college teaching. One criticized sociobiology." Oglethorpe University/Atlanta, GA 30319.

RON SILLIMAN "is the author of *The Age of Huts* (including *Ketjack*), the first stage of a long work he does not expect to finish."

E.A. SKLEPOWICH, "born in Connecticut in 1944, is a freelance writer living in New York City. He teaches modern and contemporary literature, writes stories of an experimental nature, and is completing his first novel, tentatively entitled, *Passing into the Picture.* He has received a Fulbright grant to study in Egypt, 1979-1980." 83 Washington Place, New York City 10011.

LARRY SMITH "teaches at Bowling Green State University in Ohio. His books are *Growth: Poems and Sketches* (Northwoods, 1976) and *Kenneth Patchen* (Twayne, 1978). He is currently working on a book treating *The Surrealism in American Writing* and doing a collection of his poems with the etchings of artist Stephen Smigocki."

ELLSWORTH SNYDER, pianist and composer, has also published criticism of Gertrude Stein and John Cage. He teaches music at Milton College, Milton, WI 53563.

LON SPIEGELMAN teaches phototype composition at Santa Monica College and produces student newspapers as a journeyman printer for the Los Angeles Community College District. 1556 Elevado St., Los Angeles, CA 90026.

CHARLES J. STANLEY: "Author of *The Adventures of Carlo Pittore;* compiled *Maine Moments in New York: Contemporary Maine Artists; Yurtyet: A Collection of Bowdoinham Maine Colonists,* & *Colleagues,* all published in 1979 by Pittore Euforico, P.O. Box 1132, New York City 10009.

KRISTINE STILES, born in 1947 in Denver, Colorado, is presently working "between visual art/writing/history/philosophy/social commentary/play." 2414 Union St., San Francisco, CA 94705.

ANN STUBBS is a critic and archivist, mostly of recent visual art, currently residing in New York.

MIROLJUB TODOROVIC, born in 1940 in Skoplje, Yugoslavia, took a degree in law and has been publishig poetry and essays since 1958. The founder of the Yugoslav signalist movement, he edited, for *Delos* (Belgrade), an anthology of *Concrete, Visual and Signalist Poetry* (1975).

ENDRE TOT, born in Sümeg, Hungary, in 1937, moved to Budapest in 1956 and continues to live there. He has produced films, publications, and performances; the Israel Museum in Jerusalem mounted a retrospective of his work in 1975.

FRED TRUCK/BOLON DZACAB writes that he was "born in 1946 in the 9th layer of hell. His works include *Camping Out B, Tangerine Universe in 3 Refrains,* and *The Polyp* (A Quetzalcoatl Production) *Tych, Polypytch Striking Camp.* Most recently he has turned to illuminated manuscripts in multiple form."

JOHN TYTELL, bron in Belgium in 1939, is Professor of English at Queens College, CUNY, and the author of *Naked Angles: The Lives and Literature of the Beat Generation*

(1976).

JOHAN VAN GELUWE lives in Waregem, Belgium, on Bouckaertstraat 8.

PAUL VANGELISTI: 3403 Glenhurst Avenue, Los Angeles, CA 90039.

ED VARNEY, an American currently residing in British Columbia, copublishes the books of Intermedia Press, P.O. Box 3294, Vancouver, BC V6B 3X9.

TOM VEITCH, born in 1941 in Bellows Falls, VT, has published poetry, collaborative fiction and one major novel, *The Luis Armed Story* (1978). 461 Wilde Avenue, San Francisco, CA 94134.

HANNAH WEINER has contributed prose to many magazines and recently produced an audiotape of herself and others reading her work, *Clairovoyant Journal* (1978).

IRVING WEISS. "English Department, SUC New Paltz, New Paltz, N.Y. 12562. Translator, selections from Malcolm de Chazal, *Sens-Plastique*, as *Plastic Sense* (1971). Complete version, *Sens-Plastique* (Sun Editions, 1980). With Anne Weiss: *American Authors and Books* (Crown, 1972) and supplement to *Thesaurus of Book Digests* (Crown, 1980)."

BOB WELKE "taught anthropology with U of Maryland's European Division until June. But his chosen WORK lately has been publishing *Network: Quodlibeta*, & experimenting with postal art." 11100 SW 80 Avenue, Miami, Florida 33156.

JOHN WHYTE "(Box 1083, Banff, Canada) was born and lives in Banff. Writes epic poems, monopoems, technopaegnia (in the form of dactylograms), art criticism, a weekly newspaper column, and is planning to turn a gallery into a poem. Recent book: *The Rockies; High Where the Wind is Lonely*."

MICHAEL WILDING: "b. Worcester UK 1942. Fiction — *Aspects of the Dying Process; Living Together; Short Story Embassy; West Midland Underground; Scenic Drive; Phallic Forest*. Criticism — *Milton's Paradise Lost; Marcus Clarke; Political Fictions*. Editor — *Marvell-Modern Judgements; The Radical Reader*." Dept of English, University of Sydney, NSW 2006, Australia.

KARL YOUNG, born in Kenosha, WI, in 1947, publishes, edits and usually prints both the periodical *Stations* and the books of the Membrane Press, P.O. Box 11601, Milwaukee, WI 53211.

NINA YANKOWITZ lives in New York City where she paints, writes and scripts. Her visual art is represented by the Stefanotti Gallery, New York City.

MAS'UD ZAVARZADEH "was educated at Middle Eastern, European and American universities. His essays and stories have appeared in numerous publications and his book on contemporary narrative, *The Mythopoeic Reality* was published in 1977. He is currently writing a book on the semiotics of transfiction. He teaches postmodern American literature and literary theory at Syracuse University."

ARLENE ZEKOWSKI, "Author of over 20 books, 8 in print, on open structure grammarless poetry/prose "Neo-Narrative," with her latest book *Image Breaking Images*, has been featured in over 40 radio/TV programs and newspaper interviews from San Francisco, New York City, Toronto, to London, is presently co-creator, co-host of the KENW-ETV series: *Future Writing Today* at Eastern New Mexico University."

PAUL ZELEVANSKY, born in 1946, has authored *The Book of Takes* (1976) and mounted exhibitions of his work with images, sounds and words around the U.S. His current visual novel is tentatively titled *The Case for the Burial of Ancestors,* which he describes as "21st Century illuminated manuscript disguised as a Great Book of the ancient world."

ROBERT ZEND, a Hungarian by birth, a Canadian by residence, has produced over a hundred radio programs for the Canadian Broadcasting Corp. His most recent books include *Oab, From Zero to One, Limbo Like Me, A Bunch of Proses,* and *From Z(end) to Zen(d)*.

HARRIET ZINNES: "Author of *An Eye for An I, I Wanted to See Something Flying,* and the 1978 volume of prose poems *Entropisms,* will be having a collection of her short stories entitled *Ancient Ritual* published late this year as well as a chapbook of poems *Book of Ten*. She is Professor of English at Queens College where she teaches a poetry workshop and modern literature, Flushing, New York 11367."

NICHOLAS ZURBRUGG, an Englishman, teaches in the School of Humanities, Griffith University, Brisbane, Queensland, Australia. He edtied the periodical *Stereoheadphones.*

ELLEN ZWEIG "is a performance poet from Ann Arbor, Michigan. She has performed in Ann Arbor, Boulder, San Francisco. . .She is presently teaching at the University of Michigan, writing a PhD dissertation on Performance Poetry, and working on *Orange Juice Mews,* a divinatory performance dedicated to Beth Anderson."